PENGUIN BOOKS

EATING CHILDREN

'A masterpiece of the genre, gripping and funny' – Valerie Grove in *The Times*

'In *Eating Children* she revealed with extraordinary passion the story of "The Cleft", her name for her father, "as unacquainted with love as a Scots pine", who undermined her at every step, her early exceptional promise as a ballet dancer who then grew too tall, and her first marriage in Canada, to an exiled count who while taking her on mad jaunts . . . was torturing her with his insane, possessive love' – Sally Belfrage in the *Independent*

'Her account of girlhood in the nice, respectable Home Counties family is so wildly funny that I forgot it was an autobiography and read it like a novel' – Mary Maher in the *Irish Times*

'A frank, sad and extremely funny book' – Val Hennessy in the *Literary Review*

'An extraordinary book . . . the reader is left gasping, not just at the suspense, but also at Tweedie's ability to write about the people in her life with such candour and compassion' – Carolyn Hart in *Marie Claire*

'A wonderful autobiography . . . truly remarkable' – Fay Weldon in the *Mail on Sunday*

ABOUT THE AUTHOR

Jill Tweedie was born in Egypt in 1936. One of the foremost women involved in the British feminist movement, she worked for many years as a columnist on the *Guardian* where her writing with its warmth, wit and emotional honesty spoke to thousands of women. She wrote regularly for newspapers and magazines and was twice made Woman Journalist of the Year. In addition to her career as a journalist Jill Tweedie wrote two highly praised novels, *Bliss* and *Internal Affairs* (both have been published by Penguin). Her other books include *It's Only Me*, *In the Name of Love*, *Letters from a Faint-hearted Feminist* and *More From Martha*.

Jill Tweedie died in November 1993.

Jill Tweedie

Eating Children

with FRIGHTENING PEOPLE
(FRAGMENTS)

And an Afterword by Alan Brien

PENGUIN BOOKS

PENGUIN BOOKS

Published by the Penguin Group
Penguin Books Ltd, 27 Wrights Lane, London W8 5TZ, England
Penguin Books USA Inc., 375 Hudson Street, New York, New York 10014, USA
Penguin Books Australia Ltd, Ringwood, Victoria, Australia
Penguin Books Canada Ltd, 10 Alcorn Avenue, Toronto, Ontario, Canada M4V 3B2
Penguin Books (NZ) Ltd, 182–190 Wairau Road, Auckland 10, New Zealand

Penguin Books Ltd, Registered Offices: Harmondsworth, Middlesex, England

Eating Children first published by Viking 1993
Published in Penguin Books with additional material 1994
5 7 9 10 8 6 4

Eating Children copyright © Jill Tweedie, 1993
Frightening Children copyright © The Estate of Jill Tweedie, 1994
Afterword copyright © Alan Brien, 1994
All rights reserved

Typeset by Datix International Limited, Bungay, Suffolk
Printed in England by Clays Ltd, St Ives plc

For Lucas

Contents

Eating Children

I stood at the feet of my father and looked along the thin long body that seemed to stretch as far beyond me as it had when I was a child. Father, farther, farthest. A handsome man, a handsome corpse; contained, commanding and no more user-friendly in death than in life. I shifted up to the top end of him to survey the clipped skull-cap of iron-grey hair, the long flat cheeks, the straight nose and mouth and the jut of cleft chin. You can only pore that intently over the undefended, the new-born, the new-dead, and I had not looked into my Daddy's face for forty years or more, not directly, not with seeing eyes. He did not permit such liberties. Indeed, I half-expected him to sit bolt upright now, extend his arms like a traffic policeman and shout, *Get away, gurl, for mercy's sake, what on earth d'you think you're up to?* Or point a skeletal finger at me, as he had so often recently: *You're in the front lines now, my lady, soon it'll be your turn to go over the top.*

There were tears on my cheeks, I observed; the sort of tears that come automatically whenever people confront the heavier dramas of life – birth, marriage, death. Take no notice, I assured him. Nothing personal, Daddy.

What had he taught me, this, my begetter? That you can get by without love, just as he had, neither giving it nor requiring it from others. Not a bad lesson, by any means. Something clean and innocent about it, even bracing. My father was a man as unacquainted with love as a Scots pine tree and what's so wrong with that? It makes a change, these days, when love slops out all over the place from any old bucket: preachers, politicians, gurus, pop stars, ad-men, every kind of shyster on the make flogging everything from fish fingers to eternal life. If

God is love and God so loved the world, take a quick look round and see what His love hath wrought.

> Full fathom five my father lies;
> His heart of coral made.

Maybe he knew this love business that was meat to others was poison to him, for it killed him in the end. I killed him with it, as it turned out, administering no more than a pinch, but that, lethal. The last day of his life I arrived early at the house, greeted my mother, still in her dressing-gown having breakfast, took the shopping list she'd made and was standing in the hall when I heard him above, manoeuvring his brittle collection of bones down the stairs, each as precariously perched on the next as cards in a card house.

'Where are you off to?' he asked, seeing me as he paused to regain his breath.

'To get some food. To the off-licence.'

'Pray buy some vintage hemlock for me.'

I turned away as he descended – he loathed being watched – but I couldn't stop my ears against the clacking of his sticks and the hoarse, hard breathing, so I turned back again. He was wedged, grey and helpless, between the banisters. I pulled a chair over, put my arms around him and eased him down to it. The first time we had touched for thirty years.

'Never grow old,' he gasped and looked up at me from such an abyss of confusion, from such frailty, that the wee dry walnut which was all that remained of my feeling for him expanded inside me as if it had been doused in water. I bent down, kissed his mottled cheek and dashed back to the kitchen.

'For God's sake, Mother,' I exclaimed, shocked out of tact by the change in one short week. 'Dad's not just off-colour. He's dying out there. We've got to get him into hospital,' and I bustled off to make the necessary arrangements. The ambulance came. Very slowly, blinking like a rooster disturbed by light, my father tottered to it and was driven off.

That night a blood clot, shaken loose by the upheaval of the move, rose upwards and stopped his heart. That drop of my love, the first he had been exposed to for years and years, contained a killer virus and it saw him off.

Now, standing beside his dead body, I felt nothing; nothing at all.

The night of the funeral I dreamed the dream again, the one I'd had since childhood. A forest in autumn, fallen leaves drifting this way and that over the ground, rustling in a thoroughly sinister manner. Nothing else occurs except that there am I, rooted to the spot, the solitary soul in the world who knows that under those leaves, under that ground lies a body and that one day it will be discovered and I will be revealed as the murderer.

This time, however, the dream had progressed. Instead of simply standing aghast among the trees, this time I kneel and begin to dig with my hands in the ground. Sure enough, bit by bit the outlines of a body emerge and then the pale disc of a face. Trembling, I scrape away the remaining earth and the face that stares sightlessly up at me is my own.

Hard on the heels of that video nasty the memory of something that happened to me during a working visit to Moscow floated up and snagged itself into my mind. A Russian contact had urged me to talk to some friends of his, *Good people*, he said, *they'll tell you what's really going on here*. He wrote their address on a piece of cardboard in Cyrillic script, which I can't read, and taking it I dived into the Metro just off Red Square. It was the peak of the evening rush hour and I boiled about in the crowd waving my placard like some Oxford Street End-of-the-Worlder until a kindly commuter directed me to what I had to hope was the right train. Once in, I spent the next half-hour agitating the placard at every stop to a chorus of 'nyets' from the other passengers as they gestured me back to my seat.

Eventually they all disembarked and I was alone in the carriage. After a while the train stopped. A woman with a broom got on and began sweeping around my feet. Obviously, the end of the line. Up empty stairs into a rasping, snowy wind and the sun setting on an immensity of flat white desert that stretched away on all sides, apparently to Siberia. Not a building visible to the horizon, no tree nor bush nor vegetation of any sort, no life anywhere.

I trudged about for a while, twenty minutes or so, in the vain hope of discerning some residual sign of humanity, a bus stop, the trace of a road, a house looming out of the gathering gloom. Nothing. I might as well have landed on Mars. By now the snow had become a blizzard that scythed straight at my eyes. As darkness fell the cold gripped me and started to administer its anaesthetic. Soon I hadn't a face any longer, no hands, no ears and no option but to give up, struggle back to the station again and return to Moscow. On feet that weren't there I plodded over the creaking ground to the single landmark, the square black bulk of the Metro.

The station gates were barred and padlocked. I rattled the chains, banged, shouted, cursed. No response but the wolfish howling of the wind – or was it the windish howling of wolves? Gone, the last escape route to civilization and – horrid thought dawning – possibly life itself. I stood there shaking and dumbfounded in the now total darkness, Death's icy fingers already groping furtively at me under my coat. God almighty, a mere thirty minutes from the heart of a capital city and tomorrow's commuters were going to find me frozen solid, propped like a bag of Bird's Eye peas against Station 68 of the Yugo-Zapodnaya line. Impossible, surely. Such a ludicrous fate simply could not befall me, yet unless an unlikely St Bernard turned up or a posse of Cossacks, there was no other ending on the cards.

That memory surfaced and stuck in my mind because it mirrored exactly the panic that overtook me when my father died. One minute I was jogging along snug at the centre of things and the next I was alone, marooned in a perilous place where I couldn't speak the language or read the words. Where were the travellers who had gone before? Where was the map that would get me out of this icy waste? Or was I to spend the remainder of my life trapped like some iron-age beast in a glacier, mute and immobile, moving inch by inch downhill?

What had happened was that the person I thought of as me had suddenly packed up and gone, like a lover or friend you take for granted and then discover they've been making other plans, finding another place to be, another person to be with and you're stunned and it's too late. I felt it physically, that moment of departure, standing in my father's garden under the pear tree where his deck-chair was still propped. Something shifted inside my skull, did a slippery flip, then slithered away like a fish from a net and I knew it was my self, that fish, off back to the sea. My first sensation was one of relief at being rid at last of some alien growth, the sort people talk about after operations, 'Big as a grapefruit, the doctor said, the size of your fist'. Distress came swiftly after, though, because there was such a void where the fish had been.

I was fine until then, fine right through my forties, thought I'd made it into harbour. My skin fitted me comfortably, I knew who I was, the good and the bad, and felt secure in my views on everything from religion and politics to the best way of chopping parsley (with scissors, in a mug). For the first time for years money wasn't a problem, I earned enough for my needs and wanted nothing I couldn't buy, or not badly. Work was going well and my children, after the usual alarums and excursions, seemed to me in all essentials satisfactory. It wouldn't be correct to say I looked forward to the future – who looks forward to an ever more tattered ozone layer, dwindling natural resources or, for that matter, their own old age? – but on the whole I considered that the planet and I, having weathered some quite vicious storms in our time, would cope somehow with whatever lay ahead.

Then this mature, confident individual (the ill-natured might say smug) expired overnight along with my father. Nothing remained, not one thought, belief or opinion that I could call mine and hang on to. The smallest decisions were beyond me: my decision-making apparatus had been shot down in flames. I couldn't even judge my own behaviour or the impression I made on others – did I talk too much or not enough? Did the things I said make sense or was I babbling? Were people laughing with me or at me? Had I been right or wrong to react on this or that occasion with anger or placation, indifference or jokes? I had no way of telling. Some virus had attacked my computer and wiped out every disk. *Tabula rasa*.

The common sense explanation, a mourning syndrome, a reaction to grief, did not in my case apply. Of that, if of little else, I was sure, despite the cooing of the sentimental and the dogma of shrinks. Parting from my father was neither sweet, sorrowful nor much of a parting. How can you part from someone you've never been with?

Nevertheless it terrified me, the void, the nullity. With no warning I'd lost my grip and gone skeltering back down the well of time to become some primeval organism, a jelly lacking any boundaries, *sans* any nucleus to speak of, sploshing gloomily about in the primordial soup. From the murk I cried out for my mother, though she, poor thing, had never been much of a life-belt, being more or less fully engaged in keeping herself afloat.

'Mother,' I cried, 'I'm lost. I'm not myself. I don't know who I am any more.'

Mother perked up no end. 'I can't say I'm surprised,' she responded in the enriched voice she reserved for trouble. 'Your Aunt Fay at your age, well, it took five men to hold her down. Your Aunt Abby went upstairs and didn't come down for seven years. Your Cousin Eve . . .'

She had told me all this when I was a child, it was her way of spreading before me the joys of womanhood. I'd imagined Aunt Fay's little biceps blowing up like Popeye's and her going *Pow, take that*, at five enormous stubbly chins, but what Aunt Abby had done upstairs all that time remained a mystery until I heard Mother say about a brother of hers, 'How could Richard do it? Has he gone upstairs?' When I asked what Uncle Richard had done she said, 'None of your beeswax, he's joined the Labour Party.' So then I imagined Aunt Abby at a party in her attic, waltzing about in a big ballgown, though a party lasting seven years seemed a bit excessive. As for Cousin Eve, I knew about her. She'd covered her furniture and herself too in dust sheets and when I biked round one day she came to the door like a ghost and said, *Put not your trust in princes nor in any child of man.*

'Eve doesn't fit your picture, Mother,' I said. 'She wasn't fiftyish like the Aunts, she was thirty.'

'Thirty, fifty, makes no odds. What I'm saying is, they're women.'

'Cousin Edmund wasn't a woman, nor was Cousin Vincent and look at them.'

'That was the war.'

'They weren't in the war.'

'I know what I know,' said Mother.

What Mother knew was that, whatever their age, the female sex was in a constant state of mental riot due to being Unwell, her word for menstruation and its all-encompassing accessories. Women were unwell before being Unwell; Unwell; unwell after being Unwell; unwell while expecting; catastrophically unwell having and enfeebled for at least three months after, or until being Unwell started again. All these unwellnesses, she would explain, came together at fifty to form one Great Unwellness lasting approximately ten years. Naturally this made it impossible for women to do anything much in life but have babies and go shopping and shopping had its gynaecological pitfalls too, look at old Queen Mary and Ann Huxtable-Jones, they couldn't be left on their own in Harrods for a minute. Only at her age, Mother implied, when you'd fought through everything your insides could throw at you, were you free to rest on your laurels knowing what's what and 'That's it,' she said, 'are you listening to me?'

'I don't agree,' I said for the umpteenth time.

'You never do, that's you all over,' she said, for the umpteenth time. Once, during a similar exchange, I'd said, 'What about all the inbreeding in the family?' but Mother replied that she didn't know what I was talking about, anyone else would be proud of them, your Grandfather sent his elks to the King.

I was talking about the fact that her side of the family were a lot closer-knit than the Bible approves and in some permutations it flatly forbids. One aunt married her first cousin and had a son. Her husband died so she married another first cousin who was also her ex-brother-in-law, who had had a daughter by her sister. Her son and his daughter, now stepbrother and -sister as well as kissing cousins, brought things to a Pharaonic finale by marrying each other. The family thought that perfectly normal, they had done it for decades and they weren't driven into each other's beds by some dark Heathcliff-and-Cathy passion either: there wasn't an incestuous gene in the DNA so much as a Little Englander one. An ancestor back in the eighteenth century had sold his Cheshire farm and set sail with his bride for the Ottoman Empire in the hope of making his fortune. By the 1900s their descendants, shrewd, energetic and with the Midas touch, had swarmed all over the Middle East, the largest English family in those parts. They'd kept themselves English by steering well clear of inferior natives and, since there were few other alternatives, settling for each other. Two centuries on, there came the accounting.

Grandmother, queen of the tribe in my childhood, persisted in positive thinking on the subject. 'Inbreeding refines the stock,' she used to say in her wispy voice, 'think of horses.' I did think of horses, you couldn't help it, watching Cousin Edmund paw the ground, hearing Cousin Adelaide whinny, but neither was anywhere near fifty and Edmund, or so everyone stoutly maintained, was a man.

Mother, oh Mother, have I lost my self because I'm a female of a suspect age and family, or could there be a few more things in heaven and earth than are dreamt of in your hand-knit philosophy?

One

Two things my parents did for me as a child stand head and shoulders above what parents usually do for their children. They had me in Egypt and they set me a vivid example of everything I didn't want to be when I grew up.

Not many people grasp the importance of furnishing their offspring with an interesting birthplace. They think, if they think about it at all, in terms of passports and citizenship or their own comfort, *I'm not giving birth in the Hindu Kush, they don't do epidurals*, that sort of sadly self-centred approach. But being born in Cairo gave me an enduring weapon to wield in the hand-to-hand battle that is childhood. It marked me as different, set me up as an individual at a time when individuality was much sought after and in tragically short supply. I could always fall back on the drama of my provenance and bank on arousing a pang of envy in the cockiest school rival, they'd all heard of pyramids and mummies even if they hadn't any more idea than I had where Egypt was. Naturally, I milked it for all it was worth, declaring when cornered that Tutankhamun, being my great-great-great-grandpa, had passed on to me the ability to dispense his Curse – *If you pull my plaits one more time, Mary Beasley, King Tooting-Common will melt your teeth down till they're all green and sticky like snot, just see if he won't.*

The value to a child of poor role models is also under-estimated. Parents have the idea that it is their duty to set a good example, never realizing that a bad one will do just as well, indeed better. At best, the nuclear family provides pretty skimpy material to work on and it takes a lot of pressure off children if they see from the start that their parents are hopeless instead of having to try all the time to be as clever or successful or saintly as them. More often than not this leads in later life to fits of depression, a deepening sense of inadequacy and a fortune spent on the psychiatric couch whereas all you have to do not to be a drunk like your Daddy is not drink so much; easy-peasy.

Unluckily for me, my parents set a thoroughly good example, and so I had no praiseworthy reason for neglecting to emulate them. Never once did they get drunk or do anything remotely against the law or hit each other or us or ever fail for a moment to provide us, my brother and me, with a nourishing diet, well-fitting shoes, seaside hols, presents at Christmas and birthdays, a decent education, a Christian upbringing and a lot of scrubbing behind the ears. In other words, by every standard going they were thoroughly nice people and if I was determined not to be like them I was going to have to throw out a lot of babies with the bathwater. Everyone said how nice they were, awfully nice, therefore nice was what from the very beginning I most passionately didn't want to be. Thus I set myself a fraught and delicate task. You know where you are with the baddies, no one approves of them, but what if everyone thinks your parents are goodies and only you in the whole world don't? Where does that leave you? Up a gum tree.

Of course everyone who said my parents were nice were quite excessively nice themselves. Those who have been spared any intimate knowledge of the Home Counties will not know what I know, that they are jam-packed with men and women who talk nicely, dress nicely, behave nicely, live in nice houses with nice gardens and do very nicely and I soon discovered that I'd rather be anywhere else than there, most of all in The Slums. Occasionally, steaming by in a train with my mother to buy school uniforms at Daniel Neal, I beheld this mythic region, a huddle of rackety tenements at the back of Victoria Station wreathed with smoke and washing, full of gossiping women and sharp-eyed children doing all sorts of forbidden things. Oh, to be a part of that warmth and noise and clutter!

'You need at least four new Liberty bodices, yours are a disgrace, goodness knows what you do with them,' said my mother across the carriage, not caring a bit who heard, and I knew as I cringed red-faced in my seat that they never said things like that in The Slums, not in front of strangers in bowler hats.

'Blasted miners,' said my father from behind his newspaper at Sunday breakfast. 'On strike, can you beat it? They ought to be shot,' and I knew from the way he said it that miners must live in The Slums and being on strike sounded lovely, perhaps they played drums.

'Take that look off your face,' snapped my father, who'd guessed commendably early on that he harboured an infant Bolshie. He knew about Bolshies, his own brother was one. Eldest son of an upstanding Edinburgh family highly esteemed in legal circles, with a judge for a father, Uncle Graeme had gone and disgraced all they stood for by joining the Communist Party and marrying a girl from The Slums. There could be no pardon for such trespasses. As my mother let slip one day in my presence, an unemployed, unshaven Uncle Graeme had once dared to turn up at our house, on the cadge, what else. My father had shown him the door. I never met this uncle or his sisters, my aunts, or any other member of his family, though I answered the telephone when I was ten or so and a small voice said in my ear, 'This is your Cousin Flora.' Made careless by excitement I imparted this news to my father who was hovering nearby. In a flash he had whipped the receiver out of my hand and banged it down. Bolshieness was evidently catching.

Thus my father remained to me the sole representative on earth of the family whose name I bore and I wouldn't go to Scotland for years and years in case it was filled with clones of him. His name was Alastair, I called him Daddy but in my mind he was always the Cleft, it had the right rocky sound, his chin was Cleft too and besides that's what he called himself, a Cleft of the Fraser Clan.

'Fraser, children, from the French *fraise*, strawberry. That's why our kilt is red.'

It was very red, he was right there, none of the soft blues and greens I could have stomached. Someone once bought Fraser kilts for me and my brother but the Cleft saved me from having to wear the nasty itchy thing.

'She's a gurl,' he said, 'and gurls can't wear the kilt.' That was the first good thing I ever came across about Scotland. The first – ah no, the second – bad thing was porridge. We had it every day for breakfast at the Cleft's command and watching it bloop on the stove each morning made me feel sick.

'Eat up, eat up,' my father ordered, 'and no sugar on it either, that's for Sassenachs. Here . . .' and he leaned across and sprinkled salt all over my bowl. Looking at the loathsome sludge, I marvelled. Scottish grown-ups, who could eat whatever they liked, chose to eat this. Wild horses wouldn't drag me there.

As a boy in Scotland my father had attended Dollar Academy – he always said 'attended'. I imagined a huge cavern hacked out of granite with my father locked in it being lashed by trolls and when later I read *Nicholas Nickleby*, there Dollar was,

MacDotheboys Hall. But I didn't feel sorry for the Cleft. Though his stories of childhood were full of teachers and preachers forever threatening him with fire and brimstone and made me feel Scotland was indeed hell on earth, he seemed not only pleased by his memories but distantly contemptuous of us for never having experienced such tortures. *You're a soft lot you Sassenachs*, said his curly lip, *and there is no health in you*.

He looked just as pleased when he talked about his father, my unknown dead grandfather, the judge.

'I remember one of my sisters, she'd have been twelve or thereabouts, went to the doctor one day and when she came back she started whinging to Father. She said, "Oh Father," ' – and here the Cleft put on a silly high voice – ' "the doctor scared me, he tried to do durty things under my skurt." And the only thing my father said was, "Och now, isn't that strange, he never did anything like that to me." '

Another story that appeared to give him pleasure concerned the time his mother was dying of cancer and a nurse moved in to look after her.

'They shared the same bed, of course, Father and Mother, and in the middle of one night the nurse woke him up to tell him his wife, who was lying at his side, had passed away. And Father said, "Well then, what did you wake me for, woman? It would have kept till morning." '

The Cleft never related his stories to us children directly, he preferred to address the room or my mother, but my brother and I knew they were meant for us, meant to teach us something (though quite what was a puzzle), and we laughed obediently at the punchlines. They had no reality, these figures from our father's past, to us they were one with the hobgoblins, witches and wizards of fairytales, full of unpredictable, bad-tempered creatures subject to no known rules. There were no photographs of his family in the house but for a solitary one of our dead grandmother with her thick dark hair looped up, a watercolour version of the Cleft, a grown-up twin of me. I often picked it up and stared at it, as if her shadowy features would reveal the answer to a mystery if I looked hard enough.

'Daddy loved his mother,' my mother said but then for her it was a rule of God that children loved their mothers so you couldn't take her word.

The rest of the Cleft's family annals were contained in leather-bound volumes in his study. Sometimes he would take one down and wet his fingers to riffle through the tissuey pages until he came to a favourite bit.

'Listen to this, children. A description of one of your ancestors.' And he'd read out with relish, lingering over each word: 'Adam Tweedie was. as mild a man as ever. slit. a throat.' He'd go on to regale us further, chanting particularly bloodthirsty episodes in a queer sing-song voice: '. . . and when the guests at the feast had supped their fill and lay back to take their rest, their hosts gathered apart and of a sudden descended with scabbards bared and did not draw breath until every man, woman and child of that great company had spilled their guts upon the ground.'

These snippets of ancient Scottish savagery made me wonder for some years if they explained my missing Uncle Graeme. The day he'd come to our house had the Cleft, clad in his kilt so red it would show no drop of blood, descended of a sudden and scabbarded him? It seemed very likely.

I invented stories of my own to inflict on the nearest soft target, my brother. As a little boy he was timorous and cried easily. (Wednesday's child is full of woe, my mother said.) Our bedrooms lay opposite each other across a landing and when our parents were out of the way in the evenings I would call out sweetly to him:

'Robbie? Are you awake?'

'Eth,' he'd mutter round his thumb.

'Is Little Teddy with you?'

'Eth.' His teddy was always with him, it was his treasure.

'Very well. Now I'm going to tell you a story about him. Listen.'

Whereupon, pulling my eiderdown up to my chin, I'd embark on a series of hideous ordeals my brother's teddy was at that moment suffering.

'. . . and Little Teddy tiptoes deeper and deeper into the deep dark wood and all of a sudden, woosh, an ugly great wicked witch flies out of the bushes with long black nails and she's scratching poor Little Teddy's fur all off and pulling out his eyes and he's bleeding and crying so hard boo-hoo . . .'

'Boo-hoo,' echoed Robbie, clutching his teddy to him in a passion of grief and, '*Poor* Little Teddy,' I would croon, tenderness welling up in me for this baby person I could torture and comfort all in one. What honeyed power.

Robbie was dispatched to prep school very early on. We went in the car to a place where the sea roared against high cliffs and I turned as we drove away and saw through the back window a gnome in grey flannel with a big flannel hat over his ears and one gnome hand wagging while he sucked away at his other thumb. I sniffed up my tears. 'It's because of the war,' Mother said. 'He'll be safe there.' Unquestioningly I accepted that my brother, being a boy, had to be saved from German bombs and I must take my chances. I bore him no resentment, indeed was deeply relieved I didn't have to accompany him to that bleak castle which, I supposed, was the nearest my father could find in Sassenachland to his dread Dollar Academy.

On the other hand, I was now alone with Them.

I liked school, I liked learning and found it easy enough, which was just as well, for my father, now more of a Cleft than ever in a blue uniform with gold on his sleeves and his cap, didn't believe in encouraging a gurl with her studies. He saw education as a Holy Grail not to be tarnished by the unworthy and I was unworthy on all counts. He kept his books locked in glass-fronted cupboards and ever since I'd learned to read I had pressed my nose against the glass and gazed at the bewitching titles within: *Eyeless in Gaza, An Experiment with Time, The Seven Pillars of Wisdom*.

'Please Daddy, please let me read one.'

'Certainly not. I'm not having your jammy fingers all over my books.'

Later, when I chased about after him with two pink well-scrubbed palms spread out, he took another tack.

'You may read my books when you can tell me the meaning of two things. The Pythagoras Theorem. The Pons Asinorum. Now away and help your mother.'

Around those words grew a briar hedge as thick and high as the hedge around Sleeping Beauty. I did my best to struggle through it to the enigma on the other side, but nothing worked, no one knew or would tell. I asked teachers at school but they shook their heads. *Wait*, they said, *you're six for goodness sake, all in good time*, they said.

At last a stranger helped me find the right book in the grown-ups' library. Flushed with excitement I copied down the entries and rushed home to wait for my Daddy.

He came. I stood in front of him and, stumbling a bit, read the words out. Then I looked up into his high face.

'Now can I read your books?'

'Have you not learned yet,' he crossly replied, 'the distinction between can and may? I dare say you *can* read my books, just about. But I've told you before and I'm telling you now, you. *may*. not.' And that was that. I never did read his books. I have seen them in libraries and bookshops many times since but invisible thorns stop me from reaching for them.

The vacuum created by the eerie absence of the Cleft's family was to be amply filled by the multilingual horde of my mother's. As the see-saw shot up on one side, empty of his relatives, it plunged to the ground on the other, heavily weighted with hundreds of hers. Their main habitat, my mother's birthplace in faraway Turkey, was my favourite daydream, a hot golden Utopia as different from the Home Counties and nightmarish Scotland and the dull war that had gone on all my life as any place could be.

I loved Mother's stories of her childhood, when she was little Catherine. They were rainbows of brilliant colours that sprang up from the barren ground of home, arched into the sky and lit everything around. I hung on to every detail but I didn't believe Turkey was real, any more than the Land of Oz was real or that strange place called Peacetime for, if it were, how could Mother ever have left it for the underworld of the Cleft?

But then the parcels began arriving, big stout packages tied with rope, leaking funny white beads and a heady smell. 'Rice,' said Mother, tearing open the first and the beads ran out of her hands like a waterfall. 'Sultanas,' she breathed, 'and currants and, look, oh, figs and oh, oh, dates and, God in heaven, Balkan Sobranies.' Her eyes went all blurry as she opened the little black box and together we stared inside at cigarettes God in heaven must smoke, gold tops for where His lips would touch and the colours of angels' wings for between His fingers. Excitedly, Robbie and I went on rooting in the straw and there was another box, bigger and wooden. We prised up its lid and then I knew that every one of Mother's stories was true for the smell was sweeter than my greediest imaginings and every time I breathed, puffs of sweet powder fluffed up in the air. They were like nothing I'd ever seen before, these succulent jellies buried in snow, pink and green and bristling like hedgehogs with almond spines.

'Rahat Locums,' my mother crooned, her voice low and caressing. 'Turkish Delight.'

I gazed at her, my jaw at half-mast. So there was Turkey, after all. There was a Family. There was Delight! Perhaps they were all true, then, all the wonderful stories, Oz, Cinderella, Snow White, Father Christmas, Heaven, Scarlett O'Hara. I began to ricochet round the room singing at the top of my lungs.

'That's enough from you, pipe down, young lady,' said the Cleft, but his mouth was full of Turkish Delight and he didn't sound cross.

Maybe there was even Peacetime.

There was Peacetime. Everyone cheered and clapped, I heard them on the wireless, and the grumpy man in the house across the road put a Union Jack on his garage. My father yanked the black curtains from our windows, ripped off the dingy paper that criss-crossed the panes and got Kenny, the gardener, to knock down the shelter, a crescent of corrugated iron that had curved up against the dining-room wall since time began. Mother said, 'We can go to Turkey now,' and I didn't give the smallest whoop when she said it in case the Cleft heard and said *Certainly not*. But some weeks later, after a night spent waking my brother up every hour to whisper, 'We're going to tread on Turkey grass, we're going to breathe in Turkey air,' we flew away to Paradise via Rome and Athens. In the plane even the Cleft grew jaunty. He lit a pink Sobranie and looked at Robbie and me as if we really existed while he reminisced about the awful plane crashes he and friends of his with names like Dusty and Old Handlebars had had or nearly had and how, when they were in the desert, they used to make circles of twigs, put a scorpion in the middle, set the twigs alight and watch the scorpion raise its tail and sting itself to death.

'Oh, *poor* little scorpion,' Robbie and I ritually moaned.

'Rubbish,' said the Cleft and scented smoke steamed from his long thin nostrils.

In Rome I encountered Victor, the man who could have changed my life. It happened in a lift in the celestial palace that was the Hotel Excelsior.

Glor-o-o-ria
In Excelsis Deo.

Squashed in with the two of us Mother suddenly glowed, turned her back on us and began to chat animatedly to a teddy bear of a man with a red jolly face. So absorbed were they that we missed our floor and had to descend again, the man too. Saying a lot of goodbyes, Mother backed out in some confusion, pulling us with her and whispering, 'Imagine! Victor! The man I nearly married!'

This revelation pierced me through. Wrenching my hand out of hers I dashed back to the lift. People were still stepping in, Victor still standing inside. Electric with outrage I planted my Clarks sandals tip to tip with his shoes, lifted my chin and fired death-rays of fury up at his smiling face. *Toad. Snake.* You could have been my father, you could have loved me, we could all have lived in Excelsior forever and ever amen. Be cursed! Get scarlet fever and chicken-pox both together! DIE.

By the time the gates of the lift clashed shut Victor wasn't smiling any more and I had no doubt, though I couldn't extract another word from Mother on the subject, that he shortly afterwards expired.

But this triumphant assassination paled beside the wonder of Constantinople, Mother's own beloved Con. The moment we arrived, everything dull and difficult and ordinary was swept to oblivion and the world put on spangles, like the glittering end to a pantomime. There was our new Grand Father waiting for us, exotic as a Sultan in a white shiny suit, a white shiny hat, a neat white beard and a face the colour of conkers. We were all embraced, even the Cleft, while men in strange clothes swarmed around us at Grandpa's command, whipping the suitcases from our hands and ushering us up the steps of a carriage because, of course, there was a carriage, bright as a pumpkin and covered all over – the horses too – with tassels and pom-poms.

'But what about our passports?' the Cleft said, fanning them out before Grandpa, but Grandpa just waved a dismissive brown hand. Before you could say Jack Robinson we were galloping off, scattering the crowds, past blue minarets to the blue sea and on to a boat – carriage, horses and all – and so to Mother's home where, down white stairs dripping with lavender plumes, rushed waving and cooing an astonishing number of aunts, uncles and cousins while, above, by an enormous lavender door, one lily-white hand upraised, stood our new Grand Mother.

I fell in love with them all on the spot, they were like no people I had ever met before. Throughout that glorious summer not one of them ever looked or spoke or behaved remotely like any grown-up in England, because this was Paradise and they were the Birds who inhabited it, fluttering in and out of their big white houses, twittering from their wide flowery verandas that skimmed the shores of the curly sea.

Aunts in England were thick on the ground but they weren't the colour of milky tea like mine were, with shiny haloes round the brown of their eyes like the moon before rain and voices warm as roosting doves. The uncles of my friends at home just sat about with pipes in their mouths but my big brown uncles swung me up behind them on horses and we cantered away into wild scrubby woods where guns exploded and huge hairy pigs came crashing out screaming and bleeding. Every inch of my skin grew sticky with fright when I saw the corners of their tiny fierce eyes and smelt their hot fearsome porky smell, but fright was part of Paradise too, it set you buzzing from your ears to your toes and banged your heart so hard up and down you felt ill with delight.

English grandfathers didn't fall asleep in their chairs with a canary perched on each ear and grown-up English cousins didn't climb trees and sit there shouting *Come-and-catch-me*, or tell you they were ostriches and make ostrich noises all through dinner or smell like Christmas puddings and wobble when they walked. Other people's grannies knew their names, mine didn't. Mine had lace up her neck, smelled of lilies of the valley and stroked my hair so gently while she called me Alice or Darling Yolande or sometimes Edmund or James. There was no end to the ways my Birds of Paradise were different and endlessly more fascinating and vastly superior in every aspect to any other person's relations anywhere else, probably in the world but certainly, *certainly* in dreary old England.

Everything else was superior, too. Nobody at home except dukes and the King had a footman each to stand behind their chair while they ate, but in Paradise we did and that was only one of the wonders. I had my own maid to run my bath – she was fat and smiley and her name was Crysanthe – and at night we were guarded by Hercules, Grandpa's head watchman, who sat cross-legged outside the lavender door till the sun rose again. At home we'd had nannies who took us for walks but here we had a real live brigand with four yellow fangs who went everywhere with us in case Turks stabbed us in the street. A Turk had stabbed one of my cousins that year, she came to the door and he stuck a knife in her. It didn't hurt all that much, she told me, and he said he was sorry after, he'd mistaken her for a Greek.

In Paradise the trees were hung with figs, nuts and lemons, not the hard pears and tired old apples we had in our garden, and one day I stood on Grandpa's veranda which was as big as two rooms at home and I saw at the far edge of the sea a grey wall of water that rose up and up as high as a house and came roaring and steaming until Grandpa shouted *Come in, child, COME IN*. But I stayed, gripping the balustrade, and watched the great wave turn itself inside out and scoop up every little boat and fling them all over the place like spillikins. Another time, just as I got into bed, the light that hung from the ceiling over my head began to swing gently round and round. I lay gazing at it, proud that even ordinary objects like lights did interesting things in Turkey, until the grown-ups came and pulled me out of bed and down to where the ground shuddered and trembled and the trees leaned over.

So the summer whizzed by, burning me and Robbie so brown as we tumbled in and out of the blue glass sea that our uncles nicknamed me Honolulu and Robbie Levrek after some Turkish fish. We stuffed ourselves on magic food and went on magic picnics in Grandpa's yacht to little perfect islands where we jogged about on donkeys and when the time came to leave I threw myself down on my bedroom floor and howled with misery. All the aunts gathered round giving us feathery kisses, one on each cheek and a third because we were family and I dripped tears on Granny's velvet hands while she whispered, 'Goodbye, come back very soon my dearest little Adelaide.' Cousin Howard the Ostrich made sad ostrich sounds and Cousin Vincent, smelling stronger than ever of pudding, rocked me so round and about in his arms that we both grew dizzy and nearly fell down. Mother cried too, her nose turned pink under the brown, Robbie sniffled and pushed out his mouth like a mournful chimp and the Cleft said, *Come along, you Wailing Willies, we'll miss the plane*.

I didn't tell any of this to my friends at home, especially not to my best friend Angela in case she pinched up with jealousy and did mean things to me. It was bad enough that I had a tan and had been Abroad without swanking as well, beastly things happened to you at school if girls thought you conceited, like being sent to Coventry. Besides, I was afraid if any of them realized the sadly poor quality of their own relatives they would hopelessly pine. After all, it wasn't their fault they only knew the kind of grown-ups England produced.

They had to be coped with somehow, these adults, other children's mothers, fathers, uncles and aunts, your teachers and neighbours, your parents' acquaintances. It wasn't easy but you learned some tricks to cope. For one thing, you never looked at them directly if you could help it and if you had to because they said '*Look* at me when I'm talking to you,' you squinted just enough to make their faces blur, which helped you bear it. I couldn't work out who was worst, the grown-up women with their blue-pink skins, lumpy jumpers and skirts, who never stopped wagging fingers at you, saying you shouldn't do what you were doing it wasn't ladylike, be a good girl, be polite, be tidy, don't be selfish, don't argue, never mind what *you* think, say thank you, say please, count your blessings, a stitch in time saves nine; or the grown-up men with hairy ginger jackets and bristly moustaches who tweaked your plaits and pinched your cheeks and winked as if they thought you liked them and laughed loudly, ho ho ho, at nothing at all.

Men or women, they made me feel trapped in the folds of some horrid scratchy stuff, the sort shop assistants told your mother would never wear out: navy serge, flannel, itchy wool. I used to close my eyes at night and pray that when I woke up I'd be back with the Birds of Paradise but I knew I wouldn't because I was in England and England was real life, ugly, grey and cold, full of porridge and the Cleft snapping *don't care was*

made to care and *elbows*! and real life went on and on and on in
the same boring way because no grown-up anywhere that I
ever heard of minded or wanted to change it or said, *That's
quite enough of that, I'm off.*

Not even Mother.

'Why d'you keep looking at me like that, my lamb?' she
started asking soon after the Turkey visit and I'd shrug and
mumble that I wasn't. But oh, I was. I stared as if my eyes
were two corkscrews that could wrench out of her the answer
to the riddle that nagged at me: why ever had she given up
Paradise to live in England with the Cleft? It was no good
putting it to her, she only said, 'Why, to marry Daddy, silly,'
which was no answer at all. I couldn't press her, either, she
would have clammed up and I surely couldn't say what I most
wanted to: *Mother, I hear the sounds in the walls. You made a
dreadful mistake didn't you? Please admit it and then you, Robbie
and me can all go to Turkey and live happily ever after, oh do
let's, please.*

The walls of the house growled every night, there were
ghostly moans in the bricks and mortar, they made the springs
of my bed quake, sometimes I quaked. But when morning came
the walls were quiet, the table in the dining room shone with
white cloth and breakfast china that said to me, *You dream
things, eat and forget.* Besides, I had learned that the more you
asked, the less you would be answered. Grown-ups loathed
answering questions from children unless they were about
geography or maths: what's an estuary, how much is fourteen
squared. They closed ranks the moment you opened your
mouth and as they saw you coming they hauled up the
drawbridge so they could pretend not to hear you shouting on
the wrong side of the moat. 'What?' they'd say, shaking their
heads, 'I don't know what you mean,' or, 'None of your business, run along.' The Cleft said, 'Children should be seen and

not heard,' Mother said, '*Quoi quoi quoi, trois corbeaux dans un bois, s'il y en a un, c'est toi*,' which was French for go away and do your homework.

Grown-ups who were married were the worst, the nippiest haulers-up of the drawbridge. You couldn't ask anything about their husbands or wives or any other married person, no matter how much you knew – and you always knew. Children are what mediums pretend to be, in touch with invisible forces, able to pick up vibrations from the ether and detect tiny changes in people's auras, which they can see plain as day. They watch those auras change from palest pink to stormy grey and then curdle at the edges into streaks of red, but they aren't allowed to mention it. Quite a lot of the time the children aren't that interested, but still they know, they can't help it. The grown-ups have forgotten about all this and think they can simply deny or refuse to confirm what the air quivers with, which is very confusing. What the children then have to decide is, who will they trust, themselves or the grown-ups? One way or the other they have to choose and that choice shapes the rest of their lives.

Mother's aura, which normally had the dappled sheen of mother-of-pearl, turned a watery grey to warn me off asking Why about her and the Cleft. How and Where questions she would answer.

'Granny and Grandpa sent me to Alexandria to stay with Aunty Marjie in a lovely house by the sea and one day Aunty Marjie gave a tennis party and Daddy was invited and . . .'

The Cleft was a pilot then, a Master Pilot. There were photos of him standing in jodhpurs beside big tinny-looking planes that sometimes had skis instead of wheels. He flew them all over the place but especially backwards and forwards to Egypt, where Alexandria was, and Mother. He was invited to lots of parties, he used to drink olive oil to line his stomach so he wouldn't get drunk, and at most of the parties there were girls who wanted to get married, with names no one has any more like Esme, Nesta, Lally, Molly and Mirth.

'He was very handsome, your father,' Mother usually added at about this point, though she never looked particularly chuffed when she said it. I could see that for myself, in their wedding picture, Mother small in a long tunic, slippery and shiny and with veils all round sweeping down to the ground from a circle of flowers set just above her eyes, clinging to the arm of the Cleft high above her in tall glossy boots and his jodhpurs, looking like Gary Cooper in a temper. I wanted to ask, didn't you notice, Mother, how cross he was? Why didn't you marry jolly Victor instead? Unaskable.

If the Cleft wasn't present, she'd go on to describe to me how he came to Turkey to ask Grandpa for her hand. If he was, he took over, though he related the story only to Mother, who knew it.

'So I boarded the Orient Express at Victoria and as we were nearing Istanbul,' he told Mother, '. . . or Constantinople as it was then, a porter came along the corridor to collect our passports. I thought it was for Customs but no. Your father, Cath, unbeknownst to me, was on the same train, in First of course, and he'd sent the porter so that he could look through the passports to see who was arriving and find out all about them. He was King of Con in those days, your father,' he told Mother, who knew.

But why had Grandpa allowed the Cleft to marry Mother? Men, after all, weren't impressed by other men being handsome so that wouldn't have influenced him. And he didn't have any money, which Grandpa did. Money was the thing that mostly worked in the books I read. So what was left? Love, and that deepened the mystery because the Cleft didn't love Mother.

'Amazing family,' he used to say, shaking his head as he

finished the story, 'I'd have married any one of the sisters, but there was only your Mother left.'

I would have, too, if I'd been him, we had that much in common, but Mother only looked sad when he said it, in spite of him adding, 'My joke, just my joke.' They'd spent their honeymoon at the Mena House Hotel with the pyramids, Mother said, close enough to touch. I supposed they might have been a bit happy then, until my being born had spoiled everything. I knew it had because whenever I wailed more bitterly than usual that Daddy didn't love me, Mother had once or twice failed to deny it as she usually did and said instead with a faraway look in her eyes that yes, he'd been jealous from the beginning, naturally she'd given me her attention but men were such babies themselves, weren't they, and he hadn't liked it, my goodness he hadn't, he'd wanted her love all for himself. The first time she said this I felt a quite pleasurable surge of pity for myself, the little match-girl left out in the cold, and waited with meekly bowed head for her to console me with hugs and kisses. Nothing happened so I looked up again to see that she'd forgotten all about me and was staring into nowhere with a tiny pleased smile on her face. *Poor* little match-girl.

Two

It was only after we'd been to Turkey that I understood some things that had long puzzled me about the way we lived. All the rooms of our house put together would hardly have filled Grandpa's hall, but Mother didn't seem to have remarked on how shrunk everything was and went on behaving as if she'd never left home. She called the not very big adjoining rooms my brother and I slept in when we were small the 'Night Nurseries' and the room we played in the 'Day Nursery', later to become the 'Schoolroom', and the names, which came straight from her Turkish house and which no English family we knew used, made me worry when I was little that Robbie and I weren't enough children for Mother, there ought to be lots more of us to crowd the nurseries as there had been when Mother was growing up with four sisters and five brothers. Later I worried that people would think us snobs or laugh at us for living in an ordinary house as if we thought it was a mansion.

Mother hadn't a fraction of Grandpa's servants either, and the ones she did have could hardly fit in. There was Annie the Irish parlourmaid who was dressed in a black frock with a white frilly apron and a white frilly cap perched like a snowy triangle on top of her mountain of red hair. There was our governess, Mother's name for Miss Barnes, and our nanny, Nanny Daisy, and the fat nurserymaid, Betty, and some depressed-looking women Mother called Cook-Generals, who came and went too fast to remember names and Kenny, the gardener, whom Mother said wasn't all there and I thought just as well, seeing how squashed-in we were. Anyone but her would have seen that there wasn't space for everyone. Annie answered the doorbell just as the servants did in Turkey, but there they had a special room to show callers into. We didn't have a special room. Whenever the bell rang Robbie and I would rush down the stairs after Annie, with Miss Barnes or Nanny Daisy after us, and everyone would scrum up in the hall falling over each other while the dogs barked deliriously and the caller stood bewildered in the jostle and noise while Mother called from the sitting room, 'Who is it, Annie?' so she might as well have opened the door herself.

The funny thing was, all the grown-ups went along with it just as Mother did, behaving quite as if they really were in a household as big as Grandpa's. They were like people in a play together, wanting to make the play work, determined not to notice how small the stage was and how wobbly and unconvincing the scenery and costumes. Annie, for instance, had cast herself as the maid in a sexy sort of farce. Her hair was meant to be pinned up neatly under her cap but in her rush to answer the bell it invariably unpinned itself and she'd arrive at the door with red tresses swirling to her waist and her black frock unbuttoned to the furrow between her breasts. Mother was forever tugging at Annie's uniform and trying to poke her Kirby grips back in. And if that wasn't enough drama for Annie, she'd make up more from time to time, like complaining to Mother, all blushes and tossing hair, that the Young Master had made advances to her. Goodness knows what Mother said but I knew what my brother had done. The soppy baby had run out of his room as Annie was passing and stuffed crumpled lavatory paper down the tops of her stockings. Nevertheless, I felt it was somehow our fault that we'd failed to provide the properly dashing Young Master Annie expected and it made me touchy and ashamed.

Miss Barnes, too, did her best to play a grim Dickensian governess. She wore long black frocks and pointy-toed lace-ups and frowned at us in front of our parents, but she couldn't keep it up when we were alone in the Schoolroom. Then her starchy accent would soften to a warm country burr and her starchy face dimple as she pulled off her shoes and sank into the basket chair to begin her perennial task of picking dogs' hairs off her skirt. It was obvious to me that she wasn't a real governess any more than Annie was a real maid or fat Betty a real nurserymaid or Kenny a proper gardener and the Cleft, who joined in by pretending to be King of the World, was really only King of Us. It was starting to look as if that's what being grown-up was all about: pretending. Only Mother didn't, she acted herself. She just wasn't in the right play.

I soon came across other grown-ups who took pretence even further in a quite different direction. Robbie and I had a neighbourhood friend, David, whose father, Mr Rowe, was one of the dark army of fathers in pin-striped suits and bowler hats who emerged from their houses every morning and returned every evening, ducking under the lilacs or making a glossy path through the snow. During school holidays Robbie and I were sometimes invited to tea by David's mother, who wore green dirndls and had her hair plaited in two circles, one over each ear. She gave us triangles of white bread with cucumber, and fairy cakes, after which we had to sing with her round the piano –

31

Early one mo-o-rning
Just as the sun was ri-i-sing
I spied a pretty maid in the valley below.

– until we could escape into the garden. One afternoon, when David and Robbie were in the garage counting to a hundred, I shinned up a tree to hide from them. As my head drew level with the Rowe's first floor I saw through the nearest window a dim figure tottering on high heels within. It had stockings held up with pink suspenders on its hairy legs, a hairy chest strapped with pink pouchy elastic (what Mother called a BB or Bust Bodice) and it also had David's father's face and David's father's hedgehog moustache. As I gaped, up from the french windows below soared the screechy voice of David's mother –

Oh, don't de-ceee-eeve me
Oh, never lee-eeve me

and I froze, clamped to the trunk of the tree –

How can you tre-ee-at a poor maiden so?

– and began to let myself down inch by inch, scraping knees and elbows painfully against the bark. Though I'd never begun to imagine that a grown man might pretend to be a woman, I knew as surely as eggs were eggs that if Mr or Mrs Rowe ever found out that I'd seen what I'd seen they'd both hate me.

'Good morning, my dear,' Mr Rowe said, clicking his umbrella along the pavement as he passed me skipping next morning and, 'Good morning Mr Rowe,' I chirruped politely. Perhaps yesterday was only a dream or me being cuckoo as the Cleft claimed. Still skipping busily, I peered after his immaculate back as it marched away and yes, there it was, I could definitely see it, the tiny bump in the middle of his suit, the protruding hooks of his BB.

Then, at school, a new games mistress arrived and she

pretended to be a man. She wore men's trousers, a man's jacket split to accommodate her largish bottom, a man's shirt and tie, her hair was cut like a man's and she spoke in a deep voice like a man's. Also, she held hands with Miss Parker the Latin mistress whenever she thought we weren't looking. The only way you knew she was a she, apart from being called Miss Paley, was the bulge across her shirtfront and her smooth face. I liked Miss Paley, we all did, she wasn't frightening like Mr Rowe, who did his pretending alone in a room and might very well puff up like a horned toad if he caught you watching and tell your parents what a horrid little liar you were. Instinct told me that it was the ones who hid their pretending who would cause you the worst trouble if they thought you knew, perhaps because they feared you'd sneak on them. Well, you might sneak to other children, giggling together, but never to a grown-up, they'd only pull their mouths down and look at you in a disgusted way as if you were the one who'd done something wrong. Any child with sense knew you didn't involve yourself with the adult world if you weren't absolutely forced to. We lived on our side of a great divide and we crossed it at our peril.

There was another mistress, called Miss Needham, at the school, a thin woman with her hair in a bun, the kind of archetypal dried-up spinster that infested the girls' schools of the day. One morning Miss Needham caught me running down the wrong side of the corridor and her arm shot out and gripped me as I ran past and pulled me into an empty classroom. I stood panting in the chalky air while she closed the door, resigned to a wigging and a bad mark. Then she tapped toward me on her creaky shoes till I had to tilt my head to look at her face, which was twisted, with little furrows forking off her pale lips like Norwegian fiords in Geography.

Her face swelled and she said, 'You're a hore, d'you hear me, a hore. You'll end up on the streets doing this to men and that,' and she went on for ages in a strange sing-song voice, using words I didn't know but they came out with so much spit they had to be awful. I grew ice-cold watching the purple ferns that branched on her cheeks. 'Look at me,' she hissed, 'look at me, you little hore,' and I squinted ferociously but this time the trick didn't veil her from me, only made her two eyes become a glaring four.

When she finally released me, giving me a hard shove into the empty corridor, I stood trembling as she glided silently away, but hot tendrils unfurled in my stomach. This time I didn't care. This time I would cross the divide, sneak to the grown-ups and they'd have to believe me because this time, surely surely, Miss Needham had done what I was always being warned not to do: she'd gone too far.

'Mummy?'

'Well?'

She was sewing, the basket full of coloured bobbins open on her knees. Thick shafts of sun beamed from between the velvet curtains and spread out on the carpet. Pink roses in vases on polished tables poured their perfume into the air. A tinted photo of baby Robbie and me, he all pastels and gold curls, me bald as a bullet with blackberry eyes, hung on the wall beside Mother's chair. I looked into my one-year-old moon face and it looked warily back at me.

'You were such a *dear* little lamb,' said Mother, following my gaze.

Little lambs didn't come home from school to upset their mothers with nasty stories. Lambs hadn't heard any nasty stories, that's why they were dear. I could feel Miss Needham's words sticky as grease on my clothes and my skin, making the room dirty. Still, I made the effort.

'Miss Needham said beastly things to me today and I hate her.'

34

'Hate, hate, that's not a word to use,' Mother said, tut-tut-ting. 'What things? What had you done?'

'Nothing. I was only running in the corridor and she . . .' I could hear my voice losing its rage and becoming thin and whiny. The incandescent brick I'd carried home inside me was crumbling to pieces.

'Whatever Miss Needham said, I'm sure you deserved it,' Mother said. 'Now do go up and tidy your room, you'd think a pig lived there instead of a girl.'

What was the use. Grown-ups always ganged up against you. Anyway, it gave me the shivers remembering Miss Needham's glaring eyes and blotchy cheeks. I clamped my hands round her scraggly throat and squeezed her to death and felt better. It would be dreadful, besides, if I told Mother and Mother told the Cleft and she would, I knew that. Instead I told my brother only. I said, 'Shall I show you what the mean old witch did?' and I grabbed Robbie's arm and shoved him on the bed hissing, 'Hore, you hore, you little hore,' making my lips like a funnel to huff in his ear and he twisted away, screeching, 'You're tickling me, get *off*,' and the Cleft roared from downstairs, 'Be quiet, you two,' and we stuck our heads in the blankets coughing with laughter. Who cared what grown-ups did, who gave tuppence? Not me.

So I said nothing to anyone about Uncle Gary, not even to Robbie. He wasn't an uncle, just a friend of the Cleft's, a Canadian with a fleshy dark face who had fought in the war and been shot through the neck, which was why he grunted when he talked. 'He's a Hero,' the Cleft said, while Uncle Gary looked heroically down at his feet: 'a Hero, children.' He and my father stood legs apart in front of the fire holding tumblers full of gold. 'Go on, run away and play with the other children,' the Cleft told us, so we did.

The game was Sardines and I climbed up into the attic and

hid behind the water tank. It was dusty, dark and warm there and I could feel grit and the corpses of dead flies under my knees as I knelt, but I hardly noticed, I was straining too hard to follow the squeals and muffled thuds of the pursuers below. Then came heavier, more purposeful sounds, the trap-door creaked open and King Kong swung up and edged towards me. Next thing there was Uncle Gary squatting beside me on wide khaki haunches, smelling of tobacco, and he had his hands flat on my chest with his fingers scissoring at the two currants there. I didn't move, only my heart knocked harder and harder as he scissored and the cries of the children rose and fell a long way away. 'Shsh,' grunted Uncle Gary, though I wasn't making any noise and his hands were under my frock and in my panties and I felt a toxic sweetness rise in my blood and a rush of saliva into my mouth like you do when you're going to be sick.

Robbie found us, he knew the house's hiding places. I saw his face poking up in the light from the trap-door, neckless, smirking. Uncle Gary's fingers slid out of me and he stamped off like a big jolly bear, growling, 'OK, pardner, you got us, don't shoot,' and then he was standing with the Cleft by the fire and I couldn't look at him, my eyes were too muzzy. No one to tell that time, not even my brother, who had somehow grown smaller, as if he were running away from me, a kid in short trousers, you can't tell things like that to kids.

After Uncle Gary there were suddenly men everywhere, the landscape was full of them, as if someone had opened the doors of a loony bin and emptied them out. They became a natural hazard, like wasps in your lemonade or ice on the pavement in winter. The lane I walked up and down to school was infested with them, once a week at least one of them popped out of a bush waggling his worm at me, maybe it was the same man always, I didn't stop to check. First I performed a lightning squint to dim whatever it was he was doing; then I ran. I was a good runner, my long skinny legs fairly zipped along under my navy-blue pleated tunic while one hand automatically battened upon my panama or felt hat, depending on the season. I can feel the thump of the satchel on my back now.

The man, or men, never ran after me, preferring, I reckoned, to adjust his clothing in preparation for the next target, or maybe he was put off by my wildly crossed eyes. Once I was past the danger zone I slowed to my normal dawdling pace, scuffing along in leaves singing snatches of the songs we'd done in Choir that day.

> How beau-ti-ful they are
> The Lordly Ones
> Who live in the hills
> In the hea-ven-ly hills.

Like an animal, like our cat, I'd learned how to fuel myself with adrenalin and then, when the danger was over, let it drain instantly away and return to my own peaceable concerns.

This happy trick wasn't always possible to exercise. The man on the bus I took to and from school couldn't be run from. He'd sit down next to me and in a while take my hand and dump it on his lap, where the worm was, under his trousers. Sometimes, if the bus was nearly empty, I had to sit feeling the flesh of the worm twitching under my limp hand. I tried to pull away from his grip but I was far more frightened of attracting other people's attention than I was simply enduring, which I soon did quite successfully, staring out of the window, distracting myself, so that the hand lying on the worm was just a spare piece of skin and bone, not belonging to me. Every now and then, when the worm reared up from its nest of flannel the soft part of my throat would rise with it and threaten to choke me; the swarm of bees in my stomach never entirely ceased their buzzing but I learned to cope. I wasn't there at all, it was some other girl. I was in a completely different place, by the sea or picking blackberries in the meadow at the bottom of our garden or flying off to see the Birds of Paradise, that was the best when things got sticky, which they often did. I kept empty lemonade-powder bags in my pocket to wipe my fingers clean as I got off the bus. I had become quite organized.

There was no point in wondering what these men were doing or why they did it. The adult world was incomprehensible and the less you bothered with it, the better off you were. Besides, nothing these loonies did with their worms mattered in the slightest compared to the truly unthinkable horror of the Cleft knowing about it. That eventuality had to be avoided at any cost. The fleeting image that rose in my mind of the Cleft's blinking eyes if he ever found out, the hideousness of him knowing about my hand, the worms, the stickiness, was so infinitely worse than the deed itself that there was no contest. Everything would be lost and I wouldn't ever again be free and private because the Cleft would be there, knowing. Then all the men would suddenly come alive, forcing me to look at them without my squint and see their wolf heads and alligator teeth. Probably my heart would stop.

The other person who made it difficult to cope was my brother. Loneliness engulfed me whenever I thought about what I knew and he didn't, and though I tried hard to forget it all when I was with him, it made a barrier between us, the higher for him not knowing the barrier was there. He played happily on the sunny side and never noticed that I was in shadow. I didn't want him to notice. The urgency of not wanting it bore no comparison to the extreme terror of rupturing the Cleft's ignorance, but in a milder, melancholic way it was there. My brother wasn't burdened with secrets. I was. He was grubby outside but clean inside. I was the other way round.

In a way, it had been so for a long time before the men had come along. Nanny Dora, our first nanny, demonstrated that. She wore a striped dress with an apron and she used to tell Mother what pets we were, how she loved us. It was true she loved Robbie, but she didn't love me. Almost the first memory I have is of lying in bed crying in the dark of the little room I slept in alone (Robbie slept with Nanny Dora next door), and then Nanny bending over me and pressing something thick and gluey across my mouth so I couldn't open it and had to stop crying to sniff back the tears stuffing up my nose in order to breathe.

It wasn't pleasant but I perfectly saw that Nanny's action was reasonable. She didn't want me waking Robbie because she loved him and I understood that, he was more lovable than me. He was cuddly and I liked his baby smell and the way his soft hair curled neatly into the nape of his neck instead of standing out in a shock as mine did – but it wasn't just that. Even then there was something whole and inviolate about him, where I was already half-plucked by the grown-ups, like a chicken they were readying for the pot. The older we got the more the difference increased: him still of one piece, me in bits.

They expected more of me. I had to do more and be more than Robbie but not in interesting or challenging ways, only in itsy-bitsy things like helping, not forgetting, tidying, behaving nicely, thinking of others, understanding them, being kind. Robbie was excluded from all this, it was as if they were allowing him to rest and save his strength for grander undertakings, as yet unspecified but sure to come. I quickly grew resigned to the concrete demands, they were manageable; you could refuse them and take the consequences, there was some choice. What couldn't be refused or ducked or ignored were the unspoken demands, a constant static all around which I could only block out with noisier static of my own: tantrums, crying fits, fidgeting and other efficient distractions, bursts of rowdiness and an earnest, near vocational self-centredness.

Such tactics, I discovered, had the effect of momentarily lifting from me the despairing adult weight that pressed on me; they flushed the enemy out into the open with guns roaring and then I could roar back. War was openly declared, a hostile engagement took place, the air was cleared.

Not for long though, never for long. All too soon I was back to building up my defences again, preparing to fend off the grown-ups' forays and encroachments, their awesome needs, their not half well-enough hidden griefs, their voracious inner appetites, their saying one thing and frantically signalling another. Some vital part had gone missing in the machinery of me, some baffle intended to keep all this out a filter that had never worked, so their messages came through loud and clear, night and day, like a switchboard gone berserk. All I could do was pretend I hadn't got them. Their appeals had to be ignored if I was ever to get on with my own concerns, preserve my patch, make a place of my own. Yet step by step, year by year, I lost ground and the core that was me began coming apart. That core: I could feel it curled up inside me, the foetus of the person I might one day be if they would just leave me alone. But they wouldn't. They hung over my head like a cloud of mosquitoes, emitting a subsonic hum, biting, stinging, raising bumps so that I was forced to stop what I was doing to slap and scratch and flail about.

My luckier brother came out of the womb covered in a mosquito repellent and they never bothered him. He played in a corner, all you saw of him was the dip in his neck as he sat with his fat little legs straight out and his head bent over, absorbed in his games. The grown-ups nagged him to do this and that, of course they did, but whether he obeyed or not the light around him remained bright even when he cried, even when he bawled his head off. No distracting sparks jumped between him and them, no invisible strings twanged discordantly and went on twanging into his dreams, he was not brought low by sly injections of pity. He saw nothing; therefore had nothing to ignore.

Naturally, then, they preferred him to me. He was a real child and I was a midget dressed up as one, a wolf in lambskin. Robbie – or so it seemed to me – believed what the grown-ups so desperately wanted him to, that they were in charge, in control of themselves and their world, omnipotent but benignly so and knowing at all times what was best for him. That meant if he chose to break their rules he could do so in some luxury, sure that when they remonstrated or punished him they were simultaneously rescuing him from danger, chivvying him from a thrilling excursion into no-boys-land back to the cosy security of what was right and good and God-approved.

This happy meshing of needs suited everyone. Robbie's faith that adults knew best gave him plenty of space to be himself. In turn, he neatly reinforced their faith in themselves, providing them with another cosy layer of insulation against the chill of fear, doubt and confusion which silently circled them in the darkness, threatening to rip off their elaborate disguises and reveal them as they really were, naked and frightened children themselves.

I'm aware of this only because I'm one of the grown-ups now. Ungrown, I merely sensed it, breathing in the fumes of their fright to sear my insides. The adults created their own micro-climate and when their winds blew I hunched over, gritting my teeth and fighting the drag, for I knew if I didn't

I'd be sucked in, eaten up and would emerge as somebody else entirely. The struggle, as is so often the case, didn't enhance my attractions to anyone except those other children who were battling away on the home front themselves. As it happened, as we were to find out much later, in the sixties, together we made up a fairly monstrous regiment.

Three

Constantinople and the Birds of Paradise continued to lie across what I saw as the rubble of my life like some glittering archaeological stratum left behind by profligate aliens on a visit from outer space. For a while I was sure it would seal off forever the dull past beneath and miraculously transform the future. To my chagrin, nothing changed. The war, though officially over, had a seemingly endless half-life, dragging on and on like a huge wounded slow-worm, flattening every new shoot in its path. The bright memory of Turkey that should have broadened my mind narrowed it instead to a thin laser beam that made everything under its scrutiny look tattier, more threadbare and more unbearably tedious than before.

'How amusing,' the Birds of Paradise were wont to twitter as they flew around their hot gold habitat.

'How boring,' I grumbled as I slouched off under Mother's orders to wait in yet another queue for awful offal. Nothing had changed for the better for Mother either. Her raffish bunch of pseudo-servants had scattered to the winds or, as I believed, to real Stately Homes where they tittered every time they remembered our piteous clutter of rooms. All Mother had left to remind her of better days, Istanbul days, was Minnie the daily, in a turban so tight it made her look Chinese, and Kenny the gardener who continued to loom up unexpectedly at various windows, absently uprooting the wrong plants as he gazed with an expression of infinite sorrow at the frequently unedifying scenes within.

Who would have blamed my gently raised Mamma for giving up and letting the house go hang? Not I. I'd have been only too pleased to see her languid and lazy, *couchant* on a couch, while the dust and household debris, given not much more than the odd stir by Minnie, piled anarchically up. It was not to be. Mother, dredging up some rocky subsoil in herself hitherto left happily fallow, clapped a dung-coloured overall on top of her pretty frocks and set about making our lives a misery with her brooms, her duster and a curious tin box with a long handle which she banged aggressively about until, in protest, it vomited up more crumbs, fluff and dogs' hairs on the carpets than it had initially swallowed. Like a convert to a new religion she went to the kind of extremes no cradle housewife would contemplate. Not a cushion could rest for a moment unplumped, no ashtray squat unemptied, no dish recline unwashed, no tiniest spill remain unscooped-up. Wherever you sat, wherever you hid, she'd flush you out with her household weapons and chase you off, though not before managing to make you feel, with her martyred groans and sighs, crosser and more guilty than you'd ever felt before.

The Cleft was as disturbed as I was by this change in Mother, I knew that by his eyes. He'd arrive back from London in the early evenings, a long grey-blue apparition in the Air Force uniform he still wore, sleeves braided with gold, peaked cap loaded down with it, and his eyes as he came through the door, if not exactly twinkling, held an outdoor light. But the moment he heard the unwelcoming thumps of Mother beating hell out of an upstairs bedroom or viciously clattering pots in the kitchen, his eyes would first dart about as if hunted and then shrink away under his brows, not to emerge again that day.

He never let on that he minded or that he thought, as I did, that Mother had gone mad. I wanted him to remove her armoury and hold her boxing arms down at her sides in a calm embrace until she quietened and began to smile as she used to do. Instead, he would turn on me his shrunken eyes as I stood twisting my plaits in the hall – oh, Robbie, how lucky you are, tucked safely away at school – and short, sharp barks would come out of his mouth.

'Have you nothing to do, gurl? Can't you help your mother? Get up there and see if she needs you. Pull your weight, for heaven's sake.'

Sometimes he'd not so much bark as plead, or almost. Lowering his voice so that only I could hear, he'd embark on a list of all Mother did, how hard it was for her and how it was the least I could do to lend her a hand, appreciate her sacrifices, praise and thank her and be good and tidy to save her trouble. He never looked directly at me as he said all this. He stared at the wall just above my head and I stared down at the bulgy caps of his black shiny shoes, afraid to move a muscle in case he shifted his stare from the wall to me and caused my head to sprout snakes like Medusa. When he'd disappeared into the dining room to pour himself a drink I would go to Mother.

'D'you want me to help?' I'd sulkily ask her, hovering just inside her bedroom door, every muscle twitching with a powerful desire to be elsewhere. Not only did I not want to help Mother, I didn't want to be within miles of my parents' bedroom. Its cupboards and chests of drawers, Mother's dressing table with its fine layer of Rachelle powder and lily of the valley talc, the smell of Mother's scent, Chanel No. 5, and the bed looming over everything, obscurely vibrating, made me gasp for air. I badly wanted that room not to exist. Bluebeard in the fairy story forbade his wife ever to enter one special room and stupidly she disobeyed him. I wouldn't have done.

I'd have been only too glad to have stayed away if this had been the special room and it was, I was convinced of that.

Mother looked up. She was kneeling in a welter of sheets beside the bed, her fingers hooked into the two cloth handles on the mattress, tugging at it. The mattress was thick and green, squiggled with gold. It was all I could do to touch it, its thick greenness upset me so.

'Get on the other side and push,' said Mother, her face shiny with exertion. Black wisps of hair stuck to her forehead. Full of resentment I did as she asked. Mother reared up with a loud cry and vanished behind the great oblong wodge. For a moment it stood teetering on its side and then thumped towards me into place again.

'You have to turn mattresses every so often,' Mother said, reappearing to scuff at her hair with the back of a wrist.

I was half out of the door again, aching to depart.

'That way, they won't wear unevenly,' Mother added.

I looked down at the fat expanse of the mattress and thought the world would wear away before it did.

'And it's hygienic,' Mother said, 'you'll learn, we all have to learn. Come back here, do, and take this sheet. No, turn it over. Feel the hem, that's the side that goes down.'

'What does it matter?' I grumpily said, and, 'It matters,' Mother grimly replied, but she didn't say why, she just whipped the sheets almost out of my grip until one by one they were creaseless and in position and the bed was made. When she had carefully folded back the final sheet over the final blanket, smoothing its scalloped edge bound with thread to make a frame for the picture I wished I didn't have of their two faces, Mother's and the Cleft's, lying side by side, scalloped to their chins, she stood up, panting, and we stared at each other. I felt the anger in her soaking into me and squinted to keep it and her at bay.

'That was a great help, darling, thank you,' Mother formally said. Ashamed but still resentful, I grunted gracelessly. Downstairs, under my feet, I felt the Cleft crouch.

Dancing was my escape. Mother's too. She said she had always wanted to be a ballerina but Grandpa wouldn't hear of it so I must be one in her stead. I was not at all sure how I was supposed to be Mother being a ballerina, everything about me was the opposite of her. She often told the story of how, in the hospital in Cairo where she'd given birth, a nurse had brought a swaddled newborn to her bed and it wasn't me. 'That's not my baby,' Mother had protested and gone on protesting in spite of the nurse ticking her off, saying she was being a silly girl, and dumping the bundle in Mother's arms, come along, no more fuss, feed your dear little daughter. But against all urgings Mother adamantly refused to bare her breast for the alien and eventually, after much coming and going of matrons and doctors, they'd discovered she was right and the infant wasn't hers. Mother's cheeks would flush as she approached the finale and she'd throw up her arms to illustrate her struggle, a heroine fending off a fate worse than death. It was stirring, this epic, and it proved triumphantly that mothers knew best.

Unfortunately, I knew the opposite. The doctors and nurses were right and it was Mother who had been wrong, Mother who had rejected her daughter and taken another baby in my place, which meant that I, the real me, must now be somewhere else in the world, possibly still in Cairo among the pyramids and the me who was imprisoned in this cold English house was the wrong me, not Mother's at all but someone unknown, a changeling. Whatever Mother said, the truth was obvious to anyone who saw the two of us together, we were such a mismatched pair. Mother was little, round-faced and sturdy, she was curved and neat and packed with energy, no wonder she had wanted to be a ballerina, she looked like her idol, Margot Fonteyn, only with a bit more flesh on her limbs and her chest, quite a lot more on her chest. I on the other hand was as the Cleft often described me, neither fish, flesh nor good red herring. It wasn't entirely clear to me what this meant except that it seemed to echo my feeling that I wasn't who I was supposed to be and certainly not Mother's daughter, being already, at ten, taller and miles less energetic than she was, and everything long and thin about me, long stick legs, long stick arms, long twiggy fingers and the hair on my long head, though as dark as hers, scrunched up into a frizz of curls instead of Mother's flat and elegant ballerina waves. And there was no flesh at all on my bony chest, nor, as far as I could see, would there ever be. Mother had round, chocolate-coloured eyes, mine were thin and greeny-flecked, the colour of the Cleft's. For I never doubted that the thin long Cleft was my father, however much I didn't want him to be. It was Mother's child I wasn't, there and there alone lay the root of my tragically misshapen fate.

But Mother was determined I should dance in her place, however ill-equipped I clearly was to be her surrogate, and she enrolled me for daily classes after school in ballet, with supplementary Greek and modern dance. Miss Yates, whose School of Dancing it was, saw eye to eye with my mother. Her classes were not for frivolous parents who wanted the gawk ironed out of their daughters so that they acquired something called deportment, plus a few pretty steps to show off at parties — there were plenty of dancing schools around to satisfy that need. Miss Yates, and Mother, were made of sterner stuff. The girls who attended her classes were expected to work as hard as athletes in training for the Olympics, and she took for granted, as Mother did, that the sole purpose of so much demanding exercise was eventually to pass the entry examinations to Sadler's Wells and end up as a Margot Fonteyn, a Beryl Gray, a Markova or, at worst, a thoroughly professional Swan.

Miss Yates, Mother told anyone who would listen, had danced with Pavlova, given it up only because of illness. Quite what illness had tumbled our teacher from such exalted heights remained mysterious, but you had only to watch Miss Yates walk across the boards of the dancing hall and rest one hand on the barre that ran the length of the mirror-lined wall to feel the ghost of Pavlova drifting beside her. Every one of Miss Yates' pupils sensed, in her presence, that they were marked girls. Not for us the trappings of amateurism, the silly frilly frocks and floppy hair bows that other girls at lesser schools skipped about in. For us, severe slit-sided tunics, pink tights kept taut the length of the legs with penny coins twisted at the groin, hair modestly restrained in nets and two sets of ballet slippers, one flat, *sans* ribbons, and one pair of points with ribbons, both only obtainable from Gamba in Soho. These were the slippers of professional dancers and they were, at that time, as rationed as food, yet somehow Mother always knew when Gamba was about to receive a new consignment. On those red-letter days breakfast was what the Cleft called a lick and a promise. Mother, clad in fur coat and sensible brogues, clasping an umbrella, looked like a woman off to the wars. Now and again, if the slipper call came on a Saturday, she'd insist I came with her so that she could do some other shopping while I kept a place in the queue that trailed half across London, or so it seemed to me. I suspected Mother of actually enjoying the ordeal, for the queue was full of real ballet dancers with coiled-up hair and leg-warmers, all twittering away about ballet affairs and Mother glowed in their company, perhaps imagining she was one of them or that one day I would be. Now and again — moments that made my stomach shrink — she'd turn and give me a gleefully conspiratorial look. This meant she'd overheard some significant snippet concerning the inner world of the ballet, which revelation her wiggling eyebrows signalled she was filing away in her memory, to be whipped out later as a vital boost to my dancing career. Guilt made me wiggle my eyebrows back, guilt and the gloom that descended whenever Mother showed signs of believing she and I had anything in common, any interest we could share. At such times I felt a cosmic pity for us both. Poor little Mother, so full of mis-apprehensions *re* the daughter who wasn't her daughter. Poor lanky me, so Motherless. Sometimes, brooding on the pain of these Gamba excursions, I found I could squirt tears out of my eyes and all the way down my cheeks at the mere thought of the gulf between us. How could Mother ever imagine I wanted to be a ballerina? How little she knew the real me, who might well be cantering across the wide-open sands of Cairo on a camel if only she hadn't bungled things from the start.

I worshipped Miss Yates. She was tall and ineffably slender, her waist the tiny fulcrum for a wonderful spiral of skirt that swirled smoothly around her whenever she moved, and she moved as if the top of her head was invisibly wired to the hand of a God perched far above who plotted her every step. I have never seen a straighter back, before or since, it came out of pictures in my history books of Court Ladies with powdered wigs and skirts like shelves, but Miss Yates, unlike them, conveyed no impression of stiffness, she could bend and sway like a willow in the wind and spin faster than any top. No one needed to convince me she'd danced with Pavlova. As far as I was concerned, Pavlova had danced with Miss Yates.

We worked our guts out for her, all of us, in her classes. There were no exceptions, even the clumsiest and least promising of her embryo ballerinas strove to make their limbs conform to her requirements and, most challenging of all, to her example. Effortlessly she would raise one leg to well above her waist, making a perfect arc of her skirt, and maintain it in quiverless place while she pointed out the exactly correct juxtaposition of hip to thigh, of spine to hip and of toes to heel. Without any hint of strain or scuffle she would glide across the floor in a series of *grands jetés* and effortfully we would follow her, puffing and thudding. Yet after a year or so of her tuition we were light as soufflés on our points and some of us were nearly real dancers. I, to my own astonishment, was one and loved every class, even Greek dancing with its angular poses and the frisky waggles and bounces of tap – 'Hands loose at your sides, girls,' Miss Yates would call as we clipped away at the floor with our steel toes. 'Good sharp taps now, *and* one *and* two and smile, come on, *smile.*' But ballet, with its burning twists, its wholly unnatural demands on every limb, remained my grail. To lift a long leg, as Miss Yates did, so high to one side that it made a right-angle with the leg on the ground and then, very slowly, shift around until you could feel, almost hear, the ball at the top of your thigh revolve in your hip and know that the leg was now still higher behind you, was a triumph no easier discipline could provide and made me occasionally flash a grin of satisfaction even at Mother watching beside the swing doors at the back of the hall as she frequently and annoyingly did.

I didn't like her being there, I didn't like her watching me, I didn't want to share with her the pleasure I got from what I did, and the better I did it the less I wanted her to see. The Cleft never came, the Cleft never intruded on this rite, he never once asked how the dancing was going, he showed no curiosity at all in how I passed every late afternoon of every week, which extended in the end to all the years of my childhood, he turned a blind eye to the heaps of my dancing accoutrements, the slippers, the red tap shoes, the tights and tunics permanently out on the line in the garden, the bags of resin and the wads of point-shoe stuffing and, later, the many costumes and tutus required for exams and performances. Grudgingly I notched up all this in his favour; he, at least, left me alone.

Mother didn't. She was permanently *in situ* at the back of the hall, giving little encouraging nods, moving her head as I moved, sometimes waving her hands as mine waved, up and down, out and in, stretching as best she could from her bench as I stretched from the barre. Sometimes I spied her feet arching in their shoes as if they were trying to escape and dance too. All this covert participation oppressed me. Just by being there she threatened what I most cherished about ballet and about Miss Yates.

When I was with her I was no longer a child. When Miss Yates surveyed me, I knew she saw a small machine that we both wanted to work in the best possible way. The steps and the movements of the ballet were immutable, the same for Pavlova and Margot Fonteyn as for ten-year-old me. In trying to reproduce them we were identical and all that kept me from being them was time and practice and infinite pains. Miss Yates believed that and what bound me to her was that belief. The aim that united us was to force my body to do to perfection, with effortless grace, all that it was never designed to do. To achieve that end I could rely on my teacher not to spare me or any other of her pupils and understanding this lifted us, in my eyes, far above the usual dreary, dishonest relationship of adult with child, and let me fill my lungs with what I could get nowhere else: the heady fresh air of equality.

'She loves dancing,' Mother told her friends, 'don't you, darling?'

'No, I don't, I hate it.'

Poor Mother.

*

Eating Children

I loved school as well, though I'd rather have died than admit that either. It had the great merit of legitimately distancing me for a large part of each day from Mother and the Cleft. There were grown-ups there too, of course, you couldn't escape them, but to regard teachers as the Enemy was more or less obligatory in order to avoid being accused by other girls of sucking up or being that most abject of creatures, a Teacher's Pet. Not that I ran that risk. When I first learned of the exploits of the Resistance, the Maquis, in German-occupied France, I needed no explanation as to why they'd run the risks or why the wretched bald women in the newspaper photos had had their heads shaved. The Germans marching about in their boots were the grown-ups, powerful but also ridiculous figures who spent all their time forcing the French to do what they didn't want to do – that was all too familiar. Germans were bone-headed bullies who couldn't even grasp the obvious fact that they had no right to meddle in French people's business, never mind scaring them and bossing them about. So the French shot them and blew up their trains whenever they could, what could be more natural? It only showed how stupid the Germans were that they acted indignant and punished the French. About that time an image from some film or photograph sneaked into my mind and has lodged at the back of it ever since: a big square box almost hidden in undergrowth, a bar with a handle on top protruding from it. The woods round about it are quiet and serene, a mild breeze flutters the occasional leaf, a robin perches for a second or two on the handle, bobs its tail and flies off, a butterfly alights on a swaying wild rose, it is all as pretty as a postcard. But the handle is there, it is always there, waiting. And one day you might walk quietly over to it, put your two hands flat on that handle, plunge it down down down, flush with the box, and oh, then, what would you see? Trees shooting like arrows into the sky, a robin exploding in a puff of feathers, no more butterflies, no more roses, just chunks of earth where

53

the air should be and air in a huge crater where the earth should be, everything turned upside-down. What larks, eh Pip? What larks.

At school it was vital to keep up your defences, cover your vulnerable parts with your fists the way boxers did. I had to do that at home as well but it was simpler at school, you had allies, friends shoulder to shoulder with you in the Resistance and the Germans couldn't weaken you the way your parents could because you didn't let them near enough to pick up their wavelength and be forced to listen to their signals. The more Mother and the Cleft intruded on me with their muffled cries and demands the greater was my relief at being able to turn a deaf ear and a blind eye to the adults at school.

Miss Collins, for instance. You could watch just for fun the blood under her skin rise from her neck to her cheeks, you could see her eyes swivelling from side to side and shrinking into their holes like the Cleft's eyes did but you didn't have to care, it was only Miss Collins. She taught Scripture.

'Please, Miss Collins,' someone at every class would ask, hand up. 'I don't understand what "begat" means.' Horrid snorts would erupt across the room while the blood in Miss Collins rose up to her forehead like mercury in a thermometer.

'Never mind that, just read on please,' she would say, her voice already strangled. That was the trigger for whoever was standing up to start pleading.

'But honestly, Miss Collins, none of us understands what "begat" means, honestly we don't.' Piteous whine. 'Please tell us, pleeease.'

On cue, the rest of us would add our plaints to be told what other biblical terms meant: 'what does "he entered in and knew her" mean, please, Miss Collins? What's a virgin, Miss Collins? Tell us, pleeease.'

Miss Collins did not tell us. She sat through our endless and endlessly predictable baiting as stiff and red as a red-hot poker and scuttled off gobbling sadly to herself the moment the bell released her. Probably she never twigged that in spite of our mockery none of us in fact understood what 'begat' or 'he knew her' meant or what a virgin was; we only knew the words were rude because of the way they ruffled her. We were innocents wise in deceit and hurtful forays against the Enemy. Members of the Resistance are impelled to take such actions whenever they spot a weak link in the Occupying Force – scurvy tactics but they have no choice.

I made my way through the years of school like a mole digging random tunnels through a fibrous night, deaf and blind and solitary, aware of other moles only as distant earth tremors or sudden soft collisions in the dark and with no inkling of the cacophonous world above its buried head. That, at any rate, was my inner state. I dare say others saw me very differently – a rowdy child in the thick of things – and it is only with hindsight that I myself can see how sealed off I was from all the various strands of the present that were busily becoming the future in front of my visionless, moley eyes.

Now and again shafts of light shot in and lit up my shadowy burrow, the illumination of ideas, of other people's existence and of words arranged in certain patterns. They would come at me out of the blue, bolts from a brighter place altogether that jogged me into recognizing a world beyond myself and left me amazed. Once, singing 'Jerusalem' with two hundred other girls in Assembly, my whole body in an instant filled to the brim with a powerful draught of happiness, I was happy to the tips of my fingers and the ends of my toes, the blood in my veins fizzed with happiness, I was incandescent. A little later I read Siegfried Sassoon – 'Suddenly everyone burst out singing and I was filled with such delight . . .' – and was utterly astonished, and oddly unnerved, to find that another human being had felt what I felt and said so. For all the constant chattering that went on between me and my friends I did not dream of confiding that sort of feeling, the thought never occurred. That sort of feeling belonged in the molescape, the underground place.

One day Miss Faulder, our English teacher, a cool detached woman with a pinched nose and a neutral gaze, read us a poem.

> She first deceased.
> He for a little tried
> To live without her,
> Liked it not and died.

As she reached the last economic line there was a ripple of appreciative laughter from her audience. Pausing until it died away she said, 'Hands up, anyone who doesn't think that poem is funny.' After a short silence during which no hand stirred, I put mine up. 'Ah,' said Miss Faulder. She said no more, she gave no indication of whether I was right or wrong and the class continued in its usual way. But for a moment a light had shone for me. A few dry words, removed from me centuries in time, had pierced through my earthy bulwark and struck the creature below with an antique grief. Words, I was learning, had the power to do that, as if their very sounds could set off physical vibrations in that chunk of gristle called the heart. That's how I thought of them anyway, bony fingers that poked about inside you till they found the right string to twang.

Even more peculiar was the way words you didn't understand at all could affect you. When Miss Faulder read from Shakespeare – 'For valour, is not love a Hercules, Still climbing trees in the Hesperides? Subtle as Sphinx; as sweet

and musical As bright Apollo's lute, strung with his hair . . .' –
I felt like I'd eaten too much Turkish Delight, while 'Then,
comes flooding in, the sea' made me feel as I did when we sang
'Long to reign over us, God save our King'; strong, upright and
noble. It was mysterious.

The girls, the living girls around me, didn't affect me half as
much, and sometimes, when their need was greatest, not at all.
It was rumoured that Anna Marks, a thin dark girl with mournful eyes and an accent, had rowed across the Channel from France
to escape the Germans, her mother and father left behind and
maybe dead, yet it never occurred to me to show her any
special kindness or even to question her about what had happened. Jenny Stevens I did talk to but didn't find out until we
were both grown-up and mothers ourselves that what had
vexed me about her as a child, her wan expression, her nervous
tic, was the misery caused by a brutal stepmother and a father
as indifferent to her pain as I was.

Worse, any overt hint of suffering made me very cross
indeed. Rowena had a cleft palate which distorted her speech
but I tolerated this defect because she made me laugh and
besides I admired her sleek chestnut hair and the brackets of
dimples in her cheeks. Carolyn had some unnamed ailment,
petit mal I now suppose, that caused her to halt abruptly in the
middle of reading out loud in class and stare blankly ahead for
whole minutes in silence. We were all instructed to be patient
and wait until, just as abruptly and without any sign of aware-
ness on her part, she began to read again. I didn't hold this
eccentric behaviour against her. Carolyn normally never
stopped talking, her butterfly stroke was second to none and
her eyes were quite ravishingly blue.

Sarah, however, had no saving grace. She wore dreadful
Minnie Mouse shoes for a start and the way she scuttled about
with her shoulders hunched and her head ducked down was

perfectly repellent. Her hair was horrid, sparse and greasy, there was something very wrong with the skin round her eyes which themselves were quite unpardonably small, and as for her hands with their pasty little bitten-off fingernails, well, they made me want to retch. These were the crimes Sarah daily committed and since it was clearly someone's duty to punish her for them I took on the obligation by persuading my form-mates to send her to Coventry. It is possible that Sarah never noticed her increased isolation – hardly anyone talked to her anyway – but I kept her under scrutiny and there was no doubt she hunched more than usual and her eyes more frequently wavered and blinked. I don't believe Sarah's persecution lasted long, there were too many other distractions to keep it up much more than a week and it may be that Sarah, wherever she is, remembers nothing of that far-off ordeal. My revenge on her, though, remains vivid in my mind, for revenge it was, however vague the whys and wherefores. All I knew was that Sarah had no right to make me feel almost as bad inside as being at home did.

Home was much better when my brother came back at half-terms and for the long holidays. He made the house, which weighed so heavily on me, seem lighter and brighter and while he was there the walls stopped moaning and sighing in the night. It was the old story – because he noticed nothing, everything improved. The Cleft became nearly jovial, at least for the first week or so, calling Robbie 'old son' and 'old boy', laughing when Robbie called him Pater and slapping him chummily on the back. I might have been envious that he was so much nicer to Robbie, but what I felt was relief. Mother, too, cheered up. She left off her aprons so we could see her smooth flared frocks, poked pearl buttons through the holes in her ears and put on the long rope of teeny seed pearls that was my favourite: in its pale glow her lips turned as red and her hair as black as Snow White's. She dabbed Chanel behind each ear, on the inside of each wrist and on a lace hanky which she tucked in the low V at her neck. She even painted her nails again, me watching, both of us holding our breath as she edged the miniature brush round the half-moons at the base of each cuticle that she always left untouched. Then, after fluttering her hands till the nails were dry, she'd open the silver cigarette box at her elbow, take out a De Reske Minor, tap it twice on the little silver ashtray and puff at it so charmingly, waving it about between fingers so sparkly with diamonds and spreading out around her such a lovely smell I'd sink back on my ankles at her feet quite lost in admiration. The Cleft was pleased too, I could see that. He'd come into the room, walk all the way round her and then stand in front of her rubbing the groove in his chin and say very slowly, *Well, Well, Well.* Mother always said, *Oh, Don't be Silly*, but though she wouldn't look at him her red lips smiled and once she huffed a whole perfect smoke ring that floated magically over to him.

Because Robbie was away from home for eight months of every year we had a rather more respectful relationship than if we'd been together all the time. At the start of each holiday we did a polite minuet around each other until familiarity was re-established and we could begin on the exchange of thrilling news and views. The first of the holiday events was the solemn Back-to-Back ceremony initiated by the Cleft, the ritual assessment of our relative heights.

With my fourteen-month head start I took for granted for ages that I was and always would be unassailably superior not only in height but in strength, authority and all-round know-how to the smaller, weaker, dafter brother who had been given to me by God as my personal serf. As his tsarina I could keep him firmly under either my wing or my thumb, depending on how I felt from day to day, but the operative word was 'under'. That pleasurably autocratic state of affairs endured for ten years, until the Revolution. For then the serf began to grow in height and strength. I grew too, but he grew faster. Soon, instead of looking down on him, we were shoulder to shoulder and next thing he'd stormed the Winter Palace and was up there on the balcony waving down at me.

It wasn't easy to accept, this reversal, and it was made the more dramatic because of Robbie's absences – at Christmas I'd Indian-wrestled him and won as always but three months later, when he reappeared at Easter, he took hold of my arm, slammed it flat on the table and did so again and again until I was forced to concede that barring some sudden wasting disease he'd probably do so for ever after. A bitter pill, that, for a tsarina to swallow. That fleshy bud of his I'd observed bobbing up and down in childhood baths had not made me feel deprived, who needed such a comic thing? But the thickening of thighs and calves, the hard shield that had begun to form across a once-plump chest, these male attributes were clearly desirable. I didn't exactly covet them for myself but I saw the advantage they gave him over me and I didn't see why he should have them just for being a boy. It was all quite interesting in its way but oh, it was unfair.

My brother's new prowess, it turned out, was the harbinger of a whole series of unfairnesses my gender had in store for me, but for a while, before puberty raised him up and struck me down, things stood roughly equal between us, with me still retaining the edge on him. And he was at home and a long summer lay ahead and everything was going to get better from now on.

Upstairs I sat on the bed in his room while he talked non-stop of the doings in that foreign country, his school, kindly adding footnotes on the intricate Sumptuary Laws that pertained to each garment he unpacked. This jacket has to have the top button undone. The other one mustn't be buttoned at all. This cap sits back on the head like this, you tilt the boater over the right eye like that, this tie is the School tie, that tie is the House tie, this one's for cricket, that one's the Fourth Remove, this you knot like so, that you tie like so and look, see this sleeve, it has to stick just this far out of the blazer and this is the badge we have for Cadets and . . .

For the most part I listened with open-mouthed attention interspersed with a withering 'Ooo-er' or 'Crikey', designed to keep him in his place. But it was the sheer volume of my brother's clothes that overwhelmed me. How were there enough hours and days in the year for anyone to put on so many things? Every occasion, every sphere of activity, every season had its full complement of uniforms and accessories: cricket flannels, bats, gloves, pads; tennis whites and tennis rackets, squash rackets too; rugger shirts and shorts and muddy, studded rugger boots; swimming togs and special swimming towels; running gear; Cadet gear; short-sleeved Aertex shirts, blazers and boaters for summer; long-sleeved shirts and grey and black suits and coats and macs for winter; peaked, brimmed, tasselled and beribboned caps and hats; countless pairs of shoes; whole nests of striped elastic belts; underwear, dressing-gowns and pyjamas; and everything neatly sewn with Cash's name tapes so that everyone knew this sartorial cornucopia belonged to the renowned cricketer, sprinter, Blood and my baby brother R. G. T.

There were all those words to be translated for me, too. Blood: a flash man, big frog in the puddle. A yob (boy backwards): a backward boy, lower class if not lower I. Q.'d. Yobs lived in the town, spoke yobbishly and went to the local Grammar schools or worse. Oi-guys or oiks: the day boys, much despised or maybe much envied for running home each night to Mummy. Bottom of the heap were the Toe-rags or squits, the scholarship boys, victims of a social experiment of the time which held that uprooting working-class kids from their comfortable homes in The Slums and sticking them in bleak Wuthering Heights of Prep and Public Schools, to be mercilessly bullied and despised by boys and masters alike, was the best thing their country could devise for them.

Listening to all this esoteric lore I was torn between scorn and a niggling groundswell of envy. It was stupid, that went without saying, only idiots would think up so many pointless rules and regulations, and I was glad I didn't have to obey them but oh dear, there must be something to them, otherwise the grown-ups would laugh at them too, or say 'mmm', as they did when I told them things about my school. Instead, whenever Robbie told them his stories, they leaned forward to listen really carefully and if they laughed, they laughed as if they were giving him a prize. They were much more interested, too, when he talked about his friends, scab-kneed boys called Ingham Minor or Toadspawn or Smellysocks, than they were when I talked about mine. They never asked *me* what my friends' surnames were or what their fathers did. I was missing something, I knew that, but what? Why did I have a picture in my mind of a castle being erected stone by stone, with turrets and towers and flags flying and high walls to keep Robbie in and me out? I don't care, I told myself under the blankets at night. They're only a lot of silly boys, who cares what they do.

I didn't think Robbie was silly, though. Whenever he talked about school he'd start walking up and down making fists in his pockets or rubbing his head or scratching a scab on his elbow till it oozed fascinating beads of blood, but his face didn't move like his body, it didn't move at all. He could have been talking to himself, except every now and then he'd look over at me where I sat, knees up in the big basket chair in the room that was still called the nursery – 'Go up to the nursery, you two,' the Cleft had said, and we'd gone. He'd look at me hard for a fleeting moment, as if he were searching for something in my eyes. I'd look back: it was like a message passing between us in a code neither of us understood very well: it might mean nothing or it might be life and death, you couldn't be sure.

'I got whacked four times last term.'

'Where?'

'Here, once,' he said, slapping his bottom, 'and here three times,' and he held out his hands.

'Did they make you take your trousers down?'

'Yes.'

'Did it hurt?'

'Not much. Well, a bit.'

Then he'd walk about even faster, slicing an imaginary cane through the air and go, 'Whup whup, bend over, keep still boy, whup whup,' and I'd pull my eyes down till the underneath skin showed red and erupt into loud bleats, 'No, don't, please, sir, stop, no no, please, you're hurting my poor bottom, please, sir,' and his face would start moving, with a frown at first as if he were waking up, and then loud blurts of laughter. Then from downstairs would come the Cleft's voice calling, 'Be quiet, you two,' and Robbie would nod in its direction.

'How've they been?'

'Awful.'

At which we'd both blow out our cheeks and see who could make the most disgusting raspberry noises.

Mother's frantic cleaning bouts eased off while Robbie was at home, maybe she felt a neat house was a lost cause with us in it all day, but she didn't give up on me. If anything her concentration increased, as if Robbie's presence reminded her of items she'd almost forgotten were wrong with me. When Robbie wasn't there the untidiness of my bedroom managed to sneak by her with only a weekly ticking-off, but when he was ensconced in his own equally untidy bedroom mine became a daily point of contention; it was filthy, a pig-sty, it looked as if a hurricane had hit it, it was unfit for human habitation and I wasn't to think of going anywhere until I'd done something about it.

'What about Robbie's?' I'd ask indignantly, not particularly wanting to drag him into the conflict but having, I felt, no choice. 'His room's just as much of a mess, why always me?'

'*And* you,' Mother would say to Robbie, but only as an aside, not with her heart in it, not strongly enough to redress the injustice. Apparently my mess was of a different order and so, it seemed, was the mess of my person, which was also a target. She despaired of my hair – she said so often – and I dreaded her attacks on it, cringing away and yowling as she pulled at the ball of frizz I hated as much as she appeared to do. That she acted pleased when other grown-ups told me how lucky I was to have curly hair was by the by, another example of how adults fibbed about everything. There were also my hands and especially my nails. 'It's not my fault,' I'd wail as Mother scraped away at the offending flesh with a nailbrush as hurtfully spiked as a porcupine. 'Look, see? It's the way my nails are made.' But she wouldn't look and she didn't listen when I said Robbie's were worse.

At bath-time, - and even with fuel shortages I had a bath once a week - she wouldn't leave me alone. At ten I'd become as modesty-obsessed as any Victorian spinster, squealing at the merest footfall outside my bedroom door for fear my privacy was about to be violated, making myself elaborate towelling tents in the ballet changing room before I would take off so much as a sock, all this in stark contrast to Mother's shockingly relaxed attitude – she didn't seem to mind who saw her in her undies, though I'd noticed the Cleft was more like me, he knocked at their bedroom door and said, 'Are you decent?' before he went in, and sometimes he came out very quickly again, which meant, I presumed, that she wasn't.

'You've locked it,' she'd say indignantly, rattling the bathroom door. 'There's no need for that. Let me in.'

Smothering myself in towels, I'd drip over to the door, open it and stand there scowling as she inspected me.

'Done your ears?' she'd ask, catching the top of one and peering into it.

'Yes' . . . twitching in her grasp.

'And your neck?'

'Yes.'

'Under your arms?'

'Yes' . . . sighing with exasperation, twisting away.

'And . . .' lowering her voice as if she were in Church, '. . . what about down there?'

Down There, a mythic region. Down There, the dark place where Pluto ruled, where Persephone's daughter vanished once a year, from whence Orpheus led his wife and sinned by looking back so that she, too, vanished forever into Down There. Sin, punishment, shame.

'Yes' . . . sullenly.

'Because, you know, that's very important,' Mother would whisper confidentially. 'You're a girl, you must keep yourself clean down there.'

By now my twistings were becoming purposeful. I had to free myself from her, I had to keep her words out of my ears. Not long ago when she was on about Down There she'd insisted I sit down so she could tell me about an abomination she called the Curse. I'd managed to forget almost everything about it since, except that she'd said how wonderful it was, this Curse, because it meant I could have dear little babies of my own, wouldn't that be nice, and the tone of her voice, soft and unnaturally sweet, had made me cringe. Babies? Who wanted babies? What had rotten babies to do with me?

'What about Robbie?' I wailed. '*He* smells, he really does. You should have smelt him yesterday after football. Whew, he ponged, honestly. What about him?'

'He's a boy,' Mother said, letting me go. 'It's not the same. A girl has to take much more care of herself.'

'Why?' . . . a rising note of outrage.

'She just does. You'll learn.'

The future grew dark at the thought of all the beastly things I'd have to learn because I was a girl.

Four

We always had a fortnight away during the summer holidays, though we never again went anywhere as exotic as Turkey. Mostly we stayed with Aunt Abby in Norfolk, which was exciting enough. The house, the Old Hall, sat on the outskirts of a small village and after all the miles of trundling along in the Morris, the Cleft crouched at the wheel, Robbie and me bickering and giggling in the back, Mother hissing at us to be quiet or Daddy'll get really angry, all noise would cease as we entered the village and craned ahead for that first reassuring glimpse of high chimneys and big iron gates, rejoicing in the crunch of the stones under our wheels as we drove through them and round the huge circle of pampas grass to the door. Aunt Abby was never there to greet us, she'd already gone into retreat 'upstairs', but the house was full of women from the village with Beatrix Potter names, Mrs Fox, Mrs Vole, Mrs Hare, Mrs Crow, ready with steaming cups of tea and cherry cake. They called Robbie 'Master' and me 'Miss', which immediately made me feel saintly and mellow. Two wonderful weeks stretched ahead, free from the onerous task of being a child. Already my insides were as light and floating as dandelion seed.

The house was Aunt Abby's only for the time being.

Grandfather had installed her there with her children when her husband, our unknown Uncle Patrick, died, but really it belonged to Grandpa, it had been in the family since it was built in Queen Anne's reign, like the New Hall on the other side of the village where Grandmother was born. These succulent property details I had eavesdropped from Mother and interpreted to mean that if only the Cleft had died instead of Uncle Patrick, she and Robbie and I would be living at the Old Hall instead. There or in Turkey. It was uncanny the way the Cleft was always coming between me and my heritage. Mother alone had the power to right my wrongs if she wanted. Why on earth didn't she, then?

Well, until she saw the light all I could do was to make sure nothing inside or outside the house that ought to be mine had changed since last year and all my treasured possessions were in place. While the grown-ups settled down to chat about dull things like the weather and how crowded the roads were, I would dash off, Robbie in tow, to check through my list.

There was the special smell the house had, of rotting apples, damp and sweet, the smell of Eden. There was the scrubbed smoothness of the table in the kitchen and its hidden carving, you had to crawl underneath to trace it with your finger, 1764. There were the jam jars on the windowsill, buzzing angrily with their burden of wasps: you could watch for hours as one wasp after another edged its way over the rim, got stuck in the sugary dregs and eventually, enjoyably, died. There was my bedroom, the one I always slept in, with the tiny silver-topped bottle on the dressing table, full of fragrant rose-water which had to be inhaled, and the little round window above the bed which had to be looked through to ensure that the secret path below it, so overgrown with black yew trees only Robbie and I could push our way through, remained inviolate. There were all the floors of the house, beautifully uneven, sloping this way and that, designed for our marbles to roll on them and there were all the rooms to run in and out of playing hide-and-seek, so many you could never quite remember how many, and more of them up the rickety back stairs to the attics, which were bulging with all sorts of extraordinary objects, piles of old, dusty books, trunks full of dressing-up clothes, a doll with real hair and one piercing blue eye, teddies and dogs and even a tiger all worn to their linen underskins, boxes of cups and knives without handles, stringless violins, a lurching piano, a padded woman with no arms, legs or head, a hollow grandfather clock, a bagatelle board rattling with silver balls, broken yo-yos and diabolo bats, oh, there was no end to the treasures here. But what I straightaway looked for, fearful that they might have vanished, were the two best treasures of all. The first was a chest with many slim drawers and inside, snuggled in cotton-wool nests, row upon row of enchanting birds' eggs, light as air, heart-stoppingly fragile, speckled and blotched with delicate colours and in every size from my littlest fingernail to the palm of my hand. I loved them so much that, as I gazed at them, I hardly dared breathe.

The second were the butterflies, hundreds of them pinned under glass and like the eggs all different sizes, from tiny twinkly blue scraps to ones as big as birds but brighter, and with wings so exquisitely slanted, peaked and curved they made my eyes water with joy.

Outside the house, the wonders continued. Here there wasn't just one garden, as we had at home, here there were many, all different, separated one from the other by red-brick arches or blocks of yew or little box hedges whose smell went up your nose into your head and stayed there forever. Big beech trees lined the avenue that led from the front door away into the fields beyond, and everywhere there were trees full of apples, pears and plums, and flat trees lanterned with warm peaches.

At the back of the house there was the long greenhouse, smelling strong and sweet of hot tomatoes, and outside there was
the old white-whiskered dog that ran barking up and down on
a chain. A billy and a nanny goat lived in the stables, kicking
up the straw and peering meanly through their gold button
eyes and sometimes, in a dip between two flagstones, there'd
be a stranded hedgehog which you could feed with bowls of
bread and milk. And then, round the front of the house again,
by the front door, you could inch your fingers through the
ropes of ivy on the wall, screeching at the sudden rustle of a
spider, till you came upon the rusty watch hanging on its
chain on the rusty nail. The Cleft had revealed its presence to
us years ago, pinning back the ivy leaves, telling us how an
ancestor of ours, an old man in a bath chair, had been wheeled
out each day to sit in the sun and had hung his watch, this
watch, on a nail, this nail, and then suddenly died in his chair
and the watch had hung there ever since.

Every day of those holidays, even after everything had been
checked, there was so much to do you had to get up very
early, before any grown-up stirred, and if you took care you
needn't see Mother or the Cleft for whole days long, you
needn't see any grown-up except Mrs Vole or Mrs Fox or
Chubman, the gardener. Chubman was as old as the trees and
as gnarled, and one summer he made Robbie and me both a
pair of stilts, and we spent every moment we could perched up
on them, stalking like giants about our realm, taller by far than
Mother, taller even than the Cleft. But, stilt-high or not, we
were never children at the Old Hall because there were no
grown-ups to be children for and the relief was vast. I felt like
I'd struggled out of a dark mine shaft, where I'd been forced to
walk doubled-up, into the fresh air outside, where I could
stand up, stretch to my full height, breathe into the limit of my
lungs and at last be myself.

Mother and the Cleft were certain of what I'd do if I was left alone, all grown-ups were, or almost all. Persons over five and under twenty-one were human versions of the unexploded bombs the Germans had dropped while the war was on. Everyone knew the countryside was littered with them, everyone knew that was why seaside holidays weren't allowed, the beaches were out of bounds, covered in barbed-wire to prevent the unwary from treading on what lurked deep in the sand, ready to blow them to smithereens the moment their guard was down. It was also well-known that many of these bombs, like many children, were got up to look quite harmless and even desirable – a toy, a tin of baked beans, a wallet – so people would pick them up and *whump*, that was them gone. An acquaintance of Mother's, a woman with an armful of bangles we knew as Aunty Joan, went just this way, blown up by a mine waiting patiently for her in a Cornish sand dune. Hearing about it – no one told me directly – no one ever told me anything directly – brought vividly back the square box in the forest and I thrilled to a vision of the bits of Aunty Joan, her shiny handbag, her fur stole, her pageboy hair and all her bangles whizzing up into the sky with a glorious clatter. Then guilt crept in as it usually did. Mother, I didn't blow up Aunty Joan. It wasn't my fault, honestly.

As human bombs, then, responsible adults were expected to fence us children in and keep a constant watch, for society's protection. Left unsupervised for any length of time, ticking away, who could predict just when and how we might suddenly go off? I, it seemed, was high on the list of suspects and, given half a chance, would quickly reveal the nitroglycerine at my core with an explosion of sin and crime, i.e., not going to church on Sundays, wearing dirty clothes, saying and doing unspecified dirty things, arguing all the time, never saying please or thank you, never brushing my teeth or listening when spoken to or taking that look off my face or my elbows off the table or doing my homework or, indeed, doing anything but the opposite of what my parents required me to do. Obviously, then, it was their citizen's duty to prevent me putting innocent lives at risk by going off in this dangerous and uncontrolled way.

I knew I was suspect, what child doesn't?, and I did my best in idle moments to live up to this unsought reputation, but my own reasons for wishing to be left alone were different. Long ago I'd discovered that only when I was by myself could I stop things being so oppressively real. Things, objects, places, people, life. Grown-ups had the knack of imposing reality when you least wanted it. They could take hold of anything, a glittering carriage, a liveried footman, a pot of gold at the end of a rainbow and in the blink of an eye you'd be left with a mouldy collection of leaves and veg plus a mouse or two. They couldn't help it, apparently, it was part of being adult. Like a contrary King Midas, whenever they touched gold it turned to dross. You could be in the middle of a great white hope, an earth-shattering disclosure, a daydream loud with bells and trumpets or about to waltz down the yellow brick road when in they'd clump and squash it all under their big feet, talking in their clanging voices about what time it was and how much things cost and why weren't you doing whatever it was you weren't doing. They stood there, high thick walls that blocked out the light so that your mind was trapped and shadowed over and the hope, the disclosure and the dream crumbled, there were no bells and trumpets, only the milkman outside delivering bottles.

At home I could try all I liked to get lift-off into that space where any cupboard door might suddenly open on to an unknown landscape, any tree could be the Amazon jungle and Mother's filmy scarf tied round my head could make me into the most beautiful lady ever seen, with prettier hair and redder lips even than Rita Hayworth but the adults were too close around me, mumbling and creaking, and I was earthbound by the knowledge that at any moment they might crash in upon me like a herd of bullocks and drag me back to the real. The Norfolk house and its gardens were too big for such interruptions, there were hiding places where no adult could find you, where even if they shouted you wouldn't hear them or could at least pretend you hadn't. It was like escaping from prison; they'd hunt you down in the end, but oh, how glorious the taste of freedom while it lasted. 'You two look as if you've enjoyed yourselves,' the Cleft would say sourly, surveying the marks of liberty on us, our grimy knees, our bramble-scratched arms, my bird's-nest hair. Perhaps he envied us, though why he should when he was free too, alone with Mother all day, Mother in her flowery summer frocks, her skin so brown and smooth, who could guess? As for me, 'enjoy' was no word at all for the feeling that buckled my ribs with its force. Standing on the step of the front door after breakfast was over, with all my kingdom and subjects out there awaiting my command, bliss nearly suffocated me.

Once or twice during each Norfolk holiday, Aunt Abby would suddenly appear on the gallery that overlooked the wide flagged hall, an ample apparition in long white robes with her long black hair snaking down from her head and her big handsome face white and moist as bacon fat. Immediately the grown-ups present began to scurry about in all directions, Mrs Vole shooting back towards the kitchen, Mrs Fox rushing up the stairs, Mrs Crow tugging at Robbie and me, while the Cleft made agitated gestures at Mother and Mother stood rigid, looking up. Far above this termites' nest, majestic Aunt Abby would slowly raise one arm high as the Statue of Liberty, holding a Bible aloft instead of a torch, and begin to chant a kind of hymn, a rather fierce one, I noted, but by that time, for all our clinging at the jambs of handy doors, Robbie and I had usually been prised off and shooed out of hearing. On one memorable occasion, however, we managed to hang on long enough to see Aunt Abby do a regal over-arm bowl of the Bible down the stairs; in my mind's eye it falls very slowly, floating like a leather leaf to land and flip open in a tissuey fan beside Mother's two little marble feet.

'Get thee behind me, Satan,' Aunt Abby boomed.

'Hold on, Abby,' the Cleft cried sternly, like a captain in charge of a sinking ship.

'Oh, *Abby*,' Mother breathed and a tiny tear sparkled in each eye.

I admired Aunt Abby and looked forward to her rare manifestations. Somehow, in spite of being a grown-up, she belonged in my world. Even when her eyes stared right at me they didn't see me at all.

Once there was a charity garden party at Granny's old house, the New Hall, much bigger than the Old Hall and owned now by a Mr Woodhouse, flat-capped, plus-foured, red-faced and jocund. I went dragging my feet, hounded by Mother, who was determined to have me astonish the village and, of course, do my civic duty by performing my current ballet exam solo, the 'Dance of the Rose'.

When she broached the subject I was outraged. 'Dance? In the garden? No. No. Anyway I can't. My costume's at home, so's my music and my points.'

'I brought them,' she said, 'and you won't need points to dance on a lawn.'

'You planned it.' I was breathtaken by such underhandedness.

'You'll do it beautifully, everyone will love it. And it's in a good cause. Come on, Button.'

'No, no, no, no.'

But the Cleft told me to do as my mother said or could I, perhaps, provide him with one good reason why he should continue to spend a small fortune on ballet lessons for a gurl who refused to dance?

Out-manœuvred, unable to put into words the ocean of difference there appeared to me between the disciplined performance Miss Yates had coached me in and lolloping about on some grass like the sort of soppy twerp who held out her skirt when she curtsyed, I gave way gracelessly. So that, after all, was how Mother saw me. That was what the Cleft thought ballet was for. To turn out swanks.

Burning with shame under a boiling sun, to the crackly strains of His Master's Voice, witnessed by picnicking village families, I did my best not to lollop in my rose-pink-petalled tutu with the chiffon petals of a rose on my head. The moment the record was over I dropped a perfunctory curtsy and fled for refuge to the quiet kitchen garden. Rounding an outbuilding, I ran slap into Mother.

'Weren't you watching me?' I asked, astounded. Mother always watched.

'I . . . oh dear, did I miss you? I'm sorry, Button.'

Sorry? This was unheard of. Mother must be ill. She looked ill or, at any rate, peculiar, hot and knocked sideways somehow and her hair in a mess.

'What have we here?' said Mr Woodhouse, coming round the corner. 'Upon my soul, a living, breathing rose. Forgive me, Miss Rose, all my fault. I was showing your Mother my houses. Have you seen my houses?'

I shook my head. A chiffon petal wilted over one eye.

'Come along, then.'

His houses were china, there were hundreds of them in glass cabinets that crowded one big room. Forgetting everything, I steamed up each pane in my eagerness to absorb every exquisite detail of the lines of crooked cottages and miniature castles with their toy towers and battlements and baby drawbridges. They gave me the same feeling of painful rapture as my eggs and my butterflies and I hardly heard Mr Woodhouse giving them names – Coalport, Rockingham – so overwhelming was my desire to possess each one. How could they be Mr Woodhouse's when I loved them much more?

Delivering me back to Mother, bowing gallantly, Mr Woodhouse said, 'This young lady's going to be a heartbreaker, just like her mother.'

'What nonsense,' Mother said in a squishy little voice. Her hair was in place again.

On the way back, walking with Mother across the meadow that separated the two houses, I brooded on Mr Woodhouse's remark. No one before had said she and I had anything in common, and I wasn't sure I cared for this sudden reversal. 'Mr Woodhouse likes you,' I said, trotting beside her.

'Your nose has caught the sun,' said Mother.

'Do you like him?'

'Everyone likes him. He's a nice man.'

'Are you a heartbreaker?'

She switched the basket she was carrying from one hand to the other. 'And sometimes he talks a lot of rubbish.'

It was always the same. They never told you what you wanted to know, only what you didn't. 'Why don't you marry Mr Woodhouse?' I asked.

'What a thing to say,' said Mother, swinging her basket up and down. 'Have you forgotten about your father?'

I wished I could forget him. I wished I could make him vanish like Rumpelstiltskin in a puff of smoke. Then Mother could marry Mr Woodhouse and all the china houses would belong to me.

The following summer, after they'd cleared the last bombs

from the beaches and the barbed-wire had gone, we went to the seaside for the first time. Our hotel was a great disappointment to me. I'd expected something at least as grand as the one we'd stayed in on the way to Turkey, but though this one called itself Grand it couldn't fool me.

'All the paint's chipped,' I told Mother crossly, chipping with my thumbnail at the door of my room to demonstrate. 'And there's a horrid brown mark in the bath and my lamp doesn't work and . . .'

'Pipe down, Madam,' said the Cleft, stomping in with the suitcases. 'There's been a war on, in case you hadn't noticed. And take that look off your face or we'll pack you off home.'

'Good,' I said, but under my breath so the Cleft wouldn't hear. His eyes were already blinking fast enough to warn me off. Their blinking rate was up on last year, sometimes he looked as if he might explode; even his hair gave off sparks. Mother, on the other hand, though she still cleaned like mad, was quieter. Her mouth dropped and the lids of her eyes were often puffy.

'Who does that child think she is, Lady Muck?' he said to Mother before he went out, leaving Mother to give me one of her ever more frequent talks. They weren't talks, really, more a kind of keening, full of how-can-you and aren't-you-ashamed and I-don't-know-what-gets-into-you. I listened moodily, squinting to close out her mournful face, concentrating my might on making it blur into other and cheerier faces, Scarlett O'Hara, Elizabeth Taylor, Margaret Lockwood, Audrey Hepburn, Rita Hayworth.

'. . . so will you promise to try, for my sake?' My hands were in Mother's and my stomach in my Clarks shoes.

'Daddy hates me,' I said.

'That's not *true*,' she said.

Lies.

*

77

'I hate Daddy,' I told Robbie, sitting on his bed in his room. 'I hate Daddy, I hate this hotel, I hate being here, I wish I was Rita Hayworth.'

'Let's go down to the beach,' Robbie said.

'I'm not scared of Dad. Are you?'

''Course not. Let's go, then.'

'Mummy is.'

'Are you coming or not?'

'It's all right for you, you can go back to school, you don't have to be with them all the time, it's not fair . . . No, wait, I'm coming. Wait for me.'

We had to be all together at mealtimes, though, sitting round a white tablecloth in the hotel dining room where everyone whispered so the sound of knives and forks clattering on plates was wincingly loud. The Cleft was, too.

'Well, well, well,' he'd say loudly, rubbing his hands and smiling ferociously at the waitress as she approached with the menu. 'What Rabelasian feasts have you in store for us today? What ambrosial delights is the chef brewing up? Food for the Gods, I've no doubt, eh, Mademoiselle?'

Robbie made bread pellets and I stared glassily ahead while the silly waitress simpered at the Cleft, patting her silly hair under her cap. Why did he go on about feasts and make everyone look round when he knew what was on the menu already? The waitress didn't seem to mind, though, she gave little yelps at everything he said.

When the soup arrived he sat back, making smacking noises with his lips. 'What about that, children? Cath? Brown Windsor, what could be more delicious? This is what the war was all about, children. The inalienable right of His Majesty's subjects to have Brown Windsor soup. Named after the Royal Family, did you know that? They have it all the time at Buckingham

Palace, great tureens of it steaming in every room, and wee tureens for the corgis. Though I don't imagine for a minute that it'll meet the high standards of Her Highness here . . .' nodding at me. 'Well, has the cat got your royal tongue?'

'We have this at school,' Robbie said.

'Poor you,' I said.

'What did I tell you?' the Cleft said to Mother, baring all his teeth. 'Miss Otis regrets. She's unable to dine. Today, ha ha.'

'Oh, Alastair,' Mother said.

'What is it, Queen of my soul? Speak up or for ever hold your peace.'

'Nothing.'

I invested my holiday hopes in the sea, that shining expanse entirely new to me where, wading out with nothing but the empty bowl of the sky ahead, I could pretend there was only me and Robbie all the way to France. For three days the two of us swam and splashed and squabbled in the sand, licking each other's scaley shoulders to see who tasted the saltiest. Then, on the fourth day, waking up with an ache in my tummy, I went to the bathroom and saw four bright red drops on the white crotch of my pyjama legs. I stared at them and my light heart grew leaden with foreboding. For ages I sat there on the cold seat of the lavatory and watched the cracks in the white tiles around me and under my feet shift and stealthily connect until I was pinned at the centre of a horrid web from which there was no hope of escape.

'Are you in there?' Mother rapping at the door. 'We're going down to breakfast, do hurry up.'

I would not confess. Wild horses wouldn't drag this beastly secret out of me. If no one found out, then nothing need change. I would send my treacherous body to Coventry, refuse to give a name even in my mind to what it was trying to do to me in its sly nudging way. How dare you, I screamed silently at it, how blinking dare you.

The pyjama bottoms were whisked from me and put to soak in the basin, pink fronds curling from them into the water. 'It has to be cold,' Mother instructed. 'Only cold water gets blood out, you'll learn,' and she bustled off, turning at the door with bright eyes and a conspiratorial finger at her lips, 'I'll be back in a jiffy with all the gubbins, you stay there.' I stayed, lumped miserably on the bed, a wad of lavatory paper under me so I wouldn't leak on the sheets. I had dwindled as fast as the Wicked Witch of the West into no more than a stain on things, a blotch of red ink or beetroot juice. When Mother returned clutching the gubbins I numbly moved to her orders as she roped me around with elastic and cotton, her fingers flying merrily. Looking down at her kneeling, blocking my nose from the sugary odour of Chanel N° 5 and bandages, blocking myself as best I could from the jammy warmth of her chat, I shrank from Mother. She was trying to enfold me, draw me bleeding into some dark hot nest with her and away from the clean fresh air outside. She would never succeed.

'There we are,' Mother said, getting up and crinkling her eyes as she patted my cheek. 'You're only eleven but you're nearly a woman now.'

I trudged after her into the hotel corridor, a convict in a chain gang clanking behind the warder.

'I'm going swimming after breakfast,' I said, whistling in the dark.

'No you're not,' replied Mother promptly, as I knew she would. 'You're unwell.'

In the white glare of sun, sea and sand I fidgeted outside our beach hut as Robbie squirmed into his blue swimming trunks. All about me the women basked in rows or lunged out of their hillocks of flesh — two fat mounds in front, sausages coiled round their middles, wobbling bellies and thighs and arms – to tweak and tug at their children. They weren't people, they were pink dollops of jelly.

'Aren't you going to change?' Robbie said, coming out. Then he grimaced, blinked once and looked up at the sky. 'Oh, I forgot,' he said. 'Sorry.'

He angled one eely arm behind him, scratching at the brown wing on his back. I could see each rib under his tight brown skin. The blue elastic rectangle lower down stretched emptily across the cave of his tummy to hook on the two sharp blades of his hips. Red in the face, bulky with Mother's gubbins, my two legs planted awkwardly apart, I stood mortified. Then he stretched his arms out, turned his back, and from my place among the women I watched my brother skim away from me to the glittering sea.

Mother took me to the pictures to make up, she said, for not swimming. I sat in the dark beside her and fell passionately in love. 'Well, did you enjoy that?' Mother asked as we emerged from a black velvet heaven to the gritty glare of the street, but I was too stirred to answer her. I could not bear the shock of being me again when, moments ago, I'd been beautiful, a woman adored and adoring in a swirly frock. Through acid tears I glowered around me, feeling the blight that chafed between my legs as Mother, gripping my hand, lugged me ever further from Filmstarland.

'I hear you didn't even thank your mother for taking you to the cinema,' said the Cleft at dinner. 'You really are . . .'

But I didn't learn that day what I really was. Mother shook her head and the Cleft broke off. 'Well, never mind now,' he said gruffly and turned to Robbie. 'Ice cream, old son?' I sat there transfixed with shame. She'd blabbed. She'd told Robbie, that was bad enough, and now she'd told the Cleft my secret. How could she, how dared she? I wanted to die.

Up in the Residents Lounge alone with Robbie, while our parents sat over their coffee below, I sprawled on a sofa staring up at the ceiling and tried to describe the love of my life to him.

'He's called Aldo Ray and his neck's this thick and he's really tall but what's the best about him is he talks like this . . .' and I growled hoarsely in my chest, '. . . and I'm going to get hundreds of pictures of him and keep them in my room and when I'm grown-up . . .'

'Was there any fighting?' Robbie asked, yawning so hard I could see the dangly worm at the back of his throat.

It was no good. Even Robbie was only a boy. Nobody understood. Life, which ought to be miraculous, multi-coloured, amazing, exciting and full of extraordinary happenings from dawn to dusk was grubby and lumpy and dull and ugly as a saggy old mattress and also quite dreadfully unfair. And the worst was, everyone thought it was all right like this, everyone in the world except me.

A peculiar sensation imposed itself on my lamentations. Something uncontrollable was happening Down There. I sprang up and ran for my room.

It was after that seaside holiday that the rows really broke out. I suspected my parents of waiting until Robbie was back at school, trying to cushion the visiting son from the un-nice facts of their life, but I dare say his blithe presence did its share in keeping the fires damped down. Certainly Mother and the Cleft conspired to distract his attention from the tremors and rumblings just below the surface, and though I was not so merciful my moans and complaints didn't carry much weight, my brother was accustomed to a sister in perpetual disarray, disarray, nothing unusual there. Besides, all three of us looked to him with varying degrees of desperation to confirm that nothing too untoward was happening – how could there be if a boy could go on so calmly just being a boy? The very sight of him in his sawed-off trousers kicking a ball about in the garden or grubbing in a pond for frogspawn or swinging from a tree shouting, *Hey, look at me*, must have been balm to the raw parental nerve-ends. A boy that normal, a Just William, Extract of Boy, had to be happy and if he was happy then there couldn't be very much wrong with his mother or Dad.

There was, though. What muffling my parents managed of their private explosions was not so much for my benefit as in the greater interest of keeping up a respectable front for the outside world to note and approve. That was essential, for if their cover was blown, blitzed to pieces in public like poor Aunty Joan, what would they have left to distinguish them from the Masses: the lower classes, the slum-dwellers, the villains in the *News of the World*, the promiscuous film-stars of Hollywood, the vulgar hordes who had no standards, no moral fibre, no breeding, no standing and no Christian beliefs?

Besides, and wretchedly for them, if they were ever to let down their guard, where were those who could be trusted, who would understand, help and advise? Mother's friends consisted entirely of her relations – sisters, brothers and cousins – most of whom lived in Turkey, and if she let the cat out of the bag while they were visiting England it would surely be in Constantinople tomorrow, scandalizing her mother and father. As for the Cleft, he had never been known to have a friend at all. Well, one. The one friend was a tall, gangling, dome-headed man, a Member of Parliament so extremely removed from the humdrum concerns of his constituents and the ties of family life that one day, strolling with my father in the neighbourhood while expounding on some genetic theory of his, he pointed to a lad bicycling towards them as a prime example of inherent criminal tendencies as manifested in the set of the ears. It was left to the Cleft to remind him that the lad was his son. My father told this story frequently, with evident approval, and, 'Brilliant man,' he always concluded, 'first-class mind.' I gathered that clever people, like birds, flocked together and they weren't interested in children, not even their own. Mother was. Therefore Mother wasn't clever, therefore the Cleft wasn't her friend. On the other hand, and puzzlingly, I was clever and he wasn't my friend either.

The question of cleverness loomed large in our household, it had a unique subterranean rumble all its own. We – Mother, Robbie and I – took for granted that the Cleft was clever, he said so, and besides, the way he leaned back, shut his eyes and flapped a shoo-away hand at any opinions we voiced was proof enough. To become so irritated so quickly must mean he'd heard everything we thought before and knew how wrong we were. Occasionally he'd expand on our wrongness and give examples of all the other people who had thought what we thought and were wrong, too, wrong and stupid, but mostly he'd just shake his head and roll his eyes so we knew that this time he hadn't the patience to explain.

The rows flared when Mother decided to argue with him. More often than not she left the Cleft alone to flap his hands and shut his eyes, busying herself with serving the food or saying, 'More peas?' but occasionally she'd get the bit between her teeth and start protesting that she didn't agree and it wasn't like that and so forth. This made the Cleft's eyebrows and his Rapid Eye Movements shoot up to alarming levels.

'Oh really?' he'd say. 'Is that so? Then perhaps you'd be so good as to elucidate. Perhaps you could furnish us with the relevant facts and figures, make us party to your sources of research. I'm sure everyone here would gain inestimable benefit from any pearls you care to throw our way. Do by all means take the floor.'

My father often spoke like this, as if he were chairing a crowded public meeting when he was only pacing up and down in the sitting room and the meeting was Mother and me. Nevertheless, my heart would begin to drum as if the argument were really being conducted before a concourse of thousands. To my dismay, Mother never rose to the challenge she offered. I wanted her to, badly. I wanted her to pitch in with a whole raft of facts and figures and nail the Cleft to the ground with them, squash him flat as a pancake on the floor. Instead she said things I knew were hopeless, like, 'I just know it's true,' and, 'I don't care, that's what I think,' or she'd stubbornly stick on some point anyone could see didn't make sense, giving the Cleft just the opportunity he needed to escalate to surreal heights his killing courtesies.

At some point in these predictable battles Mother, hot and flustered, would turn to me for support – 'It *is* so, isn't it? Your father can say what he likes but I'm *right*, aren't I?' – while the Cleft waved a dismissive hand at both of us, leaving me in a stew of conflicting emotions, sorry for Mother but contemptuous too, impressed and repelled in equal measure by the Cleft's tactics. I didn't wish to take sides. I wished in truth that they would both drop through a hole in the earth.

But I took Mother's side in the end because when the Cleft had stalked out with a last scornful wave of a hand, she cried. The sight of her quivering shoulders, the sound of her mewing, couldn't be borne without doing my best with pats and strokings to console her. And I felt the worse for it as she gazed up at me with her wet, sad, grateful eyes because I knew my warm front concealed an iceberg as big as the one that sank the *Titanic*. It splayed out my ribs with its freezing bulk, it was so cold it burned, and it proved that I was the meanest, most unnatural girl in the world. I should love my mother and stand up for her. Instead, even as I murmured endearments, I continued to long for the earth to open, and if no one else was aware of my perfidy, God was.

The rows went on. At night the walls of the house no longer mumbled discreetly as they'd done when I was younger, now I could feel them vibrating to the Cleft's low roar and Mother's soughing descant. I dreamed that I picked up a pretty fur glove lying on a dark road and dropped it in horror as blood seeped from it and regularly, when I first awoke, all the furnishings of my room, the dressing table, the chest of drawers, the curtained windows, the white cupboard with the tulips on it, had dwindled in the half light of dawn into inch-high toys fit only for a doll's house, and I had to rub my eyes over and over before I could force them back to their normal size.

In the mornings, at breakfast, a newspaper was all that could be seen of the Cleft, and if Mother was silent and the lids of her eyes looked soft and fat, then the house was a place to be quitted as quickly as possible and not re-entered until as late as could be. On those days, school was my refuge. I sprouted like Alice in Wonderland as I neared its gates and, once inside, erupted into day-long orgies of laughter and chat that earned me endless reprimands from the teachers and a blissful popularity with other girls. I bathed in their admiration for my rowdy refusal to knuckle down, I adored the whole gossipy, exciting anarchy of school, ecstasy gripped me as we tore down the corridors, exchanged shattering secrets in the playground and rushed from end to end of the hockey field and the netball court. At school, life nearly reached the peaks I yearned for and lines, detentions, deprivations of all sorts, were prices well worth paying to have a part in the constantly unfolding drama. Blind to everything but the action of the moment, I crashed like an unguided missile through the blazing hoops of school.

Coming home from Miss Yates' class afterwards – '. . . excellent elevation on your *grands jetés* but *do* try to hit the floor a trifle less like King Babar . . .' – I shrank with every step until at last, at our front door, I was again the pygmy they called a child. Entering, I paused in the hall to assess the evening's barometric pressure. Unsettled weather. Rain, thunder, storms threatening. Mother in the sitting room, eyes still swollen, still downcast, face all downward lines. Three days now since the last quake.

'Mummy, what's the matter?'

A shake of the head.

'Shall I help you lay the table?'

A shrug.

'When's Daddy coming home?'

Another shrug.

'Mum-my' . . . a peevish appeal, 'what *is* it?'

'Nothing.'

Nothing. Nothing to be done but listen for the jangle of the Cleft's keys at the door, jitteringly anxious on such days for any relief from the sealed hush of the Mummy's tomb.

He arrives. A lull while he, too, taps into the atmosphere. Then a burst of *son et lumière*; his voice, scorchingly cheerful.

'Well, well, well. How are we all?' A sideways glance at Mother. 'Mmm. Something smells good. Had lunch with the Minister today. He sends his regards, Cath. Funny chap. Remember him in Karachi, Cath? That wife of his didn't last long, did she? What was her name, Cath? Molly, was it? Something like that. Molly, Dolly, Lolly . . .'

'Polly.' Eagerly I join in. 'Holly. Golly!'

'That's it!' and the Cleft whacks his folded-up *Times* on the table. 'Golly. Sir Vernon and Lady Golly Wigetty-Wog. What a woman, eh Cath? Black as the ace of spades, remember, Cath?'

'Golly golly golly golly,' I squeal, doubling up with laughter as the Cleft, twanging away at his *Times*, circles Mother warbling, 'Black hands I loved, beside the Shalimar . . .'

Sometimes it worked. Mother's tight lips would tremble a moment and a reluctant smile edge across them. 'It was Lally,' she'd say, 'and she wasn't black, don't be so silly.' Triumph! The Mummy had spoken! The clouds were passing, we could breathe again.

More often it didn't. This time it didn't. She turned her back on us, twitching and frowning, she got up and walked rigidly out to the kitchen. The Cleft's song faded, my laughter died. After a long silent dinner I came upon him standing by the window in the sitting room, staring out. His back was straight and hard as a board but his fingers were drumming away like billy-oh on the windowsill. As I prepared to slink out again he turned his head and glanced at me. His eyes were two holes the wind whistled through. Oh, lonely Daddy. I paused at the door, feeling my heart move towards him.

'What is it?' His voice, icy.

'Nothing.'

'Well, get on with it,' he said.

I wrote a gloomy poem about a mad girl screaming in the wild winds and won a prize, climbing up the stairs on to the platform to receive it from the Headmistress in front of the whole school. Mother said, 'Clever. You are clever.' The Cleft said 'Mmm. Don't let it go to your head.'

I won another prize, a nation-wide competition this time, for an essay. It was printed in the school magazine and I rushed home, waving it triumphantly. Mother read it and was full of praise, saying, 'Wait till Daddy hears. He *will* be pleased.' I waited impatiently for the Cleft to come, running out at frequent intervals to watch for his tall figure striding down the road.

When he finally arrived there was an ominous set to his jaw. He thumped his briefcase on the hall table, shifted out of his coat, slung it over the banister and, brushing me aside, marched to the sitting room where Mother sat repairing my Dying Swan costume.

'Idiots,' he said. 'What a bunch of idiots I have in the Department. Half of them, I swear, are barely literate. If I want a decent report I have to write it myself. And the train was late again. *And* standing all the way. Pity we didn't lose the war. Hitler would have had them running on time.'

'Oh dear,' said Mother. 'Well, we've got some good news, anyway.' She bobbed her head at me and, glowing, I stepped forward.

'I won a prize,' I said. 'For essays. It's printed here. Mummy's read it. She thinks it's good.'

'What your mother knows about essays,' said the Cleft heavily, 'could be written on the head of one of her dressmaking pins.'

'Alastair!' Mother, reproachful.

'As for you, young lady. Fine, you've won a prize. Just don't go thinking what you win at school has anything to do with the real world out there. You think you're clever? Let me tell you, you haven't half my brains, never will have so don't give yourself airs. And I'll tell you something else. It's not clever that counts, it's hard work and character. Without them, you'll end up no more than a smart alec and you're well down that road already. You may be smart or you may not but it's a whole lot better to be wise like your mother and your brother. It's she who ought to be your example. Look at the way she sacrifices herself, sewing away at your dratted ballet frocks. Work on your character, that's my advice, and never mind the scribbling. I'm telling you this for your own good, so you can take that look off your face and listen for once.'

With that look on my face I looked at Mother, but she was looking up at the Cleft and there wasn't any room for me.

I tried hard, after the tears had dried, to sort out the muddle of it all. The way the Cleft said 'clever' made a sort of clack, as if someone had trodden on a cheap tin toy. There was a smell of metal about it, too, the dingy smell of pennies. And when he said 'wise' it sounded like music, lyrical and sweet. So I was dingily clever and bad and Robbie and Mother were wise and good. But then, the Cleft being cleverer than me, did that make him badder? After earnest deliberation I concluded that it did, which rather cheered me.

Yet in spite of the Cleft's repeated lectures on the theme, I could never quite bring myself to believe in the badness of clever, not all the time, not in everything. What being clever felt like was having a tiny bagatelle board in your head. When you wanted to think, you set the cue against a silver ball and off it went, pinging here and there against the rings of nails until, with an utterly satisfying clonk, it found its proper hole and settled. Besides the satisfaction, there was something orderly and upliftingly remote about this exercise that reminded me of dancing: if you did it right it wasn't you doing it any more, you'd somehow escaped from your own messy self into a wider, calmer place. It felt good, too good to be bad.

That, of course, had to be weighed against the bad things cleverness made you do whether you wanted to or not, like thinking cruel and agitating thoughts about your parents and other grown-ups and even Jesus and God the Father, even Virgin Mary. Good people didn't spend time thinking that if God made Jesus really human he'd have to go to the lavatory, or that Jesus couldn't love everyone the same or it wouldn't be always the Africans who starved. It seemed inescapable that playing bagatelle in your brain led you into the paths of the unrighteous and, if you wanted to be good and wise, you had better stop. Mother didn't think sinful thoughts about Jesus, she had a picture of Him in her room and a silver medallion of His mother that had once been pinned on my cot, and I hated myself for the searing impatience I too often felt with her. As did the Cleft, the bad clever Cleft, our father which aren't in heaven. The odd thing was, when the Cleft made me cross I didn't hate myself for it as I did when Mother annoyed me, and the relief of that was enormous enough to make me fear I might occasionally prefer him to Mother. What could show more clearly how bad I really was? Please, God, let me take no notice of either of them, like my wise brother.

But it was against Robbie that I committed my worst cleverness crime. 'Ye Gods,' said the Cleft, reading a letter at breakfast, 'will you look at this, Cath.' Mother read the letter too and put her hand on her mouth.

'What? What?' I asked. 'What's happened?'

'Nothing,' they said in unison, and then, 'Go up to your room.'

I spied, I eavesdropped, I pressed my ears to the relevant walls and shortly amassed enough fragments of the whisperings and mutterings to realize, astounded, that for once wise Robbie was in trouble, not me. He'd done something terrible at school, something so terrible they were sending him home a whole week before the Easter holiday was due to begin.

'Why?' I implored them again when they informed me of this officially. 'Has he been expelled? What's he done?' A sudden thought occurred to me, one of those other questions I'd asked before to no effect. Maybe this time if I cunningly combined the two I'd trick them into an answer. 'Has Robbie done what Oscar Wilde did?' I hopefully inquired.

My arm was gripped by a furiously blinking Cleft. 'Is your daughter insane?' he demanded of Mother. 'What does she know about . . .?'

'Nothing,' said Mother.

'Nothing,' wailed I. 'Nothing, nothing, nothing. I never know nothing about nothing. You always say nothing and I always know it's not true. Why don't you ever tell me anything I ask you? Why, why, why?'

'For heaven's sake,' said the Cleft, 'we've got enough on our minds without you making scenes, Sarah Bernhardt. Go up to your room, go on. *Now!*'

Naturally, the moment I got Robbie alone, looking blotchy but otherwise none the worse for running the parental gauntlet, I asked him and he told me. He'd pinched a bar of chocolate from Smellysocks' tuck box; well, Smellysocks was always pinching his tuck, but he was unlucky and got caught by a beak. I was piercingly disappointed.

'Is that *all*?' I asked glumly. 'That's *nothing*.'

'They think it's awful.'

'They would. So you didn't do what Oscar Wilde did, even?'

'Who's Oscar Wilde?'

'A man who drives Daddy wild,' I replied and snorted appreciatively at my wit. Robbie didn't join in. He got blotchy again, slumped down in the basket chair and squashed his eyes shut. A thread of water appeared across each tight lid.

'I've got two rats,' I said hastily. 'A white and a black. They're in a cage in the shed. You can feed them if you like.'

Robbie went on twice-weekly outings that holiday, with Mother in the car. She told me she had to buy him things, shoes, shirts, underwear, she couldn't keep up, he was growing so fast. No, I couldn't come, I'd be bored and start complaining, better that I cleaned out those nasty rats' cage, it was my responsibility and mine alone to keep them clean and fed, that was the agreement, remember?

The white rat was pudgy and exasperating, she wouldn't come out of her straw box no matter how I tried to coax her down the ladder with trails of grain. I left her nameless as a punishment. The black one was much more fun; he had bright beady eyes and if I hunched up and spread my arms out he would skitter on his pink birdy feet all the way from one hand across my shoulders to the other. One morning he leapt from the back of my hand to the floor and vanished. I was still searching for him under sacks and flower pots when Robbie appeared.

'Tommy's gone,' I said, close to despair. 'Where have you been?'

'You know. Shopping with Mum,' he said.

'You haven't.'

'Have.'

'That's a lie. A big whopper.'

''Tisn't.' But the click of marbles in his pocketed hand was suspiciously loud.

'You don't go shopping. It's something else. Tell me what, you've got to, come *on*.'

'I promised I wouldn't.'

'They only make you promise for *their* good,' I explained patiently, 'not for yours, don't you see?' Then, grimacing horribly, '*Tell me.*'

He was going to see a man. Mum stayed in one room and he sat with the man in another room with a plant and some toys.

'Toys?' I sneered.

'They're not for me. I'm just supposed to talk.'

'What about?'

'Anything I like, he says.'

'What for?'

'I dunno.' The marbles were clicking again. 'Let's look for Tommy. I'll look for him with you.' He knelt and began a vague scuffling among some bamboo sticks. I seized his hair and yanked him up.

'Bet you said things about me.'

'I didn't. Leggo.'

'You did' . . . shaking him.

'Only a bit. Nothing. Just about . . .' and he looked truly bewildered, '. . . about nothing.'

I never found Tommy. I imagined him living under the house, getting bigger and bigger until he burst through the floorboards, ravenous with hunger, and chewed us to pieces. I spied some more, hoovering up every available mutter from behind windows and doors and walls. Robbie had pinched the chocolates because I was domin. I heard the Cleft say it. 'She's domin.' Then he said 'Robbie', and then something that had my name and 'clever' in it. The spy grew cold, the plot thickened, that word again. Somehow it was my cleverness that made Robbie pinch the chocolates. I was responsible, like I was for Tommy, and Tommy was lost. As I was absorbing this disagreeable news, far worse happened. I forgot to feed the female rat without a name. I forgot one day and remembered on the following with a guilty jolt. But I didn't feed her then, either. Invisible chains shackled my feet, I dragged myself around, a big yellow spot blew up on my chin, so big my whole face tightened round it until all of me was one hot pulsating spot. My head buzzed. Rat, Rat, Rat, it buzzed, every minute of every hour of the following three days, and in my dreams at night. Then, clammy all over, I trudged down to the shed, and opened the door. It smelled bad inside. Behind the bars of the cage, no rat. Grinding my teeth, I unhooked the catch to the side of the nest box and lifted it. She was inside, dead, and stuffed round her like tiny pink pillows were the heads of six eyeless baby rats; she'd eaten the rest. First I was sick over the flower pots. Then, scooping up the little heads one by one, I walked down the garden to where the brambles started and squatted there for a long time with my hands out, heaped with bits of corpses, waiting for God to see and strike me dead in my turn for being the wickedest, most evil, most domin person in His world.

Every holiday until he left school altogether, Robbie always came home with a cup, sometimes three. Little cups at first, then bigger ones, silver, with his name on. Cups for running, jumping, archery, fencing, shooting, hurdling, I lost count. I remember the praise, though, in the early days. It started after the choc-pinching episode.

'Well, well, well,' the Cleft said, stepping back from the mantelpiece in the dining room where he'd ceremoniously placed the cup of the term. 'Look at that, eh? What a clever chap you are. Well done, old boy, well done, my goodness yes. What do you say, Cath?' Then Mother came and picked up the cup to read Robbie's name aloud and say yes, indeed, he was awfully clever, how on earth did he do it, she was dashed if she knew.

I was taken aback by the unwonted vigour of the Cleft's enthusiasm, though Robbie's cup pleased me too and he never added to the ache of my disjointed nose by swanking. However, I felt impelled to redress an imbalance, not caring to have things askew. 'You swam the Hellespont when you were young,' I pointed out to Mother, 'so you *do* know how Robbie did it.' I'd gleaned that surprising fact during the summer with the Birds of Paradise. What the Hellespont was I had no idea, but swimming it had to be worth at least one of Robbie's trophies.

'How did you find that out?' said Mother.

Swiftly I added, 'And *I* won two prizes, didn't I? *And* my ballet certificates.'

'Never mind all that,' the Cleft snapped, riffling his fingers at me. 'This is Robbie's feat we're talking about. First-class job, sonny boy'.

Jill Tweedie

I didn't push my luck. After all, they hadn't found out that I was the sort of girl who first made babies fatherless and then, on purpose, starved them to death.

Five

When the time came for Robbie to return to school, shriven, forgiven and armed against Satan with a tuck box full of humbugs – also acid drops, lemon fizzers, Mars Bars, bulls-eyes, liquorice bootstraps, one of Mother's fruitcakes and Playbox biscuits iced with lions and monkeys – I went with Mother to see him off. It was an unsettling experience, this seeing-off ritual in the great echo-chamber of Paddington Station. I could never resist the chance to gawp at such a swarm of boys, it was as intriguing as kicking the top off an anthill, but it was also like being in the middle of a flu epidemic, boys and parents feverish, flushed or ghostly pale, eyes and voices over-bright, faces garlanded with sickly smiles. Two planets were in collision, ours and the grown-ups', and the impact stripped everyone, leaving them horribly embarrassed by their sudden indecent exposure. Every family weft became instantly warped: love splintered into resentment, pride into shame, pity into guilt, a bewildering hybrid of motives emerged. Little boys, shrunken terrapins under their new shells of blazers and flannels, peered out wrinkled with fright from behind their mothers' skirts while the bigger boys pecked maternal cheeks and pumped paternal hands, loyal in gesture but turncoats in spirit, their attention already focused on other boys, friends and foes.

I watch the parents, who are too caught up in the farewell
ordeal to notice my bead on them. I see the few fathers, pin-
striped, hacking-jacketed, punch their sons with unnatural
bonhomie, palm them off with a furtive fiver, ho-hoing away
like Father Christmas while taking swift squints at their
watches. They say to their boys 'best days of your life', and,
'pull your socks up this term, eh?' and, when a boy looks
tearful, 'Oh, come along now, no blubbing, be a man.' I see the
mothers, the ones who smell of sugar as they pass by, the ones
with high heels, scarlet mouths and jaunty hats who make
kissy noises at their sons that don't quite reach the target and I
see other mothers blowing watery noses while they pat their
boys' heads, saying, 'Once you're there you'll love it, Daddy
did,' and, 'It's for your own good, you know, really it is,' and
quietly but clearly enough for the skilled lip-reader, 'I'll miss
you, darling.'

'We'll miss you, darling,' Mother says to Robbie, blowing
her nose.

'He doesn't have to go,' I say sternly.

Mother groans. 'Oh please, not that again.'

'But he doesn't, it's *true*. If you really missed him, you
wouldn't send him. He could stay at home and go to Whitgift.
We could go on the bus together, Whitgift's only two stops
further . . .'

'Whitgift?' says Mother, 'but that's not a public school.'

'Whitgift?' says Robbie, 'that's for oi-guys.'

'It's all right for me, though,' I burst out, now thoroughly
churned up. 'I can go to school with oi-girls but not precious
Robbie. Why am I always the one left out?'

This isn't what I want to say at all. The words have come
out charred and twisted, stoked by the scenes around me to a
mean blue flame. The grown-ups were at it again, doing all the
wrong things for the usual grown-up reasons that never made

a bit of sense. They knew it in their hearts, you could see they did, they looked shifty and had to pretend too hard that it was for the children's good. And the stupid boys believed them even while they were feeling sick, it was obvious Robbie was feeling sick, he kept swallowing the way you do when your mouth fills with water just before. Grown-ups were awful, they absolutely were, and any child who trusted them was goofy.

The whistle blew, the train shuddered, the ants swarmed towards it. Robbie shoved his tuck box up the carriage steps, Mother heaved his suitcase after him. I watched him through the window jostling for a seat, whisking off his cap to whack another grinning boy. I saw him forget us or not want to remember and I didn't blame him. To waves, to calls of 'bye-bye', 'be good', 'don't forget to write', the train loaded with fun and adventure chugged cheerfully away.

Mother dabbed at her face and I turned on her, outraged by her hypocrisy but most of all by my forlorn, deserted state. 'Why can't I go?' I howled indignantly. 'Why is it always *me* left behind? I want to go to boarding school too. It's *so* unfair.'

That night or soon after, the occasion all too memorable if not the date, I dreamed I was drowning in a mountainous sea and flailed up through nightmare layers of blankets and sheets to see a dark figure ribbed with moonlight rocking to and fro at the end of my bed. The figure had Mother's voice and Mother's voice sobbed out over and over words I only half heard and can never forget.

'He doesn't want me any more. Your father doesn't want me any more.'

I would have none of this. Blocking my ears, holding my breath, I turned and dived instantly back into sleep.

By the time I reached fifteen I'd given up on adults, always excepting Miss Yates, the mythic stars of stage and screen and the faraway Birds of Paradise, who continued to glow in my memory like jewels locked up in a box. The rest, the grownups I encountered daily at school, in the shops, on buses, in the neighbourhood, at home, appeared to have no other purpose in life but to go on and on about a hundred things you didn't want to know, refuse to tell you about anything you did and fill up the time in between keeping you in what they called order. The only way I was ever going to escape was to grow up and up and up until the walls of the prison of childhood cracked apart and set me free.

Living with this jailbird under their roof, constantly itching for the end of her sentence, couldn't have done much to add to the jollity of Mother and the Cleft, themselves imprisoned by holy matrimony. Perhaps my obvious urge to break out too clearly reflected their own frustrations – at any rate they did what they could to damp me down in their different ways. Mother, in between mourning my general unsatisfactoriness as a daughter – 'Why don't you ever want to come shopping with me? Why won't you wear that pretty dress I bought you?' – and nagging me to be tidier, cleaner, quieter, more thoughtful and altogether nicer than she had any reason to hope for, tried to lighten things with rosy pictures of what lay ahead if I would only be patient.

'When you're grown up you'll meet a man and you'll marry him and have your own house, perhaps quite near me, and then, later, you'll have some beautiful children and be very happy. I know you will.'

Reciting this litany she sounded wistful, as if she needed to convince herself that I wasn't altogether a lost cause and everything might turn out all right in the end, however black things looked now. Mostly I responded to these maternal dreams with hideous writhings and grimaces, meant to convey

the extreme unlikelihood of their fulfilment and my own
fathomless disgust with them, but occasionally, just once in a
while, seeing that flicker of hope in her eyes, a desolation fell
on me. Mother's real daughter, the one left behind in Cairo, the
one she'd muddled up with me, would have loved pretty
dresses and happily gone shopping and dreamed identical
dreams of weddings and babies. That daughter would have
been Mother's best friend, the companion she longed for and
deserved. As for my mother, my real one, well, if I ever met
her I wouldn't mind what she was like just as long as she
deeply approved of me. What a waste it all was. Poor little
Mother, poor us.

The Cleft's tactics were bleaker and harder to comprehend.
It was obvious he wanted me to grow up and leave home as
badly as I did, but instead of holding out juicy carrots to hurry
me up, he painted a picture of the adult world so riven with
Sturm und Drang as to give any sensible child an ingrained
Peter Pan complex. The way the Cleft talked about Life was the
way other people might talk about Hell.

'You think Life is easy? You think Life is fun? Let me tell
you, it's anything but. Life is hard. Life is a battle. Life is a
vairy lonely furrow we all have to plough, and if you can
count on one hand . . .' and here he'd hold up in front of
my nose five long, strong fingers, '. . . *that* many friends at
your funeral, you'll be lucky. You think the world out there is
waiting for you? Oh, I fear you're very much mistaken. I
suppose you imagine when you're grown up you'll have a
gude time? Is that what you think? A *gude* time? No, no, no,
no.'

At the thought of the gude time that was never to be mine
he would often fall into a kind of reverie, brooding over the
phrase, repeating it to himself with varying degrees of scorn,
drawing it out or contracting it – a gude time, a guuude tiiime

– as if, by hitting the exact intonation, a door would swing open or, better, shut. After a while he'd come to and continue with an ever longer list of the awesome hazards and impossible obstacles that Life was at that very moment readying for me. People out there, he informed the sitting-room curtains, were so many dunderheads who despised those cleverer than themselves and did everything they could to keep them down, That was England for you, be warned, my gurl. At other times the people out there were far smarter than I would ever be and no school certificates or poems or amateur essays were going to impress them, no siree. As for the men out there, he told the sitting-room ceiling, they were to a man Only out for what they could get from a gurl, oh yes, you'll learn. Other days he'd say the opposite, that the men out there had no respect at all for gurls of a flighty disposition. Such gurls might fool themselves they were popular but, in truth, they were despised and soon came to a sticky end. What this end might be he did not make clear and I dared not ask, though once, during a particularly doom-laden tirade, he did mention linen.

'They may be pretty, some of these gude-time gurls,' he said, pacing up and down in his fox-red jacket addressing a rebellious Persian rug, 'but they're durty linen. Remember that when you think you're the bee's knees, my gurl, because you might well be nothing more by then than a snotty handkerchief.'

Years of school jokes had fairly well inured me to snot in any guise, and though I winced a bit at the Cleft's metaphor I swiftly decided it was a far far better thing to be pretty and have a good time even if you did end up in the washing. At fifteen I was already engaged in an in-depth analysis of my chances of turning into Rita Hayworth or possibly Cyd Charisse. At every ballet class now, in front of the mirrored wall at the barre, I scrutinized my physical assets and drawbacks at least as carefully as my entrechats. Good: legs, figure in general, hands and eyelashes (long), eyebrows (Elizabeth Taylor). Bad: nose (too big), hair (too frizzy). Perfectly hopeless: no breasts to speak of and already too tall and too skinny. These last barriers to eventual Ritadom had only dawned on me recently and filled me with despair. They were, of course, the Cleft's fault, they had to be. Mother was little and curved nicely on top, enviably filling the pink 36C cups of her Kestos BBs, but the Cleft had turned what were advantages for him, his height, his thinness, his hair cut too short to show the frizz, into defects so crippling when passed on to me as probably to cancel out any hope of a gude time, ever, never mind being Rita. Mother only laughed when I bewailed my blighted hopes and added insult to injury by refusing to buy me a bra on the senseless grounds that I didn't need one. I stole one of hers from her lingerie drawer, discovering in the process a hidden book which I also pinched. The bra I padded with handkerchiefs and wore out of the house, where no one would comment on my newly sprung if bumpy bust, and the book I read under the sheets for a week. It was called *Precious Bane* and its heroine had a hare lip but one night, when she took off all her clothes to help out a friend, the Lord of the Manor passed by and fell in love with her. This depressed me further, revealing as it did a future in which my only hope of winning a Lord of a Manor was to hang grimly on to my clothes in a sitting position so he'd never know how tall I was or that my breasts were hankies.

Of all these crosses the burden of my tallness now weighed most heavily. Ballet had for years been my light at the end of the tunnel, a micro-climate in which I flourished, safe from the storms outside. But now my height, something quite beyond control, was imperilling that refuge. When I passed the penultimate exam before the all-important final that would see me triumphantly into Sadler's Wells, Miss Yates took me aside and revealed some facts of life more daunting than anything the Cleft had so far disclosed.

'A ballerina,' she said, tilting her neat chignoned head to look up at me, 'must devote her whole life to her *métier*. She must work all the hours God sends if she wants to succeed. You, my dear child, due to your height, will have to work harder than most because already you are too tall for the corps de ballet, where most dancers start, and too tall, also, for the average male partner. Therefore, like Beryl Gray, you will have to go straight into solos, character parts, and to do that requires enormous skill and dedication. You will have to take the leap straight from school into stardom, if you follow me. I will help you in every way I can if you decide you want to go on, but think about it, won't you?'

'I didn't know Beryl Gray was tall,' I said, trying to evade the impact of this dreadful speech. 'I never noticed.'

'Exactly,' said Miss Yates. 'Because she dances alone. Think it over, child.'

She smiled kindly up at me before she glided away, head high on its invisible wire, and she left me numb. How could I work any harder than I was already? And oh, cruel Fate, to know that however hard I worked I'd never be the Prima Ballerina Assoluta of my dreams, dancing a *pas de deux* in her partner's arms to wild applause from the downy darkness beyond the footlights, but only a lonely satellite of those heavenly bodies, twirling and whirling all by herself, no more than an interlude on the programme. And that only if they let me dance at all. I clopped miserably into the changing room, empty now, and said to the mirror, *Why me, why ME*? Then I wept into the upturned flap of my tunic for the fame and fortune that had just been wrested from me and the dustbowl that stretched ahead. Unwinding the pennies from my tights, unlacing the ribbons on my points, easing my crushed toes from the blocks stuffed with wool, I breathed in the smell of resin and sweat that had meant hope to me for as long as I could remember, the smell of the only place I really belonged. What was there for me now? Nothing, nothing. Other girls who were not as good as me, Jennifer, Marian, would be whisked through the pearly gates, leaving me shut out, abandoned in a desert of marriage and babies. And it was the Cleft's doing, of course it was. Once again his long shadow, cause of my present misery, had fallen across me and barred my way. Trudging home, dragging my case full of suddenly redundant ballet gear, my thoughts were all of parricide.

But the Cleft lived on. Somehow he survived the dish of poisoned mushrooms, the lorry whose brakes had failed, the fatal heart attack, the train crash, the drowning, the sudden choking on a piece of meat, the fall from a great height. Murderous glares did not fell him, he merely repeated yet again, 'Take that look off your face.' I knew he knew what I was about, the dagger that I saw before me, but when I stood ready over his chair what he said was, 'Kiss me.' Every morning as I came into the dining room for breakfast he put down his newspaper and said, 'Well. Give me a kiss.' He didn't want my kiss and I didn't want to give it, that knowledge lay stark between us, but he turned one flat hard cheek towards me and gave me no choice but to put my pursed lips to it as he stared across at the window. Each day, therefore, began with that little humiliation while Mother, all unknowing, nodded her approval for the filial scene before offering her own unforbidding cheek. How could she be so blind, she of the puffy eyes, whose life had been blighted almost more than mine by the Cleft's existence? Well, that was adults for you. To them, ritual was everything, truth nothing, I'd learned that years ago. Their lives were one long, insistent pretence and so they hated, were hostile to anyone who wasn't fooled by their masks and masquerades. Mother, I saw, was the one of us who clung most strongly to her set of pretences, she let herself believe in the game of Happy Families and even, sometimes, in the game of Happy Wife, and so it was Mother who got most upset when the game went too terribly wrong to ignore. The Cleft, on the other hand, wasn't lulled for a minute. What made him angry was if you broke the rules of the game, if you threatened to stop pretending. Oh, that was when his face went bony, his eyelids quivered, his fingers writhed and drummed. On those occasions I wished he'd hit me, hit Mother, hit anyone or anything and get it over with. I wished it furiously and feared it, not for the sting of palm or the thud of fist but because of the tornado I sensed inside him, which one day would surely rip itself out of his body and, yowling like a banshee, lay waste the whole world to flotsam and jetsam and set the globe reeling off into space to crash against the sun and moon and blow the lot to Kingdom Come. Then we'd know where we were. Wouldn't we just.

However, the Cleft soldiered on. He didn't froth at the mouth and crack apart, no one got hit, nothing got wrecked, the universe remained intact and day continued to follow night in an orderly fashion. It was all a sad disappointment, and since I could neither change, escape nor liquidate the adults, I directed my energies to blotting them out.

'*Will* you take your nose out of that book,' growled the Cleft. 'You're *always* buried in a book,' complained Mother. 'Put that book down and *listen* for a moment,' ordered the Cleft. 'Are you *still* reading?' asked Mother in despair. 'That's enough. *Give* me that book,' said the Cleft and snapped it shut under my nose. But he couldn't shut out funny Mrs Gummidge, gallant Sir Percy Blakeney, smart Miss Marple, tempestuous Cathy, brooding Heathcliff, the three gallant musketeers or the heart-breaking hunchback of Notre-Dame, they went on in my mind laughing, weeping, shouting, clashing steel, more alive and far more thunderously real than the cardboard cut-outs around me, who grew quite transparent, thin and pale as if the blood was being tapped from their veins. No wonder they try to stop me, I thought. They're afraid the book people will undermine them, undo their careful work, challenge all their stupid rules, and so they did. Book people were giants among dwarfs, who did all the things dwarfs never dreamt of doing and that's why they lived a hundred times more vividly in worlds a hundred times grander and more enticing than the grey one my parents knew. I read in bed, in the bath, as I dressed, on the bus, in the garden, in my room, up a tree. I balanced books on the edge of the basin as I brushed my teeth, I spread them on my knees below the tablecloth as I ate, my eyes saw only books, wonderful books that kept Mother, the Cleft and the rest of them at bay, dwindled and powerless to disturb.

For a while my book fortress held fast against the enemy forces camped outside its hardback walls. Very little news of the non-fiction world managed to filter through and it was ages before I became vaguely aware, from snippets of parental conversations, that another and much disapproved-of vicar was about to take over from the Reverend Atkins, wispy-haired incumbent of the church Mother and I attended and the Cleft did not. Vicars as a category were about as dreary as adults could get, and Mr Atkins existed for me only as a foggy outline droning in the pulpit and a fishy hand extended at the church door. His purpose, other than this, remained obscure and certainly had no connection with my occasional violent attacks of religiosity.

These attacks, endemic since childhood, came over me in malarial waves that, retreating, left me and those I'd caused to suffer while under the influence weak and shaken. At a tender age I was already inflicting good deeds on Mother, tiptoeing from bed to prepare her evening's toilette by squeezing toothpaste on to her toothbrush, filling her tooth mug with water and then tiptoeing back to check in the mirror for signs of a back-light round my head. I expected the most ardent appreciation for these saintly acts, falling asleep a-tingle with anticipation for the next morning's orgy of gratitude, and Mother tried hard to live up to my expectations, a task that must have taken a lot out of her. The Cleft's toothbrush and tooth mug I stopped molesting early on, since his praise was too frequently diluted by an unsettling quid pro quo.

'I'm most grateful,' he announced to the breakfast table after one of my first Good Fairy excursions, 'for a certain little person's nocturnal contribution to the well-being of my dentures . . .' (the Cleft never attempted to tailor his language to my age but with Mother translating I caught his drift pretty well) '. . . and in return I intend to reward her with a rare, albeit fleeting, glimpse of the Eighth Wonder of the Wurld.'

Thus saying, and with much gestural flurry of the Rosencrantz and Guildenstern variety, he bent down and began very slowly to hitch up his trousers, meanwhile intoning, 'Roll up, roll up, Ladies and Gentlemen. Gird yourselves for the ghastly spectacle about to be revealed. As seen by the Crowned Heads of Europe.' Inch by inch the trousers rose to expose legs astonishing for their cadaverous pallor and skeletal dimensions, two long hairy bones incongruously poked into socks and shoes. The sight convulsed me, though I struggled hard to maintain the dignity required of one soon to be beatified. Sometimes he'd prolong my discomfited shrieks with a further freakish display. Out of pursed lips he'd gradually unreel a snakey tongue that protruded ever further until, unfurling, it rose like a meaty blanket to lap lovingly over the top and both sides of his nose. I watched this performance agog and goose-pimpled, giggles erupting against my will. Mother had mixed reactions too, she said, 'Oh Alastair, don't,' wrinkling her own nose, or, 'That's enough now, the food's getting cold,' or, if it was one of her puffy-eyed mornings, merely hunch her shoulders *à la* Richard III. On good days, when she joined in my laughter, the Cleft might get carried away enough to pull out from the cupboard half-way up the stairs a whiskery banjo and proceed to bang hell out of it as he sang 'Lily of Laguna' in a George Formby voice.

'I. Know. She loves me. I know she loves me. Because she said so,' he'd quack, making moony faces at Mother. And if mother didn't flinch he'd go on through his whole repertoire, from 'Poor Old Joe', which put tears in my eyes, to 'When Father Papered the Parlour' which, combined with the way he capered about like an unhinged stick insect, reduced me to a hiccuping heap.

Afterwards, though, as ever when the Cleft made me laugh, I suffered a queasy sort of hangover. His manic grin rattled me, it sat weirdly upon his habitually immobile features and, besides, I considered a proper father ought to respect his daughter's spiritual stirrings and not coerce her into merriment when she didn't wish it. Laughing was all very well, but sometimes it left a nasty taste in your mouth and a creaky lump in your tummy. I used to wonder glumly whether St Bernadette would ever have been visited by the Virgin Mary if the Queen of Heaven had had to contend with the Cleft bashing his banjo in the sacred grotto. How was I supposed to flower into holiness, given such unsuitable surroundings?

I persisted however, with intermittent lulls, until, one Sunday morning, while charting my soul's course for the coming week, I hit upon a couple of uncomfortable blips in the religious system. It was well-known that Death was the Wages of Sin, but the more I thought about it the more likely it seemed that Death was also the Wages of Virtue. After all, everyone died, whether they were good or wicked. My own gentle Granny had just done so far away in Turkey and no one, surely, could be virtuouser than her. Of course Granny was in Heaven and a wicked man like Hitler in Hell but they both had to be dead first, which made the Wages business not strictly true.

But that wasn't the worst of it. The worst of it was my growing suspicion that the Wages of Death caught up with the virtuous a lot faster than the sinners. Mother said St Bernadette died young because God loved her and wanted her to come and live with Him, so that was one reason the good died quicker. But according to my calculations, being good was a high-risk occupation in itself. I worked out that if I were to start on Monday doing exactly what Jesus said every day I'd be dead very shortly, whereas if I didn't, I wouldn't. For instance, Jesus said to leave everything and follow Him, so I'd have to leave home, saying to Mother as I went, 'Woman, who art thou to me?' which I quite relished the idea of. But then I'd have to give everything to the poor, from my sixpence pocket-money down to my socks and vest. Admittedly, the poor weren't thick on the ground in the Home Counties but a woman I saw at the bus stop every day had darned stockings and a poorish smell; she'd do. After that, clothesless and penniless, I'd either starve or freeze to death or they'd lock me up in a loony bin and a Mad Axeman inmate would kill me. Even practising a less drastic virtue like speaking the truth – say about Mr Rowe dressing up in women's BBs or who really broke the Cleft's watch – was guaranteed to bring about a life-threatening situation.

The second problem concerned the poor again. When Robbie and I were little and wouldn't eat something, Mother conjured

up starving Chinese or Indian children to reproach us, and at
Sunday School they were always wanting our pocket-money
for Black people in Africa. But if Jesus really loved everyone
the same, why did He let millions of Chinese and Indians and
Africans starve all the time or die in floods, earthquakes and
volcanoes but never millions of us? It was disgusting to pick
on people, specially dear little piccaninnies, just because they
were born black in Timbuctoo and not white in Surrey. In fact,
it was just the sort of disgusting you expected of grown-ups. It
struck me then that God might be very like the Cleft, who
wasn't a bit keen on Black people. He said they were lazy and
never worked unless you shouted at them, he knew that from
being their boss in the British Empire. Well, they could say
what they liked but these things proved in my opinion that
God was just as hopeless as the rest of them: unfair, untruthful,
untrustworthy and very bad news if He loved you. Since I
didn't a bit fancy dying and was anyway exhausted with being
good, I decided to drop God, at least for the time being.

But going to Church – Sunday Service, ll a.m. – went on and
on. Mother insisted on it, as did the Cleft.

'Why don't you ever go?' I asked him once, standing hot
and fretful in Sunday frock, gloves and hat beside his deck-
chair in the garden.

'Because,' he said, tilting his panama further over the tip of
his reddening nose, 'I am a member of the Kirk, not the C. of
E., and there are no Kirks among the Sassenachs.'

'What does that mean?'

'It means I don't need church. You do.'

So one Sunday, five years after my renouncement of God, there
in St Marks, at a suddenly brighter and perfumed altar, stood our
new vicar, the gaunt and haunted-looking Reverend Mr Vaughan.

'What worries me most,' said Mother to the Cleft afterwards,
'is it'll be Mr Vaughan preparing her for Confirmation.'

Catching my name I dog-paddled up from the depths of *Pride and Prejudice*. 'What's wrong with Mr Vaughan?'

'Nothing,' she said as ever. Too late. The spy was already on full alert. Over the next three weeks I gleaned via my usual keyhole sources that the new vicar, unlike the worthy Mr Atkins, was High Church, an apparently tasteless spiritual state marked by too many candles and vulgar smells. This High Churchness also involved the Pope, a sinister figure who lived abroad, and Mother voiced the dark suspicion that Mr Vaughan might himself be foreign.

'Taffy was a Welshman, Taffy was a thief,' was the Cleft's cryptic contribution.

'Well, anyway, not English,' said Mother. 'And not at all the sort of person Abby would have allowed to be vicar at the Old Hall.'

Sunday services now left her with ruffled feathers and she wasn't the only one – after Church most of the rest of the congregation gathered by the wych-gate to grouse to each other. The candles and smells upset them too, but what elicited the loudest squawks were Mr Vaughan's sermons. Here I was foxed. Sermons were for eyeing likely lads and only peripherally for listening to, so I hadn't yet gathered what it was that made the new vicar's addresses so objectionable.

Communion Classes, when they started, soon enlightened me. Mr Vaughan, like the Cleft, had an irascible glitter about him and chose to address the ceiling rather than his six pupils, but there the resemblance abruptly ended. The vicar's fiery eyes seemed to see visions beyond our ken, just looking at him made you feel uplifted and expectant, as if the crucified Jesus on the wall might suddenly move, or choirs of angels descend and miraculously vanish away your spots. But Mr Vaughan, for all his otherworldly appearance, was a tough shepherd. During the weeks that followed, we listened breathlessly as he took the familiar Lamb of God by the scruff of its neck, shook it free of its infestation of Gentle Jesus stories, fleeced it to the bone with the skill of a seasoned shearer and dumped it down in front of us, a different beast altogether, muscled, dangerous and raring to go.

I couldn't believe it. For the second time in my life, here was an adult stepping out of the Enemy ranks to haul me from my quagmire and set my feet on solid ground, rooted in things you could see and touch and hang on to. Ballet, the foothold Miss Yates had afforded, was small in comparison, and anyway crumbling from under me. Mr Vaughan's territory was gigantic, the entire planet in fact, and from his description a calamitous place it seemed to be, chill as the dark side of the moon, rocky with suffering, toxic with cruelty and swept by typhoons of injustice. Not much fun, I concluded, listening avidly, but all the same a jolly sight more interesting than the Home Counties. But the world wasn't quite past any hope of reclamation, so Mr Vaughan assured us, given colossal inputs of human energy and God's hand on the plough. For God, it appeared, wasn't to blame for its poor condition. The rocks and flinty outcrops, the howling winds, weren't burdens He'd dispensed to be meekly borne, nor had they any connection with the state of the inhabitants' souls or their sins or their failure to worship Him. God was a decent chap, God was a sport. The world was in a bad way because of the selfishness of a few greedy human beings who made life miserable for the majority by hoarding the good bits for themselves. Mr Vaughan inveighed against these villains so wrathfully as he glowered down at our partings that I worried for a moment that he included us. Then he burst into 'All Things Bright and Beautiful', singing in a manly bass that vibrated ever more thrillingly as he punted up the hymn's lesser known reaches:

'The rich man in his castle,' he boomed, 'the poor man at his gate, God made them high or lowly, and ordered their estate.' And without drawing breath he dived into prose again, demanding to know if we really thought that sort of injustice was what God wanted, pointing out with curling lip how convenient it was for the rich, not having to give up anything or share anything with the poor, just so long as they could make the poor believe their poverty was God's will. And ever and anon he dinned in his refrain: 'A *man* wrote that hymn, remember that. Not God but *man*. D'you see?'

My goodness, I saw. I could hardly keep still in my chair for seeing. We weren't steeped in television as teenagers are nowadays and this dose of *realpolitik* came as a bolt from the blue. It galvanized me. Here was someone talking about things you didn't have to believe in because you were told to, you could feel their truth digging into your bones. It wonderfully fitted my vague but vehement conviction that a lot of life's rules were wrong or stupid and the adults who made them weren't half as good or clever or right as they thought they were. Now it appeared that some of them were downright bad. Not as bad as Hitler, no. About as bad as the Cleft. But the greatest revelation came as the greatest surprise – that here was an adult who felt as I did and if one, then maybe more. So perhaps the world wasn't set for ever in concrete, like it or lump it. You might be able to change it. You might be able to join up with others and chip bits away or add bits on. Or even – delicious possibility – blow the whole kaboosh up and start again. Rapturously I gazed upon Mr Vaughan who gazed rapturously out of the window.

For the rest of the period of our Instruction I sat smitten at the feet of my hero, gulping down his every word, and on Confirmation Day, dressed all in white and clutching the ivory-backed prayer book Mother had given me, I knelt in a haze of commitment and incense to receive the Body and Blood of Christ from the hands of His Rehabilitator.

Afterwards, gripping the edge of the pulpit, looking more spectral than ever, Mr Vaughan let fly. Raking his congregation of kid-gloved maters and waistcoated paters with a sharpshooter's eye, he took aim and blasted the perky smiles straight off their faces with a salvo of invective re the practitioners of what he called False Christianity, all form and no content, all talk and no deeds, sugar and icing but no honest bread. Jesus, he informed them witheringly, contrary to what they might think, was not meek and mild, a resident of some celestial Grove, Avenue or Crescent, fond of kiddies and birds, whose idea of virtue was mowing the lawn. Jesus was a revolutionary. Jesus was a warrior. Jesus wanted to change the world.

At this the vicar emptied over the heads of his flock the contents of his favourite can of worms: suffering, injustice, poverty, plague, pestilence, famine, drought and so on, disasters no one present, comfortably off and expensively clothed, could begin to imagine, he said. But these children – here he pointed a quivering finger at our six bowed heads – are the hope of the future. They are on the march, recruits to a new Church Militant, foot soldiers in a Christian Army preparing to go forth from this day on to fight the good fight and root out these evils wherever they might be.

At this point one of our number, a nervy girl named Pamela, was so overcome with emotion that she slumped to her knees, greeny-pale, whereupon her mother arose, clucking indignantly, and bore the wounded foot soldier away. The pews rustled and creaked sympathetically, a fusillade of coughs rang out, a man said 'Shame!' not very loudly. For St Markians this was tantamount to storming the Bastille. Undeterred, nostrils flaring, Mr Vaughan cantered on and when finally the choir broke into 'Onward Christian Soldiers' it more or less drowned out the sound of Pamela being copiously sick in the vestry. Drinking in the hot and bothered faces around me I felt mine was a Confirmation devoutly to be wished.

'Just wipe those daft ideas out of your head,' the Cleft commanded my left ear at dinner, Mother having genned him on events. 'Your precious Mr Vaughan is nothing but a damn Bolshie hiding behind a dog collar. The nerve of the man, to say that people here haven't suffered. What does he think we were doing in the war – eating smoked salmon at the Savoy? We need a Senator McCarthy here to see off the likes of Comrade Ivan Vaughanski and his Communist claptrap. Why, he couldn't tell a decent law-abiding citizen from a Loch Fyne kipper.'

'But you said,' I protested, 'that when you were a child the Rector made Mistress McKenzie stand up and told her in front of everyone she'd burn for ever in Hell.'

'Mistress McKenzie,' he answered crossly, 'was quite a different kettle of fish.'

'What was she then, a Loch Fyne kipper?' I inserted daringly.

'You see?' said the Cleft to Mother. 'Already, the rot's set in. Damn Bolshie. I shall write to the Bishop.'

Maybe he wrote, maybe not. Whichever way, disaster soon after struck me down in the full flood of my plan to become a nun and devote my life to the service of the poor, preferably the poor on the side of the planet furthest from Surrey. Only a month after my Confirmation rumour reported that Mr Vaughan was leaving St Marks. He was going to work in The Slums – and a good job too, rumour gloated. The Slums! My yearned-for Shangri-La! I was racked with envy and mortification. Once again, as on the day my brother ran away from me to the sparkling sea, I had been abandoned to the Enemy. If only I could go with Mr Vaughan. Didn't he see that I wasn't like the others, that I knew all too well why he couldn't abide his suburban flock and needed to throw himself into a worthier project, a higher struggle? Instead, he'd tarred me with the same brush as them. He'd lumped me with the greedy selfish few of his sermons, just as I'd feared on that first Instruction day. Me, his champion. Me, prepared to follow him to the rockiest corners of God's far-flung globe or at any rate to The Slums. How unfair, how wretchedly unfair. Smarting with the humiliation of it, the unmerited rejection, I was forced to rethink my position and for the remaining three weeks before Mr Vaughan's departure I scowled at the traitor in the pulpit as fiercely as anyone. Beastly man. Damn Bolshie. Oh please take me with you, *please*.

Mother had somehow convinced herself that one sip of the Body and Blood would automatically transform me into her dream daughter: neat, loving, interested in clothes, shopping, babies and other womanly pursuits, and her disappointment at receiving back from First Communion a distinctly rattier version of the old model was grievous. So much so that I was once or twice tempted to give up and be what she wanted – it might have its rewards and at least I'd please someone at last. But most of the time I saw Mother as a Venus fly-trap from whose seductive jaws no traveller returned and so I turned my back on her and struggled on, trying to keep ajar the escape hatch Mr Vaughan had opened. To this end I began to read *The Times* and the *Telegraph*, the Cleft's newspapers, poring over them in the bathroom while I washed and at breakfast before he came down. It was an undermining experience. The grey cramped columns were largely incomprehensible, you seemed to have to know simply masses already to make any sense of what was going on and the Cleft was no help, he didn't take any more kindly my intrusion into his newspapers than he had my childish efforts to read his books. He fought back with a slightly adjusted version of his old jammy-fingers routine.

'Tut tut,' he'd say, taking up *The Times* from where I'd snuck it back under his napkin and inspecting it. 'Very distressing, this Korea business. It says here that the troop landing at the port of Inchon was held up by several lumps of porridge. And the US 5th Marines had to wade ashore through a spreading slick of fried egg while being heavily bombarded with scraps of back bacon. *What* an ordeal.'

'It's not me,' I lied. 'I didn't do it. You don't allow me to read it, do you? I'm not even allowed to put my elbows on the table and I'm fifteen.'

'There's no doubt *The Times* is becoming sadly parochial,' continued the Cleft, undeflected. 'These days its columns provide me with very little real information beyond certain clues as to the contents of our larder and a brief insight into the volatile nature of the talc powder in the bathroom. Both of which are, in my humble opinion, not quite as internationally significant as, say, the Chinese invasion of Tibet or the assassination of the King in Jordan or even . . .'

The Cleft could ramble on in this vein for ages but the underlying message was succinct enough. World affairs, politics, newspapers, indeed practically everything that didn't actually happen in our house, was his, i.e., male territory and females trespassed at their peril. Mother, I noted, kept well within the permitted borders. She read – often aloud – the little advertisements on *The Times* front page, the columns of engagements, weddings, births and deaths, anything about Monsieur Dior's New Look, reports of sticky divorces, stickier murders and what Princess Margaret Rose was up to, plus she kept a weather eye open for news of Edwina Mountbatten because they had been at school together. I was deeply contemptuous of Mother's taste for what the Cleft called tittle-tattle and fretted a lot about the shameful fact that I secretly liked it the best myself, especially the murders and Monsieur Dior. Maybe the Reverend Mr Vaughan had seen all along that I wouldn't do. Maybe I was doomed to end up the sort of person he despised. I might even turn into Mother.

This dreadful possibility, which I pictured as a large Mother-shaped blanket hovering just above my head, threatening to descend and suffocate me in its folds, drove me to further paroxysms of prayer. Our Father which art in heaven, if I can't be a ballet dancer would you kindly arrange for me to go to Africa and minister to the poor? God's intervention was vital if I was ever to leave home and lead an adventurous life without becoming either a snotty handkerchief or, worse, a secretary. Fulfil now, O Lord, the desires and petitions of Thy servant. Amen.

A week or so later, God moved in a mysterious way, not to dispatch me to Africa but to send me rather further than that from Him. He accomplished this with a book, C. S. Lewis's *The Screwtape Letters*, which I picked at random from the library shelves, innocent of any knowledge of the author's background or beliefs, and began to read in bed the same night. Five pages in and I was already squirming with unease, the same unease I'd once experienced hearing Lord Haw-Haw on the wireless, not knowing who he was, only knowing there was something violently awry about what he was saying. By the time I'd finished the book two nights later its pages seemed to me to reek of rotten eggs – Satan's smell, what else? – and I was on my way out of the world of gods and the whole business of religion.

That conversion on the road from Damascus was as sudden in its miniature way as St Paul's. My whole body, gut, blood and sinew, shrank in revolt from every word. Screwtape, the eponymous demon, listing the ways he lured human beings away from God, at first puzzled and then appalled me, for they were exactly the ways I had assumed led to God, it was my own list somersaulted. The book's definition of sin was my concept of virtue, its bad my good, its truths my lies, my lies its truths, a world turned topsy-turvy that reminded me . . . of what? . . . of the Cleft, yes, that was it. Like the Cleft, this C. S. Lewis regarded the brain as the Devil's Kingdom, seat of all evil. He sneered, like the Cleft, at cleverness, counting it a devilish weakness. To him the wonderful workings of the mind formed barriers between Man and God, therefore people who used their minds were sitting ducks for Satan. Only those who stopped thinking and had faith, the blinder the better, would escape the Devil's blandishments and be saved.

Well, that's how I interpreted it, though admittedly I was no great shakes at analysis. I hadn't the patience nor any real idea of how to hunt down arguments for or against the Screwtape contentions and, anyway, it didn't occur to me. I felt only, and strongly, that if this was what God wanted, for you to give up thinking about anything but Him, if He didn't dare let you question Him and His works, then He couldn't be much of a God at all and I didn't want anything to do with Him.

But then it occurred to me that perhaps Mr C. S. Lewis was a well-known loony or his book was an elaborate grown-up joke I didn't understand. So I turned it over to see what it said on the back about him and learned that everyone thought the book was wonderful and that this C. S. Lewis held all sorts of grand positions in grand places like Oxford and Cambridge. It wasn't a happy moment, finding that out, though it didn't unduly surprise me. Once again I was all by myself clinging to the branch of a tree that was creaking ominously under me. The world out there, which had gleamed with promise during Mr Vaughan's brief reign, looked dull and hostile now, unchanging, unchangeable and stacked to the brim with men whom everyone thought important, intelligent and right and I thought nasty bullies and very wrong.

'I bet C. S. Lewis smokes a pipe,' I said aloud to my face in the mirror. 'I bet he wears awful hairy jackets and baggy trousers and spends ages puffing out smoke from his awful hairy mouth before he says one word because he thinks he's so important you'll have to stand and wait and listen when what you want to do is jump at him and poke out both his piggy eyes.'

Just then came the voice of the Cleft from the hall, proclaiming from the depths of his lungs as he did each morning: 'Every day and in every way, I am getting better and better.'

The face in the mirror scrunched up like a prune. 'No, you're not,' it snarled. 'None of you are. Every day and in every way you're all getting worse and worse.'

Goodness, I felt lonely.

A year later, I passed the School Certificate and Mother, possibly worn down by the strain of containing me and the Cleft under one roof, told me I could leave school now and go to Switzerland.

'Switzerland?' I said, dumbfounded.

'Your grandfather,' the Cleft said, 'for reasons we can all appreciate, thinks you ought to be finished off at a Finishing School. We have found such a school. M. Delange, the Headmaster, seems to believe that for an understandably vast sum of money he can just about turn you into a lady.'

'Grandpa's paying,' Mother said, giving him a look before she turned back to me. 'On Saturday you and I are meeting M. Delange at the Dorchester and if he likes you, you can go in September.'

'For that kind of money,' the Cleft grunted, '*I* would like her.'

Thus the Birds of Paradise, whose exotic existence I had almost forgotten, swooped to my rescue. There was, to my astonishment, a not entirely favourable reaction from various teachers when I crowed to them about when and where I was going. Some, for reasons I couldn't fathom, raised their eyebrows or shook their heads disapprovingly and one or two actually said they thought finishing school was a waste of time and what about university. Perhaps they were jealous? Nevertheless.

'What about university?' I said at dinner.

'What about it?' said the Cleft.

'I don't know.' It was the truth. I didn't know a thing about university except that it was at Oxford and Cambridge and that men like C. S. Lewis taught there. 'It's just that some of the mistresses at school think I ought to go there instead of Switzerland.'

'Oh do they?' The Cleft put down his fork and knife rather noisily. 'Well, the choice is yours. Isn't that right, Cath?'

Mother looked worried but she said yes, it was.

'Your choice,' the Cleft continued. 'You may leave school and go to Switzerland now or you can stay on at school for two more years, take another much harder set of exams and, should you pass, then you could go to university. Which will it be?'

'Switzerland,' I said.

Six

Le Château du Lac was in an ancient farming village not far from Lake Neuchâtel. In many ways the school was the village, or at any rate its only industry. The dozen or so large houses all belonged to M. Delange, the largest being the château itself, perched at the top of a web of cobbled lanes lined with ramshackle cottages. Its elevation marked it out along with its most distinctive feature, a mighty heap of manure that stood gently steaming at its main gate. The majority of our daytime activities took place at the Chat; in the evenings we returned to the dormitory houses nearby.

There, we were roused at dawn each morning by the rural sounds of mooing, bleating, milk churn clanking and the mad soprano shrieks of pigs being slaughtered. Setting off for the Chat, hopscotching from cobble to cobble to avoid the leftover deposits of the mooing and bleating, we had to pass huge vats of boiling water wherein were sunk the murdered pigs, their trotters poking through the vapour in silent protest. The sight and particularly the smell of those pigs was somehow grue-somely familiar, as if it might be some cousin or uncle quietly simmering there, and by the time we arrived at the Chat, via the manure mountain, our appetite for the breakfast of doorstop bread and cherry jam had been severely curtailed. Later I suspected the pigs were there for that very purpose – M. Delange was never a man to pass up the possible saving of a franc or ten.

I discovered immediately that I wasn't going to be happy at Le Château du Lac and for the first month or so the knowledge that an unimaginably long year of not being happy stretched ahead drove me to spend as much time as possible locked in the lavatory, partly so that I could cry in secret and partly because, being unaccustomed to boarding school, I craved for privacy so badly that any reminder of my room at home, unbelievably big, incredibly empty, guaranteed a fresh waterspout. Mother's face swam frequently before me, dolorous and oddly baffled, as if some inner organ she couldn't quite locate was hurting her. How long had she looked like that and why hadn't I noticed? I wanted to put my arms around her and rock her better, as if she weren't my mother but an orphan child. Nothing was her fault and all I'd done was blame her. Biblically, I thought: she has fallen among thieves. Among the Birds of Paradise was where she belonged, in the warm, undemanding embrace of her enormous family. I could see her through the blur of tears, a laughing girl with splendid teeth, arms round and golden in the sun, black hair bobbing as she bounced about a tennis court or stood silhouetted against the blue sky before diving into the shining sea to forge across the Hellespont. We weren't her sort, the Cleft and I. She was loving and kind, we weren't. She liked hugs and kisses, we didn't. She was no good at arguing and she didn't want to be, all she wanted was for us to be happy, for us all to love each other and be happy like the Birds of Paradise and we wouldn't and weren't. Sitting on my lonely loo I cried and cried for Mother.

The Cleft I didn't cry for, things never got that bad. But he stalked about in my memory more often than I would have guessed before this exile. I would have guessed I'd never think of him at all but there he was, long, thin and cold, a stalagmite in the cave of my mind, and I thought that he must feel colder to himself than anybody, that his insides must be frozen stiff. Sometimes he looked as if he hurt, too, not in the way Mother did but in the way Scott of the Antarctic might have done, stranded in Polar wastes, or Captain Oates before he said, *I'm going outside, I may be gone for some time*. The Cleft had gone outside and like Captain Oates he'd not come back. When and where had he gone and why? Mother's photograph of him as a boy showed him fine-looking, in a kilt hung with a great white sporran and gaiters up his legs. He stares ahead expressionless, a lock of dark hair bisecting his forehead, eyes wider than they were now but already wary, on guard. Had he always been that way or had something happened to change him? I tried to imagine the Cleft as a jolly, smiling child and couldn't. While I was about it, I tried to recall when he'd ever touched me, and couldn't. He must have some bat-like radar in him that steered him clear of touching me, even by mistake. Perhaps he had when I was a baby, but never after. It was strange to realize that. Other girls' fathers hugged and kissed them the way their mothers did, I'd watched them and found it hard not to titter rudely or wrinkle my nose, it looked so drippy. The Cleft wouldn't ever act like that, the very idea made me pimple all over. Lone wolves don't kiss you, do they? Wild cats don't hug. It wouldn't be natural. Well, then.

From the safety of a Swiss loo I felt faintly proud of the undomesticated Cleft.

After a while I settled into that state of suspended emotion adopted by generations of boarders for survival purposes. In the case of the pupils of Le Château du Lac this was blessedly relieved at the weekends when we all had hysterics. Fay-han, the only Turkish girl, usually led us into it, throwing herself

down on the nearest soft surface, rolling her black grape eyes
and emitting a series of razor-sharp shrieks. This triggered
Maria, a glamorous Belgian, into kicking off her skyscraper
high cork wedgies and jumping up and down, screeching almost
as loudly as Fay-han. Then into the fray leapt the Italian
contingent, six sexy, faintly moustachioed older girls, most of
them Contessas, who flung themselves energetically about,
chests palpitating *con brio*. Triggered off by the seismic tremors
the whole lot of us set to: Germans, French, a brace of swarthy
Portuguese sisters, one plump Swiss-German, a little gaggle of
Spaniards, three athletic South Africans, a very plain Austrian
Princess, one representative each of Lichtenstein, Luxembourg
and Monaco and, finally, us Brits and the five Scandinavians.
The walls of the Tower of Babel came tumbling down and
everyone enjoyed themselves hugely – I, for one, soon became
an addict and whenever Fay-han showed signs of flagging took
over and drove the Harpies on, puncturing ear-drums for miles
around. What the villagers made of this cacophony we never
discovered. Perhaps they'd already been deafened by the pigs.
As for those nominally in charge of us, they all took off at
weekends except for the keepers of the dormitory houses who,
if they heard us, kept mum.

Monsieur Delange, short, squat and shrew-eyed, was the
only adult who lived at the Chat, somewhere in the upper
regions where no pupil ever penetrated. We worked out
quickly enough, however, that the photograph in the school
brochure of Monsieur sitting on his balcony with the snow-
covered peaks of some Alp gleaming toothsomely in the
distance was either a fake or a once-in-a-lifetime climatic
phenomenon; none of us ever caught a glimpse of an Alp in all
our Château year. Needless to say, the manure heap didn't
figure in the brochure either.

Our headmaster had a few other tricks up his sleeve. One of

the classes on our *Horaire* was *Repassage*, ironing, and I wasn't alone in wondering why learning to iron was an attribute of Young Ladyship. After all, Mother had her maid Minnie do hers and we weren't rich. Austrian Princesses and Italian Contessas must have castlefuls of Minnies to iron out their creases. Why was Grandpa paying for what I heartily hoped I'd never have to do? That question was soon solved. In the *Repassage* room, suitably equipped with rows of irons and ironing boards, we were doled out piles of undergarments of a style none of us had encountered before: starchy bodices, ample petticoats and knee-length bloomers, all trimmed with Swiss *broderie* laced through with pink and blue ribbon. You didn't have to be Miss Marple to suspect you were ironing local undies, presumably for some nearby laundry. Cunning M. Delange!

'*Mon Dieu, c'est un peu épais,*' we English exclaimed to each other. '*Shockant, je l'appelle. Quelle cheek.*' The other nationalities merely shrugged and said in rather better French tolerant things like, '*Eh alors?*' We were on our honour to speak French and daily signed a book called *Le Livre d'Or* to that effect, and I brooded over the fact that M. Delange allowed himself to lie – what else were the Alps in the brochure but a lie, never mind the *Repassage*? – but assumed we wouldn't. And we didn't, not the English contingent at least. We didn't even cheat in tests, unlike many of the others who covered their knees and inside wrists with scribbles, concealed bits of paper all over their persons and didn't mind us knowing. Fayhan, who attended every test looking like a tiny Tattooed Lady, was baffled when I questioned her.

'Eet don't make no difference to you,' she assured me, beaming benignly.

'*Mais c'est cheating, quand même.*'

'Cheating oo? Monsieur Delange? *Il s'en fout.* He just want ze money. *Ils sont tous les mêmes, les grands.*' And she rubbed her fingers with their tiny bitten red nails under my nose and giggled. Clearly our view of *les grands* had something in common. Why couldn't I accept their shortcomings, anyone's for that matter, in good spirit like Fay-han instead of so often feeling sore and swindled? More than anything I longed to meet the perfect person, a pillar of purest gold against whom I could lean. Where were they, for goodness sake?

Monsieur Bernard, our ski master, looked pretty perfect. He was tall and Gary Cooperish and all the girls were in love with him. Being in love with someone was compulsory at the Chat, you were no one if you weren't. It was just permissible to be in love with someone at home and flash his photo around or, better, his letters, but the real status symbol was a Swiss boy, because he was a concrete ingredient in a drama we could all observe and discuss. The difficulty was meeting a suitable Swiss boy, i.e., one good-looking enough to arouse envy and enhance prestige. There was none in the village and on our occasional trips into Neuchâtel we were heavily chaperoned, Mme Hubacher on one side, Mam'selle Eloise on the other, both intent on shooing us as fast as possible through the various parks and shops to their desired destination, any one of the hundreds of al fresco cafés. There we sat hungrily eyeing the passing males, meanwhile devouring huge cream coffees and huge cream cakes. I had two favourites: a leaning tower of squiggly chestnut worms topped with whipped cream, and a Tête de Nègre, a chocolate mound bulging with whipped cream, served with yet more dollops of the same. Once I broke the current school record by eating twelve Têtes de Nègre at a go without ill effect, but it was no consolation for not being locked in the arms of M. Bernard or anyone else, for that matter.

But every second month our chance came with invitations to dances at Neuchâtel University. These engendered indescribable excitement and our weekend hysteria sessions were stepped up beforehand to two and sometimes three midweek. We were all equipped with at least two ballgowns, as per the Chat's Dress List, and we all without exception hated our own and coveted someone else's, which led to prolonged and bitter bargainings, during which friendships withered and vendettas bloomed. Dressing on the night itself was fraught almost beyond human bearing. Jennifer came out in red patches all over her strapless bosom and nearly died. Marie-Louise found a spot on her chin, burst out crying and then cried a lot more on account of the crying having ruined her eyes. Valentina split her waspie, couldn't squash herself into Jennifer's dress and ran screaming *Madre di Dio* from room to room like Dante in Hell while Britta, pinioned in a slinky gown of Susi's, screamed Nordic oaths in a stationary position because the tight fit showed the ends of her Kotex. My own Armageddon was the futile attempt via kilos of cotton wool to fake a cleavage where there was none. Only Trudy, the prettiest girl in the school, tossed her curls and smiled radiantly upon the infernal scene. How we loathed her.

In the end, perched wonkily on unaccustomed heels, we got to the ball, where we huddled together at one side of the ballroom under M. Bernard's supervision and pretended not to notice the boys gathering at the opposite side. When the music started the boys walked across and chose their partners and all of us instantly fell in love. M. Bernard, superb in black tie, conscientiously danced with each of us in turn, whereupon we fell in love with him again. And so, with the added bonus of a sudden gift for French, we danced the night away. On the road home, fragrant with sweat, we fell fast asleep in a jumble of wilting finery, like so many dolls dropped from an Alp.

But the ball was just the first hurdle — next we had to wangle forbidden meetings with the loves of our lives. This involved the setting up of a complex network of moles and carrier pigeons who could be relied on to deliver and receive impassioned instructions as to lovers' trysts. Then came the truly hazardous part, the creeping out at night through windows, down drainpipes and past insomniac House Mistresses' rooms to the murky silhouette of the waiting lover. Uncounted kilowatts of brain power, enough to split the atom, were spent organizing these moonlight flits but, alas, the most ardent and eternal of loves had the oddest way of collapsing like a punctured balloon when at last you were in the arms of the loved one or, in bleak fact, sitting awkwardly together on a garden bench saying nervously to an even more nervous student, '*Comment allez-vous?*' and '*Très bien, merci.*' Nothing seemed the same without the support of the companions in crime left behind. The kissing (and even kissing wasn't always on the menu of nice girls and boys in that pre-Pill age) was hard on the teeth and prickly on the neck and besides, the bench was awfully damp.

'*Alors?*' came the whispers from bed after bed as the fallen woman loomed again at the window or tiptoed back through the door. 'What did he do? *Qu'est-ce qui se passe?* Did he embrace you or did he *baiser* you? Come on, spill the beans, do.' The mixing up of *embrasser* and *baiser* was a dependable source of hilarity to us, for though both could mean kissing, '*baiser*' also signified that momentous deed: going all the way.

Who had or hadn't gone all the way was a school obsession, so much so that a Martian dropping in on Le Château du Lac might well have reported back to Control that that was what a finishing school was for: pupils studied, discussed, researched, debated and did practical work on the subject and when they finally went all the way they were officially declared Finished and given a diploma, hurray.

And in one sense, finished they were. We knew the saying 'nice girls don't' and we dismissed it as the usual adult rubbish. Who cared about niceness? Our rule was much more down to earth and effective: pretty, smart, popular girls didn't and plain, dumb girls did. This rule was no artificial imposition, it was organic and it worked. For the observable fact was that since a man would sleep with anyone if he got the chance, it was no testimony to a girl's attractions and, besides, once he'd done it he'd cast you off. What incentive was that for going all the way? Pregnancy, the adults' direst threat, was unreal, not to say unimaginable, compared to the lively certainty of losing the man while being ridiculed behind your back by the girls. Virginity at least gave you the illusion that you were up there among the Beauty Queens, who didn't because they didn't have to.

None of this, of course, detracted in the least from our intense interest in the matter or the pleasure of egging each other on. Angry red blotches on necks and shoulders, called euphemistically 'love-bites', were sported with pride and the ins and outs of deflowering were mulled over in fantastical detail. The outcome of these discussions was always the same, a general agreement that the first girl who managed to lose her virginity to Number One Heart-Throb M. Bernard had to pay for her luck by vowing to give us all a blow-by-blow account, cross her heart and hope to die.

'*M. Bernard, c'est un vrai homme,*' said Fay-han, crouched Turkish-style on her cushioned bed, and, '*ah, oui,*' we all sighed, '*pas moitié.*' Not half.

M. Bernard, however, though he continued to cause mass swoonings whenever he gave one of his shy smiles, showed no sign of being ready to do his duty and appeared to be unaware of the female ripples that spread out around him wherever he went. The ski season, which started earlier than usual that year, snow falling picturesquely enough for any brochure from September on, meant delicious hours on the nursery slopes behind the Chat, standing sometimes but mostly collapsing within the steadying ambit of Monsieur's strong arms.

'*Monsieur, Monsieur,*' went up the cry from top to bottom of the slopes, '*je ne peux plus, je suis si fatiguée, oh là là, je vais tomber, sauvez-moi, je vous en prie, Monsieur, sauvez-moi!*' And the darling man, tanned to a turn by the winter sun, swooshed heroically up and down on his short hooked skis and saved us, every one.

And so it went until Christmas, which emptied the Chat for a fortnight of all the Continentals and left the field clear for the English. We, because of still stringent foreign currency restrictions, could not return home, nor could our parents visit us. But by then, four months into the school year, my own homesickness was a good deal less acute, and though I was still aware of a kind of vacuum inside, the momentum of school events kept me jogging along without much time to brood. The pre-Christmas week we spent at Wengen, a real ski resort with a real funiculi-funicular. The excitement of being suspended in a swaying carriage hundreds of feet above white mountains cross-stitched with pines, and the heart-clenching pause at the peak of the downward run – skis dead ahead, crouch, breath in, ski-poles *whuff* into the snow and *schwuff* away – that challenge drove any remnants of self-pity into deep freeze. For me, the *après-ski* doings in Wengen, as later in Canada, were a penance. The endless ski-chat, the bronzed ski-hearties, the bawled-out choruses of boring songs, the Teutonic jollity of it all leaves me to this day unable to see ski-gear in a Lillywhites window without gagging, but skiing itself, the fear, the loneliness, the whistling speed, the blissful swish of blade on snow, was very heaven. Down we whizzed one after the other, slaloming grandly from side to side while in and out between us wove M. Bernard in a shower of snow, the bobble on his cap wobbling madly, his voice floating thinly back to us.

'*Gardez les genoux ensemble, jeunes dames! Toujours les genoux ensemble!*'

That classic instruction to young ladies, keep your knees together, caused instant and dangerous wobblings in the ranks and Margaret Tulley, quite unbalanced by laughter, promptly closed with a tree, which doomed her to a Christmas in plaster, a casualty of love.

Christmas Day dawned. With Margaret hobbling between us we trudged through the snow in our snowboots, singing out *Joyeux Noël* to all who passed, and gathered in the dining room of the Chat in our gladdest rags, velvet, taffeta and lace. We ate suckling pig and Kugelhupf, pulled crackers and moaned that our zips were busting. Then Mme Hubacher announced that we were all invited to join M. Delange in his inner sanctum. Following Madame's bombazine rear up the Chat's last and hitherto forbidden flight of stairs, we entered what seemed to be a hunting lodge perched at the top of the house. A huge log fire blazed in a stone hearth below stone walls spiked all over with rows of guns and the antlers of dead beasts. Beyond french windows that gave on to the famous balcony lay a winter wonderland that stretched as far as the eye could see but did not, I noted, even on that sparkling day, include the notorious missing Alp. On the far side of the room glimmered a majestic Christmas tree and beside it, arranged as in a Nativity scene, sat Monsieur himself, squat, smiley and poacher-checked as Mr Toad, backed by a group of young men in casual wear, which is to say razor-creased trousers, immaculate blazers, striped shirts topped by impeccable ascots and hair so slicked it looked like the skin of their skulls had changed colour. Even M. Bernard, who to our joy was among their number, had been rendered almost unrecognizable by grooming.

Awed by this vision of masculine perfection, we sank as directed upon the pelts of various animals that lay scattered about.

'*Alors. Joyeux Noël, Mesdemoiselles,*' said M. Delange with a regal wave in our direction.

'*Joyeux Noël, Messieurs,*' we chorused in our turn.

'I ave invite you ere,' continued Monsieur, 'for a leetel Christmas glass of champagne. Jean-Claude?'

He clicked his pudgy fingers and one of the young men shot up to dispense from a tray what were indeed leetel glasses of champagne. When everyone had been supplied there was a formal clinking and a toast by M. Delange to the health, happiness and general well-being of his dear pupils. The champagne having vanished in one convivial gulp, our Headmaster's expression became sepulchral.

'But we must remember zat Christmas eez a appy time becoz we celebrate also ze burss of ze bébé Jesus. Please zerefore *taisez-vous mes enfants*, and I will read for you from ze Eenglish Beeble.'

He indicated an outsize tome which lay open upon a nearby table formed of zebra skin and elephant tusks. Once more Jean-Claude leapt to his glossily moccasined feet, picked up the Good Book and laid it reverently across M. Delange's checked lap. Monsieur pinched his nose, cleared his throat and began the reading from St Luke.

'. . . And Marie brought forse er firstborn son and wrapped eem in swaddling clozzes and laid eem in a manger; becoz zere waz no room for zem een ze een. And lo, ze angel of ze Lord came upon zem and ze glory of ze Lord shone round about zem and . . .'

Listening to the familiar story, beautiful even when wrung through M. Delange's mangle and even though I no longer believed, I drifted off into a dream of home in which Mother, the Cleft and Robbie stood gathered together with sad uplifted faces thinking of me. When the Cleft fell to his knees sobbing about how much he missed his dear, good, clever daughter the daydream collapsed under its own weight and I turned my attention to something less abstract; the clean-cut features and firm jaw of M. Bernard, heart-stirringly masculine as it jutted out above the rash of horseshoes on his silk foulard. The other men too were more than averagely good-looking and hadn't I seen one of them before? Wasn't the one with the shortest back and sides the same man who helped his mother, Mme Houlot, at the village shop, except that now he looked altogether smarter, cleaner and . . .?

'. . . but Mary kept all zeez sings and pondered zem in er art,' finished M. Delange and closed the book with a thump before saying briskly, '*Et maintenant, amusez-vous bien, Mesdemoiselles. Au revoir.*'

No sooner had we trooped downstairs again and were flopped on the sofas in the sitting room ready for an intensive post-mortem of the episode than Jennifer, closing the door behind her, rounded dramatically upon us.

'Shut up and listen,' she hissed, her neck above its pearl choker ricked with agitation. 'M. Bernard. I've just realized. He's a homo. So's M. Delange. They all are.'

This bombshell, too cataclysmic for mere hysterics, was greeted with Bunty's usual dismissive '*Oh, va pee-pee sur les rosiers*', after which fell a silence as long as Remembrance Day as we scanned each others' faces open-mouthed. Eventually little Jane piped up – she came from Lincolnshire and was unworldly. 'What's a homo?' she asked, peering at the statues around her.

Someone took her aside. The rest of us, after the first wordless babble of protest, began to wrestle with the awesome possibility.

'Why d'you think so? He *can't* be. I don't believe it.'

'All of them? M. Delange too? But he's *old*.'

'Jennifer, you're *mad*. Homos aren't like M. Bernard. Look, they hold their hands like this. They walk like this, look.'

Everyone scrambled up in order to demonstrate to everyone else their superior knowledge of homosexual behaviour. The room heaved with girls mincing and flapping.

'Not much like M. Bernard, huh?' I squealed, pausing to wave a limp wrist at Jennifer still standing at the door.

'You don't know anything,' she said with accuracy and, addressing the turmoil behind me, added loudly and firmly, 'I'm willing to bet. Why hasn't M. Delange ever married? Why are they all up there together on Christmas Day? And Mme Houlot's son from the shop, what's he doing there unless he's one too? That's why M. Bernard isn't interested in any of us. Because he's queer as a coot. They all are, so there.'

Queer as a coot. The words, so emphatic, so odd, hung in the air. Jennifer, after all, was nearly eighteen, the oldest among us. She wore doe-eyes, had a house of her own behind Harrods, knew what went into a White Lady and was going to be presented at Court. Besides, the evidence she'd marshalled didn't look good.

'What about all those guns and things?' said Margaret defensively.

'What about them?' Jennifer snapped.

'There certainly aren't any homos in the Quorn,' said Bunty, who had a three-barrelled surname and claimed to have been born on a horse.

'My grandfather,' I joined in, 'is the best shot there is, he sent an eland to the King and he's certainly not queer as a coot.'

'Oscar Wilde,' said Jennifer, raising her eyebrows in a lordly way, 'shot tigers and hunted and look at him.'

This hitherto unknown fact confounded us. It became clear that Jennifer was right and none of us would ever be deflowered by dearest M. Bernard, or any other man probably, because if M. Bernard was queer, who wasn't? Really, adults were even more disappointing than any of us had imagined.

'We have coots on the lake at home,' announced little Jane.

Sunk in contemplation of our virginal fate, no one bothered to reply.

After a while, little Jane said, 'Anyway, what do homos *do*?' At this, there was a general perking up and what remained of Christmas Day passed serenely enough explaining to her and to each other, with appropriate lardings of 'ughs' and 'yuks', exactly what it was that we imagined homos did.

M. Delange never regained his authority once these revelations had been relayed to the other girls on their return from home sweet home. Fay-han was particularly struck, and took to producing the most realistic retching noises whenever Messieurs D. or B. were mentioned. Once M. Bernard, coming unexpectedly into the room, put a solicitous arm round her heaving shoulders and urged her to lie down until she felt better.

'Do stop,' I said irritably to her when he'd gone. '*Ça devient trop ennuyant, quand même.*'

Fay-han butted her head affectionately into my angular shoulder. '*Ah, mon pauvre chouchou,*' she cooed. 'Per-aps you are also, ow you say, queer like a coot, *n'est-ce pas*? My dulling, *je t'adore.*'

The rule of law at the Chat started to disintegrate. Issued with new *Horaires* after the Easter holiday, all but the most dedicated swots crossed out every class that required any work and turned up for a maximum of two a day, spending the remaining hours lounging in the sun, trying different hair-dos out on each other and sucking away at thick tubes of condensed cream like so many greedy ewe lambs. Once we spent an agonizing day stabbing at each others' ear lobes so that we could wear the gypsy earrings we'd all bought at a Neuchâtel fair. Margaret swore she'd done it hundreds of times.

'All you do is put a cork behind, like this, and you stick the needle through like this . . .'

'Aaagh,' I shrieked, but I stood my ground as she jabbed away while Jennifer, clutching my hand, chanted ever more loudly, '*Il faut souffrir pour être belle.*'

'You're supposed to sterilize the needle first,' said Bunty, kindly mopping up the blood as it dripped down my neck.

'Oh yes? Pass the bunsen burner, then,' Margaret said sarcastically, pausing for a breather.

'Is it done?' I whimpered.

'Give me half a chance, do.'

Little Jane, coming in unexpectedly upon the gory scene, gave a pitiful gargle and had to lie down. Nevertheless, at the end of the day all our ears were punctured and despite the fact that a week later the jabbings had to be repeated because throbbing pustules had sealed them again (this time the agony was worse than having a baby, Bunty said), when it was over we flashed our rather lop-sided earrings well satisfied. '*Nous avons souffré* like hell and *maintenant nous sommes* hell-ishly *belles*,' was Jennifer's bilingual verdict, and so said all of us.

At night there were now more girls out of their beds than in. Having placed the obligatory bolsters under the duvets, a device in which we had boundless faith, we racketed into town on trams pungent with garlic and perched ourselves like a row of starlings on the banks of the lake to meet and canoodle in the twilight with François and Jean-Pierre, Mathieu and Henri.

These young men displayed true Swiss stolidity, generally confining themselves to tidy kisses and earnest nibbles at what little flesh our well-gusseted Horrocks frocks revealed. We, for our part, remained half-wittedly English, straining around the various male necks and shoulders to make faces at each other instead of concentrating on the work at hand. None of us, in practice, went more than a millimetre of all the way; not my circle at any rate. That one rule held, abetted by instant panic at any masculine strategem designed to distance us from the group and by the bras and suspender belts we wore, multiply stitched and rubberized, which held out stoutly against attack. My own special terror, that exploring hands would discover a pair of old stockings instead of a breast, gave me all the incentive I needed to defend my honour and gained me an envied reputation as one of the icier *dames sans merci*.

Sometimes, sitting around after these outings comparing notes, we were forced to admit that things hadn't turned out quite the way we'd planned. Almost eight months of opportunities had passed and in spite of our big talk here we were, still deplorably virgin.

'If only M. Bernard wasn't a you-know-what ...' sighed Margaret.

'Oh, if only,' we sighed back.

'It's all his fault,' said Bunty crossly.

'His fault,' we echoed.

'I mean, Henri and François and the rest, they're just boys.'

'Just boys,' we sneered.

In the glum silence that followed I got up and trailed over to the mirror to give my lips a third coating of Joan Crawford violet. Margaret, peering from behind me, spat into her mascara and Elizabeth Taylored her eyebrows. Jennifer, gazing out of the window, absently squashed her breasts together into a Wicked Lady trough while Bunty munched fretfully away at her nails and little Jane surveyed us all with her wistful Margaret O'Brien expression. Finally Bunty spoke up again.

'Well,' she said brightly, 'all the same, there's one good thing. We're none of us real virgins any more. What we are is *demi-vièrge*.'

'Yes, oh yes,' we agreed, cheering up no end. 'That's it, that's what we are, *demi-vièrge*.'

I rolled the words round on my violet lips. '*Demi. Vièrge*. You know, that actually sounds chicer than going all the way, don't you think?'

They did and there were smug smiles all round.

'Am I one too?' inquired little Jane, who'd never been seen within miles of a male.

Relief made us generous. 'Yes, Titch, you too,' we said.

One Chat activity that no one opted out of was swimming. The summer was hot, the beach pleasantly sandy and there was always the hope of encountering boys. The proper swimmers among us, the crawlers, the butterfliers, promptly abandoned the breasties doing their sedate old-lady strokes close to shore and struck out for the Mine – a large metal buoy with a runged prong sticking up from its middle – that bobbed up and down a decent distance away.

'OK, line up for the Strapless Stakes,' shouted Bunty one particularly roasting day. Bunty was the fastest swimmer of our group and also the possessor of a unique strapless bra so intricately boned and foamed that in it the averagely developed girl ballooned into Jane Russell and even my spartan equipment became two decent-sized tennis balls. Naturally, this engineering marvel was coveted by all and the deal was, in the unlikely event that you beat Bunty to the Mine it was yours. But this time a dark horse trotted towards us, Carla, one of two new arrivals that term from the unimaginably glamorous land of America.

'OK if I join you?'

Bunty, taken aback by this limber, streamlined apparition, allowed rather grudgingly that it was. We lined up, we dived in and before we'd come up for our first gulp of air Carla had forged effortlessly past us and was swinging on the Mine with a wide grin as, gasping, we finally scrambled aboard. This was a disaster. An American from a land choc-a-bloc with miraculous bras had wrested from us our one meagre trophy. Through gritted teeth Bunty conceded it and Carla, grinning even more widely, said no, thanks a lot, keep it. How wonderful Americans were, how fine and generous. What perfect teeth Carla had. She was clearly perfect through and through.

Happily we sprawled over the warm surface of the swaying Mine while Carla clambered up the prong and clung at the top, rolling herself energetically to and fro and the Mine and us with it. Then she dived off.

Clasping my knees, I sat and watched as she reappeared, hovering just beneath the surface a yard or so from my feet. How long her eyelashes were, softly fanned on her cheeks. She looked like a sleepy mermaid, her long hair floating out on the lazy lap of the waves. I watched until the skin on my body became suddenly much too tight.

'Carla! Carla! Hey, something's wrong with Carla!'

Floundering into the water beside her, I cupped her cool face in my two hands and lifted it to the air. Her eyes stayed closed. Then they were all around us and Bunty was yelling from the topmost rung of the Mine: 'Oh my God, help help! *Attention! Au secours! Un bateau, vite, vite!*'

We held her up, the dozing mermaid, kicking hard against her weight, shocked tears soaking our soaked cheeks, until after what seemed an aeon of time a man in a boat arrived and somehow we heaved her in. On the way to the beach, lying pale and still in our arms, Carla's eyes flickered and opened. Oh joy! We clustered above her, clucking, murmuring, stroking.

'I can't feel my legs,' she whispered and tenderly we whispered back, 'It's nothing, don't worry, you'll be all right, you'll be fine, everything's fine.'

But it wasn't. Five days later Carla died.

We were instructed to wear black for her funeral but no one possessed more than one or two black garments and those mothball-smelling and wintery. Snuffling, I dug up a woollen skirt, Monique, weeping, found grey wedgies, Bunty dragged out a blouse and coat, Jennifer a belt and skirt, Jane a floppy black felt hat, Margaret a grey jacket and a long black nightie, red-eyed Fay-han and the Italians a black dress each. Mournfully we shared out this sombre collection as best we could.

Outside the village church we gathered. The bells tolled. The sun boiled furiously in a brilliant sky. I staggered slightly in Monique's wedgies, yanked Margaret's nightie from my damp armpits and dripped slowly like a long black candle. Beside me a black coat stood all on its own with little Jane sweltering somewhere inside. Fay-han and the Italians, hanging about by the church door in their skin-tight black numbers looked like tarts in a Rossellini film, while Margaret in Fay-han's black crinoline with Jane's felt hat pulled over her ears looked like an ancient puffball waiting to be kicked.

In the pews we waited again. Two tall strangers walked up the aisle, the woman with a hectic smile on her face, the man vacant. Carla's parents. Then came Carla, heaped with flowers. Carla, who was and now was not. In my mind I could see her living eyes, wired with tiny fronds of green. I could feel her wet hair and her cool skin. The organ boomed, the priest bade us pray and Fay-han's dress as she bent to obey ripped across with a noise like a fart. In the electric hush that followed, someone snorted. Someone else gulped alarmingly. The tinderbox rasped, ignited, flared. Ahead of me, Britta convulsed and slumped on her prayer cushion; Trudy beside her gave an eerie gurgle. On my left the puffball began to quake, on my right the black coat shuddered. A sound that had started in my throat as a sob emerged from my mouth as two loud snickers. Then I couldn't stop. None of us could. Crushing gloves against rictus lips, stuffing hankies into racked throats, covering bleary eyes with scarves, clutching bruised stomachs, we rocked and writhed. I saw her, Carla's mother, beside the coffin, I saw her cheek crumple as she half-turned our way and the shadow in the long jaw of Carla's father; still do. On that blazing afternoon, to an agonized chorus of whickers and whin-nies, they laid their daughter in her grave and in our beds that night we ached as if an army had galloped over us.

The summer died with Carla and the Chat year meandered to its end. We took our final exams. The standard M. Delange set – with a canny eye to satisfied customers and future prospects – was discreetly low and, as we were meant to, all of us passed and received impressively scripted and gold-leafed diplomas for our minimal pains. Then came the farewells – an anguished affair. Poor Fay-han, whose parents had sentenced her to three more Chat months, was Ophelia abandoned, wandering tear-streaked through the mounting piles of luggage wailing the Turkish equivalent of 'There's rosemary, pray, love, remember, hey non nonny' and so on.

'Ah Djeel,' she sobbed, winding herself vine-like around me, '*je vais mourir quand tu pars, tu es l'amour de ma vie, qu'est ce que je vais faire sans toi*, my dulling sweetie-pie?'

Reduced by her brilliantly watering eyes to tears myself I hugged her passionately, swearing to write, to visit, to keep her *toujours dans mon cœur*. It was all deeply affecting and I hiccuped with grief as I tenderly helped her unwind her limbs from me and entwine herself around Margaret.

Little Jane was almost equally distraught and had to be

passed like a soggy parcel from one consoling embrace to the next. Sentiments of undying love were scribbled in *livres de souvenir* by girls who had barely exchanged two words with each other the whole year long and when the final parting came between Margaret, Jennifer, Bunty and me, emotion so choked us we could hardly cram down a single triangle of our very last shared Toblerone. *Adieu, au revoir, arrivederci, hasta la vista, servus, auf Wiedersehen* we cried and felt our hearts crack as we waved and waved.

Now I was seventeen and Finished. Now I was on my way home, a young lady. Now life, wonderful life, would begin.

Seven

'Look!' Mother opened my bedroom door. I looked. A strong whiff of paint nipped up my nose. The chipped old furniture had gone. No more nursery cupboard, no more chest of drawers with its wooden frieze of animals marching two by two, no rickety lamp, no braided rug, no toy-box. Now instead of the old brown linoleum a soft carpet spread from wall to wall and on it stood a proper wardrobe, a matching full-sized chest-on-chest, a slipper chair and a grown-up dressing table complete with a gold-edged three-piece mirror and a stool tucked under, all trimmed, padded and upholstered in a rose-covered chintz that matched the new curtains and the new button-back bedhead and the frill around the new bed table. And on the bed table was a vase full of roses.

'Welcome home, darling,' Mother said shyly. 'D'you like it? Oh, I hope you do.'

I hugged her and thanked her and she went away downstairs with her cheeks almost as pink as the roses. I closed the door, sat down at the dressing table and watched in the mirror as the tears flooded my eyes. I hated it. The old sickness came rushing back and took up its place in the pit of my stomach as if it had never been away. This room was for the daughter Mother wanted and should have had; her real daughter. This room said, *your mother loves that one, she doesn't love you*. This room yelled, *Get out of here you alien creature, you don't belong and never will. These roses, these frills, they're for that other altogether nicer girl.* I could feel the very walls closing in around me, trying to squeeze me out like toothpaste from a tube. *Begone, imposter! Go hence!*

That was the worst part. The girl the room was meant for was meant to stay in it for a long time, perhaps for ever, and I wanted to go hence immediately and stay hence, wherever hence was, for a long time, if possible for ever. I hadn't known that, quite, when I crossed the threshold, I'd thought things might be different now, but the chintz and the roses were telling me they weren't, chivvying me out with wee chintzy voices, pushing at me with wee rosy hands. My room didn't understand me. Oh if only Margaret, Bunty and Jennifer or even little Jane were here. If only Robbie wasn't at school. It was going to be so terribly lonely at home.

I did try not to let on at first. I lied a lot, one way and the other, to keep Mother thinking I was happy, because that made her happy and someone might as well be. The trouble was the more I lied, the more I fell in with her plans and her views, the happier she got. It was like blowing up a balloon, knowing all the time you'd soon run out of breath and have to watch it shrink to nothing with a sad, wet sound. Or else? Or else I could give up being me and become what Mother wanted, the way a shoe takes on the shape of the foot. Either way it would end in tears.

The Cleft came into my room, harrumphed and went out again, saying well, it certainly cost a pretty penny. I didn't think he liked it any more than I did, but he thought I liked it all right, because I was a gurl and gurls liked that sort of thing. He wasn't pleased I'd come back, I knew that the moment I saw his head sticking out of the crowd at Victoria, his eyes round and madly blinking, like a chicken woken by a fox in the night. Luckily, the next day he was cock-a-hoop again on account of a letter he got with a large crest on it.

'Well, now that you've been finished off,' he said, flapping the envelope in front of my nose, 'how'd you like to go to a garden party?'

'I'd love it,' I said ingratiatingly.

The garden party turned out to be at Buckingham Palace, which cheered me up. The only way out of my impasse with Mother was to be whisked off by a Prince Charming and where better to meet one than a palace? Mother may have had the same idea because she bought me an expensive whisking-off outfit at Harrods as well as a mother-of-the-bride frock and hat for herself. 'Don't tell your father how much it all cost,' she reminded me.

'How do I look?' I asked that evening, prancing up and down in ivory grosgrain, sucking in my cheeks under the little veiled hat, hardly more than a jumped-up hairband, that clung to my head.

'Lovely,' said Mother.

'Better than a slap on the belly with a wet fish,' said the Cleft.

We set off in the Daimler the Cleft had acquired while I was away. I thought it looked like a funeral hearse but I ummed and aahed over it to keep in with him while I wondered whether we were rich or not. You couldn't tell with the Cleft, you could never tell anything with him, most especially not if you asked. Some of the girls at the Chat had been rich, though I'd only found out when they wrote their addresses in my souvenir book – Palazzo, Château, Hall, Manor, Schloss. Our house was just a number on a street. On the other hand, there was the Old Hall in Norfolk and the New Hall where Granny was born and Grandpa's other house in Turkey, which was so enormous and important that you only needed to write its name and 'Istanbul' on the envelope and your letter got there. Probably it was what I'd always suspected: Mother had been rich and wasn't any more because she'd married the Cleft, so Grandpa paid for the things she could no longer afford, like Robbie's school and the Chat and my new room and my whisking-off clothes, maybe even the Daimler. Perhaps Grandpa bought that for Mother's sake, to keep the Cleft in a good mood. If so, it'd take more than a Daimler. What would it take? For me and Mother to die, I supposed. Then he could load our corpses into his brand-new hearse and drive to our funeral in the same top hat he was wearing now. Singing, as he was now, 'De Camptown racetrack five mile long, doo de doo dah day'.

It was thrilling to glide up the Mall to the Palace with a big number on the windscreen and people on the pavements pointing and staring. I smiled sweetly out at them and thought what a pity it was, if I wasn't rich, that I wasn't. I'd make such a very good rich person, gracious, kind and yet remote, therefore admired and loved by all. Look how nice I'd always been to the servants in Turkey and Norfolk. That was the best thing about servants, they improved your character so.

The King's back garden was packed out. The Cleft's top hat sailed above the crowd and Mother and I jostled in his wake, me looking haughty to impress passing Princes, and Mother smiling vaguely in every direction as if she were about to meet a distant cousin she hadn't seen in years. Her smile didn't last long.

'Of course,' said the Cleft loudly as we stalled alongside a table loaded with sandwiches and cups of tea, 'the King gets all this wholesale, you know. Food, cutlery, china, the lot. From one of Lyon's Corner Shops. The Queen was a Bowes-Lyon before she married, old Joe Lyon was her uncle. A grand old man, Joe Lyon, though a Jew, of course. Once told me he felt Lisbet had let the family down, marrying that little German. Couldn't have him serving in one of my tea shops, he used to say. Not with his stutter. The teacakes would be cold before he got a word out.'

'Alastair, *please*,' Mother said out of one end of her smile.

'Calls himself Windsor now, the German. Like Mountbatten calls himself Battenberg. He's a Jew too, if you ask me. They don't marry out.'

His remarks, unmuted due to his height, reached the ears of all in his neighbourhood. They glanced up as they shuffled by, their eyes flickering uneasily. Mother ducked her head to her teacup and I dumped mine and edged hastily away from the source of embarrassment. Better be all alone in the crowd than allow the Cleft yet another go at spoiling my chances. No man, never mind a Prince, was going to whisk away the daughter of such a father. Every day and in every way, the Cleft was ruining my life. Why did he do it? Because he hated me.

Between crammed bodies, I spotted the white flank of a marquee and struggled towards it. As I squeezed to the front of the crowd I came upon a group so instantly familiar that I felt I'd known them all my life.

There on a clear patch of emerald lawn stood the Queen with her pink-and-white skin, her frizzy perm and her dear smile and, beside her, also smiling, the two Princesses shaking their way down a line of hands. I stood transfixed, hoovering in every detail, and soon I was smiling just as the Royals smiled, tilting my head in perfect time with the Royal head tilts, moving my lips simultaneously with the Royal lips. The four of us were as one, though I had to acknowledge to myself that I performed rather better really, rather more to the manner born, with a surer and more Queenly touch or, in view of my age, more Princessy. It wasn't Lisbet's fault that she was dowdier and less graceful than me, it wasn't Margaret Rose's fault that my waist was waspier than hers. As their friend, their best friend – and already they and I were bosom pals, sitting cross-legged on the Royal beds confiding secrets just like at the Chat – I would help them over these disadvantages, advise and encourage them in an utterly unswanky way.

Cradled in this daydream – 'Oh,' Lisbet was saying, 'whatever would we do without you?' – I was rudely awoken by a real voice; the Cleft's.

'Where are ye, daughter?' it was calling in a music-hall Scottish brogue. 'Oh, daughter, where are ye? Dinna abandon your poor blind faither. Will ye nae come back again?'

I froze. Then, hunching to conceal myself, I peeped behind me. The fearful figure of the Cleft, eyes shut, arms extended piteously, was approaching, guided towards me by solicitous guests. 'I need ye beside me, daughter, I canna do without ye. Please, I beg ye, dinna leave me on my ain.'

Red as a raspberry, my heart jammed half-way up my neck and thumping fit to burst a vein, I swivelled away from the advancing phalanx of the Cleft's bodyguards and burrowed as fast as I could for sanctuary. As the grass petered out and the crowd thinned, a wide flight of steps rose ahead. I scuttled up them and hid behind a pillar, gulping down sobs of outrage and struggling to resettle my hat. After a while, when my heart was back in its proper place, I peered from my pillar at the garden below. It looked an unattainable dream in its frame of high spiked walls and trees, brim-full of flowers and long flowery frocks bright against the sober grey of the men. Somewhere amongst those men could be my Prince. He'd be kissing my hand and asking me out to a nightclub by now, if it weren't for that *salaud* father of mine. I scowled at the back of a toy-size man encircled by a crowd at the foot of the stairs and thought up ten ways to assassinate my father. *Va pee-pee sur les rosiers*, Cleft. *Ta gueule*.

I was just wondering if '*tu*' could properly be applied to someone as implacably '*vous*' as the Cleft when the toy man below did a half turn towards me. Hadn't I seen him somewhere before? He looked a bit Indian, very sunburnt.

'See the King?' said the Cleft, loping up out of nowhere. 'He's wearing make-up.'

The King? Why, so it was.

'Make-up?' I said, startled out of my eternal vow never to speak to the Cleft again.

'Greasepaint all over him. That thick.'

Heavens to Betsy, could a King be a homo too, like Messieurs Bernard and Delange?

'He's wearing it because otherwise he'd be white as a sheet,' the Cleft said. 'The King's dying, you see.'

Dying? On such a lovely summer's day? Carla had died on a summer's day. The sun, I was learning, offered no protection from catastrophe.

'Does the Queen know?' I whispered. 'Do the Princesses?' This was terribly worrying. If they did, then they were behaving much better than we had about Carla. I felt a surge of pity and admiration for them and for the poor brown little King.

'Know it or not,' the Cleft went on, 'Princess Elizabeth will be Queen before the year's out. Elizabeth the First for me. The Second for you.'

There was some veiled insult here that I couldn't pin down. The Cleft made a habit of reserving all the tastiest tit-bits of life for the Scots, i.e. him, and chucking the left-overs to the English, i.e. me. I imagined him dying and me taking over his throne.

'The King is dead. Long live Queen Elizabeth II,' I said, gripped by revenge and history.

The Cleft glanced at me and his lips thinned. 'Don't get carried away. It's all rubbish, this King and Queen business.'

'But you . . . you've always said . . . you . . .' I stopped and breathed in. 'If it's rubbish, why are you here?'

But the Cleft had had enough of intimate moments. 'Go and round up your mother,' he said. 'She's the one with all the answers. Go talk to her.'

The problem of how to co-exist with Mother and the Cleft became ever more complicated. Pleasing her meant skirting the minefield of my own thoughts and opinions and keeping within the domestic heartland where she resided. But that was easier than pleasing him. Might as well expect a cat to please a dog, Nature herself had ordained against it. To be fair, the Cleft clearly didn't wish me to please him. What he wished was me out of his way and when I got in his way the efforts I'd made to please Mother were cancelled out. If I was in his bad books so, automatically, was she. *Your daughter*, he said, *your daughter*. Neither of them, I saw, had any idea what to do with me and I had no idea what to do with myself, other than refusing point-blank Mother's suggestion of a secretarial course.

'But why not? Afterwards, you could work somewhere nice for a while, just until you get married.'

'I don't want to be a secretary,' I retorted, 'and I don't want to get married.'

Nevertheless, the thought of getting married was a good deal less grim than the thought of being a secretary. Apart from all else, secretaries went on living with their parents, or the ones I'd heard of did, whereas marriage ensured an immediate change of abode. Despite the Cleft's frequent assertion that no man would ever marry me due to my being a useless blatherskate, a blitherer, half-baked, a pain in the neck and neither fish, flesh nor good red herring, I didn't believe him for a minute. He might not like me but plenty did. I'd found that much out at the Chat so boo to you, Cleft, with brass knobs on, you're a mean, miserable old man and I wish you were dead. I didn't say any of this to his face, I dared do no more than glower at him, despising myself for my cowardice, but I said it to Mother often, omitting only the death wish, that she would not have let pass. Mostly she'd just sigh, which she was forever doing, and say what she always said: 'He's proud of you really.' This was so obviously a Gargantuan whopper that even if I'd yearned to believe it I couldn't. Oh Mother, can't you even lie convincingly? Lord, what a pair.

In the meantime, in between paternal eruptions, I led a submarine existence sunk in books at home, and lunged up for great gulps of air whenever the outside world beckoned. Fortunately, it started to beckon often. I went to my first Hunt Ball at my Chat friend Jennifer's place and discovered a useful talent – I could drink lashings of champagne and stirrup cup without any effect whatsoever while strong men lay snoring under the table. I also discovered, as one man led to another, that strong men were weak in all sorts of ways apart from a general inability to hold their liquor. You could wind them round your little finger, though what you did with them then was harder to know. Also, it was pricey, the winding. You had to become the Incredible Shrinking Woman. You had to make yourself smaller than them in every way possible: small ego, small brain, small voice, small talk. Pretence, with men just as with parents, appeared to be obligatory if you were to be liked, approved of or adored and, despite the cost, adored by men I devoutly wished to be. Luckily I was good at pretending by now, I'd had practice. Some useful sixth sense, a sort of Feminine Intelligence Agency, efficiently briefed me on the quirks and foibles of this man or that so I could decide what role to play for maximum effect. This game had its challenges, excitements and rewards, it even gave an illusion of choice when, in fact, there was none that I could see. Either you joined in, played the game well and were invited everywhere or you didn't and weren't. What choice was that?

Yet now and again, nudged by some film or book or poem into my old craving for a grander, freer, more purposeful life – crossing the Sahara alone but for a faithful camel, saving the needy from some vague fate – the job of pleasing men became heavy going and the rewards diminished sharply. They took up such acres of time and space, men. They consumed everything, no other life-form survived in their presence, not unless it was carefully camouflaged or hidden away. The moment a man came into the room he created an instant vacuum into which whatever you were thinking or feeling or doing or talking about got sucked away from you to him and was swallowed up. Sometimes, in the dark before I fell quite asleep, up flipped a cardboard cut-out of the Cleft in his peaked hat with the scrambled eggs on it and behind him, like fairground targets moving this way and that, a gallery of cardboard men in perukes and periwigs, helmets and busbies, birettas, mitres and cardinals' hats, bowlers, homburgs, mortarboards, toppers and gangsters' fedoras, there was no end to the hats they wore and every hat said 'I'm extremely important. Listen to me or else.' Oh, the weight of men. However much you wanted their company, more often than not you ended up fagged out and flattened, as if you'd been propping up a three-legged elephant all night.

Still, men were my escape route, no other presented itself, so it seemed the best thing, for fun and for enlightenment, to sift through as wide a range as possible in order to sample the flavour of each, a sort of marriage-tasting I suppose, and I suppose they were doing the same with me though, being men, not as diligently – they had another focus, the mysterious world of work. That first year after Switzerland I went out with Jonathan, round-faced and immaculate, who wore a bowler at work in the City and a cloak lined with scarlet when he took me to the opera; David, a bearded beatnik, who took me to espresso bars and the Festival of Britain; Rolt, in advertising, who called me Baby and boogied with me at 100 Oxford Street; Roger, a lieutenant in the navy, who used up every leave escorting me to *Oklahoma*, *Ring Round the Moon*, Ionesco, Beckett and every other modish show in town; Denby, the ten-foot-tall Guardee – he took me dancing to nightclubs and balls in the country, as did Robin, Perry, Victor, Denzil, Graham and goodness knows how many others.

Habitually, in those days, no one expected exclusive rights over the evening's partner. We rode around on a crowded carousel and were only occasionally a couple. 'Let's make up a party,' was the frequent cry and off we'd roar, full of ourselves squashed into assorted jalopies, to squash ourselves further in some tiny house in Walton Street or Beauchamp Place for cocktails before 'going on', the next cry, to Danny La Rue's in Piccadilly or, for a lark, the Mecca Ballroom off the Strand.

What my partners required of me was to look pretty and be frightfully vivacious about nothing at all, so I was and they fell in love with me, or swore they had, which led to sweaty lunges in taxis, a lot of smooching on pocket-hanky nightclub floors, the odd knee-jerk display of jealousy regarding other men and occasional attempts to get me into bed. Since none of my escorts had beds that weren't ruled over by battle-axe landladies or inconveniently sited in Shropshire or Suffolk, this hardly posed a threat. The old Chat rule, if you're pretty you don't have to, held in London as it had abroad. Sometimes these men spent a lot of money on our evenings at the Bagatelle or the 400 Club and sometimes they hadn't any money and we went dutch on the cheap Chinese in Shaftesbury Avenue and snogged at the flicks afterwards or, in suitable weather, by the lake in Green Park. The affluent bought me bouquets of flow-ers, Gucci scarves and silver and gold toys, pens and pencils, earrings, necklaces, compacts and champagne swizzlers, all of which I instantly lost. The broke wrote me poetry and presented me with a single perfect rose.

And they proposed. Every man proposed to every girl on every possible occasion, if the gossip in nightclub Ladies' or country-house boudoirs was to be credited. We sat there powdering our noses, heaving up our breasts in their straplesses, rearranging our *décolletages*, dabbing nail varnish on new-sprung ladders and told each other that Charles had just proposed, or Edward or James or that unspeakable berk Ralph Patton-Jones, would you believe? I believed it all right; Charles, Edward, James, the unspeakable berk and Henry *and* Robin had just proposed to me. That's what men said when their lips were crushed against your earhole on the dance floor: *Oh God you're such a little dazzler I can't help myself, do marry me, what?*

No one in the wide world, I supposed, wanted me to marry as much as the Cleft but with typical perversity he rolled up his sleeves and set himself to lay waste to any budding bridegrooms who came his way. Invitations to country-house dances had to be accompanied by a letter from the inviter's mother guarantee-ing my virginity under her roof, or words to that effect. Any London entertainment too extended for me to return home the same night required the production of a detailed curriculum vitae of my unfortunate hostess, from her address, marital status, general reputation and social circle to her family pedigree plus a personal telephone call from her so that the Cleft could make trebly sure she existed and, in so doing, check her accent. All this caused me exquisite embarrassment and kept me in a lather of fury *vis-à-vis* the Cleft.

But the embarrassment and the fury soared to astronomical levels on the evenings I had to come home. The Cleft's outer limit was midnight, a Cinderella target set without the slightest regard for the vicissitudes of late-night transport or my dependence on unreliable Princes. Again and again, as the clock struck, my carriage turned into a pumpkin that either wouldn't start or broke down half-way. On its eventual arrival, spurting up the drive in a series of explosions that rent the quiet suburban night, the Cleft was inevitably waiting, a lowering figure at the door, ready to loose his humiliating arrows.

'What time do you call this?' (Eyes wildly blinking, fixed on me.)

The unfortunate prince would stammer apologies. 'Um. Oh God. Sorry, sir. My fault. The dratted car, there's something wrong with the carburettor and . . .'

'I'll deal with you later, sir. I'm talking to my daughter. I said. What. Time. Do you call. This?'

Rat-tat-tat went my trusty machine-gun and the Cleft fell in a hail of bullets, never to rise again. Meanwhile I mumbled whatever came to mind that might curtail the hideous scene.

'Upstairs. Go on.' A jerk of the head in my direction. 'Now, as for you, sir . . .' And I was forced to retire, leaving my father to tear strips off my wretched escort and thereby cause to wither yet another shoot of happiness. What man, I asked myself, furiously chucking my shoes across the bedroom, would ever be prepared to fight through the Cleft-barrier for the prize of me? None, that's how many, and I'd go to my grave a dried-up spinster, victim of the most sadistic father since time began. At least Elizabeth Barrett Browning's father acted the way he did because he couldn't bear to lose her. The Cleft could bear to lose me all right, yet still he did everything to forestall my departure. Why else than that he was a misery himself, and didn't see why I shouldn't be miserable too. Rat-tat-tat, take that, Cleft. Straight through the heart and hope to die.

Mother remained invisible during these nocturnal eruptions. While the Cleft was on the rampage she lay low in her room, though the faint sound of snuffles that came from within, as if there were piglets under her bed, proved she wasn't asleep. Of course she wasn't, who could sleep while the Cleft turned the house into a gong. As I bolted upstairs from the storm below and slunk past her closed door I pictured her flung across the bed, white arms raised in supplication, with 'All Hope Abandoned' or 'The Curse of Drink' written across her in curly script. The image made me feel all kinds of awful: wrenched with guilt, full of resentment against the Cleft – all his fault for carrying on so – and frequently wrung with compassion for my own little self, cruelly persecuted by Father, abandoned by Mother. Oh, if only she'd just once hold back her tears, screw up her courage and come out fighting, as mother birds did for their chicks. I imagined Mother in a flurry of feathers swooping ferociously down on the Cleft, walloping him to his knees with her wings, then pecking his eyes out and, while she was about it, his liver too.

For I never doubted that Mother was on my side, however useless she might be in action. The snuffles signified she was as mad at the Cleft as I was and dreaming of how happy life would be for her poor children and for her without him. After all, it was she who was really stuck with him, so it stood to reason she must feel even more fed-up than I did.

I never doubted her until one night, unavoidably detained yet again, I returned to find no Cleft strobing on the doorstep. This was unprecedented. My escort, Robert, Roger, Richard, groaned with relief – by this time the Cleft's reputation fell not far short of Himmler's – and gratefully backed off up the drive, wagging a moonlit hand from a window flap. With a safe-cracker's skill I turned my key, sneaked into the hall and crept up the stairs, to catch Mother's muffled voice down the passage, squawky, insistent and 100 per cent snuffle-free. As I was tiptoeing past their door there came a renewed bombardment from Mother, a driven kind of yodel from the Cleft, the drum of feet across floorboards and out he charged, head down and snorting. In that instant of collision I clearly saw in the whorls of his eyes not the triumphant gleam of the hunter but the batty white goggle of the hunted.

Two heartbeats later things were back to normal, him fuming, me spraying tears. Next morning the usual cloud over breakfast, though again, no Cleft. Your father has the flu, Mother said, her neck bowed under its permanent yoke. But this morning my heart refused to twist to order, it lay still as a toad under my ribs while I reviewed the logic of events. The Cleft hadn't wanted the row last night, he wasn't well, maybe hadn't even heard me return. Yet Mother, instead of being glad to let sleeping dogs lie, had commenced to snipe away until she'd succeeded in hounding him up and out and at me. And if she could do that when he was feeling ill, perhaps she did it routinely. Which meant that though the Cleft was the bullet, it was Mother's finger on the trigger, Mother who fired the gun. Over my bacon and eggs I narrowly studied her downcast mien, her downturned mouth, the defeated slope of her shoulders. Mother, I thought, you don't love me either, and the thought caused a hole to gape open inside me, not bloody but urgently pulsing, like the gills of a fish. Nobody loves me, nobody loves me, nobody.

'Nobody loves me,' said Mother aloud. Her face was empty but her wet red eyes sucked at mine.

'I do,' I mumbled and looked away and ate my toast, appalled.

Eight

One day it struck me that the ads in the magazines I read –
'She's Beautiful, She's Engaged, She Uses Pond's', 'Which
Twin Has the Tony?' and other alluring cameos that promised
eternal happiness for half a crown at Boots – must be
someone's job to think up and write, so why shouldn't it be
mine? In secret, in my bedroom, I produced six tensely plotted
playlets involving love and lipstick and sent them to two
advertising agencies. Near one hundred letters and three
months later, to my astonishment and jubilation, I was hired
by one of the largest London agencies as a junior copywriter.
The Cleft was even more astonished, so much so that when I
announced my triumph he eyed me quite closely and
directly.

'Have you got it on paper?'

'Yes.'

'How much do they say they'll pay you?'

'Ten pounds a week.'

'Ten pounds a week?' He shook his head as if there was
water in his ears. 'Whatever for?'

I shrugged uneasily, trying to appear confident and casual.
In 1954 £10 was good money – typists got £2. 'To write
advertisements,' I said.

'But you don't know anything about advertisements. You don't know anything about anything.'

For once he wasn't being insulting, he meant what he said, he was genuinely flabbergasted. 'They're going to teach me,' I muttered, shaken.

'Then why aren't you paying *them* £10?'

Why wasn't I? I had no idea.

'Well,' the Cleft concluded after a long pause, 'if you ask me, there's something very fishy about it.' And from this opinion he was never to waver through the years ahead, maintaining it stoutly and reiterating it about every job I ever took on. 'What's the job? How much are they paying you? Well, I call that *very* fishy.'

Mother was equally consistent in her reaction. 'But why not be a secretary, darling, you'd meet far nicer men,' she wailed and ever after, whenever she wrote me a letter to wherever I was in the world, from between the pages would flutter out a scrap torn from *The Times* or the *Telegraph*: 'Managing director of highly reputable City firm requires discreet and efficient Secretary P.A. . . .'

Despite the lukewarm reception and my resulting butterflies, within a fortnight I was officially a trainee copywriter and had begun what turned out to be a stint in heaven, surrounded by what I supposed were the cleverest, funniest and most eccentric individuals that had ever existed outside books and films. Everything they did, said and wore bowled me over in wonder at such wit, wisdom and *savoir-faire*. Wilbur walked about with a Siamese cat perched on his shoulder! Ronald wasn't married to Sonia but they lived together! Harry went to Russell Square Turkish Baths and sometimes spent the whole night there! Hedda (Hedda!) blew smoke rings from a long amber cigarette holder, Xanthe (Xanthe!) cooed at us all from behind the perkiest little veil and they all expected me to call them by their first names even though they were much older than me! No wonder the company I'd kept till then, the richards-rogers-jennifers, faded rapidly into an anonymous blur like the new Polaroids. So boggle-eyed and open-mouthed was my admiration for these elders and betters that they could hardly help taking to me in their turn, thus completing my euphoria. Not since Miss Yates had anyone I looked up to approved of me. Determined to please, I set about learning every last esoteric fact concerning the agency's most important account, a heavy-duty detergent, peppering everyone with penetrating queries like, 'What exactly do men *do* to get their overalls so dirty?' They bore up surprisingly well.

At the end of three months I also fell in love. Jimmy was one of the three commercial artists who sat in the next cubicle to mine, drawing wasp-waisted glamour girls elegantly perched on top of the great bell skirts of Dior's New Look. I was stirred by his famished face and lank hair and strangely aroused by the skill in his skeletal fingers. Luckily, he was aroused back and we embarked on one of those explosively unconsummated affairs that smouldered everywhere in the fifties like campfires the night before Agincourt. At lunchtime, along with hundreds of other couples, we clutched each other in Grosvenor Square or Hyde Park, upright when it rained, horizontally when it didn't, and tottered back to the office at two o'clock half senseless from the toxic effects of prolonged internal combustion. Most of us lived with our families so we were forced to do our courting in the open like the beasts of the field. Jimmy, for instance, had a room in the house of his older sister Iris and her husband.

This unremarkable fact, like others that concerned Jimmy, was pounced on by the Cleft, scrutinized for clues as to how it might be used against me and filed away, ready to be whisked out whenever he judged the time was ripe. He'd had to concede that my job meant the end of the more or less absolute control he'd had over my movements, so quick as a flash he switched tactics and began setting up a kind of Deuxième Bureau over my mind instead.

'They tell me,' he remarked one morning with the baffled air of a judge confronted with some lunacy of modern life, 'that you now consider yourself to be what I believe is known as "in love". Have you any comment to make on this? Could you tell us, mayhap, what the word "love" signifies to you? Prithee do us the honour of expounding upon the subject. I assure you, we are all ears.'

Though I ardently longed to slash my tormenter to ribbons with my rapier replies, I was usually reduced to a piggish sulk with occasional humiliating Mother-type snuffles.

Then Mother would compound my shame by saying in her most depressing mothery voice, 'Oh do leave her alone, Aly' or, to me, 'He's only teasing, you know what he's like,' which dragged me into her camp and left me feeling a good deal worse. I could see she expected me to chum up with her and couldn't understand why I wouldn't. I couldn't either, except I was afraid that if I did I'd be throwing in my lot with her, admitting that I was like her, a weepy woman on the losing side.

At other times the Cleft would put on his absent-minded professor act, lowering his newspaper abruptly at breakfast, popping his head round a door, sidling without warning into a room or suddenly appearing from a bush in the garden, to ask with furrowed brow, 'In love, are you? In love, eh? I see said the blind man as he took a cup and saw-cer. In love. Well, well, well.' And away he would wander mouthing the words as he went – *lurve, een lur-ve* – like a man learning an unusual foreign language; Sumerian, say, or Kyrgyz.

'Iris,' he said out of the blue at dinner one evening, examining the rim of his plate. 'Iris,' he repeated broodingly. Then he fell silent.

I waited, determined to rise above question or comment. The Cleft munched stolidly on. Mother informed us there'd be a frost that night. Mother brought in a sponge cake she'd made. 'Oh, lovely,' I said. Then I cracked. 'What about Iris?'

As if surfacing from a deep sleep, the Cleft said, 'Iris? Iris? Ah yes. The Christian name of your loved one's sister, I gather.'

'Yes,' I said. 'What *about* it?' I'd not come across the name before and thought it glam. Why was it now beginning to sound vaguely suspect?

'Nothing, not a thing, merely thinking aloud. Have you met the lady?'

'Not yet.'

'Aha. And are we permitted to inquire as to the occupation of the esteemed Iris's spouse?'

'Haven't the faintest.'

What was the old beast up to? Did he know something I didn't? Was Iris's husband in prison or a Russian spy or what? The next day I checked with Jimmy. Glancing up from his sketch pad, grinning his sweet ravenous grin, Jimmy said, 'Ken? He's a plumber.'

Given the choice, I'd have plumped for a multiple murderer. Well, wild dogs wouldn't drag the truth from me so the Cleft need never know. I rather wished I didn't know myself. Jimmy's accent, a mild sort of Cockney, only enhanced his exotic charm in my eyes and, anyway, he was an artist. But however you looked at it there was nothing exotic or artistic about being a plumber or having one for a brother-in-law. It dropped my sweetheart several rungs further down the class ladder than I had bargained for, and filled me with a squeamish foreboding. No good will come of it whispered a voice in my head and I cursed the Cleft, he spoiled everything, he was the malevolent King Midas bent on turning my golden love to dross. Well, he wouldn't succeed. Every day, enclosed in Jimmy's arms, my head reeled as our lips met, but the dizziness no longer entirely distracted me from keeping one jumpy eye out for any sighting of richard-roger-robert-jennifer. I loved Jimmy, I thought him wondrously talented, but curiously didn't wish anyone I knew outside work to meet him. Love, meant to be generous and outgoing, was fast becoming a strictly limited company.

'When are you going to bring Jimmy home?' Mother asked, 'I do want to meet him.'

'We all want to meet him,' agreed the Cleft, but he said it as though he were Scotland Yard and Jimmy was John Reginald Halliday Christie, with a backyard full of women's bones.

'Soon,' I said loftily, 'when he's not so busy,' and a cold sweat chilled me.

Then I met sister Iris and brother-in-law Ken, steadying myself on Jimmy's arm in the tube as if going (via Plaistow and Dagenham) to where no white woman had gone before. Iris was as chubby as Jimmy was thin but she had the same tender gaze and sweet smile. Ken, older and shorter than his wife, was sandy all over, with a Friar Tuck fuzz of sandy hair sticking out from under the woolly cap he wore and hands that were thick and calloused. Iris was shy, Ken bouncy, but they both made me feel whole-heartedly welcome, circling round me like tugs round a liner, alert to my every need. Tea came, and bread and jam, and then sausages, bacon, baked beans, eggs. Attentively they watched me eating, Iris bobbing up and down, 'More tea? another sausage?', while Ken joked and winked at Jimmy and said, 'She's a corker, my son, you don't deserve her,' and Jimmy gazed benevolently upon us all.

'And what did you think of your prospective in-laws?' the

Cleft inquired, extending a leg from his armchair and circling one bony ankle. 'Were they right up your street? Fit in with them, did you? All cosy and chummy, was it?'

'They were lovely,' I said vehemently. 'Just as kind as could be.'

'Hearts of gold, eh? Salt of the earth? Backbone of old England? I take your meaning.'

'What meaning?' I shrilled. 'There's no meaning. Iris and Ken are good people, they work hard, they're kind, they're . . .'

Creak creak went the Cleft's rotating ankle. '. . . honest as the day is long?' he said. 'Ah ha. I'm with you now. They're the good people who, when they go for a drive, resist the easy lure of mountain, forest or sea and instead pick a spot right beside the road for their picnic. Out they get with their wee chairs and tables, set them up in a nice puddle of oil, unwrap their fish and chips and sit there gawping at the traffic and filling their lungs with petrol fumes.'

The Cleft did not depend solely on words for effect, he mimed as he talked. A Dad scratched his belly as he guzzled invisible chips, a Mum sat bolt upright, knees prissily clamped, sipping with dainty pinkie raised an invisible cup of tea. Also in his repertoire a half-witted lad with a peashooter, a leaking baby and a truly repellent Gran. Meanwhile he kept up a whistle and roar for the passing traffic, his head swivelling back and forth, left to right. The scene ended as he choked on petrol fumes and coughed himself to a disgusting death.

I heard myself hiccuping. I tried to gulp back belches of laughter. Then between the belches it all blurted out, 'Iris and Ken's house is called Myrtle Villa and it's squashed in a line and lunch is dinner and dinner high tea and there are bottles of ketchup and vinegar and some brown goo on the dining table and they put the vinegar on their chips and the goo on their sausages. And they say pardon and serviette for napkin and toilet for lav and have bits of cloth on the backs of their armchairs in what they call the lounge and the carpet looks as if they'd dropped fried eggs all over it and . . .'

But I couldn't go on, I was laughing too hard.

The Cleft grunted. His eyes were two tiny lighthouse beams winking far away across a black sea. Tears streamed down my face. 'They were lovely, Iris and Ken. You don't know. They were about a million times nicer than you.'

The room went quiet except for my gulps. Probably the Cleft would now explode in some awesome way, spattering rage across the walls.

He didn't though. He said, 'Be that as it may, I'm relieved to note that you now refer to these saintly folk in the past tense.'

That remark and a wretched sense of kinship with Lady Macbeth — Will all great Neptune's ocean wash this blood clean from my hand? — left me with no choice but to compensate for my treachery by accepting the next of Jimmy's marriage proposals. 'I will,' I said, gazing sorrowfully into his adorable, adoring face, and my heart tolled like a funeral bell thinking of Myrtle Villa and the lace mat under the ketchup in the centre of that dining table at which I would shortly take my place for ever, changing day by day from radiant bride to wrinkled crone as one high tea led to another.

Why I was so sure that my married life would inevitably unwind all the way to the grave *chez* Iris and Ken I don't know, but Myrtle Villa was a sore tooth I couldn't help probing, and each time the nerve jabbed — serviettes, *ouch* antimacassars, *aargh* — I betrayed poor Jimmy in thought, but also by sneaking out with other men. Being in love was all very well in stories but in practice it hurt, after a bit the whole business got you down dreadfully and you had to have a change, the company of big bluff Roland, for instance, or cheery Peter, or hep-cat Rolt, at a pinch even the roger-richard-roberts, men who were happy to go through the motions – compliments, flirting, dancing cheek to cheek, all the formal gestures of desire – but could be relied on to steer well clear of touching the heart. Roland, as it happened, made himself quickly surplus to requirement by trying to rape me (I foiled his evil plan by making hideous retching noises at a key moment), but Rolt made a useful stop-gap while he waited for the American visa he needed before he could take over Madison Avenue, and Peter, the nicest, was also the safest, being already married. After these surreptitious sorties it took only one glimpse of Jimmy's dear starveling self to make my heart hurt all over again, but by this time thoughts of him were fast being shaded over with the cloud of marriage. The day he approached me with a small box on the flat of his palm, clicking it open to display a ring, my whole Myrtle Villa future flashed before me as if I were drowning. Jiminy cricket, I'd left it too late. A juggernaut was heading full steam towards me and there didn't seem to be any way to avoid it except by throwing in the towel and revealing all to the Cleft and Mother. And that, I felt deeply, was a deed so fell it would have made even Lady Macbeth blench.

But just when there seemed no way out of the dilemma there came galloping to my rescue in full Wild West regalia an uncle hitherto unknown and, tottering two paces behind him on the highest possible heels, a new aunt. Uncle Harry was Mother's eldest brother, so much older than her that they'd never laid eyes on each other. By the time she was born he'd already left Istanbul for Oxford where, so Mother explained, he fell in with a fast set, took to gambling and was eventually sent down. Grandpa, enraged at this stain on the escutcheon, instantly bought a stretch of forest up in Northern Canada and dispatched the black sheep thither, with instructions not to darken the family door again until he'd either proved himself an upright citizen or made his fortune.

Sensibly, Uncle Harry plumped for the latter. After a year's logging he struck oil, whereupon he married the daughter of a neighbouring oil millionaire, used her dowry to finance his own operation and in a remarkably short time was one of the richest men in Canada. Naturally Grandpa forgave him, but his ensuing visits from Vancouver to the old Turkish homestead never thereafter coincided with Mother being in residence and he had remained a stranger to her. Now the two of us – Mother in an uncharacteristically saucy hat, me nipped into a green Dereta costume I fancied matched my eyes – were advancing on Claridges with a view to rectifying this unnatural state of affairs.

Uncle Harry turned out to be a Beanstalk-size giant, as big as Mother was little and wider than two of her put together. He was so big that, tall as I was by then, five feet ten inches if you didn't count my hair, I could only see up his nostrils and survey the velvety underbrim of his enormous stetson.

'My baby sister,' he boomed and, rising, obliterated Mother in a bear hug. Then, releasing her, flustered but all smiles, he swung round on me. 'And whadda we got here?' he said, revolving the thick green stub of a cigar between giant's teeth as he looked me up and down. 'Uh huh. Mmm mm. Trouble.'

This snap judgement, coming out of the blue, shook me dreadfully. True, Uncle Harry winked as he said it but men, in my experience, were given to winking for no obvious reason and to say such a thing in front of Mother, who would tell the Cleft, who'd immediately use it against me, boded no good at all. Wasn't anyone, ever, going to be on my side?

'Oh now, Harry, give over,' said a Tinkerbell voice, and there at the door appeared my new Aunt Jen. She wore baby-blue pumps, baby-blue stockings, a baby-blue costume topped by a baby-blue fox stole and perched on her amazing baby-blue curls was a baby-blue pillbox hat. She had tiny feet and slender ankles and calves but from there on she swelled out and out to a bust so voluminous that she looked like an Easter egg on legs.

'Why, she's just darling, aren't you, honey?' said the blue angel. Teetering over to me she laid a tiny diamond-covered hand on my arm and, indicating Uncle Harry with a bob of her head, tinkled to Mother, 'He always called our own Sugar trouble, our daughter, you know? But she really wasn't and this little gal isn't gonna be either. Isn't that right, honey? No trouble in the world.' Then, before she'd properly greeted Mother, she took my sleeve and tweaked me across the room. 'Come see my wigs, honey bun, tell me which ones I should throw out,' she said, opening a door. To my astonishment, there they were lined up on a sideboard, nine wigs on nine fabric heads, some curled, some straight, some short, some long and each in a spectrum of delicious pástels from blush pink to palest violet. 'One for every day of the week and two on Sunday,' Aunt Jen said and squeezed my arm. I looked down into the flour-white face, cheeks blobbed with rouge, pansy eyes set in a halo of mascara, crayon eyebrows high above and a weeny silent-movie mouth. The sight melted me down to my toes.

The afternoon passed in a dream. There was tea, there were bite-sized sandwiches and iced cakes, there were strawberries and cream and other rare treats. I wasn't in the least surprised when the Lord Mayor of London turned up to kiss my hand and flatter Mother. At first Mother only smiled in a rusty kind of way but soon she was laughing quite hard. After tea, some important-looking men in dinner jackets arrived and a waiter followed with a trolley full of drinks, plates of hors d'œuvres, bowls of olives. 'Mezes,' said Mother under her breath but

Uncle Harry heard and said, 'Mezaliques, yep,' and brother and sister smiled a family smile at each other. I stuffed myself and gazed about me, happily inhaling cigar smoke and wondering at the immensity of Uncle Harry's fortune. He was so rich he could afford a suite at an hotel, with two bedrooms and a sitting room; so rich that though he and Aunt Jen were leaving for Istanbul the next day and staying there for a whole fortnight he could keep the rooms on, paying for them while they were empty just so they could leave a few clothes there until they returned and flew back to Canada. Richer than that I could not imagine.

'A criminal waste of money,' was the Cleft's verdict when Mother told him, but his mouth crooked as if he were pleased and pretty soon he was cavorting up and down singing about putting on his top hat and Mother was saying *Don't be silly* in her cheeriest voice. The very idea of such abundance, even though it was Uncle Harry's and not ours, bucked all of us up, there was something about the thought of it that was like fur or thick carpet, muffling sharp corners and tinny noises, soothing you and making you feel warm and safe. I was registering this delightful sensation when I overheard Mother whispering.

'Who?' I said sharply. 'Who's been invited?'

'You,' said Mother. 'Aunt Jen took a shine to you. She's invited you to stay with them in Vancouver.'

'I put it down to Jen's age,' the Cleft said. 'Women get very peculiar around that time. If, that is, they weren't already.' He frowned in my general direction. 'Be that as it may, don't think I'm paying your fare, young lady. You're the one who's earning the fortune. If you persist in this madcap scheme to depart for the Colonies you'll have to pay for your own chuck wagon.'

As his meaning sunk in, a pair of iron gates that had been locked and barred swung suddenly wide, letting in a great and glorious gale to blow away the stagnant air. A way out at last from the prison of marriage! And sanctioned by the Cleft! I felt like Sydney Carton, told seconds before the guillotine was to fall that he didn't have to do a far far better thing after all. Whew, the relief.

Woebegone and tearful, we clung to each other. 'How will I bear it?' I whimpered into Jimmy's duffle coat and, 'How will I?' Jimmy groaned. The day after my momentous Claridges visit I'd broken the news to him of the Cleft's cruel plan to separate us by banishing me to the snowy wastes of Canada and here we were a month later, saying our farewells before the journey – paid for, in the event, by Mother.

'Only a month and I'll be back in your arms,' I sobbed.

'And then, I don't care what your Dad says, we're getting married.' Jimmy's poor nose was pink with grief.

'I'll write every day,' I promised, my heart misery-logged.

'I'll never love anyone else but you.'

'Me too,' I cried, 'boo hoo.'

At Heathrow, Mother hugged me, her eyes swollen, and I hugged her back, already overcome with a homesickness the worse for being unexpected. What was I doing, leaving everything familiar – lover, job, friends – for unknown Canada? And deserting poor Mother, leaving her alone with the Cleft, a rat leaving a sinking ship. More tears dripped down my cheeks.

'Away with you now or you'll miss the plane,' the Cleft said, making shooing gestures towards the departure gate. I squeezed Mother again and shuffled miserably off. As I turned to give a final wave the Cleft strode forward to the barrier and beckoned me back. I stood before him and looked up through swimming eyes at his set face. He cleared his throat and I became aware that he was struggling to say something momentous, perhaps that he'd always loved me, that I shouldn't go because he'd miss me too much.

'Always remember,' he said in a low, urgent voice, 'that whisky should be taken neat. Never on any account add water, soda or ice.'

Then, without further ado, he turned away and I watched the long oblong of his back recede into the crowd.

Nine

At the end of my first week in Vancouver my image of Jimmy was fraying at the edges and by the second he was inch-high and still dwindling, overlaid by wonders. Uncle Harry's chauffeur had met me at the airport in a car longer than I could have imagined, a black Cadillac with a built-in bar and tinted windows that hissed smoothly up and down at the touch of a button. Aunt Jen, now apple-green from wig to toe, had ushered me into a bedroom so exclusively yellow it was like being dunked in a soft-boiled egg. Everything was yellow: walls, floor, ceiling, bedhead, bedlinen, curtains, pictures. There was even a matching yellow Ronson lighter on the table by the yellow slipper chair and the carpet looked as if it had been sheared from the backs of a flock of yellow sheep. Off the bedroom was my own private bathroom, complete with yellow towels, a yellow towelling robe, yellow soap, a jar of yellow bath salts and a spare roll of toilet paper edged with yellow. Hot air blew at the touch of a dial out of grids in the skirting boards and all round the yellow frame of my dressing-table mirror were stuck invitations to lunches, dances, afternoon teas, cocktail parties and mysterious events called Showers.

'All the girls are dying to meet you,' chirped Aunt Jen as I read them. 'Oh my, having you here is going to be just the way it was before Sugar married and went away.' And she reached up and patted my cheek with a tiny soft hand.

It didn't take long for me to discover that I was startlingly ill-equipped for Vancouver's social whirl. Like most London girls of my acquaintance I prided myself on my cool, anarchic, highly individual style, achieved by slavishly copying Juliette Greco and ensuring that every garment I wore, from the beret that clung to the side of my head to the flatties on the ends of my fish-netted legs, was undiluted raven black. The unavowed aim was to look as much like one of the pros, or prossies, who thronged London streets and were thought by us virgins to be awesomely seductive figures. Naturally, then, I was taken aback at the uniform worn by Vancouver virgins: tartan skirt, matching pastel twin-set or white blouse with Peter Pan collar and pearls. Among them I looked like a bat let loose in an ice-cream parlour and oh, the dawning shame of it, a dingy bat at that.

Nothing had prepared me for this humiliation. In Britain the war, with its fuel shortages and soap rationing, had not only made almost unavoidable a certain scruffiness of person, but had given it a kind of patriotic cachet – if the King sluiced down his Royal person in the two inches of water allowed in Palace baths and considered the results satisfactory, who were his subjects to require higher standards? As long as I could remember, having a bath had been something of an event, if not because of the scarcity of fuel then owing to the eccentricities of English plumbing. At the Old Hall in particular, anyone who announced such an intention – 'I think I'll have a bath, is that all right?' – incurred an automatic ripple of attention and a general beetling about, as if some ocean liner were about to set sail, demanding a sudden stoking of boilers and checking of pipes.

And for at least a decade after the war nothing changed. Baths remained an event and the relaxed wartime attitude to personal hygiene persisted. You did what you could, but the decrepit state of most geysers, complicated by meters in lodgings, made a lick and a promise the sensible option. The upkeep of clothes was equally fraught. Nylon stockings were too precious to discard until they were so laddered they had virtually ceased to exist and therefore, in summer, when your legs were decently tanned, you painted seams down the backs of them and, if you were artistic, added ink clocks on the ankles. After that output of energy you weren't anxious to wash it all off so you didn't, or not often. Dry-cleaning skirts and coats and jackets cost too much and took too long, so you scratched stains away and learned to ignore the patchy results. Deodorants were hard to find so everyone at one time or another smelt of perspiration, and menstruation, if not a public event, was not a wholly private one either. You might not like it but you were accustomed to it. That was life.

Unhappily for me, it wasn't life in the New World. Here men, women and children were squeaky-cleaner than the wildest dreams of the Old Country, and standards of hygiene that would have been considered near neurotic at home would not begin to pass muster in Vancouver. I was daunted by the cleanliness I saw on every side: rows of graded pearls for teeth, hair lit up by an unearthly glow, necks, hands and fingernails buffed to perfection and shining skin showing never a trace of blackhead or a run-of-the-mill spot. Even people's features were neater and more ordered, while clothes were impeccably band-box. How did collars get to be so snowy? How did tight skirts manage to conceal any sign that their wearers had been born with bums?

'You need a girdle,' said Aunt Jen as together we regarded my silhouette in the mirror, black skirt bagging over rear parts. 'Let's drive out and get one, huh?' Soon, swaddled firmly in rubber, I was respectably mono-buttocked, and the pencil skirt Aunt Jen had also bought me showed almost no trace of an occupant. In fact in less than three weeks, thanks to Aunt Jen's charge accounts and a daily pelting under the shower, I was transformed from a musty-smelling night creature to a flower-scented butterfly, albeit a rather flat one. My hair, being congenitally unflattenable, never did scale the tailored heights of Canadian bobs and fringes, and my nails remained unreliable, starting the day pink and shell-like and then sneakily reverting to their dirty old grime-gathering London ways.

Aunt Jen was pleased with my progress, tottering round me on her spindly heels purring approval while I, though I hardly felt myself any more, blushed modestly and said it was all due to her, which it was. But something more would have to change. My manners weren't up to scratch either. At home it was quite normal for compliments to bring on a kind of fit. The recipient either writhed, grimaced, pretended she hadn't heard or muttered tetchy denials – *This dress? It's as old as the hills*, or, like Mother, *Don't be silly*. But Canadian girls sailed through the ordeal, never failing when they met to praise every aspect of each other's appearance in detail, out loud, and when praised themselves to bend their heads in gracious acknowledgement while saying enviably poised things like *Thank you kindly, sir, she said.*

In the evenings, instead of answering one of my now-bulging drawerful of letters from Jimmy, some of which I felt too burdened with guilt and irritation even to open – why did he have to go on and on about love, why couldn't he give it a rest for a while? – I put my New World persona through its paces in front of the mirror in my room, cocking my head this way and that in a hostessy manner, extending a gracious hand to myself, saying, 'Thank you kindly, sir, she said,' in a Canadian accent while bestowing upon my reflection brightly confident Canadian smiles.

'What in hell are you up to?' growled Uncle Harry, pausing before my open door during one of these sessions. 'Damned if you aren't as crazy as your aunt,' and he snorted out a horsetail of cigar smoke before stomping off, muttering until the front door slammed – 'Women. Hell. *Women*.'

I'd noticed already that Uncle Harry could be as rude as the Cleft, ruder really (the Cleft never said hell or damn), and yet somehow make you feel pampered and cute instead of freezing your blood. That was the way he behaved around women, even Mimi, the housekeeper, and I watched how they pouted and pretended to be vexed while their cheeks dimpled and their eyes flashed. They didn't mind what he said at all, and the gruffer he got the better they liked it; me too. Aunt Jen minded though, and I could see why – when he was rude to her there was no grin lurking under his chomped cigar. The words were the same but the temperature wasn't. Together the two of them reminded me powerfully of the Cleft and Mother. That was marriage, it seemed. Husbands bullied and wives cried, husbands were brusque, wives pathetic and you wanted more than anything to shoot them both dead or anyway lock them away somewhere so their gruesome antics didn't impinge. Though Aunt Jen didn't quite fit that pattern. Unlike Mother, she joked instead of sulking or crying. That should have been better, but somehow it made things worse.

Like when she came in to dinner. One of the many things that astonished me about Canadian mores was how much time women spent together when they didn't have to. In London, once a girl had left school she'd rather have been lightly burned at the stake than seen in public in exclusively female company, which could only mean she couldn't find a man or she was a lezzy. But such dire conclusions didn't seem to worry Canadian women. In Vancouver there were actually all-women clubs. Aunt Jen belonged to a sumptuous one, all deep sofas and carpets, and spent two or three evenings a week there, dressed to the nines.

'How do I look?' she'd flute, wobbling after her bust into the dining room in a series of full-length evening dresses, each more spectacularly sequinned than the last. Staggered by so much sparkle on one little woman – and so much energy spent to wow other women – I'd murmur about how lovely she looked and if Mimi was in the room she'd join in. But though Aunt Jen thanked us both enthusiastically her pansy eyes remained fixed on Uncle Harry like a little dog begging for a tit-bit, and he never said a word. All that happened was his face would close round the stub of his cigar and he'd grunt and shut his eyes as if he hoped when he opened them that she wouldn't be there.

'Where are you going?' I'd ask to distract her.

'Why, nowhere at all. Just to the Club, to play mah-jong with the girls. You wanna come with me, honey?'

'*Girls*,' Uncle Harry said and I had the feeling he'd have spat if there'd been a spittoon.

'OK, hon,' she'd say perkily. 'Old biddies then. But old biddies or not, we know how to have fun. We have our beaux, oh yes we do,' and she'd wink at me and put her hands out flat and rock a little from side to side like there was music playing.

But Uncle Harry had stomped from the room.

One time, as she was sitting down to eat, hitching up her long skirt and tucking in her bosom, he swivelled his chair round to me and said, 'You know something? Your Aunt Jen hasn't a hair on her body.'

This news flummoxed me. No hair. Was that good or bad? Was it all right to mention out loud or was it terrible? Into the silence that followed, Aunt Jen inserted a crystal titter. 'Harry!' she said.

'True,' he went on, still looking at me. 'Not a hair anywhere. See those curls on her head? They're some other woman's. Those eyelashes? False. The eyebrows? Chalk. Why hell, naked she looks like a plucked chicken.' He tipped his chair back and glowered at the ceiling.

Impassively Mimi circled the table collecting dishes. 'Well, Jimmy crack corn and I don't care,' Aunt Jen said, hunching up one sequin shoulder like a little girl flirting. 'I've got a beau thinks I'm cute as pie, so there.'

I saw that it was terrible.

Time passed and I settled into Aunt Jen's daily routine, not caring to think about going home yet. Each morning after Uncle Harry had been chauffeured off the telephone would ring. 'Madam, the *Sun*,' Mimi would holler, and Aunt Jen, swooping upon it in her négligé, her unmade-up face almost perfectly blank, a wig on but crooked, would settle down to chat with the Vancouver *Sun*'s social columnist about where she'd been the evening before, who she'd met and what she planned to do that day. The gossip took a good half hour to impart, during which she'd cover the receiver and hiss asides at me.

'Old buddy of mine – Angie. Angela Grant Butterworth as was. Imagine, her husband Tommy Lukowiak – he was worth millions, Downhome Cookies you know? – well, he died last year and Angie didn't get a cent. The Lukowiaks were always mean as they come, I warned her when she married him, she was his third wife, he tied up all the money in some trust but oh Tommy was handsome, I'll give him that, never marry a handsome man, honey, so I got poor Angie this little job on the *Sun*, through Johnnie Klatz, an old beau of mine, and now I help her out dishing the dirt, you know what I mean . . . Yes, Angie, I'm here. So what Ruby said *was*. . .'

After this lengthy accounting Aunt Jen would retire for an

hour to put a face on, colour code her ensemble and drench herself in White Shoulders, whereupon we would head off together for the social whirl: an all-woman lunch, an all-woman tea or a shower, each of which events she would preface for me as we whizzed from venue to venue in the Pontiac – 'The party's for little Mary O'Brien, the biscuit people, new money, she's the bride-elect of Austin Dangerfield of Dangerfield's Manure, they're an old Vancouver family, Austin's Daddy was a beau of mine. Mind you, Austin isn't a patch on his Daddy but then Mary's a plain little thing so she's done all right . . .' Later, crammed to the brim with cakes and canapés, we'd return to the flat and Aunt Jen's nap before we headed out again for the evening to a dinner, a dance, a cocktail party or maybe the Club for mah-jong, Aunt Jen playing, me all eyes and ears.

Then there was Aunt Jen's weekly ritual, her Visits to the Ruined. Every Thursday Mimi would pack into the Pontiac several hampers full of biscuits, tins, cake and fruit and Aunt Jen, soberly bewigged in dove grey, would take the wheel. Her mission, she explained, was to call on those poor souls whom Uncle Harry had ruined. As we drove into Vancouver's meaner streets, Aunt Jen would recount the details of their ruination through buy-outs, mergers and other largely incomprehensible business tactics that Uncle Harry had engineered and from which he had invariably emerged richer than ever while his erstwhile partners leapt out of windows and widows and orphans wept in their wake. Absorbing the impact of these dramatic deeds I was at first full of trepidation as to our reception by the Ruined. Surely anyone broken on Uncle Harry's wheel was bound to deny the wife and niece of such a monster entry to their newly humble abodes? Might they not assault us with oaths and blunt instruments or, at the very least, turn proud backs on the ill-gotten hampers, refusing succour from our tainted hands? My heart knocked with foreboding as we stood in ill-lit corridors waiting for battered doors to open, but when they did Aunt Jen swept all before her. Within moments she was chucking the chins of wide-eyed children, pressing threadbare women to her dove-grey breast and waddling in upon the men to galvanize them with technicolour tales of their youthful exploits.

'Why, Hayden Jacobs,' she trilled at one man hunched disconsolately in a cabbage-smelling kitchen, 'I swear you're better looking than ever, how many hearts have you broken since I last laid eyes on you, you devil you? Honey,' turning to me, 'let me tell you about the time Hayden here . . .' and on she'd go piling up more and more flamboyant Jacobean acts while the man's stooped shoulders slowly unhunched and the drooping moustache took an upward turn. Next thing there was Mr Jacobs brushing his moustache on Aunt Jen's hand, Mrs Jacobs flushed and laughing and the little Jacobses jumping all over like Mexican beans.

I was glad they were glad and I admired no end Aunt Jen's talent to distract but I didn't entirely approve of so rapid a sweeping under the carpet of my uncle's sins. Forgiveness was all very well for Jesus, but it looked rather disappointingly spineless in the wide-open country of Canada's West. One day, I thought wistfully, Uncle Harry would come with us and there'd be a proper cowboy shoot-out or at the very least a Victorian-type showdown, with snarling lips, clenched fists and shouts of *Begone!* It wasn't that I personally wanted Uncle Harry punished – the truth was that all this rather added to his charisma – but for him to get away so easily with his misdeeds offended my sense of cause and effect. I never asked Aunt Jen if Uncle Harry knew about our hamper outings, so I never found out.

At the weekends, if there was no glossier entertainment on

My parents' wedding

Me

My father, the Cleft,
in the early 1930s

The dancer

Aged about twelve

The holiday in Turkey

Family holiday

On the slopes in Switzerland

István

In Montreal with István

My wedding photograph

The proud mother with Michael

the agenda, Aunt Jen, Uncle Harry and I drove out of town to their country place, called Moda after Grandpa's house in Turkey. For me that was by far the best entertainment, and my spirits, never low, soared to new heights as we turned in off the road up the boulder-lined drive to where one-storey Moda lay long and curvey on the bluff above, like a snake basking in the sun.

The first time I saw Moda, though, it was through a veil of tears. That morning, a Friday two weeks after my arrival, preparations were under way for the usual exodus. Uncle Harry was away on some business trip, the chauffeur was off for the weekend and I helped Mimi pack the Cadillac and Aunt Jen's Pontiac with the supplies to be transported to Moda for the start of the summer season.

'Now,' Aunt Jen said to me when both cars were crammed full, 'I'll take the Caddy and you follow in the Pontiac, OK hon?'

Caught off guard, I nodded.

'You do drive, don't you? Well, of course you do, all you girls can drive these days.'

That did it. I had my pride. If all girls could drive then so could I, and the fact that I'd never been behind the wheel of a car in my life was neither here nor there. On the other hand I suddenly felt rather ill.

'Oh,' I said, as if it had just flitted into my mind, 'there is one thing though. I've never driven an automatic before so I don't think I should . . .'

'I can teach you that in two shakes of a racoon's tail,' replied Aunt Jen with ghastly confidence. 'Here, come look. Nothing to it.'

Thus it came about that I started the Pontiac and with frightful roars and squealings of tyres lurched out of the driveway after Aunt Jen, narrowly missing a street light, a mail box and a stunned mailman, progressed in bumps and horrid grinds to the highway and then, stepping on the gas in a desperate bid to keep the Caddy in view, belted 150 miles up the Hudson River to Moda. By the time I drew up at Moda's gates three hours later my T-shirt was a rank and wringing rag, my hair was standing out like a dandelion clock, every bone in my body had come unhitched and my eyes were phosphorescent. But now, like every other girl, I too could drive. At that triumphant moment, as the car's engine died and the peace of the countryside broke over me, birds tweeting, brooks babbling, trees rustling, the Cleft rose up like Excalibur.

'I know you,' he thundered at me. 'You may impress others with your flashy ways but you don't impress me. Do you realize what you've done? Do you realize, you vain, selfish gurl, that you're no more than a common criminal now?'

Who cares, I answered him, trembling all over. I feel wonderful, I feel on top of the world, I'm here and you're not. It was clear to me as I sat there gasping in lungfuls of pine-scented air that I'd stumbled upon my guiding principle in life. From now on, whatsoever the Cleft was against, I would be for. Whatsoever and whomever he loathed, I would love. Whatsoever he would not have me do I would do and whatsoever he would have me say no to, I would say yes.

'Honey!'

I scrubbed my red eyes and peered into the sun. Aunt Jen was standing in the paddock by the house waving a scarf and beside her, towering above her, stood silhouetted an extraordinarily large horse. From the way it stomped its hoofs and kept wrenching its huge head away from the man hanging on to its halter I could tell it wasn't a bit glad to see us.

'Honey,' piped Aunt Jen, 'come and meet Hiawatha.'

Still shaking, I fell out of the car and dragged myself up the hill. In the glare the horse grew bigger and blacker until its massive bulk blotted out the sun. I squinted up at its gnashing great teeth and the mane on it, feathered like Hiawatha's head-dress.

'Do you ride?' asked Aunt Jen and then fatally added, 'Well, you're English. Of course you do.'

My heart dipped, my stomach dropped, my head swam and all hope withered, but grimly I hung on to my new principle. 'Yes,' I said. The result of that lie led directly to the next and equally fearsome ordeal, but when it was over I could ride as well as drive, or at least stay on the right side of the saddle.

After I'd been in Vancouver six months I came upon a scrap of newsprint enclosed in an airmail letter from Mother. I smoothed it out and saw Jimmy's name. It said he had died, flowers to Myrtle Villa. Mother explained that it had come in an envelope addressed to me, there was nothing else in it, no details of how or why. 'Sad, isn't it,' she wrote. 'Perhaps it was cancer, it spreads awfully quickly when one is young. Don't be too upset, I know you were fond of him; God moves in mysterious ways.'

That evening, as I soaked my way through a box of Kleenex, Aunt Jen stretched her two arms towards me and twisted them over. Girding the base of each palm was a thin knotted rope, two fleshy bracelets. 'See this one?' she said. 'That's for Mary-Lou Tomalski. And this was Kathie Buckerfield, Kathie Sweeney then.' Then she laughed. 'After them, I ran out of wrists.'

I blinked at her through puffy lids, unsure what she meant. 'Honey,' she said, 'I'm telling you. Give it a while and the worst thing in the world gets to be so much dirty water under the bridge.' Settling the pink chiffon stole round her shoulders she glanced out of the window at the dark sky beyond and began to sing in her high tinny voice: 'Every mornin', every evening, don't we have fun . . .'

*

The indigestible fact of Jimmy's death shook me up so much that after the first storm of remorse I locked it away in some cellar of my mind along with any thought of going home. The two were sickeningly intertwined and I couldn't face trying to unplait them. Inertia took over. Vancouver would do for the time being, though I knew already that it wouldn't do for ever. The town, for all its beauty, edging the sea, mountains rearing up behind it, mild in winter and warm in summer, was too far away from the rest of the world. You had to be born there to feel at home, otherwise a kind of claustrophobia clutched you, as if your oxygen supply was being cut off by the Rocky Mountains and the endless miles of the Saskatchewan plains from the lively pulse at the centre of things. I was an alien without the right breathing apparatus and time was slowly running out.

In the meantime life went on. That weekend in Moda Aunt Jen put on one of her special country dresses, a riot of ruches and tucks, tied a sun bonnet over her country wig – Doris Day blonde in two bunches – tucked a pannier in the crook of her arm and, looking like an overweight Fragonard lady, staggered out on three-inch wedgies to cut the roses that bloomed fatly everywhere. I wandered after her in a bikini warbling a selection of the highlights from *The King and I.*

'Jesus H. Christ,' bawled Uncle Harry from his den, 'stop that caterwauling, will you, before I go loco!'

'Harry, don't be so ornery,' twittered Aunt Jen from a rose bush. 'It's a lovely day, why don't you come out here and . . .'

'Hell, I can't afford to lie around, I have to work my guts out to keep you two. Jen, have you forgotten who's coming to lunch?'

'No, honey, that's all under control. I've ordered . . .'

Her voice cut out. In the sudden silence I looked up the garden to where emerald lawn was swallowed up in the maw

of the forest. I could see Aunt Jen's frilly back but now, in the
shadows a couple of yards beyond her, there stood a tall dark
stranger. For a long pulse of seconds the two of them froze face
to face with each other and then Aunt Jen, with excruciating
care, pivoted on her wedgies and began tiptoeing towards me.
She looked like the mouse in the cartoon trying to sneak past a
sleeping Sylvester. Puzzled, I shaded my eyes against the sun
and squinted hard at the dark figure. It appeared to be wearing
a fur coat. Fur belly, fur arms, big furry head and oh what big
teeth you have, Granny. The stranger was a huge brown bear.

She made it. Teetering and tottering, clutching her pannier,
she made it down to where I was and together, arms wrapped
round each other, we fled into the house. 'Golly, Aunt Jen,' I
shrieked as we shot through the french windows into Uncle
Harry's den, 'he could have eaten you!'

'She's a tough old bird, your aunt, she'd give him heartburn,'
said mean Uncle Harry. 'They come down all the time, those
bears. Inquisitive creatures. So what are we having for lunch,
Jen?'

'Abalone, asparagus, T-bone steak,' panted out brave Aunt
Jen.

For me at least, the day's shocks weren't over. When the
table was ready and laden with Aunt Jen's roses, Mrs O'Brien,
Moda's resident housekeeper, opened the sitting-room door
where we sat and a second tall dark stranger walked in. For one
breathless moment I thought it was the Cleft, come to upbraid
me and drag me home but it wasn't; it was Gary Cooper.

'Coop,' said Uncle Harry and they smacked each other's
backs.

'Jen,' said Coop and gave Aunt Jen a funny bobbing bow.
Then he shook my limp hand. 'Gary Cooper,' he said.

Foolish with shock, I mumbled, 'I know.'

Over the abalone, the asparagus and steak he and Uncle

Harry talked money and then dogs – Coop was about to pick himself some puppies from a litter of one of my uncle's three champion Labrador bitches. In the meantime I scrutinized the heavenly guest as intently as was possible while still eating a lot, amazed that any man could look so like my father yet so different. The same lanky arrangement of bones, the same long planes of flesh, but within that dour structure, changing it utterly, a gentle, guarded but friendly spirit. Could someone so cataclysmically famous be shy? Apparently. As I ate and gazed, gallons of Hollywood clichés rose up and sloshed about in my head. A whirlwind romance, strong arms about me, a boyish grin, then a yearning. My darling, can you ever love me, could I dare to ask you to be my wife even though I'm old enough to be your father? To which I replied, already luminous with adjacent fame, who cares, darling Coop, I love you too and anyway I never had a father, be mine, be mine.

We met again later, at a restaurant in Vancouver's Chinatown, he took my hand in front of all the rubberneckers and touched his stubble to my cheek, bending over me in a way that struck me deaf with adoration so that I remember nothing of what he said or what I replied. But the banked warmth of his presence and his bashful regard gave me the first inkling I'd ever had that there might be nothing wrong with me the way I was, that I might be liked, even loved, without trying, without effort, without armoury, and that a man could be a source of happiness and well-being instead of the hereditary adversary. Years later when I heard that Coop had died I felt half widowed, half orphaned.

The social whirl went on and I whirled with it, escorted around and about by that assortment of young men Aunt Jen insisted on calling my beaux, sons of the men who had been her beaux; in those days Vancouver was not a big place. These escorts, tall, square-shouldered, square jawed, crop-haired, rich and hard to tell apart, had punchy first names like Chuck, Judd and Jip and surnames that ended in Junior or, like the Kings of England, Second, Third or Fourth, and they were all much politer than boyfriends at home. They invariably appeared at the door bearing a corsage, that tortured arrangement of flowers convention obliged New World men to buy and New World girls to pin on, no matter how badly it clashed with their frocks. Thereafter they ceaselessly buzzed about you opening and shutting doors, heaving you from cars, helping you up and down steps, pulling and pushing you in and out of chairs and rushing to provide you with plates of food as if you were frail, old and fatally ill instead of eighteen and, like June, busting out all over.

These dizzying attentions were kept up until about midnight, by which time the drink had caught up and they either fell asleep at the table or crashed around a dance floor that soon resembled the sole clearing in a logging camp. This collapse was mainly due to British Columbia's incomprehensible liquor laws, which prohibited drinking in any public place other than those furtive taverns set aside for rough men who lined up drinks along the bar and grimly downed them until they too collapsed. Thus any function or dance held at an hotel required bedrooms to be booked and stacked with bottles which then had to be emptied before the dance was over. I thought it all very odd but stoutly did my bit towards the emptying and hardly missed my escorts as they fell by the wayside since all they ever talked of while still upright were dollars, stocks and shares. The one man I dated who didn't was a poet with hauntingly hollow cheeks whom I'd met while walking in Stanley Park and he hardly talked at all, only stared, sighed and wrote another poem. He caused an unexpected stir when I asked him to one of Aunt Jen's cocktail parties – unexpected by me at any rate. *Who is he?* people kept asking me. I told them his name but they only looked puzzled so I added, *He's a poet*. That wasn't the answer either, for still I could hear them behind my back asking each other, *But who* is *he?* I should have thought them snobs but for the well-known fact that there were no snobs in Canada or America either because there was no Class, which was manifestly proper and fair. The Cleft was very fond of Class, so I wasn't. He also despised fairness. He couldn't say the word – 'Fair? *Fair?*' – without looking as if he'd swallowed a lemon.

But it was when my cousin Charlton started arriving most evenings to take me out that my time in Vancouver began to run out.

'Charlton. You again,' said Uncle Harry as Mimi showed him in for the fourth time in a week.

'Sir.' Charlie gave his stiff little nod and looked a trifle uneasy but angelic all the same, with his shiny gold hair and his white shirt and black tuxedo.

Two of Uncle Harry's brothers, lured by his success, had followed him to British Columbia, though neither of them had subsequently ruined anyone so they hadn't done half as well. Uncle Hugh, Mother's youngest brother, spent all his money on women who played musical instruments. He couldn't resist them and married four in quick succession: a violinist, a pianist, a harpist and his wife of the moment, a hefty Ukranian accordianist. Uncle Willie, Charlie's father, was retiring and had been married to the same woman always. 'My, but he was a dreamboat when he was young,' Aunt Jen told me. 'Handsomer even than Harry, but killingly shy. The Bakker twins fell for him like a ton of bricks, chased him up and down dale, but he dithered and dithered till they put their names in a hat and made him pick one. And oh, how the other twin cried all through the wedding. Even when the organ played 'Here Comes the Bride' you could still hear her sobbing, she wailed like the curlews on Grouse Mountain. My *heavens* it was romantic.'

Charlie was a dreamboat too, and besieged by girls. Unwisely perhaps Aunt Jen had assigned him as my first escort, and though for ages we behaved like brother and sister, earnestly discussing the pros and cons of our passing flames, the kiss he gave me at the end of one evening was not brotherly at all and soon we were spending every evening together. The necessary secrecy – we knew first cousins were not supposed to feel what we felt – added fire to our attraction. One weekend, lying like troopers as to our plans, the two of us met and drove up beyond the mountains into the interior. This was gold rush country, hot and empty except for the ghosts of the old Forty-niners and their shuttered ghost towns, shingles and rafters perfectly preserved in the dry air. All day we swam in lonely lakes and walked and talked and all night under the brilliant stars we wriggled together in our sleeping bags like a pair of amorous worms. Sadly, it was all fore and no play. So implacable was the taboo against sex before marriage, so unyielding the respect of an upright man for a *virgo intacta* that even alone in that deserted moonscape we never quite toppled over the brink of 'all the way'. In the morning, giddy with sleeplessness, I blundered from the tent into the dazzling outdoors and squatted behind a locust bush at the edge of a lake to pee. In full flow I heard a twig crack behind me, craned my neck round and saw, enormous against the wide sky and not two yards away, my second bear. It is not easy to freeze while you are squatting, and impossible to stop a morning pee in its tracks. Hopelessly I peed on while the bear looked down on me and I looked up at him. Midges clouded his muzzle and crept in his fur and his smell was chokingly strong. No sound in the world but the soft sussuration of urine sinking into sand and my heart clonking. Years passed and then modestly the bear looked away, scratched his (or her) belly, bared a rocky ridge of teeth in a yawn and lumbered off. Until my thighs would take it no more I stayed squatting, then I hoiked myself up. The bear was nowhere. The land lay vacant, the lake shone ahead like a bright silver dish and beside it I wept as quietly as I could with the joy of having been so near to so huge and wild a creature. And then, to spill over my brimming cup, out of the blue sky an eagle swooped, skimmed the silver dish and rose again in a silver spray with a silver salmon spiked on his claws. The night's heavings paled beside such solitary excitements.

We returned to a great scampering around – the family had found out that Charlie and I had been together and we were called to account, the two uncles harrumphing, the two aunts wringing their hands. Aunt Jen had her dove-grey wig on, which wasn't a good sign. The room was sticky with embarrassment.

'Didn't I say so? First time I laid eyes on her? Trouble,' said Uncle Harry, shoving out his jaw and pulling down his eyebrows. 'Time you went home, Missie.'

'Sir, that's not fair,' Charlie said, moving protectively towards me, but Uncle Harry's scowl was too black to be entirely convincing, I guessed he was more annoyed at this waste of good money-making time than at me. Still, I was upset. Of course I couldn't stay in Vancouver for ever, but what sin had I committed to be dismissed so peremptorily?

'We haven't done anything wrong, Charlie and me,' I appealed to Aunt Jen. 'We're in love, that's all.'

This statement caused everyone but Aunt Jen to look extremely shifty. Aunt Jen said, 'Aaah.'

'Shut up, Jen,' said Uncle Harry.

Uncle Willie said, 'Son, I thought better of you.' Charlie said, 'Now *look*, Dad,' and Uncle Willie put his head in his hands. The situation was deteriorating.

'Hell,' and now Uncle Harry's scowl was real. 'Never mind who did what to whom or didn't. Missie, as long as you're under my roof you're my responsibility.'

'I see that,' I said placatingly, 'but there's nothing you need be responsible for.'

'Maybe so. But the fact remains that this young whipper-snapper here is your cousin.' Perhaps I didn't look abashed enough at this. At any rate he added, rather violently, 'Your *first* cousin.'

'Oh that,' I said. 'That's not even in the prayer book any more. No one minds about cousins these days, honestly.'

'*I* mind.' Uncle Harry was suddenly angry. 'Your father minds, your mother minds, Willie and Mary here mind. I'm getting you your ticket home and that's where you're going.'

'But . . .'

'But nothing.'

I was bewildered by his unwonted ferocity. 'Why does everyone mind so much?'

'I'll tell you why.' Uncle Harry, breathing heavily, leaned forward. 'You and Charlie carry on this way, you could end up having a baby. How'd you like it if that baby wasn't normal, huh? Huh?'

Aunt Jen jangled her bracelets in distress, Aunt Mary moaned a little and Charlie drove his fists so hard into his pockets you could hear the seams give.

'But why shouldn't it be?' I asked, too bemused to protest at this phantom pregnancy. 'Charlie and I are perfectly healthy. What . . .?'

Uncle Harry slammed his two fists on the arms of his chair. 'Listen, Miss Cussèd. You've been to Turkey. Remember those cousins of yours there? Adelaide, Edmund, Vincent? D'you think they were healthy? Normal? Just like anybody else? They're dead now, God rest them, and thank the Lord they had no children, but why do you think they were the way they were? Because their parents, all of them, were first cousins. That's the hell why.'

A black hole opened inside me. I couldn't speak. My lovely Birds of Paradise, my joy, my secret pride. I saw them skittering towards me as they had on that first wonderful Istanbul day, leaning over the flowery verandas, waving and calling. Howard making his gobbly ostrich noises. Adelaide hugely grinning and clapping like a seal. Wilfred up a tree, Vincent smelling of Christmas pud, my sweet Granny stroking my hair, saying darling Yolande, dearest Tom. And Aunt Abby who went upstairs and Cousin Eve and . . .

Unexpectedly, I recalled a book I'd read about Virginia Woolf. Now she rose up, long and white, with water weeds in her hair. Mad as a goat, her sister called her and everyone laughed because they knew she didn't really mean mad, only eccentric, a bit dotty, as geniuses are. But Virginia locked herself away, saying her head hurt terribly, she hadn't closed her eyes for thirty nights, food made her retch. Behind closed doors, where her sister never saw her, she screamed and clawed at herself, covered her ears to stop the voices, talked faster and faster, babbled and gabbled until she fell down half-dead from exhaustion.

Eccentric is what I called the Birds when I told friends about them. I was pleased with the word, it lifted me into the airy ranks of people in books, the Sitwells, the Mitfords, King Ludwig of Bavaria, all those grandees past and present whose idiosyncracies (another good word) only went to prove their ineffable superiority over ordinary people, the kind who said 'We're all mad here' when someone forgot to put salt on the sprouts. For years I had boasted about my family's curious ways for the curiouser the grander and the better for me.

But now that bright memory cracked apart. Worse, it meant there was no alternative to the Cleft and Mother and all those awful scratchy grown-ups at home and the world was what I'd always feared: dull, mean, miserable, boring and suffocatingly small.

'Honey, hon-nee,' crooned Aunt Jen, her arms around me, 'don't cry, don't cry.'

Ten

The train journey to Montreal via Chicago took three days and two nights, during which time the steward who came in to make my bed tried to make me as well. He wasn't an appetizing sight or smell. His belly flopped over the belt of his trousers, the few strands of hair he had left were stuck to his skull in zebra stripes and fumes of sweat formed a pungent nimbus around him. In those close quarters he took up most of the room and I backed up against the window while he heaved the seats into position, repulsed but ashamed of my repulsion – how awful it must be to look so like Sydney Greenstreet. For fear he'd read my mind and go home and hang himself I began to smile and chat with great animation.

Unfortunately this must have led him to believe he looked like Clark Gable. With a suddenness that knocked my legs from under me he pinned me flat on the newly formed bed and kneed my thighs apart. I opened my mouth and yelled blue murder, but the train yelled louder as it rushed through the night and nobody heard. I still don't know why he abruptly heaved himself off me but he did and was almost as suddenly gone, digging his shirt back into his trousers as he wrenched the door open and disappeared, leaving me splayed out as if I had been dropped from a great height.

The next day, much shaken, I considered making an official complaint but the Cleft, his nose twitching fastidiously, remarked in my ear that I had only myself to blame and how typical of me to be mixed up in such an unsavoury episode, so I didn't. Instead, as mile upon mile of flat unchanging prairie slid by, I brooded upon the tragic wrongs done me, forever chivvied from pillar to post, forever outcast from love, doomed like the Flying Dutchman to a lonely circling of the globe. On the third day, waking to brilliant sunshine, the train's rhythmic lament of dear-dear-dear-poor-poor-you changed as we neared Montreal to a series of excited yelps. For the first time ever I was quite on my own, no one had their eye on me, no one on earth knew exactly where I was and I needed to account to no one. Like the boy in the story, one bound and I was free!

As it turned out, that freedom was about as fleeting as the fleeting train, and I was heading full-tilt towards a more barred and bolted existence than even the Cleft had managed to impose, but for the moment Montreal, with its French road- and shop-signs, its clamorous trolley-cars and river traffic and its multitude of multi-lingual cafés serving multi-national food, looked thoroughly alluring. The pulse of the outside world that had fluttered so weakly in Vancouver pumped away here almost as strongly as in London. Fresh snow covered the city, the air was needle sharp and Christmas trees twinkled icily at every corner. I cashed in the plane ticket Uncle Harry had meant me to use to fly straight on to London and put down a week's rent on a room, share kitchen, that advertised itself outside a rickety house on St Catherine Street. The next day I found my way to Montreal's biggest department store and got myself hired as the last recruit in Santa Claus's Reindeer Shock Troops.

Compared to the other shorter girls on the team, already

decked out in fake suede costumes and looking like so many plump rabbits who'd mysteriously sprouted antlers, I made a rather better reindeer; more of a moose, really. Our job was to make ourselves available all over the store, filling in whenever the permanent sales staff went down with flu or swooned in the face of besieging waves of Christmas shoppers, and we scooted all day from department to department, the bells on the tips of our antlers jingling merrily. A week into the Christmas rush our bells were still merry but we were not.

'Jeez,' groaned the runt of our pack, wobbling on one foot while massaging the other, 'I got no hoofs left.'

'You're lucky,' said another reindeer, 'mine feel like I'm walking on knives.'

'Me too. I wish an Eskimo would come along and harpoon me out of my misery,' said the third.

The four of us were huddled, against the rules, in a fitting room attached to the Rich Uncle's Boutique, socks stuck over our antler bells to muffle give-away jingles. I had spent the last exhausting half-hour ladling a large and bad-tempered matron into a Playtex girdle and then, with the aid of a tin of talc powder, lugging her out again. My hands were as white as my face.

We puffed in tired silence. Then, 'You got plans for Christmas Day?' inquired the littlest reindeer of me.

'Yeah,' I lied and screwed up my eyes to seal off possible leaks of self-pity. It hadn't occurred to me when I changed my London plans, but what *was* I going to do at Christmas? It was unthinkable to be alone but who was there to be with? My housemates – Roman, a Bulgarian who wore his hair in a net and Hans, a fat Swiss-German – had kindly invited me to join them for Christmas lunch in our shared kitchen, an invitation I declined on the grounds of a mythical previous engagement and a concrete conviction that I'd rather die than sit with them in that squalid kitchen under the piece of greasy holly that Hans had thoughtfully attached to the fly-blown overhead bulb. Now it looked as if not only would I end up with nothing to do but I'd have to do it outside on the street. I took a last puff of my cigarette, stubbed it out on a wad of chewing-gum and sighed so deeply my sock slipped and my bells gave an unhappy tinkle.

'Reindeer! *Nom de Dieu, ou êtes-vous maintenant?*'

It was Mme Tremblay, Führer of the Reindeer Squad. Moaning, we stuffed our hot lumpy feet into the compulsory stilettos and hobbled back to the fray. I limped along behind the fitting rooms into the Rich Uncle's Boutique and came face to face with a customer. We did a little jig backwards and forwards to the tune of my bells, then I stepped back and said weakly but bilingually, as the job required, '*Excusez-moi*, sorry.' The customer looked me up and down.

'You are not French,' he said.

Wearily I replied that I wasn't a reindeer either and waited for him to stop laughing and let me pass.

'Well,' he said in a heavy accent, 'that is a good thing for you because I like to hunt reindeer' – and indeed his eye was fixed on me like a man peering down the barrel of a gun. I made to move aside and again he moved with me. 'You are English,' he said. 'I like the English sense of humour. Have you been long in Montreal?'

'A week.'

'And where in England do you come from?'

'London.' Any minute he'd be asking like everyone did if I knew this friend of his who lived in London too, or was it Brighton, or maybe Aberdeen. 'I must go now,' I said.

'Please . . .' he put out a hand towards me and as I paused bowed his head, '. . . will you do me the honour to have a drink with me when you are finished your work?'

I looked at him properly for the first time. He was tall, taller and older than me, perhaps thirty-something, broad-shouldered and well-dressed. A faint perfume floated from him. He had not checked his coat at the cloakroom as most people did but wore it loosely over his suit, arms dangling, like a cloak. His hair was blond and crinkled and his features blunt except for a short, hawkish nose. There were bags under his eyes and the eyes were compelling, pale and polished as mirrors and slightly convex. They disturbed me.

'No, thank you very much,' I said and fled.

He was waiting for me by the staff exit when I came out an hour later. There were flowers in his gloved hands and he put them in mine. I clutched white roses in the snow. 'I can see,' he said, 'that you are tired. I know a nice club round the corner. Let me buy you one drink before you go home. Please?'

They knew him at the Tour d'Eiffel. 'Hi, Count, how you doing?' came from the dimmest reaches of the bar. He ordered a bottle of champagne and we sat down at a small table in a pool of pink light.

'Count?' I said.

He inclined his head in formal assent.

'Count Dracula, I presume,' I said wittily.

'He was an ancestor of mine.'

This ridiculous answer triggered a transport of giggles. He watched me, calmly sipping his champagne. I stopped and said snippily, 'Well please don't sink your teeth in me.'

'I promise not to yet,' he said. 'First we shall know each other better.' He filled both glasses, shrugged his coat off his shoulders, twisted a cigarette into an amber holder and flared a match. The gold signet on his little finger glittered. He took a slow drag and blew out one perfect smoke ring.

'Let us introduce ourselves. I am Count István Karl-Maria of Hungary. And you . . .?'

*

I spent Christmas Day in a more or less unfurnished flat shared by Erica, Annie and Janet, three English girls I'd got talking to in the store on Christmas Eve, just as I was planning to celebrate Noel by sticking my head in my third of the oven. Ten of us, including four Englishmen, an Austrian and one Canadian, gathered round an old door stretched across orange boxes and demolished a turkey and trimmings in the festive light of candles stuck in chianti bottles. Our drink we scooped out of the bathtub – the men had half-filled it with moonshine alcohol cut with egg whites. You had to add egg whites, they said, to reduce the chances of alcohol poisoning. Hoagy, the Canadian, called the frothy brew caribou juice and told us that the old-timers in the bush made it out of anything to hand, potato peelings, wood shavings, pulped paper, but they didn't add egg white so they soon went loco and their eyeballs spilled down their cheeks.

In a couple of hours, despite the egg whites, my own eyeballs felt none too secure in their sockets. 'Bewitched, bothered and bewildered,' we chorused to a tinny old record-player and collapsed, overfed and vision-impaired, on the only other furniture in the room, some fraying beanbags that excreted small pellets over the floor like incontinent rabbits. Hoagy, whose lanky cowboy looks I was finding more interesting by the minute, draped himself around me, nuzzled up and began singing drunkly into my neck. 'Wild again,' he droned, 'whimpering shshimpering child again . . .'

Then the doorbell rang. Perhaps it had been ringing for some time, it was hard to know. Erica detached herself from her Austrian swain and wove an uncertain path to the door. Through the din in my ear I heard an accented male voice asking for me and, like some schoolgirl caught with a boy behind the bicycle shed, tried to straighten my skirt and look decent. Before I could pull myself properly together the Count, impeccably suited and groomed, bearing in his arms a beribboned bouquet, stepped across the threshold. At that moment the record player stopped. As silence fell he stood looking around and his pale eyes came to rest on me. Giving one of his odd little bows to the other occupants of the room he said formally, *'Mesdames et Messieurs, je vous souhaite un joyeux Noël.'* Then he walked across, stood before me and, like a mourner tending a grave, laid the bouquet upon me. 'To wish you a most happy Christmas,' he said, ignoring Hoagy, and bowing around him again stepped back to the door and vanished, leaving an aromatic cloud in his wake.

Banjaxed by this apparition, no one spoke for a moment. Then 'Ooo-er,' said Erica vulgarly.

'Who's the Ruritanian dude?' drawled Hoagy, making an unsuccessful effort to prop himself up on a dislocated elbow. 'Dig the perfume, man. He swing both ways, or what?'

Annie wagged a finger at me. 'We were going to ask you if you'd move in here but we don't allow gentleman followers.'

'He's not,' I protested, pink with embarrassment. 'I hardly know him. Goodness knows how he found out I was here.'

'Love will find a way,' said Janet. 'I like older men. They're romantic.'

'You mean they've got money,' snorted one of the Englishmen.

Janet raised prim eyebrows. 'That too,' she said.

Hoagy wound a lock of my hair round one finger and frowned at me. 'Seriously,' he said, 'are you and he, you know . . .?'

'No. I don't even like him. He gives me the creeps.'

'OK. Come here.'

We snogged horizontally for a bit and then vertically, to music, tenderly carting each other about like the victims of some natural disaster, and I almost forgot the visitation. Almost but not quite. Every now and again, in the spaces between one kiss and another, the Count's stiff and solitary figure intervened while the Cleft, watching from the sidelines, said, 'Look at him, will you, with his flowers and his bows. I can smell him from here. Well if that's your type you'll come to a sticky end, my gurl, and don't say I didn't warn you.'

'He doesn't ... he isn't ... Oh, you're just horrible,' I answered and felt such a number of curious aches and pains I thought I must be coming down with flu.

As Boxing Day dawned I fell asleep on a beanbag and when I awoke all the flowers in the bouquet were dead.

Two days later I moved in with my three new friends and István began his siege of me. He was there with a car to move me. After work he was waiting to collect me for a drink, dinner, a movie. Weekend after weekend, before I'd had a chance to make plans, there he was at the door, with plans. When it was my turn to do the food shopping he drove me, and when it was my turn to cook, he cooked. If something went wrong in the flat, a leaking cistern, an intransigent boiler, a dud radiator, he found a Hungarian to repair it.

'Where do you find them all?' I asked.

'They are my serfs,' he said.

On the increasingly rare occasions when I managed to evade him and go with my flatmates and other friends to a dance, a concert or an ice-hockey game, he was disconcertingly present as well. As I danced, as I clapped, as I laughed or ate or talked, I could feel his eyes on me, watching. The Mad Magyar, my friends nicknamed him and I called him that too when I was with them, but I knew that for all my protestations to the contrary they suspected me of carrying a secret torch for him or why would he persist in this extraordinary way? I don't know, I told them continually, I expect he's mad. Mad about you, they said, he never leaves you alone. They sounded half awed and half reproachful, as if to say why won't you tell us the truth? What I wanted to say more and more was *help me*, but that was silly and the words wouldn't come.

Faced with such ubiquity I began to drift into a sort of trance. After all, I hadn't so much else to do and very little money to do it with – the reindeer job had folded soon after Christmas and though I was looking for something else nothing had turned up and what savings I had were dwindling. Of course I would drop him soon, when a man I really liked came along, but until then it seemed perverse to refuse István's invitations to delicious meals in riverside restaurants or picnics up north in the mountains and hang about alone in the flat instead, washing my hair or trying to get a tan on the small back balcony. Besides, whenever I did refuse, which I sometimes did, when the other girls were in for the evening and it would have been nice to stay home and gossip, he used such a concentration of argument and persuasion that I flagged and gave in.

He turned upon the details of my life the same concentration, which made his company more enjoyable than it would otherwise have been. Until then I'd assumed that all outings with men apart from Jimmy – but I refused to think of Jimmy – consisted of them talking about themselves while you sat there saying, *Did you really*, and *I do so agree*. István, in startling contrast, seemed to want to know everything about me, and having so far accumulated hardly any details worth mentioning I was charmed to oblige, chattering away with vivacity as my ego inflated deliciously.

Thus I didn't really notice when he started edging me away from the wider Canadian scene into his own *émigré* domain. Soon, no matter where we began the evening, we almost always ended up at his favourite haunt, a battered kind of parlour-cum-brasserie called Dolly's, whose largely Hungarian staff and clientele, with a sprinkling of Austrians and the odd (very odd) Pole, appeared to live on the premises; eating, talking, reading, dozing, arguing, gossiping and entertaining friends as if they had no other home. Indeed, as I later learned, some of them didn't – one room in some ramshackle boarding house was all they could afford, to be retreated to only in the small hours or if they were terminally ill.

The first time István took me to Dolly's I caused the sort of stir among the natives that a white explorer might have, paddling for the first time up the Limpopo. Everyone looked up and some even stood up as we came in, and István solemnly paraded me from table to table to be introduced and have my hand kissed. The fuss made me nervous.

'Anyone would think I was some fiancée being inspected by your family,' I hissed when the greetings were over and the polyglot babble had started again.

'They *are* my family,' István replied. 'I have no other now. They will love you, don't worry.'

'I'm not worrying,' I snapped, but he took no notice. 'Come, we will sit over there with Dönci Bácsi. Bácsi, that is uncle in Hungarian.'

The old boy he was pointing out heaved himself to his feet as we approached, seized my hand to cover it again with whiskery kisses and made a great business of moving the other guests down the table so that I could sit next to him. 'Is good, is good,' he said frequently, which I was shortly to discover was about all he could say in English other than 'Cheese on rye'.

'Well, you've got an uncle at least,' I said to István, pleased not to have to feel sad for him.

'He is not my uncle. He is a Jew. He managed the estate of a cousin of mine. Bácsi is a word of respect we use for old men.'

'Like boy for negroes.'

'Please?'

'Never mind.'

The food came in random batches as it always did at Dolly's, and was shared out as it came rather than to order. I asked for pancakes and got cold cherry soup and goulash but it was all exotic to me, and delicious. As I ate, István gave me a *sotto voce* précis of the backgrounds of customers and staff. 'See the tall woman in red? She is a Countess, her mother was lady-in-waiting to our Queen. The man over there with the moustache, he had the best stables in Hungary, he is a Prince. The Russians when they invaded burnt his horses alive. By the door, that woman, she comes from a very old Austrian family, they are Barons who had . . .'

This bloodstock information impressed and irritated me in equal measure. After a bit, I let the irritation out. 'Oh, do stop. Who cares about all that? I think it's silly.'

'Silly?' The soup spoon that was halfway to István's mouth paused in mid-air. 'How, silly?'

The Cleft, who'd been totting up the titles with approval, told me to cease blathering and learn something for a change. I shrugged.

'But please, why?' István asked. 'The English have Sirs and Milords and Dukes. It is the same for us.'

I stared at the middle-aged Baroness behind the counter hovering over the espresso machine. I watched the Prince, white-haired and stooped, stacking plates as he joked with the Countess at his side. There was no one of my age, they were all older and, to my parochial eyes, extremely foreign.

'It isn't the same at all,' I said grouchily. 'It's ridiculous, people calling themselves Princes and what-not when they're in Canada and not in castles and are running cafés and . . .'

'Selling cars?' István sold cars.

'Yes.'

István drew himself up. 'I am a car salesman and I have no castle now, it was stolen from me, but I am still a Count,' he said. 'Why should I not call myself so? It is my name, they can't take that. If you married me, you would be a Countess.'

'Not a *real* one.' I was busily shredding my paper napkin. A burst of laughter made me glance down the table and when I looked back at István he had turned into an iceberg, hard and white and glacial. The tiny shock that jolted through me did my own temper no good. 'What's the matter with you?' I said tartly. How pompous to take umbrage when someone told you the truth.

He pushed back his chair, closed his fingers round my upper arm and rose, pulling me up with him. 'Hey!' I protested. 'Do you mind, that hurts. I'm not . . .'

His grip tightened and now he was smiling. '*Servus*,' he said, bowing to the lifting, puzzled faces. '*Auf Wiedersehen*,' and, smiling all the while, marched me to the door. He didn't speak a word as he drove me to the flat and neither did I. When we arrived he stopped the car, got out and opened my door for me. 'Good-night,' he said, and drove off.

I watched his car disappear. Him and his precious aristocrats. If I'd been a bit ruder than I intended, it was just as rude of him to go on as if he might do me this great favour, making me some no-account Countess. Why, I wouldn't marry him if he could make me Queen of England. I was glad he was angry. With any luck he'd never call again and good riddance.

'It's all over, me and the Mad Magyar,' I announced to my flatmates, flouncing in. 'I'm not going to see him any more.'

'Goodness, how sad,' said Annie. 'Of course he was a bit old but still, rather dishy. Those eyes, too much. Poor thing, though, he did dote on you.'

Erica said briskly, 'Good. Now you'll have time to do some of the housework round this place for a change.'

But Janet, trailing from the bathroom in her nightie looking Ancient Greek and tragic, turned a white mask of cold cream towards me and said in a Cassandra-like monotone, 'Mark my words. You won't get rid of him that easily.'

Two evenings later István drove me up to the top of Mount Royal and we stood under the great crucifix at the peak looking down on the lights of the city below. A busload of black teenagers from some school in the States were whooping around us and I thought how beautiful their cropped heads were and their little neat ears.

'I'm sorry,' I said, 'about the other night. I didn't mean . . .'

His blunt profile with its beakish nose, silhouetted against the light from the Cross, was beautiful too. 'Will you marry me?' he said.

'No.'

'Why?'

'Because I don't love you,' I said as gently as I could.

He turned his whole body to face me. 'But I love you enough for two. I will *make* you love me.' Then he said, 'Please, how shall I be for you to love me? I will be it. I will be anything what you want.'

I couldn't bear it. 'I don't want you to be anything. I like you but I can't love you.' Down at the foot of the mountain the lights sparkled and beckoned. I longed to be there, not here.

'Please,' he said and his pale eyes glinted in the shadows, 'I must talk to you. Come to my apartment.'

I didn't want to go but I went. He had one room at the top of a house, with a kitchenette concealed behind a curtain in the corner and lino on the floor; the pattern looked as if someone had upset a box of coloured matches over it. In the room was a bed, an old sofa covered with a rag rug and a lot of books on shelves held up with bricks. He apologized for its lack of comfort. 'I make money selling cars,' he said, 'but I will not spend it here on this room. It is just to sleep, that is all.'

Two pictures on the wall caught my eye. One was a poster of Stalin, his countenance scored with jagged holes. 'I use it for target practice,' he said and, picking up a knife from the table, threw it unerringly at one of Stalin's eyes. 'That monster,' he said. 'Alive or dead, I hate him, by Jove.'

He pronounced Jove to rhyme with love, but I didn't have the heart to correct him.

The other picture was a small oil painting of an old man in a sort of night-cap peering anxiously out from a halo of yellow light. I gazed open-mouthed at its beauty and István came to stand behind me. 'That is my Rembrandt,' he said.

'Rembrandt?' Now, verily, I was impressed. 'Not painted by him? A copy, is it? You'd never know.'

'No, truly. It is a Rembrandt. It hanged in my father's study. My uncle was Ambassador in Paris. He got it out in the diplomatic bag and gave it to me. It is all I have from home except this ...' From under the bed he pulled out a battered leather suitcase, delved in among layers of rolled socks and held up a tiny box. Inside, in the velvet interior, a ring. Two large diamonds and clasped between them an equally large emerald. 'Here,' he said, taking my hand, 'I will put it on. *Now* will you marry me?'

'Oh István,' I said helplessly. The diamonds sparkled, the green at the heart gave out a steady glow. 'It's perfectly lovely but I simply can't.'

'I bringed that ring out of Russian prison camp inside a bar of soap. It was with me always, all through that bad time. Now I know why I did it. It was for you.'

'No.' There was damp under my armpits, on my forehead too. 'Oh, I'm so cold,' I suddenly wailed and, indeed, I felt quite perished.

'Wait, my baby,' he said. 'Sit down.'

I plummeted on to the sofa while he wheeled over a Calor

gas-heater and lit it. As it flared and reddened, he poured two glasses of wine and brought one to me. 'When you are warm,' he said, 'I will tell you my story and you will understand why you shall marry me.'

He told me his story while he chafed my hands and it was the saddest I had ever heard about someone I knew. A little István, born of loving parents in a fairytale castle, with two protective older brothers and faithful peasants who adored the family who in turn adored them. No cloud on the horizon. Long summer days spent riding, fishing, hunting boar – like the Birds of Paradise, only more so. Then, when István was twenty, the blue skies darkened. War broke out. Beloved eldest brother enlisted and was killed in action. István fought and miraculously survived. But the Reds invaded – no, not the Russians but Mongol troops who knew nothing, not even what country they were in. They swarmed into István's castle, bound hand and foot his father and raped his mother, pillaged and looted, peppered the paintings ·on the walls with bullets, smashed every treasured plate, statue and figurine. Then István, wandering on the streets of Budapest, was rounded up at gunpoint and trucked with other prisoners to Sverdlovsk in Siberia, where twenty years before they'd shot the Tsar and his family. Four years of hard labour in the ice-bound tundra, four years of hunger, sickness, despair, no hope of escape.

'Then the Russians made an uncle of mine Prime Minister of Hungary. I remember how, before the war, he took out a silver cigarette case from his pocket and threw it in the river, saying he was no longer a Count but a Communist. They released me then from the prison camp, with other Hungarians. I made my way home but there was no home – mad people had been moved into the castle, my parents were living with the peasants in the village, my mother's beautiful hair was snow white, my father could not stop his hands from shaking. He arranged for me to be a chauffeur for my uncle, that Ambassador in Paris, and I escaped there with nothing. Nothing but this ring. Then I came to Canada to be a car salesman. So it is, now.'

There were tears in his eyes. I felt a grinding pity and put my hand to his cheek. He grasped it. 'So I have lost everything,' he said. 'Parents, brothers, home, country, everything. But if I have you, then I shall be happy again. You will make up for all that I lose.'

'Oh, István, no,' I said, pleading, but he laid his head on my breast and wept, so I put my arms round him and wept too for the misery of it all and the next thing I knew I was in his bed.

The Cleft had a field day with my fall from grace and no wonder, he'd predicted it for long enough. For weeks, at unguarded moments during the day and in dreams at night, up he would jump, gleeful as a winning punter, one bony Lord Kitchener finger pointing straight at me, full of jibes about dirty handkerchiefs and soiled goods and how he washed his hands of me, consigning me and my lost reputation to that gutter whence no woman can hope to return to the respect of decent people or the love of a good man. Mother did her bit as well, though in my dreams as in life she remained in the background, like the sea in a holiday snap, the Cleft gesticulating full frontally while she lapped and moaned somewhere behind him, heaving oceanic sighs of how could you, how *could* you. It was all most disturbing and left me with what threatened to become chronic gastro-enteritis.

I did not conceal from Erica, Annie and Janet my fallen state. Propelled by vague fears of contamination I confessed in their interest, though I found it difficult to believe, hearing my own voice mouthing the dreaded words 'all the way', that such disgrace should at last have enveloped me.

They took it on the chin, merely inquiring discreetly (for their ears alone) whether the Fall had been painful as such – they of course being pristine goods still, themselves. Nevertheless in the next few weeks I caught them eyeing me surreptitiously, as if awaiting some subtle change, some outward sign of the stain within: a slow deterioration in dress perhaps, wrinkled stockings, hanging hems, a coarsening of the complexion. Eventually I confided that I'd felt sickish ever since. They rallied round.

'Canadians don't say sick, they say sick to the stomach,' Janet informed us. 'Doesn't that sound awful, like you're going to sick up your liver and kidneys all over the floor.'

'Mrs Fuller at the office is always saying she feels naw-shus,' contributed Annie. 'Or sometimes that she's going to throw up. She spends half her time in the lav throwing up. We all think she's preggers.'

'Maybe you're preggers too,' suggested Erica helpfully, 'maybe it's morning sickness.'

'I've got the Curse,' I said.

'I suppose you'll have to marry him now,' said Catholic Annie.

'I dunno,' I glumly replied.

'Or perhaps he'll cast you off, now that he's had his way with you. Men do that a lot. And then no other man will marry you because you're not a BV any more.'

'Huh?'

'A Blessed Virgin.'

'Oh,' I said, and went to the bathroom, where I threw up.

István, however, had no intention of casting me off for my non-BV state. Rather, he radiated a new and disturbing confidence, like a man who has pulled off a particularly tricky business deal. Where before he had been discreet with me in public, at Dolly's for instance, now he was forever patting and stroking my hair or my cheek and when I drew back or dislodged his arm with a twitch of my shoulder, which I did all the time, he merely chuckled, seemingly delighted. 'My cold little English girl,' he called me and made no objections when I refused to sleep with him again, apparently approving of this further evidence of my coldness. 'I understand,' he said, chucking my chin, 'there is no need to rush, we have all our lives before us.' And so sure was he that my yielding to him my precious maidenhood was as good as saying I'd marry him that he didn't propose again, which might have reassured me except that when he talked of this and that – a visit to Europe, a business plan, the amount houses cost or what he liked for breakfast – my presence beside him was taken for granted, which sent new tremors through me.

My own feeling, contrary to his, was that my life was already behind me. The future, far from brimming with inchoate possibilities, was setting like concrete before my eyes, yet I couldn't see any way to stop it without crushing István. His words, often repeated – that having me would make up for all his grievous losses – beat in my head like a funeral drum. I saw myself clad in Grecian drapes, a cross between Justice on the top of the Old Bailey and the Statue of Liberty. Send me your poor, your huddled masses yearning to be free. It was a mighty role that Fate had handed me, the salvation of the dispossessed, and who was I to reject it just because I'd much prefer to be giggling with Erica, Annie, Janet and the rest?

Anyway, by this time I no longer seemed to have that choice. István's constant and curiously intimidating presence had quite severed me from my contemporaries, and I was left to make the best of his. Yet once resigned to that, it had its compensations. At Dolly's, old Dönci Bácsi and the rest bestowed upon me the tender care usually reserved for invalids, and their cosseting was addictive, though it did occur to me now and then, with a prickle of skin, that Hansel and Gretel probably felt the same as they scoffed the delicacies the wicked witch fed them while fattening them up for her table. Did Dolly's inhabitants like me for myself or was I being prepared as a sacrificial repast for their favourite son?

'István, he loves you, oh, so much,' crooned the Countess, holding my hand and feeding me grapes.

'So many girls try to capture him,' said the Prince, 'but now you have brought the great stag down. How did you do it?' and he winked as one hunter might to another, coaxing me to reveal my quiverful of curare-tipped arrows.

'Is good, is good,' growled Dönci Bácsi, 'he adore you very much. Please, eat more goulash.'

But none of them ever asked me if I loved István. Over that subject they drew a curtain of iron.

I didn't love him, though. Pity was the source of my sickness, unwelcome, unshifting and unshiftable. But pity was at least an acceptable emotion which, with effort, I could winch up to near-mythic levels, the Greeks and all that. Alas, there were less elevated layers: apathy, a sagging into dependence, the easy rewards of being cared for, no decisions to take, no unpredictable hazards to face, in fact all the seductions of prison life. There are many, ask any old lag.

It was at this stage of stagnation that I was offered work by Mike Gutwillig, an acquaintance of Erica. Mike, when he wasn't wholly absorbed in turning himself from a 115-pound weakling into Mr Universe with the aid of a steel-spring contraption, was the onlie begetter of a monthly newsletter that supermarkets and shopping-centres throughout Canada were urged to subscribe to so that they might boost their sales to unparalleled heights. The newsletter was entitled *Gut Promotions* and my job was to think up the promotions while Gut promoted his biceps. Armed with my London copywriting experience I soon became rather good at this. My Canada-Goes-Fishing promotion had shopping-centres from New Brunswick to Vancouver Island stuffing their salesgirls into mermaid gear while exhorting their customers to Catch Your Own Trout in Our Special Trout Pond! Make a Tastee Trout Timbale for Your Own Fisherfolk! Net Junior His First Fishing Rod (A Bargain Catch, This!) and Treat Yourself to a Genuine Aluminum Fish-Poacher for the One That Didn't Get Away! And my Batten-Down-The-Hatches-for-Winter Event, with its notions for flogging everything from snow-chains to storm windows (Beat the Freeze But Never Our Prices!) was a Coast-to-Coast wow.

Or so Mike and I fondly believed. In fact, we never checked to see if my ideas were put into action because we never went further than the corner drugstore for maple-syrup waffles. Nevertheless there was a while, in that cubbyhole ten floors above St Lawrence Boulevard, when I fancied myself queen of a shopping empire, dictator of a million menus a night and the builder of a better world.

The third member of Gut Promotions, Jo-May, a black girl who put out the mailing shots, didn't see eye to eye with us on this. Whenever her tongue was envelope-free she shouted, *Oh man is this the pits, oh man, this sucks*, and whenever Mike had enough puff between hauling on his Mr Universe springs he'd yell back, *If you weren't a schvartzeh, Jo-May, I'd kick your black ass out of here*. Then she'd shriek, *Oh yeah, just you try you skinny little kike*, and so it went on, yid and nigger, o-fay, honky and Jew-boy, until the day Jo-May screamed at me, *As for you, you dumb Limey* . . . and Mike yelled, *Who do you think you are, you horse-faced English asshole?* That day I felt happiness shoot through me from top to toe for the first time since meeting István.

'You like this Mike,' István said.

We were drinking in the Tour d'Eiffel, icy dry Martinis.

'Yes.'

'And he likes you?'

'I suppose.'

'You suppose?'

'He calls me an asshole and a Limey. I suppose he does.'

'I do not understand.'

'You wouldn't,' I said.

'I love you. I do not call you asshole and Limey.'

'No.'

Later, as usual, we sat eating pancakes at Dolly's. For once we were more or less alone; no Prince, no Countess, no Dönci Bácsi. István was silent for a long time. Then he said, 'I think you are in love with this Mike.'

'Don't be stupid.'

'Stupid? I am not stupid.' He was freezing up again. 'I see you yesterday. Across the street when you come out from your work. You kiss him. I see you.'

This instantly rendered me speechless with rage. I had recently discovered this rage that boiled just beneath the surface, like lava trapped within a volcano. 'So what?' I managed to stutter.

István said, in a voice of ice, 'You are mine. I will tell this Mike so. He must leave you alone.'

'Don't you dare,' I hissed. My hands were trembling again.

'You want to see how much I love you?'

'No.'

'Would your Mike do this for you?' He took his cigarette out of its amber holder, tapped its ash away, dragged at it until it glowed red hot and pressed the tip into the mound of flesh below his thumb, never taking his eyes off me, never ceasing to smile.

*

216

I had some money saved but not enough to pay for a passage by ship to England. Erica said she knew people who put ads in the Montreal *Star* and got their passages home paid. 'You offer to be a courier or something,' she said. 'Try it, why don't you.'

I did, and the day the ad appeared a man rang. He said he wanted two suitcases delivered to a London friend, and if I met him with my down-payment he would make up the rest and buy the ticket then and there. He named a café along the St Lawrence River and I went. He was sharply dressed, with a hand-painted tie, and he showed great sympathy for my plight. He ordered two coffees and we chatted for a while.

Then he said, 'Now, you give me your third and I'll go right across the road to the travel agent and buy your ticket, OK?'

'OK,' I said, handed over my money and watched him disappear. After half an hour tears began to slide out of my eyes. The proprietor came over and I gulped out what had happened. He patted my shoulder. 'Honey, you've been done. No charge for the coffees.'

I reported the theft to the police, anger overcoming the shame of my gormlessness. The policeman who drove me home afterwards stopped on the way and got back into the car saying, 'Here, some flowers to make you feel better.' I was touched and invited him into the empty flat for a thank-you coffee, whereupon he exhaustively and exhaustingly attempted to get me into bed.

The next night the telephone rang again. I picked it up and a man said, 'About your ad.'

'Thanks for phoning,' I said, 'but . . .'

'I'm with Weston, the tyre company? We're shipping over to England a football team, yeah? It's a team we sponsor. You wanna go back to the Old Country, right?'

'Well I . . .'

'So OK. How old are you?'

'Eighteen.'

'Nice-looking gal, are you?'

Wonderingly I replied that friends considered me attractive.

'Fine. We'll buy your ticket. First-class cabin, all facilities, all comforts. Does that suit?'

'But what do I have to do for that?' I asked, honed slightly by my last encounter. It could be drugs.

It was worse. 'Well, honey, nothing really. Just be a little friend to the boys, know what I mean? Home comforts, some drinks – we'll provide them. Open house kind of thing. You get me?'

I got him and slammed down the phone. How many were there in a football team? My God, men were hell.

No details of these encounters did I dare to reveal to István – what further terrifying self-mutilations might he go in for if he knew I was trying to escape him? The smell of charred thumb was sharp in my memory, that and the white, tight smile. I hadn't mentioned István's act to my flatmates, too quelled by the image of their shocked faces or, worse, one of Erica's oo-ers, and the Cleft, thank goodness, hadn't cottoned on yet. His reaction I could neither face nor imagine, so whenever he popped up I said rhubarb rhubarb or switched my mind instantly somewhere else to prevent him getting a word in edgeways, though he'd found out almost immediately about how I'd been conned and pronounced his verdict: 'You haven't the sense you were born with, gurl.'

Eleven

Then it was full summer and Montreal blazed day after day under a sun whose presence was as constant and often as enervating as István's, though on me István cast the deeper shadow. The cigarette episode had blistered me as well as him, and whenever the memory reared its ugly head above the fence I'd thrown up around it my whole body turned into one of those test tubes in mad-scientist movies, full of sinister liquids bubbling and smoking, the very stuff Dr Jekyll brewed up to become Mr Hyde. It wasn't a pleasant feeling.

Still, I had Mike, Jo-May and my shopping empire to distract me, and enough money in the bank now to afford a whole passage home. Ironically I'd been able to save it largely thanks to István; I paid my rent and bought my own clothes but he footed the bill for most of my meals and entertainment and wouldn't hear of any contributions from me. This fact plus the niggling fear that he would do something a lot more destructive than singeing a thumb if I suddenly departed held me in a state of suspended dither. After tense encounters with him I would silently vow to buy a ticket the very next day and then some gentle gesture, some pleading word, the sadness that never quite left him and, most of all, his struggles to be what he imagined I wanted and his anxious attempts to make me laugh with terrible jokes would arouse a stifling pity and I'd let my plans drop.

Then two things cropped up to delay those plans even further. I was offered continuity work at a local radio station, which I accepted with much excitement and many rude but fond farewells from Gut Promotions, and Hoagy came back to town. My first sight of him was a nose and two grinning lips squashed against the glass of the studio wherein I was nervously addressing the mike under my new CFCF Montreal's Weathergirl hat.

'But I don't know anything about the weather,' I'd protested beforehand to Marty, my new boss, 'except that it's hot.'

'You got it,' said Marty. 'Just say that plus a bit of newsy chat, old ladies drop dead from the heat, truckloads of fish stinking in the harbour, a plague of locusts, that kinda thing. That crazy English accent'll slay 'em. Oh and hey, you'll need this.' He chucked something at me that looked like a mummified tarantula, felt like it too.

'Yuk. What is it?'

'You mean you don't know?' He frowned, shaking his head. 'Maybe this job's not for you after all.'

'Oh, Marty.' Disappointment threatened to sink me. 'I'll learn very quickly, I promise . . .'

'OK, Toots, I'm a big man, I'll give you a break. What you hold in your hands is standard equipment for all meteorologists. A piece of seaweed. When it's dry, like now, tell the listeners humidity's low. When it softens up, tell 'em it's high. You dig?'

'Marty, you're joking.'

He wasn't and with some reason – Montreal's weather had none of the countless variations of weather at home, necessitating solemn scientific analyses BBC-style. Here it was either boiling or freezing, with a week or so at either side of the year for a rush of spring blossoms or a firework display of autumn leaves. Montrealers were never in doubt as to how things were going climatically, so CFCF's weather reports relied heavily on the ingenuity of the reporter to hook listeners, with the odd hurricane alert thrown in to keep them on their toes. It was during my final minutes of seaweed-divining that Hoagy's squashed face appeared. 'Idiot,' I said when I came out, 'you nearly made me dry up. Anyway, where've you been since Christmas?'

'Up on the Dew Line. I was skint. Now I'm rich and I'm gonna spend all this loot on you. Here . . .' He stuck a hand in his pocket and pulled out a thick roll of bills. 'How does that make you feel? Bright-eyed and bushy-tailed? When d'you get off?'

'A half-hour' I said before I could think. Hoagy looked so relaxed in his worn jeans and T-shirt, so seductively slapdash, so *young*. I telephoned István, told him I couldn't see him that evening because I was working late and put down the receiver full of gratitude to CFCF where, unlike Gut Promotions, working late was the norm.

We boogied half the night away at a dance hall the size of an aircraft hanger where the music hit the walls and bounced back to ring round your skull like a gong. István, who'd have been the stiffest of fish out of water here, was an excellent dancer – to glide in his arms across the floor with his hand firm and commanding at my back summoned up instantly waltzing Hussars, rococo ballrooms, great chandeliers, swirling frills and furbelows, all the romance of Old Vienna or, in his case, Old Budapest. Hoagy, his sun-bleached mane of hair flipping every which way, possessed no such finesse. He loped into the throng, beat them back a few paces and proceeded to slide and yank and bounce me up and down like a Harlem Globetrotter with a basketball. It was hard work, and by the end of the evening the two of us were wrecked, soaked, and I was aching all over. At four a.m. we walked back to my flat swinging hands along the empty streets in the cool of a brand-new morning. As we kissed on the steps in the rosy dawn we were cheered on by men waving from a huge street-sluicing truck and I thought with a thrill that the whole scene must look just like a *Saturday Evening Post* cover and for this luxurious moment I was inside the picture with Hoagy instead of outside, with István.

The moment passed. 'Pick you up tomorrow, same time, same place?' said Hoagy, treading backward down the steps.

The worries I'd fended off all evening came at me like a plague of mosquitoes. I stood stone dumb.

He stopped and squinted back at me. 'You got other plans?'

'No. Yes. I mean . . . Oh Hoagy, it's so complicated, I don't know how to . . .'

'What? What is it?' He came back up the steps and took my hand. 'Is it some other man? Go on, shoot.'

I shot. It all came pouring out and I was surprised at the depths of my woe – until then I hadn't grasped just how much I minded, how manacled and caged I'd felt for so long. Holding my hand Hoagy listened quietly, his face wrinkled like a puzzled monkey.

'Gee Willikers,' he said as I tailed off, sniffing, 'so it's that guy, the Christmas weirdie. What a sonofa . . .' and he did a quick one-two punch in the air. 'I get my hands on him, I'll . . .'

'No,' I said anxiously, 'he's not . . . It's not his fault, it's just . . .'

'You're kidding, not his fault. The guy's an asshole, he's . . .'

I looked up at him while he banged on, at his long, good-humoured Canadian face, his bleached flag of hair, his crinkled-up eyes, the dust of freckles across his nose, and felt uninnocent beside him, a burdened androgynous creature pretending to be a carefree girl. He and István came from different planets, Hoagy's green and fresh from the melting pot, István's battered, shell-scarred and a million years old, and me strung between them, belonging nowhere. I wanted badly to be on Hoagy's planet but my chances of making it seemed low.

'Look,' Hoagy said, 'the whole thing's crazy. This is a free country. I wanna see you and if you wanna see me, no frigging bohunk wearing frigging perfume can stop us. You're gonna be working late tomorrow too, OK? Just tell 'im, or I will.'

'I'll try,' I said and waved him off with a spurt of hope inside me. Maybe István wasn't my fate after all. Maybe there was light in the tunnel.

For the next month I managed to juggle the two of them, but the lies I had to tell István, the energy required to deflect Hoagy's threats to confront him and my nagging fear that we would be spotted together by a spy from Dolly's or István himself took a lot out of me. I grew jumpy, swinging up and down a gamut of contradictory emotions – dislike for my lies, resentment that I had to tell them, the old drag of pity for István that caused outbursts of affection switching without warning into irritation while, with Hoagy, though I revelled in the freedom he afforded me and often swooped to great heights of exhilaration in his company, his refusal to see that there might be real hazards in a break-up with István and his goading of me to 'Go on, tell 'im, *do* it,' plunged me into despondency. Or was I the blind one? Or cowardly or a masochist, perhaps? Was I purposely exaggerating István's feelings so I could play the *femme fatale*, had I blown the whole thing up out of all proportion? There was no shortage of questions here, but answers came there none. Meanwhile I kept Montreal informed on the fluctuations of seaweed and took on besides the presentation of a cooking programme, niftily recycling my left-over Tastee Tuna Timbales and the like. One silver lining – I had quite lost any nerviness in front of the mike. What nerves I had were all used up backstage in my private life.

Hoagy bought a car with his Dew Line earnings. The Dew Line, he'd explained at some point, ran across Upper Canada from coast to coast; for all I know it still does. 'Dew' stood for Distant Early Warning and served as North America's first radar defence against Soviet attack – let one MiG stick its nose across and all hell would break loose, or so the theory went. But the Dew Line played a far more vital role in the eyes of many Canadians than merely repelling the Commies. It was the place you could always go to solve your money problems. If bankruptcy threatened or a quick injection of capital became vital to get some project off the ground, you upped sticks and went to work there as anything from a cook to a plumber, for which you were paid extremely well to compensate for having sweet Fanny to do in your spare time but stare out at millions of acres of tundra.

'Maybe I'll go up there,' I said to Hoagy, struck by the image of a bolthole out of István's reach.

'You hafta be a Canadian citizen,' he said.

'I could get that.'

'And male.'

Another escape route hit the dust.

Hoagy's car was only an old Chevy grainy with rust, but it nicely widened our range to the restaurants and clubs in the mountains up north, and soothed my nerves – less chance of bumping into István a hundred miles out of town. Late one evening, two a.m., three, after just such an outing, Hoagy stopped the car as usual outside the darkened windows of my flat. Under the sulphurous light of a nearby street lamp we sat chatting for a couple of minutes and then Hoagy shifted along the seat, slipped a hand inside my blouse and began to kiss my neck. With my head to one side I gazed dreamily out of the window, sunk in his caresses, half-drunk, half-asleep. There was a car parked opposite, a dark silhouette. As I gazed, the driver's door swung open and István got out. In two strides he was across the road and in front of our car. I jerked up, my heart thudding fit to bust a rib. 'Hey,' grumbled Hoagy, rolling away. István's face loomed at the glass, yellow in the lamplight, expressionless, his eyes two yellow pools.

'What the . . .' Hoagy was sitting bolt upright now, raking at his hair.

'It's him. Oh God.' Panic-stricken, I scrabbled at the door on my side, trying to find the lock. Hoagy dived across me and clicked it down. István put an elbow on the hood. He was smiling now, gesturing for me to get out.

Frantically I shook my head. For a long moment nobody moved. We stared out, István stared in. Then he lifted his shoulders and let them fall, turned on his heels and walked back to his car. He'd given up and I gasped with relief. Hoagy said, 'Jeez,' and came alive, pushing at his door.

'I'll get the bastard. This is it. Who the hell does he think . . .'

No sooner had he got one foot out than István was back. This time he was holding a pick-axe.

'Christ,' yelled Hoagy and slammed the door. 'Christ, the guy's crazy!' He fumbled for the ignition and gunned the engine. István rather slowly and gracefully swung the pick-axe back and then fast forward. With a sickening crunch the windscreen shattered. Glass flew everywhere. Cursing, Hoagy scraped wildly at his face and put his foot down. The car jerked forward, István sprang back, the tyres screamed and we shot off down the street. I turned as we went, splinters showering from my hair. Under the lamplight István stood, smiling.

Hoagy drove me to his parents' house. They came downstairs blinking in dressing-gowns and were anxiously kind, his Mom bringing us strong cups of coffee, his Dad stomping up and down, bewildered. I was shaking so much I could hardly drink the coffee. Hoagy brushed me down and himself. Glass fell on the floor and his Mom swept it up, saying, 'Oh my my, what a thing to happen, he coulda killed you both. Hoagy, you OK?'

Hoagy's Dad said, 'I'm gonna call the police.'

'No,' I said, supplicating. 'Please, please don't. It'll make things much worse. Please, I couldn't bear it.'

'Honey-bun, you gotta face it,' Hoagy said, going down on one knee beside me. 'The guy's out of control, he should be put away.'

I don't remember much more, except that they gave way and didn't call the police. Hoagy's Mom found a nightie for me and took me up to a bedroom where I fell fast and deeply asleep. At once, the Cleft pounced.

'Is this how you intend to lead your life, causing mayhem wherever you go, waking perfect strangers in the middle of the night to minister to you? You're a menace, that's what you are. Encouraging madmen for your own purposes, have you no shame? D'you know what's going to become of you? You'll end up a headline in the *News of the World*, "Brunette, 36–24–36, found in some squalid little room with a scarf round her throat and her eyes bulging out." As for that so-called Count you're mixed up with, words fail me. For God's sake, pull yourself together, gurl, before it's too late.

In the background Mother hiccupped and sobbed and so it went for the rest of the night, just as if I were at home.

By all the rules, that eventful evening should have brought about the death from unnatural causes of whatever there was between István and me: closed its eyes, laid it out and buried it in unhallowed ground. Something died, that's certain, but it came to life again: a pity there wasn't a Van Helsing or a Jonathan Harker around to drive a stake through its heart. Hoagy did what he could to finish it off but was soon daunted and who can blame him – few men much relish the prospect of coping with a mad axeman who could leap out at any time of the day or night and hack you into gobbets without so much as a nod in the direction of the law or M'Naughten Rules on Sanity. For Hoagy saw István as indisputably mad – what else would you call a man without respect even for another man's car, for Christ's sake – and, sure, it'd be a privilege to knock the mad bastard's teeth down his throat if, say, he, Hoagy, and I were engaged or had ever had a roll in the hay, for Christ's sake. But how was he supposed to react when the woman he risked having his balls cut off for wouldn't admit that the guy was off his nut and instead kept mumbling that he, Hoagy, didn't understand, didn't grasp the complexities involved, actually defended the bastard, for Christ's sake? He, Hoagy, was no dummy, no sir, and he didn't mind telling the world that the way he saw it someone wasn't coming clean and there was more to this business than met the eye, one heck of a lot more, yes siree.

I sat and listened as he let off steam and, yes, I did mutter the odd word in István's defence, but I quite understood, was resigned to, more or less expected Hoagy's reaction and, besides, Erica, Annie and Janet joined forces to make sure I did.

'That Count person of yours, he's not setting foot in here again, we've voted, it's unanimous,' declared Erica, pacing up and down in my bedroom like an expectant father. 'It woke us all, that crash, and then you weren't in your bed and we looked out and there was glass on the pavement and then we saw him getting into his car and Janet guessed something had happened and . . . are you listening?'

'Honestly, it is a bit thick,' said Janet, coming in from the bathroom with a towel over her head. 'We were worried sick. I mean we're fond of you and everything and . . .' She scrubbed aggressively at her wet curly hair.

Annie, perched on the bed where I lay, said, 'I mean, we can all see what you might see in him, but if you ask me he's also crazy, and that's not funny, he might come and murder us all in our beds. No wonder Hoagy . . . Oh for goodness sake, will you *listen*!'

I propped myself up and tried to look alert but in truth I could hardly keep my eyes open. It had been so for days – ever since, in fact. A somnolent blanket had fallen on me, distancing me from everything, muffling every sound. For all that the outside world impinged I could have been huddled in a cave in a mountain or under the sea or down a mine. Where had I read about someone living in a treacle well? Whoever it was, I knew how they felt. Quite peaceful really, except that you risked getting stuck in your ways.

'I said it's not *funny*,' snapped Erica.

'Sorry,' I whispered from my glutinous retreat and closed my eyes again so that I could go back to watching István slowly and gracefully swing his pick-axe. And then – oh that wondrous explosion! That starburst of glass! I could feel again how my heart had sprung from its moorings and gone whistling up into the night sky, a little red comet lashing its tail, not seen in the heavens since Aunty Joan was blitzed to bits by that old landmine. Whoof! Pow! That's what was needed! Smash the glass, crash through the wall, kick in the door, set fire to the house, blow up the whole bang shoot!

Janet was leaning over me, her hair damp on my cheek. I opened my eyes. 'You're right,' I said meekly to her, 'he is mad and I won't let him come here any more, cross my heart.' That should keep them quiet.

I kept my promise and they kept quiet. Once upon a time they'd have garlanded the front door of Apartment 3, Maupassant Avenue with garlic and nailed up a horseshoe upside down. As it was, within its chambers István's name was pronounced anathema and he ceased to exist. Hoagy evaporated also, a job in California, or so he said, *I'll miss you baby, stay clear of Dracula, you hear?* Alas, the effect of this well-meant quarantine was to push me ever further towards that cliff edge that was István's natural habitat. He came the morning after, and five mornings after that, with armfuls of flowers, and when I wouldn't answer left them at the door, so many of them the porter put on a long face to inquire whose loved one had passed on.

'Don't give way,' Annie instructed me sternly. 'He's only trying it on. Keep your nerve and he'll give up soon. No point in wasting the flowers, though,' and she gathered up the latest arrivals and set off yet again for the Poor Clare Convent down the street.

'Those nuns get any more bouquets, they'll make our Annie a saint,' said Erica.

István didn't give up, however; I gave way, though I didn't dare breathe a word to anyone and anyway, by then, there was no one to breathe to. I gave way because István wouldn't. For what seemed aeons after the flowers had petered out but was probably only a couple of weeks he took to standing at the gates of CFCF. There he was in the mornings when I arrived and in the evenings when I left. He did not approach me, he made no attempt to communicate, he simply stood sentry, like the guards outside Buckingham Palace, erect, expressionless, immobile. Only his eyes followed me; they follow me still, eyes without colour, two shards of silvered glass, empty as mirrors in an empty room.

'Who the heck is that cigar-store Indian back there?' Marty

asked once, coming into Reception with a group of us. 'Is he KGB or FBI or what?'

'Dunno,' said everyone. 'Dunno,' said I, and heard, above the roar of rush-hour traffic, a cock crow.

Eventually, the giving way. Somebody's birthday at the station, bourbons all round. When the party was over, there István stood, as ever. Propelled by Dutch courage I advanced on him. He watched me come, not stirring. A yard away I opened my mouth to let my anger out and abruptly closed it again. The mirrors weren't empty any more. He held out his arms to me, not caring who saw him, a tall man in a light-weight thin-striped Ivy League seersucker suit holding a briefcase and weeping. For a long moment I stood stock-still in the milky twilight and then, as a woman, any woman, goes to comfort a crying child, I went to him.

Very little in this life endures, least of all reflex tugs of emotion. We shared a kind of happiness for a short while, István because he had me again and I because that made him happy. To be given, at eighteen, the opportunity to fulfil another human being's dream is not to be sneezed at, and when that human being has suffered in ways you cannot fathom and lost every other dream he possessed, well, frankly, Herr Hitler would have had to steel himself to say *Up yours, pal, I'm off*. Or so I argued to myself when the implications of what I'd done began to sink in. When it comes to matters of the heart you cannot be an Indian giver, doling out goodies one minute, grabbing them back the next, particularly if you've reason to believe that what you might get for doing so is death by strangulation. And that fate, or some variation on it, seemed ever more likely as time went on and the spectre of holy matrimony began to dog me, rattling its chains.

I had nothing against matrimony *per se*. Along with every other female extant at the time I took for granted that marriage was the be-all and end-all of a woman's life. But when the issue was marriage to István, any attempt to cheer myself up by contemplating the be-all — good riddance to the Cleft, a lot of bridal fuss and drama, and the licence to shop day in day out that, in the New World, was written into the marriage lines — all these joys were immediately swamped by a vision of the end-all, which I couldn't exactly put a shape to but which tallied with much of what I'd heard about the Somme.

István never did apologize for his pick-axe outing, but then I didn't wish him to. 'Bourgeois' was a term he used a lot, and it struck a deep chord in me; I took it to mean the dreaded 'nice' of my childhood, the Cleft, Mother and all those other grown-ups who talked eternally of upholding the law, going to Church, respecting your elders, telling the truth, doing as you would be done by and then going home and being beastly to their daughters or, in Uncle Gary's and Miss Needham's cases, beastly to other people's daughters or, in David's father's case, dressing up in women's clothes so other people's daughters nearly fell out of trees or, in Robbie's masters' cases, whacking other people's brothers and making them blub. They were fine ones to talk. Out of the whole dreary bunch only the Birds of Paradise weren't bourgeois, they didn't care, they were what they were and of course, now I came to think of it, that could explain why Uncle Harry had said all those things about them. Probably none of it was true and he was just embarrassed by them, as bourgeois people were by the bold and the free. Though Uncle Harry hadn't seemed particularly bourgeois himself, what with ruining people and so on, and Aunt Jen, teetering about in her wigs and dyed furs, surely wasn't.

István surely wasn't either, the pick-axe proved it, that and the fuss Hoagy and the girls made about it, saying he was mad. The truth as I saw it was that István didn't give a brass monkey what the world thought about him and the world couldn't take that, such sweeping indifference was too rich and rare and upset their little tummies so they called him crazy and made petty rules to keep him at bay. I was fond of Erica, Annie and Janet, they were fun to be with and kind and all that, but the chips were down now and they stood revealed as the bourgeois they really were at heart. Good, that was them neatly pigeonholed.

God knows I needed to explain things away, for other things were going from bad to worse. To the great delight of the Dolly crowd, who gathered round us clapping, István announced one evening over bowls of borscht that we were going to be married and asked the Prince to be his best man. The Prince mopped his rheumy eyes and made a long speech in Hungarian with many courtly gestures and bows towards me. Then Dönci Bácsi took the floor and crippled them all with his jokes, also in Hungarian. After that, because they had such exquisite manners, each of them took turns in translating to me every word of the Prince's speech and Donci Bácsi's jokes. I listened hard, nodding appreciatively in all appropriate places, laughing gaily at the jokes, my every reaction eagerly watched so that everybody nodded when I nodded and laughed all over again when I laughed; István too. I rather enjoyed the attention at the time but that night in bed I wept into my pillow, with another pillow over my head so that Erica in the opposite bed wouldn't hear and ask awkward questions.

One evening István, waiting for me where he now parked round the corner from Maupassant Avenue, said we were invited to visit a German he had met and taken to because, he explained, Gunther had been in prison camp too.

'Where?' I asked, remembering the German prisoner I'd come across, who'd worked on a Gloucestershire farm I'd visited as a child and made me a ring out of a threepenny bit.

'In Russia,' István said, 'like me.'

The hows, whys and wherefores of the war weren't at all clear to me, in history at school we'd only got up to the First World War. I pondered for a while and then said, 'But why were you both in Russia?'

'Why? How do you mean?'

'I mean, the Germans were enemies of the Russians but you weren't.'

'Of course I was.' He glanced at me sideways as he drove.

'But the Russians were on our side.' I was mystified.

István said heavily, 'For Hungarians, no one was on our side.'

'Then why choose the Germans to be on the side of? Nazis?'

'Choose?' he said and bumped the car to a jolting stop on the curb. 'Choose? We had no choice. The Germans marched in, they ordered us to the Russian front. They knew Hungarians hated the Russians, always that has been so.'

I was stunned. How could anyone hate the brave Russians? Or fight for the Germans? Mother had seen a film of Jews gassed by the Nazis, she'd said it was everyone's duty to see and I'd wanted to but she said no and the Cleft wouldn't go. When she came back I heard her being sick in the lav, the Cleft said it's something she's eaten. It was obvious to me he didn't like the Jews, he spoke of them as if they were quite different from us, a bit as István did of Dönci Bácsi. Plucking up my courage – István was staring straight ahead but I didn't much care for the hawkish strut of his profile – I said, 'So. If my brother'd been older he'd have been fighting you in the war. Him and the Russians against you and the Nazis.'

István turned and his eyes held that empty menacing look. I shrank back.

'The Russians killed my brother and put me three years in prison camp,' he said and placed a thumb and one finger quite delicately on each side of my throat. 'Please,' and he was smiling now as he pressed, 'we will not speak of this any more.'

That wasn't the last of our quarrels about the wretched war, not by any means. In little flashes here and there I saw István in German uniform, those helmets hooded like turtle-shells instead of the cheery tin plates our Tommies wore or, worse, in a Nazi peaked hat and jodhpurs, with swastikas on his arm. Who could tell, being on the German side, how many of our brave boys he'd killed? Maybe he'd even gassed the odd Jew. How could you be sure of anything about someone who was wrong about Dunkirk?

For he was; very wrong. We'd just been to the movies to see *Casablanca* and he'd started lecturing me about the war, he was always lecturing about things, but that was men for you, they all did it, you just had to pretend to listen while you thought your own thoughts. Then he mentioned Dunkirk as if it were some battle we'd lost and that I couldn't let pass. 'Shows how much you know. Dunkirk? The little ships, the Armada and all? It was a terrific victory. I remember. They told us so at school, gave us flags to wave.'

'No,' said István flatly, 'it was a terrific defeat.'

Flash! and he was marching in his turtle's hood across the Siegfried Line, the one we English hung our washing out on. Flash! and there he was in that Belsen place poking Jews into what looked like showers and weren't. Smiling.

'It wasn't, it wasn't, we won, you Nazi,' I shrilled, 'and I won't see you any more.' I didn't get far. He came up behind me as I skittered off and caught hold of one little finger, which he bent upon itself until the sidewalk blurred before my eyes and I was forced to halt.

'I hate you,' I whimpered.

'I love you,' he replied.

Not long after, I kissed another man as István and I left a party, one kiss on one cheek, one on the other, thank you, lovely evening, see you soon, bye-bye.

In the car home, a silence that choked like smouldering rubber. Then, as we drew up, 'You like that Franz don't you?'

I knew it. 'Franz? He's OK.'

'You dance with him too much. Cheek to cheek.'

'Don't be silly.' How many times had I said that already? Hundreds of times. Don't be silly, silly, silly. Please don't.

He said, 'I do not want you to kiss other men.'

I couldn't help it. That yellow mask, the two glittering mirrors fixed on me, the challenge. Dangerous laughter welled up. 'I'll kiss other men if I like.'

He took his cigarette out of its holder but this time he didn't stub it out on him, he stubbed it out on me. Then, while I clutched my hand, too shocked to make a sound, he rammed his foot against the accelerator, took off and drove so fast and furiously through the sleeping city streets that my snivels turned to shrieks.

'I hate you!' I screamed.

'I love you!' he yelled.

Cute little lap-dogs, pekinese, poodles, jumped from their cosy baskets to yap madly in our wake.

The wedding date drew closer. It was now a month away. The church was booked, the priest too, the friends invited, his, not mine. Mine still knew nothing.

'I have to go home,' I said in a panic. 'I must tell my parents.' Deviously I added, 'I need their blessing.'

'Of course,' István said, fondling me. 'I understand.'

Perhaps he caught my sigh of relief. At any rate the hand that was stroking my neck rose to grip my chin, directing my gaze to his. 'You go, by all means. I wish I could come with you . . .'

I already knew he couldn't. Persons who had applied for Canadian citizenship were not permitted to leave the country until the citizenship came through.

'. . . but do not think, my darling, that you will not return to me.' He bent so close I could feel his whispering breath. 'Because if you do not, I will come after you. Wherever you go in the world I will come after you. You will never escape from me. Never.'

Such melodrama. I giggled. He smiled. 'You see, I love you more than all other men together shall ever love you. I can never let you go. Do you see?'

The Cleft, blinking furiously, shouted in my ear, 'There's no man in the world who's going to put up with you, gurl.'

For the first time, I wished he was right.

A month's stay in Canada had stealthily become a year, and though I left Montreal assuring all concerned that I'd be back in three weeks I was not so sure myself. Options had to be kept open. The fates might conspire to save me from the altar in unforeseen ways. Fiancés could be struck by lightning, couldn't they? Fall under buses or in love with someone else? You never knew.

Meanwhile England would serve as a temporary sanctuary, an István-free zone wherein, the moment my feet touched ground, he might somehow cease to exist, wiped off the map in some bloodless coup by the everyday familiarities of life. Excess did not flourish in England and he was excess – maybe the very climate would shrivel him, as a hot-air balloon shrivels, exposed to fog and rain.

It was raining as we sighted land. The white cliffs of Dover had no bluebirds over and looked as if they could do with a good scrub. The fields were minute squares on the sort of boring board game aunts made you play. Already I missed the great green sweeps of Canada's forests that took hours and hours to fly over. You never saw them if you lived in the city but you breathed deeper and took bigger strides because they were there. Here everything was jumbled together like the bolts and nails at the bottom of a tool box, no room to move.

Still, that might be all to the good when it came to exorcizing István, and my spirits lifted further when the wheezy Glaswegian sitting next to me, hearing where my father came from, asserted with heartfelt authority that och aye, Edinburgh folk were full of empty pride. Perhaps the Cleft would go the same way as István, shrivelling from the Caliban of my memory to the runtish dimensions of any old man. And Mother might go the other way, expanding instead of contracting, a woman writ larger and altogether grander than memory described: tearless, shrewd and a refuge in trouble. Luck, be a lady to me.

Mother wasn't tearless when we met but then neither was I, tears at reunions didn't count. The Cleft's pat on my cheek was more like a slap, but he seemed to mean well. Once we'd arrived home and he'd brought in my suitcases he said, 'Well, now, what have you been up to in the Colonies, young lady?' and before I could answer disappeared upstairs for several hours. Mother and I settled together in the sitting room and I readied myself to tell all, but after she'd mentioned that my brother had been given the next weekend off from Sandhurst to see me and asked a few desultory questions about my journey, about Montreal, her eyes almost immediately filled and she embarked on her own true confessions which began as they always had with a variation on the Lord's Prayer; not Our Father but Yours.

'Your father,' she moaned, applying the prettiest lace hanky to the lids of her eyes, which were fast swelling into the puffy pink domes of my earliest memories, 'your father has become quite impossible to live with. He won't talk to me, he hardly talks at all. He just sits in that chair every evening and reads. Never a word. I have been so lonely you can't imagine. What am I to do?'

I gazed at her, bemused. I leant across and patted the hands that squirmed in her lap. The veins stood out blue against the ivory loosening skin, the diamond ring slipped sideways with a sad little wink. How worn and thin her wedding ring was, how worn and thin was she. The old pity, the old impatience burned up into my throat like dyspepsia.

'I know I shouldn't tell you. You're my daughter. But you're grown up now and who else can I tell?'

Wildly I looked around for some distraction. The room was as tidy as a tomb and as still, velvet chairs and sofas in their accustomed places, the Turkey carpet creaseless before the fireplace, plumped-up cushions everywhere, crystal vases of roses from the garden on polished oak tables, scattered photographs in polished silver frames and nothing more promising to be seen through the velvet-rimmed bay window than the two old lilacs and the ancient chestnut tree. Silently I prayed for the telephone to ring, the Cleft to appear, a visitor to call, an escaped convict to plunge through the window or, lacking these, a plane to crash miraculously on the roof.

Mother edged closer and clasped her soft hands on mine. Tears made shiny snail tracks down her powdered cheeks. 'Your father, you see, he hasn't wanted me for ages, not really but now, well, not at all. He won't discuss it, he just says it's over, that part of our lives. You understand what I mean?'

I nodded, unable to meet her eyes.

'It isn't normal. I know it's not. But he insists it is, perfectly normal at our age, he says, and he won't go to a doctor, absolutely refuses.' Her voice rose thinly. 'What does he mean, *at our age*? I'm forty-five and I've been without the physical side of life for ten years and now with you children gone there's no one to talk to, even. I can't bear it. I can't, I can't,' and to my unutterable dismay her head drooped to my lap and a deluge of sobs broke over my knees.

I wish memory could report from me a flooding of compassion, tenderness, wise words, love. Certainly I stroked her hair, dabbed a bit at her wet cheeks, muttered *oh dear* and *I'm sorry*, as one might if one stepped on a stranger in a bus, but I felt as if I'd swallowed a bottle of Javex that was scouring my insides and shrinking every organ. Then my toes jerked up into such spasms of cramp that I was forced to cast poor Mother aside in order to stamp the rebellious feet back into shape. All in all, my response was woefully inadequate and Mother, kneeling where I'd discarded her, following my contortions with doleful eyes, must have heard then the knell of her last hopes for a daughter, confidante and bosom friend. Meanwhile a bell tolled in my ears too: England. Mother. Misery. Go back to Canada. Go.

Mother was right about one thing, though, the Cleft had clammed up. No more outbursts of manic glee, no more polly-wolly-doodles on the guitar. Indeed he appeared to be as vowed to silence as a Trappist monk, and whenever he was addressed – 'pass the butter could you,' 'what time is it?' – he blinked so hard and looked so alarmed that it seemed only decent to desist. He stalked off to the station in the mornings and stalked back in the evenings and perhaps because, unlike Mother, he confided in no one, the solitariness that cloaked him was palpable. I almost began to feel sorry for him, there were moments when hesitant tendrils emerged, but he hacked them back with all his old skill – *Are you sickening for something, gurl? You look like something the cat brought in. You know nothing at all, you great blatherskate, so cut the cackle*, or (particularly effective), *Only a man who thinks he's a teapot would take on a featherbrain like you.*

It was one such remark that braced me to tell them about István and tell them, moreover, as if all were decided. 'And I'm going to marry him,' I ended defiantly, which was not in the least the prayerful whine I'd intended: *stop me. I don't want to. I'm scared*.

Mother twittered for a moment, strung between excitement and sal volatile but, by God, the Cleft rose to the occasion. In a jiffy his cloak of silence was off. 'A Hungarian?' he bellowed. 'A Count? What the dickens do you think you're up to, gurl? Do you not know that Counts are ten a penny in the Balkans, if he's a Count at all, which I very much doubt. You've picked a con man and he's turned your daffy head. Typical, typical. Well, it's not on, take my word for it. No comic-opera Ruritanian Count is going to marry a daughter of mine and that's flat. For the Lord's sake, the Hungarians were in the pockets of the Huns in the war.'

'Oh, the war,' Mother sighed.

'The war?' I squawked. 'It wasn't István's fault. Hungarians didn't have any choice. They had to fight for the Germans. He lost his whole family. He was in prison camp. You're so *unfair*.'

The Cleft did one of his cut-it-out gestures. Then he reached over and picked up the photo I had of István, holding it at arms' length as if it bore the plague.

'What's this when it's at home?' he said.

'It's István when he was in the Hussars.'

'He looks very handsome,' Mother said, taking a peek.

'He looks like the Grand Panjandrum,' said the Cleft. Everything on him but the kitchen sink. Plumes, gold braid, the whole Transylvanian olla podrida. Done up like a blithering Christmas tree. I suppose he's seduced you already, has he? Come on, out with it.'

'Oh now,' breathed Mother, riveted.

The secret relief that had surged up in me at the Cleft's first clamour evaporated on the spot, turned into steam by scalding shame. 'He didn't! I'm not! Oh you're awful,' I screeched and yet more shamefully burst into tears and fled the room.

There were other rows, some short and sharp, some long and tiring, but then they died down. With a certain bitterness I ascribed this calming of the waters to my brother's approaching visit. It had always been thus. Robbie must be spared. Robbie must be shown the best there was and the worse there was the more they strained to cover up. But then, so did I, and it was worth it to sense the lift in the atmosphere as he trundled in, dumping his kitbag and hugging me, full of good cheer and stories of Sandhurst doings. There was no one else I could tell the truth to so I told him, only snipping off the cigarette-burning and the pick-axe episodes, too embarrassed to pass them on. Robbie responded by telling me a long story involving someone called a sarntmajor, some jewels and King Hussein, who was currently with him at Sandhurst, presumably recalled because Hussein too was a foreigner with a title. Then he frowned, scratched his shorn head and swore he'd plaster the blighter to the wall, Count or no Count, if he did anything to hurt me. The moment he said that I countered with István's various attributes and, in the end, puzzled, he shrugged, said, 'OK if you say so, what do you want then, what do you want?' To which there came no answer.

When Robbie had gone and real life had begun again, Mother indicated that she was on my side, talking of wedding dresses and bridesmaids, saying, 'I'm sure István's awfully nice, I long to meet him,' and, 'Take no notice of your father,' but all I thought were mean things like *István? Nice? At least he's not that*.

The Cleft, after subjecting me to barrages of questions and greeting my answers with much curlings of lip, laid down a condition. 'I want a reference,' he announced. 'No, there's no point arguing. I require a proper reference from someone in authority who knows this so-called Count. A professional man, d'you understand? I want assurances as to his character, prospects and background – no fooling about. And unless I'm fully satisfied with the results you can forget all this tosh about a wedding or going back to Canada, is that clear enough for you?'

The bit between my teeth (*I'll show him, the beast*), I relayed the request on to István. Rather heart-sinkingly, he said he'd comply. A week passed and my time for leaving or otherwise was drawing near. Then one morning a crackly envelope arrived, addressed to the Cleft. He opened it as Mother and I watched. The impression lingers that the letter inside was engraved on a roll of parchment hung with red seals. At any rate it came from the Empress of the Austro-Hungarian Empire, Queen Zita of the Habsburgs, at that time residing in Texas, and whatever it said, which I can't now remember, calmed the Cleft down no end. He didn't let on that it pleased him, no, but he hummed 'Ten Green Bottles' for quite a while after and no more was said about Panjandrums.

Mother said, 'So I'm going to have a Countess for a daughter,' and told me again how she'd saved the life of her schoolfriend Countess Mountbatten, 'Edwina Ashley as she was then', by nursing her during the great flu epidemic when the mistresses were dropping like flies.

As she chatted I slumped on the sofa and sank into a daydream which involved catching the Great Flu and going into a coma that would last so long that when I emerged from it (like Rip van Winkle, no, like Sleeping Beauty) István would be too old to marry anyone or, alternatively, dead for how else was I going to evade him while remaining both guiltless and all in one piece?

Now that this dismaying parental accord had broken out, I

realized how much I'd relied on both of them, but especially the Cleft, to thwart my marriage plans, brutally reject István as a son-in-law and, if necessary, ruthlessly forbid me to go back to Canada. Elizabeth Barrett Browning's father would have. Why didn't mine? Obviously he couldn't force me to obey him, but that had never before stopped the Cleft from laying down the law. Look at all the storms he'd raised about truly nice, well-behaved boyfriends, Roger, Richard, Rodney et cetera. Look what a fuss he'd made about poor Jimmy, nicest of the nice. Yet when István came along, a fire-breathing dragon compared to any of them, what happened? Did my wicked father buckle on his armour, get on his high horse and fight the bad fight? Not on your nelly. He let off a couple of damp squibs and collapsed. Coward. Turncoat. Snob. Damn and blast Queen Zita. The truth was, my parents didn't love me, never had, never would, and now they were selling me off for a mess of potage, whatever that might be.

Mother said, '. . . pity the wedding can't be here but I see that's not possible if István can't come over, so I'll come ahead of time and arrange things, caterers and so on and . . .'

I left her in mid-sentence, ran out into the garden, flung myself down under the old chestnut tree and threw a fit of hysterics that surpassed Château du Lac's finest.

Twelve

Reader, I married him – or so I was informed. Since the service was conducted entirely in Hungarian with some Latin thrown in, at what exact point I changed from spinster to wife was hard for me to ascertain. For ages afterwards I entertained a vague hope that the priest, who, being Catholic, waved his hands about a lot in various directions, had married me to another man: Dönci Bácsi, perhaps, who gave me away, or István's best man, the old Prince. One day – or so went my fantasy – that same priest, suitably decked out in sackcloth and ashes, would knock on my door, confess to making a hideous mistake, proclaim the marriage invalid there and then and set me free to scamper off.

The news that I was actually going to wed you-know-who had floored my flatmates, but after a few exclamations concerning my powers of deception – 'You sly-boots,' said Janet quite nicely; 'You whacking great liar,' said Annie, not so nicely – they recovered well. After all, marriage meant me moving out of Maupassant Avenue, not István moving in. Erica, however, was made of sterner stuff, and when I asked her to be my bridesmaid, refused point blank.

'I can't,' she said, going very red. 'I'm too fond of you and . . .'

'You think it'll be a disaster,' I finished for her.

'I do.'

'I understand. So do I,' I said and we put our cheeks together and mingled tears quite as if we were holding a mutual grieve-in for some unfortunate third party. She had a further ordeal in store, for I spent the whole night before the wedding wildly weeping while she sat beside me holding my hand and saying over and over again, 'You don't *have* to go through with it, you can just not turn up, you don't *have* to . . .'

To which I replied, tossing myself about in a hurricane of sobs, 'I do I can't he'd kill me he'd kill himself Jimmy did he'd come after me I'd never get away . . .' and so on and on until nearly dawn, when weary Erica placed damp camomile teabags on our ravaged eyes and side by side, laid out like two brass rubbings on my sopping pillows, we fell finally asleep.

Later that inauspicious day, kneeling with István at the altar of Our Lady of Hungary in a white grosgrain dress, with my feathered head drooping like a shot bird, I thought to myself as the Dolly-packed congregation sang in foreign tongues, 'Oh Lord, I am now making the worst mistake I shall ever make in my life.'

And so, indeed, it proved.

Luckily, however, even the curate's egg was good in patches and simply being young and greedy for life was to see me over quite a lot of the bad parts. Understandably Mother wired that she was deeply hurt to be excluded from the wedding but calmed herself somewhat when I wired back to say we were on our way over on the first leg of our honeymoon – István having pulled mysterious strings to obtain compassionate leave for the purpose. We stayed a week with my parents, during which time, to István's frustration, I refused all overtures from him. The thought of the Cleft lying sternly in bed a mere two walls away was appalling to me. Why, at any moment he might charge in shouting dreadful things *re* dirty laundry. There was also Mother to consider. It seemed indecent, unfair, to do under her roof what she couldn't, particularly since she so minded its absence and I didn't in the least.

'No,' I hissed under the blankets, wriggling away from my new husband's touch. 'I can't. Not while we're in this house.'

'Thanks heaven we do not have to live here then,' he growled feelingly, 'or my family name would die out.'

I didn't much care for the implications of that remark but put it from me hastily. Enough that I had gained a brief respite from marital chores; a good patch.

The Cleft was excessively polite to István and István was excessively polite back. They circled warily around one another saying *Is that so?* and *How interesting,* and *What d'you think of this vintage, eh?* Every now and then the rapport cracked a bit, as when István launched into the epic saga of some great-uncle of his who had galloped on horseback up a flight of marble steps and into a Viennese opera house to challenge a rival in love, or how another ancestor had managed to cuckold the Emperor Franz Josef himself while also keeping three famous actresses well-supplied with his bastards.

'Ah-er-hum, ha-achoo,' went the Cleft on each occasion trumpeting into his handkerchief with such convulsions of shoulders and knees as to send Mother scooting for water. She, on the other hand, had gone all soft and moony since we'd arrived, wearing her laciest dresses with a lot of Chanel and straining to catch István's every word between the Cleft's eruptions.

'I think Mother's rather fallen for you,' I teased when we were alone.

'Why not?' he answered. 'She is a pretty woman and I am a strong man. We could make beautiful music together.'

A short Cleft-like spasm seized me. Recovering, I said indignantly, 'She's forty-five. And my mother.'

He rolled his eyes and shrugged in a peculiarly irritating European manner.

I reminded myself that we had only one more day to go.

We flew to Zurich, where István had arranged for us to stay with some relation of his – 'Joachim is his name, Joachy. You will like him, he drives like a madman,' was all the information he had vouchsafed. I envisaged a Teutonic Hooray Henry boring on about how grand things used to be before he was reduced to driving buses or waiting on tables and was taken aback to be met by a uniformed chauffeur who ushered us into a huge black Mercedes and spread a fur rug over our knees before conducting us smoothly over the border into Germany. I was even more flummoxed when the Merc eventually turned in through high iron gates liberally punctuated by the shapes of crowns and up a long drive towards a building so colossal and multi-winged it made Buckingham Palace look an outhouse.

'You didn't tell me this Joachim worked in an hotel,' I said nervously. 'If he's putting us up here I haven't got the proper clothes.'

The car drew up, the chauffeur hooted and leapt out. Two liveried footmen stalked down the steps towards us, causing me to wince at the shame of our decrepit luggage being handled by such very upper servants. In the great marble hall a sudden throng poured in through the various arches – just as the Birds of Paradise had in Turkey, I thought – to embrace and exclaim over István in a polyglot babble while the antlered heads of innumerable beasts looked stuffily down their dead noses at me.

Then István turned and came towards me accompanied by a chunky fair-haired man and an elderly couple. Introductions were effected: Uncle, Aunt and mad driver Joachy – Prince, Princess and Prince again. The Princess and Joachy warmly kissed the air round my ears, the older Prince bowed over my hand and I watched it briefly vanish beneath a Niagara Falls of a moustache. Then he said in excellent English, 'Welcome, my child, to Donaueschingen.'

It quickly became clear that in such elevated circles there was no quarter given to honeymooners. Probably, I thought, honeymoons were considered bourgeois or even vulgar, on a par with Hollywood songs about moon, June and spoon, and I didn't have to ponder long before I wholeheartedly adopted this point of view. Nevertheless I was rather rocked when István was led in one direction down a long corridor and I in quite another. My bedroom when I finally reached it – was it in the same country as István's? Had I crossed into Switzerland again? – was as big as the whole of Maupassant Avenue, with a bed in the modest shape of a boat but the size of an ocean liner. Then, to my horror, the maid shadowing me made a lunge for my suitcase. Obviously she meant to unpack it, and this I could not permit. What? My bargain-basement clothes, my safety-pinned slips and off-colour undies exposed to the gaze of a maid accustomed to far better things? With desperate gestures I drove her off and sat quite at sea on the boat bed, surrounded by so many tables bearing so many Fabergé eggs I felt like the first chick hatched in an incubator.

We stayed a month at Donaueschingen and in that time I managed to maintain myself in a constant high lather of querulousness which I let froth all over István on the few occasions we were alone. There were no obvious reasons for this state of mind. Nobody could have been kinder to me than Joachy and his parents. Nothing could have been cosier than life at Donaueschingen. Despite its scale and opulence – there were poor relations ensconced there whom no one had seen in public for years, there were pure silver basins in every room, there were paintings on the walls that would have turned the National Gallery green – we gathered every evening as any family might to play parlour games: Monopoly, Old Maid, Happy Families, Canasta, Confidences, charades, even Snap. In the daytime we went for walks and the old Prince pointed out the spring in the grounds whose waters, trickling up from the earth at my feet, flowed on to become the white and then the blue Danube. We drove into the Black Forest, István and I fearfully fast in Joachy's winged Porsche, the others more sedately in a fleet of Volkswagens, and the men shot things while I wandered about under the trees thinking of the Brothers Grimm. We gathered in one of the family's dozens of hunting lodges and ate the first slaughtered pig of the season with gold forks and knives, getting up and jumping round the table now and then to tamp down the food and make room for more, after which the men went hunting again and I retreated to a bush and was sick. Visitors came and went: I remember distinctly only two. One was Joachy's sister who, like me, was newly married and, unlike me, had been escorted to and from her nuptials by the whole village dressed up in the family's uniforms, dusted off from the remnants of what was once their private army. The home movie of the wedding showed them lining the roads and cheering the bridal carriage, a proper gilded royal carriage, more ardently than Londoners had cheered the Queen and Prince Philip. The other visitor was a stiff and scary Baron who glared out at me through a web of duelling scars, clicked his heels at every turn and gave me a guttural lecture on the glories of the Fatherland. Clearly he had no idea the Germans had lost the war and, eyeing his bullet-head and glinting monocle, I decided not to be the first to let him know.

'I am so sorry,' the Princess said to me at the end of the first week. 'Please forgive us but tomorrow is Sunday and the servants are off. Zo. Only cold food, I am afraid. Is that *convenable*?'

On Sunday, there were only servants behind every other chair and only mounds of caviar, smoked salmon and baskets of curious knobbly things to eat.

'Truffles,' explained István at my elbow. 'A kind of fungus and . . .' he kissed his fingers '. . . ambrosia. You know, here in Donau, if you would like a truffle even in the midst of the night you have only to pick up the telephone by your bed and call the Obertruffeljaeger, the head of truffle hunters. He will bring them to you.'

It was when he said things of this sort that I tended to froth over. I couldn't stand him teaching me about what I didn't know and since I knew very little this was hard to avoid. Indeed, at the time I couldn't stand much at all. The awe I felt for István's ability to switch from English to German, French, Italian or Hungarian I strove to dilute with a measure of contempt – was there not something suspect, ingratiating even, about knowing so many languages? His every gesture altered as he spoke each one, too. Wasn't that reason enough to feel uneasy?

My judgement on such matters was made the more erratic by a scratchy conviction that my clothes weren't right, that my hair was a mess, that I was too thin or possibly too fat, that I talked too much or not enough: i.e., everything about me was subtly awry. I stared despairingly into every available mirror, tweaking and grimacing at myself, yet whenever István assured me I looked fine, lovely, I turned on him, enraged. But what most infuriated me was the way he spread Donaueschingen's luxuries before me, truffles and the like, as if they were his gift to me, as if he were Sir Walter Raleigh spreading his cloak before the Queen to save her little feet from the mud. He did it to wrest my independence from me, make me grateful for what he could bestow, or so I was convinced. Therefore, more often than not, I churlishly kicked the cloak aside and aimed an accusing finger at the mud beneath.

'Just *think* of how the villagers live,' I protested as we sat one morning by the Danube spring, István attempting to draw my attention to the beauties of the tended park around us, me distractedly twiddling my new wedding ring. 'Not much better than *cattle*, most of them, and they have to pump all their water from a well. It's *awful*, a few people having everything and the rest nothing.'

'We will have everything one day, I promise,' István said.

'I'm not *talking* about us,' I snapped. Why did he wilfully misunderstand? 'I'm talking about the poor *villagers*.'

'It has always been so,' István soothed. 'They are peasants and happy in their way and they love the Prince, all the family, just as our peasants loved us at home.'

Aggravation fizzed over. I knew a good deal less about peasants than István, peasants being thin on the ground in the Home Counties, but I felt strongly that I wouldn't have been one bit happy sitting outside Donaueschingen's gates looking in.

'Well, they *shouldn't* love them,' I pronounced crossly.

István looked bewildered. 'But they are so lovable, the Prince and Princess. Do you not find so?'

I gave a great exasperated sigh. 'That's not. At all. The point.'

But what the point was escaped me. All I knew was that a most combustible mix was brewing in my guts, a hateful unrest that made me hateful. Vivid images of the birds' eggs at the Old Hall, the butterflies, Mr Woodhouse's china houses rose up. So beautiful yet so cruelly out of reach of those who ought by rights to own them because they adored them and understood in the marrow of each and every bone how rare

and exquisite they were. Instead they belonged to unapprecia-
tive others by some accident of fortune, inheritance or the
grossly vulgar fact of simply having more in the bank than me.
I wanted to weep at the injustice of it all.

István tried to kiss me but I fended him off. He got up and
said quite kindly, 'Oh, my cold little English wife,' yet he
looked crestfallen, my moods were having their effect. I
wondered why he loved me and could only think the less of
him for it.

The month was almost at an end the day we set off to visit
another of the family castles in a neighbouring province. We
were a crowd as usual – Joachy, István and me plus a couple of
Hohenzollern Princes, a skinny Austrian Count, an Italian
Marquesa and a small Baroness of uncertain provenance. It felt
quite natural now, bowling around the countryside with this
pack of Court cards.

'I have some business there,' Joachy had said beforehand,
'and I would welcome your company. If, that is, you would
not be too bored and have no better thing to do.' The family
prefaced all suggestions for outings thus; as if they were tearing
us away from unimaginable pleasures – an interminable round
of nights at the opera, fancy-dress balls, skiing in the Alps,
Malibu beach parties, Himalayan expeditions on elephant-
back.

'I think we would not be too bored,' I answered graciously.

The castle was the smallest of four belonging to the family,
this one not broad and massive in a sweep of parkland like
Donau, but an eyrie on a mountain peak, a conglomerate of
towers capped with delicate wimpoles and corbelled turrets
whiskery with the nests of storks. I caught a first glimpse of it,
shining against a wide sky, as we streaked from an overhung
forest ravine into the white glare of a winter sun and jolted

back into first gear to climb the steep helter-skelter that spiralled up the mountainside.

'*Nein, das ist nicht,*' István said to Joachy, 'my *dummkopf* wife cries always when something pleases her.' He squeezed me fondly and my eyes dried.

Joachy disappeared when we arrived and while he was gone I left István with the pack nursing schnapps by a roaring fire to wander from room to raftered room, clamber up winding turret stairs and pace the battlements above, the wind whistling through my hair and all Germany below. I gazed down at the splendid panorama, gripping the stone balustrade against the gusts, and happiness, not a frequent visitor recently, swooped down, pierced me with talons and swung me high in the sky.

At tea – heaps of newly baked scones, sandwiches and plates of sticky cakes served by lines of maids – I asked Joachy who lived here.

'No one,' he answered. 'Well, the servants of course. My father used to come in the summer sometimes, for a week or three, but that is all. My mother finds it inconvenient now she is older, my brothers live far away and my sister, ah, my sister, she is always occupied.'

Fancy-dress balls, expeditions to India and such, I supposed.

That evening, back at Donaueschingen in my room before dinner I expressed amazement to István. 'It's hard to believe. That whole wonderful place, all those servants, kept there just in case once a year somebody thinks oh, I've got a spare moment, why don't I drop by for tea.'

'Come over here,' István said. He was lying on my bed watching me wriggle out of my jeans.

'No, but really . . .' I kicked the jeans aside, too worked up for blandishments, '. . . it's such a waste, it's criminal. Couldn't you get a job managing it for them? We could live there then.' Coaxingly I added, 'And you could shoot things all day long.'

'You wouldn't like it.'

'I would.'

'In two minutes you'd be bored.'

'I wouldn't. I never get bored. Why does everyone keep saying that?'

'Joachy maybe will use it when he marries,' István said to distract me and, seeing that this had no effect, added, 'The British, you know, were there in the war.'

'British soldiers?'

'Not soldiers. Officers. As also here.'

'Here? At Donaueschingen? Where did the family go?'

He arched his eyebrows. 'It is a big place, no? I think there is room for all. The Princess was happy with them, she said to me so. Ah, the English, she said, they were gentlemen, they took care and damaged nothing, they were the best of guests.'

I sat down abruptly at the foot of the bed, overcome by this new view of the war. Not blitzes and torture in cellars, not blood, guts and chaos but guests and hosts, German ladies and British Majors dancing sedate minuets. Conversing politely over crystal epergnes, sipping Liebfraumilch out of silver goblets, playing Old Maid and charades together while the chimneys of Belsen smoked industriously a few miles away.

Lowering my voice I said, 'I'd have thought they'd bomb Donau, turf the family out, send them all to prison camp or shoot them or something. They were the enemy, weren't they? Isn't that what armies are supposed to do in wars?' It wasn't, I realized, in the best of taste for a guest to be advocating mayhem for her hosts under their very roof but there was a principle at stake here.

'That is what the Russians did,' István said. 'Used our paintings for targets, bang bang bang. Threw all our dishes at the wall, for fun. Their arms were full to the elbow with stolen watches. They are barbarians. The British are not.'

I had given up defending the brave Russians lately, having temporarily run out of ammunition. 'And Joachy? Where was he?'

'In the army, of course. Also his brothers, the two you have not met.'

'What army?' I had to get to the bottom of this though I felt like the one maggot in an otherwise perfect apple.

'Ah, that is interesting. Joachy, he was in the German army, his brother Fritz in the Italian and the third, I forget his name, with the British, in Yugoslavia. The family have lands, you see, in all those countries so . . .'

'Honestly,' I interrupted, swelling up with indignation, 'you aristocrats don't give a fig which side you're on as long as you and your castles survive. You're like those hydra thingamijigs. Cut off one head and up pops another. After all, why bother to fight for any particular land when you've got land simply everywhere?' I put on a mincing voice and flapped my hands. 'War's frightfully bourgeois, doncha know. Let the peasants fight for their one pathetic acre, they enjoy it, what what? As long as they're back in time to get my tea.'

With a sudden jump of the heart I realized that István was looming behind me. I swivelled. His face, inches from mine, was drained of colour, his lips stretched and white. He laced the fingers of one hand in my hair and yanked my head sideways. Then he swung his arm back and brought it whacking at my face. The fist stopped short a fraction of a second before it hit my chin. Shock galvanized me. I wrenched myself from his grip and then I saw how he trembled.

'I fought,' he said, and his voice shook too, 'and my country, my family, *my* home did not survive.'

My anger fell away, pulverized by remorse. Why did I have to spoil everything? 'Oh, I'm sorry. So stupid I am, I didn't mean . . .'

My arms went around him and I rocked him like a baby. He leant for my lips.

There came a tap at the door and the maid entered, fresh towels over her arm, saying something in German.

'She is going to run your bath,' István translated, still holding me.

The maid, always the same one, was big, raw-boned and dour, with greyish-blonde hair nipped into plaits that vanished up under her cap. Flash! Irma Grese at Belsen. Flash! Back again in maid's uniform.

'I hate that,' I said uncomfortably, 'I can perfectly well run my own bath. You'd think I was a cripple.'

The maid, giving a stiff little bob, disappeared into the bathroom. István walked me over to the bed and pulled me down beside him. I struggled to hoist myself upright again. 'The maid,' I said, flustered. 'We can't while she's there. There are always maids creeping around here. How anyone ever makes love I don't know.'

'*Devant les servants*,' said István.

Two days before we were due to depart the old Prince heaved a sigh and said how much they would all like us to stay on for Christmas. 'But I understand if you must go. You are young and it is boring for you in the country with us. You want to dance, you want to have fun. But still, if you would like . . .?'

'Would you like?' asked István when he had gone.

'Like? Like?' I said testily. 'I would like to stay here for ever, but we can't.'

'But for Christmas?'

'No. A month is enough. He's only being polite, don't you see? We can't keep sponging, being the poor relations.'

István, stretched out by the fire with his feet balanced on the sleek grey back of a sleeping Weimaraner – there were almost as many dogs at Donau as there were servants – said, 'Please. Do not be so bourgeois. There is no question of sponging. They know I would offer them the same hospitality if they were in my castle.'

Stung by the dreaded B-word I retorted, 'Well, you haven't got a castle any more so that's easy to say.'

The floor shook as István swung his feet off the dog and banged them on the floor. 'You do not believe me? I give you my word. That is the way it would be. Enough now.'

I turned away from István, cupped my hands and blew a muted raspberry at an oil painting of an old boy sporting a Kaiser-type helmet. 'You know what I'd have done with you,' I mouthed at him. 'Turned you upside-down to spike up rubbish in Hyde Park.'

No sound but the crackle of burning logs and the odd whitter from the dog, twitching and dreaming.

OK, I'd have to use the only generally acceptable reason for leaving Donau. 'István,' I whined, 'I'm *bored*.'

We left that branch of the family in their German schloss to move on to a palazzo outside Venice. Our host, once a poor relation like us and still slightly hunted-looking, as if the time he had spent in the wilderness had left its scars, had finally managed – by using his title as bait I guessed – to trap an American heiress and was now being kept in the manner to which he had previously had little hope of becoming accustomed. I never found out what he did, if anything, but he was only with us for the two days before Christmas, after which, with many unnecessary apologies – we'd descended quite unheralded upon him – he took himself off somewhere and his wife was not seen throughout our stay. In the whole palazzo, gloomy as I remember it, there only remained a leftover child and his tutor to celebrate Christmas together.

We passed the feast day in another palazzo, one of those crumbling edifices that rear up from the lapping waters of Venetian canals and provide a good deal more pleasure to tourists than they do to those who inhabit them: in this case a Colonna Prince whose family history began, I gathered from István, a couple of days after Romulus and Remus had weaned themselves from the wolf. As far as this poor Prince was concerned things appeared to have spiralled downhill ever since. Cold is what I recall of that day. Dank, marrow-chilling, blood-clotting cold. At lunchtime a gong resounded throughout, and through me, chattering my teeth a fraction harder than they were already. A manservant appeared, appropriately clad in penguin gear, and ushered us through Arctic reaches into a vast stone igloo which contained not a stick of furniture save a refectory table and some chairs. I retain the impression that no one said a word throughout the meal, though this cannot have been so. Probably they spoke Italian and it didn't register on me. The only sounds I do remember were the manservant's shoes tap-tapping on the flagstone floor as he fetched and delivered dishes and the drip-drip-drip of water trickling down the moss-streaked walls. I also observed the water at the end of the manservant's nose drip-drip-dripping into the tureen of soup as he ladled it out.

'This is a lovely way to spend a Christmas,' I sang to myself in the cavernous loo, and meant it.

There must have been many impoverished old aristos lurking behind those Canaletto façades, for our host's daughter Nica had been married in Venice a few weeks before and her father described how half the guests – his half presumably – appeared with mould on their top hats and tails, moss-streaked like their walls. I pictured the scene as a kind of matrimonial All Soul's Night, the tombs creaking open and the skeletons in mildewed wisps of tattered shrouds climbing out to dance till dawn, clickety-clack, round the bride. Lucky Princess Nica, to have a wedding so very different from the usual kind. How I wished I'd been there. As it was, all that was left to show for the occasion were the wedding presents – she too was currently honeymooning.

'Would you like to see them?' asked her little leftover brother, Claudio. 'Come, come, you must,' and he tugged and chivvied me up endless flights of stairs to where the presents, canteens and services of silver and gold, mounds of fine linen, hundreds of vases, bowls, candlesticks and figurines, stacks of cut glass and heaps of porcelain stretched wall to wall on five enormous tables in two enormous rooms.

Describing them to István afterwards I faltered for a moment and then said – for surely even he wouldn't be jealous of an eight-year-old boy – 'D'you know. Going up the stairs the little brat pinched my bottom. He did. A real sexy pinch and when I turned round he winked. I said don't *do* that but it was so bizarre. Eight, he is.'

That night we dined alone with Claudio's tutor, an earnest bespectacled New Zealander. Over coffee, when the servants were out of the way, he cleared his throat awkwardly, lowered his voice and said, mostly to István, 'Would you mind if I asked your advice about something that's been very much worrying me? You see, there's no one else to ask.'

István, settling himself comfortably in his chair, indicated that he was willing to dispense advice and I craned forward, intent on missing not a single word. Then the dam broke. The tutor, his eyes tumescent behind his glasses, confided that for the whole time he had been in residence, five, six months now, the mother of Nica and Claudio had been giving them both daily injections.

'She'll come in at his bedtime, Claudio's that is, and do it, and I saw her going into Nica's bedroom too, with the syringe.

I asked her what it was but she wouldn't say, she just shrugged
. . .' and the tutor did his best to convey an insouciant shrug.
'When she was away I had to do it. But now I've found out
what it is.' His face creased with distress. 'Hormones. Sex
hormones.'

'No!' I gasped, nearly falling into his lap. I had no inkling of
what hormones were but they sounded pleasingly scandalous.

'Yes. That's why Nica looks and behaves like, well, a tart,
when she's only sixteen. They had to marry her off quickly
or . . .'

'And that's why Claudio pinched me on the stairs!' I
squeaked and told the tutor what had happened.

'There you are, you see. Isn't it appalling? What should I do
about it? I told the Prince but he just made excuses, said that
was la Principessa's business, not mine.'

'The Prince is frightened his income'll dry up if he has a row
with la Moneybags about it,' I said and turned on István. '*You*
must say something to him, he's your kith and kin. Those poor
children, it's too awful.' I contemplated the acres of wedding
presents upstairs. All that in return for a daily injection? It
seemed a small price to pay.

Goodness knows whether István ever brought the hormone
question up with his cousin. He swore he had, but when your
host only pops in fleetingly for breakfast it isn't easy to corner
him over the espressos and accuse his wife of handling a loaded
syringe without due care and attention. The probability is that
Claudio was abandoned without further ado to the squalors of
female buttock abuse which, as I was rapidly learning, merely
put him a couple of years ahead of most Italian males. Perhaps
we'd misjudged la Principessa and she was simply doing what
all good Italian mamas did. One step out of the house and it
seemed highly likely.

In the early fifties in Italy – things have calmed down slightly now – any foreign female not hunchbacked or senile was tailed everywhere by curb-crawling Topolinos, baby Fiats bulging with young men in such an explosively libidinous state that they would have run over their own Mamas if they'd got between them and their quarry. Or so I diagnosed them, pursued down every lane and by-way by a barrage of hoots, shouts, vigorous gestures and, if I wasn't sufficiently nimble, gropings and pinchings. István, however, informed me that I had it all wrong.

'No no,' he said, 'it is not just sex. It is a theatre. The Italians are not like the English, cold and repressed. They are virile, they appreciate women, and like to show them so. It makes the girls happy.'

Unsure of my ground and not relishing the role of repressed odd-girl-out I forebore to argue, but I did wonder at István's sudden access of tolerance. How was it that in Canada he could throw a convulsion over a good-night peck on the cheek while in Italy any old passer-by apparently had his full permission to appreciate me black and blue? But then I hadn't yet plumbed the depths of approval my husband felt for everything and everyone Italian.

Our next stop was Rome and here he was enthusiastically received by yet another array of titles. Years later I caught up with the fact that István's Roman circle, Crespis, Sforzas, Corsinis, Crescenzis, Borgheses, d'Estes, the moss-ridden Colonnas, were the city's history incarnate and highly glamorous names to drop. At the time all that struck me – but that with the force of a bomb – was their unutterable sophistication, more immense and intimidating than I was able to handle without frequently sobbing out loud. Every man looked as groomed and pomaded as a champion at Cruft's and wore clothes in fabrics so rich yet so lissom they could have been pulled through my wedding ring. As for the women, the first sight of their *soignée* chignons, their scads of gold jewellery, the svelte little black numbers they sashayed about in and their burnished high heels whose very soles were magically unscuffed set up such powerful emotions that my neck, always a barometer for insecurity, developed a painful and visible crick.

Never before had I met, in such numbers, females so pulverizingly feminine. Positively edible they were, with their olive skins, chocolate eyes, cherry lips and fruity perfumes. Vivacious too, simply seething with little charming moues, flutters and flirts of shoulders and lashes and unfathomably meaningful gestures made with exquisitely manicured hands. Beside them I felt as prickly and static as a cactus stuck among hothouse orchids and it didn't improve my morale one bit to hear the Cleft in the background rumbling out one of his favourite put-downs: 'If you lack the vocabulary to say what you want without waving your hands about like a Sicilian ice-cream vendor, then better say nothing at all.' István, on the contrary, was besotted with all this hand-animation and spent several hours reproducing them to me along with their accessorizing noises – Uh! Ma! Ech! Ow! – and explaining in detail what each signified. Meanwhile I stood like a zombie with my mute English hands hanging like dead fish by my side. Nor did it help to catch István remarking to one of his friends that I resembled a horse.

'How could you *say* that?' I shrilled, the more upset for fearing that there was indeed something equine about my appearance.

'Oh, you,' István chuckled. I hated that chuckle, it meant I'd got the wrong end of the stick again. 'What I said was that you were an unbroken filly who needed a strong hand to guide her.'

Should I be flattered or offended? As so often with István I couldn't decide and let it pass. The same indecision cropped up again and again in Italy. Was István getting at me when he sucked his teeth with admiration for the dark tufts of hair that sprouted rudely from under the arms of passing women? My own armpits were as devoutly shaven as a nun's head and for much the same reasons. Body hair was a venal sin – at the very least, superfluous to any normal woman's requirements and, I felt strongly, any normal man's – yet obscurely I sensed a sexual reproach and veered away showing the whites of my eyes. Then my girdle came under attack, my Maple Leaf Forever standard bearer and by now my second skin.

'Why do you need it?' István asked, running his hands across my severely restrained rear and chuckling again. 'You are not fat and old, you are slim and young. It is stupid.' Who knows, I might have agreed and flung the wretched contraption away but he added, 'No Italian woman would wear such a thing, they are pleased to show they are women,' so I hung tenaciously on.

'If you think Italian women are so great you should have married one,' I snapped.

'Ah. You are jealous,' he said, looking unbearably smug.

'I'm not,' I retorted, and I wasn't, I fear, not of him. Let him leave me and plunge into an orgy of hirsutism and wobbly bottoms if that was his wish. What churned me up was the image he conveyed to me of myself, straight up and down and depilated, a plastic doll without a single secondary sexual characteristic and maybe not even a good primary one. I remembered Uncle Harry going on about Aunt Jen's hairlessness. I remembered her poor scarred wrists. It was she who had got me into a girdle in the first place, had she been wrong? I recalled Mother endlessly scrubbing herself and everything around her, Mother hanging over me in the bathroom, have you washed yourself, you know, *down there*, are you clean, you're a girl, girls must keep themselves clean. The Cleft carrying on about dirt and hankies, his face all screwed up. Silvana Mangano had flopped about in a thoroughly ungirdled fashion in *Bitter Rice* and didn't look very clean at all, or as if she had ever heard of a Lady Shick razor, yet she made all the men sit up and beg while Mother and Aunt Jen . . .

'And you don't need all that deodorant, either,' István continued, rubbing his nose into my neck. 'It is good, the smell of sweat on a woman. It is sexy. Italian women know that.'

With grim determination I heaved on my girdle and daubed my shaved armpits with lashings of Odorono. Through the long windows of our beautiful room I could see the moonlit hills of Rome punctuated by the dark exclamation marks of cypress trees. Stars trembled in the indigo sky and an undermining warmth, fragrant, seductive, wafted in. Tears of frustration rose up to blur the scene. Fake. Theatrical. Untrustworthy. I decided there and then that I disliked Italy and every Italian in it as much as István adored them and probably more. It was becoming glaringly obvious that whatever my husband stood for, I was against. Why was that feeling so familiar? I couldn't think.

Bent back like a scorpion's tail I confessed hoarsely to the ceiling of the Sistine Chapel, 'I'm late. You know? Late.'

'Late? What do you mean?' István's puzzled face swam across my line of vision.

'This month. I've missed. I may be pregnant.' I flipped upright and a black bag descended over my head. I swayed and nearly fell, would have done if István hadn't caught me in his arms, held on to me, cradled me saying words in Hungarian I took to be tender. Already the bag was disintegrating but he wouldn't let me go.

'My angel, *tesora, gioia,*' he said, grinning fit to bust. 'Come, you must sit down. Rest. Relax. Oh . . .' and he gave a loud Indian whoop to the consternation of the other Sistine viewers '. . . what a lovely news. I will have a son. Oh darling, my darling. Come, take my arm.'

I took his arm, my jaw slack. That dizziness, it was what I'd often felt in church when I got up too quickly from kneeling. It was nothing, surely. As for missing a period, did that really, always, every time mean you were pregnant? And if I was, what did I think about it? I had no idea.

'I shall arrange an audience with the Pope,' István said when we got back to our room. 'Here, drink a little coffee and lie down.' Carefully he led me to the bed. I lay down and reached for the coffee, only to find it being whipped away. 'No, no. Coffee is not good for my son. I will get you a glass of water.'

My mind still curiously woolly, I didn't object. 'What d'you mean, the Pope?' I asked instead.

'We have three days more. I want His Holiness to bless our son.'

'Oh well then,' I said facetiously. 'By all means ask him to drop in for tea.' Had the merest hint of fatherhood unhinged the man?

Two days later the doorman hailed a taxi and uncomfortably hatted and gloved I got in. István followed in his best dark suit. 'If this is a joke . . .' I muttered but I knew better. István's face was at its most hawk-like and solemn. *'Il Vaticano,'* he instructed the driver and off we went.

On arrival at the Vatican we joined quite a throng lining a long quadrangle, arches everywhere, green gardens beyond. Nothing happened for ages. Then a rumble of voices growing louder . . . *'Viva Papa, viva Papa'* . . . and in the distance a white figure who seemed to be sitting on a stretcher.

'Viva Papa,' the crowd roared, reaching out, and István, transformed, roared and reached out too. A kind of balloon

blew up inside me full of unnameable burnings and yearnings but I shut my mouth firmly, kept my arms down and watched the white figure draw ever nearer until he was there in front of us, an erect waxen-faced old man on a gilded throne, moving one hand up and down like a doll. He passed and was gone.

'He's very old, isn't he?' I whispered. 'D'you think he can walk or is he . . .'

But István had my hand in his and was tugging me along. 'Come, our audience. It is now.'

'I thought that was . . .'

We sat alone in another room on red hard chairs and waited some more. At last two men in red to match the chairs opened the doors and the old man came in. I was glad to see he still had the use of his legs but I didn't much take to his tall hat, it savoured too much of the Ku-Klux-Klan. Probably he didn't know about them or he wouldn't be so keen on it.

István put an arm around me and we walked forward. István knelt and kissed the Pope's ring and the two of them spoke for a minute or so in Italian. Then I felt myself being nudged forward. The old voice crooned and the white-as-death hand, bent back, thin and seamless as a Communion wafer, made movements at me. Two seconds later His Holiness Pope Pius IX was gone.

'Don't be upset,' I said, patting István. 'He was really very nice.' I didn't care to see those mirror eyes turn into lakes. Then we got into the taxi again.

'I didn't once shout "*Viva Papa*",' I said with some pride, watching Rome skim by. 'I wanted to, rather a lot actually. My eyes got quite wet but I kept thinking of Hitler. All that *Sieg Heil*, all those hands in the air. Isn't it interesting, the way just hearing other people yell makes you long to as well? I suppose men like the Pope count on that. István?'

But he was miles away. Perhaps he was in what they called a

spiritual rapture. Certainly the look on his face was very much like some of the saints in the paintings I'd been seeing. St Theresa especially. Gently, I tweaked at his sleeve. 'Tell me what you said to the Pope.'

István took out a hanky and blew his nose. 'I told His Holiness how precious was this coming child to me. Because I do not have my country, my family. Because they are in Communist hands. I asked his blessing on the child and he gave it, he gave it.' He had cheered up now, he was hugging himself.

'Oh,' I said. A bit further on, as we drew up to the house, I said, 'But the baby, if there even is one, well, why are you so sure he'll be a Catholic?'

István paid the driver and leaned back to chuck my cheek. 'But of course he will, my silly sweetheart. He is my son. Of course he will.'

Thirteen

As far as István was concerned, the Papal blessing was the ecclesiastical version of a pregnancy test and all the proof he needed that his son (it was always a son) was on the way. Within the week we were back in Montreal – no more travelling, he said, not good for the baby – and a fortnight later we had moved into a rented flat on Côte des Neiges, a steep hill with apartments at the bottom, ranch-style houses mid-way up and pseudo-Palladian mansions with large gardens, swimming pools and extensive views at the top. Thus newlyweds at the foot of the economic ladder were provided with a concrete incentive to work their guts out for the rewards of climbing rung by rung up the hill until at last they reached Maple-Leaf Heaven. In fact, what Côte des Neiges most reminded me of was those Temperance samplers full of primrose paths signposted 'To The Demon Drink', which might have served as a useful warning if we hadn't all known that most of the mansion owners had risen to their present heights by boot-legging liquor.

Once a week dumpsters filled with the cast-offs of the Top People were trucked downhill and stacked by our apartment house awaiting collection. There was not much to collect after we Bottom People had helped ourselves. I got most of our furniture from those dumpsters and was proud of myself for doing so, arguing with István, who was himself proud of his earnings at Volkswagen, that the Top People's chattels, having fallen for the most part off the backs of lorries, were a good deal less run-of-the-mill than the La-Z-Boy chairs and knotty pine stocked by the dull but respectable furniture marts we could afford.

Rather to István's surprise – he presumed expectant mothers spent their time languishing on *chaises-longues* – I went back to CFCF, not telling them I was pregnant partly because, despite a medical test that confirmed the Pope's, I didn't yet believe it myself. I knew no one of my age who was even married, never mind pregnant, and though I saw the odd pram being wheeled about on the Côte des Neiges slopes I felt no curiosity whatsoever as to its contents. Babies and I inhabited different planets. They were east and I was west and never the twain would meet. Nor were there any physical signs to make me reassess the situation. True, my breasts were now able to hold their own without the aid of padded bras, but all I thought was: and about time too. Beyond that, I gave pregnancy no quarter. Even when inner movements began I treated them more like some pet dog's tricks – Oh look, Fido's doing his somersaults again, isn't he a hoot! – than evidence of developing life. To the outside observer I must have seemed a fine example of a no nonsense young woman taking pregnancy in her athletic stride.

No one saw the underside, the fears that rose up like spectres in the night to gibber at me while István slept soundly at my side. Those thoughts came unbidden and acknowledged only too absolutely what was denied during the day – the reality of the child inside me. Thoughts for which, if put into action, I would have been arrested and imprisoned in Catholic Quebec. In the night I knew beyond any doubt that I didn't want this baby or its father, that I longed for quite another future with another kind of man entirely and that my life was in the process of being destroyed. It seemed a tragically premature end to my dreams of Liberty Hall and in those low moments my one ray of hope was the prognostication of Mme Les Etoiles.

The Star Lady, fat, middle-aged and multi-braceleted, with a hairy mole just to the left of her nose, was CFCF's own expert on matters occult, an astrologer, palmist, medium and clairvoyant who, just before the six o'clock news every evening, informed *tout* Montreal of their various fates as determined by the planets and her own close connections with the upper classes of the Spirit World. After one such broadcast I cornered her as she came out of the john in the women's washroom and begged her, please, to read my hand.

Smoothing down over hefty hips the layers of embroidered cloth that constituted her professional outfit Madame said, '*Eh bien, mon enfant, j'ai un cab qui m'attend . . .*'

'*Oh, s'il vous plaît,*' I pleaded, putting it to her that I was in deep trouble, in shit in fact, a perfectly acceptable word in French-Canadian society as opposed to the stuffier English.

'*Bien*, OK,' she agreed, '*mais* quick *alors*, I aven't got much time.' I stuck my hand out with its gleaming rings and she took it in hers, rambling on for a minute or so about lifelines and mounds of Venus. But then she turned my palm sideways and smoothed the skin at the base of my little finger.

'Aha. Ere we ave it. *Oui, voilà, mon enfant*, you see these lines? *Un, deux, trois. Ça veut dire* you av one usband now but you will av two more. That will keep you busy, *n'est ce pas?*' and she gave a rich chortle. '*Assez maintenant*. Two dollar please.'

She left me elated, beaming at my newly regenerated self in the chipped mirror. There was life ahead! There was hope!

However black things looked now, I had a future and, somewhere out there, two whole other men were waiting for me. It was written on my flesh so it had to be true and that meant that, somehow, I would struggle through. Three cheers for the Queen and all who sail in her.

I managed quite skilfully, however, to keep these clandestine upheavals from cracking the smooth veneer of my marriage and it was smooth now, very. As my belly shaped up into a smallish football and I was forced to relinquish for the time being a certain freedom, and later my job, István became ever more solicitous, hovering around me, helping with the household chores, carrying the shopping, bringing me flowers, doing the cooking at weekends and exhorting me continually to put my feet up and rest. On the surface I was appreciative and grateful, on the surface our relationship was better than it had ever been. Underneath, well, that was another story, in which I no longer starred as Mrs Goodie approved by all but slunk on stage to boos and hisses as Miss Baddie, the fly in the ointment, the mole beneath the verdant lawn, the anarchist busy planting bombs where'er she trod. I wished, often quite violently, to be what I seemed in the brightness of day but the misgivings of the night simmered on and I could not turn them off.

He is good to you because he has you where he wants you. Dependent, uninteresting to other men; his property only. No more need for unsettling jealousy, no arguments, no opposition. No wonder he's good.

How mean you are, how untrusting. He treats you like a Queen because he loves you, why can't you accept that, you ingrate?

Is a Queen bee in her Royal cell, fed by hundreds of slaves, really the Queen or the most abject of the slaves? Did the peasant in the fairytale cherish his goose for her blue eyes and sense of humour or did he put up with her squawks and flaps for the reward of her golden eggs?

All of which led me back to the Pope. Was that meeting some kind of man-to-man pact with me piggy in the middle? Had His Holiness blessed a living woman or a flesh-covered incubator for István's son? Why, he hadn't bothered to find out a thing about me or my feelings on the matter or even whether I was a Catholic or not. All he'd done was what István had wanted.

That poor little Virgin Mary. I saw it now. They set about making her feel important, gave her brownie points for not having gone all the way, organized a famous angel to drop in and chat her up, found her a husband to stop tongues wagging. And all the time what they really wanted was a nine-month lease on her immaculate all mod. con. womb so that the Father could use it to produce his Son.

Disturbing thoughts and lonely, they'll do you no good, my gurl. Look on the bright side for once, come on. The sky is blue, the clouds have gone. Count your blessings, including the Pope's, and get on with it, do.

I got on with it. One thing about pregnancy, you don't have much choice. The baby was born, a Count as ordered. István was ecstatic, I was too. My confinement was over, my body my own again with no line or residual bulge to show for its temporary tenant. I had snapped back into shape again a mere twenty-four hours after the child was delivered and the child was perfect, all fingers, all toes present and accounted for. I lay back in radiant relief to receive the Dolly contingent, who turned up in full force, a battalion of aristos that made up in numbers for the lack of three Kings, bearing gifts of matinée jackets and shawls in lieu of frankincense and myrrh. They were worshipful, they were kind, and I realized as always that they saw me only as István's lucky wife and, now, the even luckier mother of his child. How my cup must brim over.

A female in her late teens is probably in top-notch condition for the physical feat of bearing a child, but how she deals with the outcome may be many notches lower, particularly if she's rocked with astonishment at the baby's arrival and has no notion in the world of infant requirements.

'What do you mean, night feeds?' I inquired of the nurse consigned to me.

'Baby,' she said (Why did everyone leave out the 'the' before 'baby' in that sick-making way?), 'baby needs to be fed for the first two months at least every four hours, day and night.'

'But who will do it at night, when I'm asleep?' I asked, belatedly curious. Perhaps they sent somebody home with you or gave you some sort of pop-up bottle to attach to the cradle, with a timer on it, like ovens.

With sadistic relish the nurse said, 'You're breast-feeding. You will.'

That bald statement heralded the beginning of the bad times again. 'After the Lord Mayor's Show come the dustmen,' intoned the Cleft grimly from across the Atlantic and so it was. No sooner had my bouquets faded than there I was at home again, alone with the baby, the two of us shipwrecked together on a desert island. Now, after three more children, I am puzzled as to why I found that first baby so hard to cope with but the memories of suffocating panic remain. Hopelessly I fumbled among the mysterious lengths of cloth that made up the old-style layette Mother had sent, trying to determine which way was up and which tiny limb went where. Desperately I stared into the red screaming face, sure that he was starving or about to burst with too much milk or in terrible pain from some unknown disease, certainly caused or transmitted by me.

'Now, now,' said the paediatrician at the clinic, 'you have nothing to worry about. Babies, you know, may look fragile but really they're tough as old boots,' and he dumped the old boot back in my arms with a carefree laugh and a merry wink. The cheer this engendered lasted exactly as long as it took me to wheel the baby home. Once inside the empty flat, the door sealing off the comforting bustle of the outside world, it was panic stations again.

I learned, of course, and the worst of the panic ebbed. As it did, loneliness, shot through with another more perturbing emotion, flooded in. It took me a while to give it its name, so ashamed did I feel, but when the name came, it was Boredom.

I know only too well, I knew it then, that boredom is a very minor irritant to most well-adjusted people, about on a par with missing a bus or being pestered by a mosquito. If afflicted they sigh a couple of times, twitch a bit perhaps or sit staring blankly ahead of them, yawning. To me, even today, boredom is torture. Since that first virulent attack I have faced with reasonable equanimity a share of human discomforts: hunger, thirst, exhaustion, guns, bombs, my own imminent extinction by drowning and, more rarified, by stampeding camels, but none of these affected me half as much as the uniquely wretched combination of frenzy and guilt that boredom induces in me. If ever I am driven to take the life of a fellow human being it will not be out of fear and loathing but because they have bored me into homicide.

In small extenuation, I didn't hold the baby personally responsible for my psychic travail. Indeed I assumed he was as bored as I was – how could he not be, poor scrap, with his prison routine of feeding and sleeping and only me for company in between? By this time, a curious change had occurred. My baby had ceased to be a baby to me. He might appear so to visitors, lying swaddled in his crib or propped in a chair: he might seem so to his father, dandling him in the evenings after work, but when these transients had gone and we were alone together again he grew like Alice in Wonderland until he reached my size or surpassed me, swelling up on the worst days to fill the room. When he and I were equally proportioned he was my friend in adversity, my cellmate, and I tended him gently, burdened with gloom for our shared plight. Sometimes we sat for hours gazing at each other, he on one side of the sofa, me on the other, I aching for him to do something entertaining to pass the time – sing, dance, tell a joke – and he, I supposed, longing for me to do the same. Sometimes I tried. Sometimes I played Al Jolson, kneeling in front of him with my arms outspread, 'How I love ya, how I love ya, my dear old Mammy'. Sometimes I did one of my old tap routines, doffing an invisible top hat to him, collapsing beside him at the finish while the silence closed in again.

'Go on, your turn,' and I'd give him a nudge. 'Sing me "Melancholy Baby", it's only fair. Oh come on, Twinkletoes, let's see you do a cartwheel at least. Or how about a duet on the old pi-anna?' But he wouldn't budge and my voice grew resentful. 'All right then, don't. You're not a barrel of laughs you know, Mister. You can't just sit there expecting me to amuse you all the time. Can you? *Can* you?' Then I'd either scoop him up and kiss him all over or burst out crying or both. Often we mewled miserably together, wetting each other with our tears.

Those were the not-bad days. On the bad days he loomed over me like a Magog, his mouth the fiery maw of a volcano spewing out an unstoppable lava of noise, flaying me to the bone with decibels, not caring one whit how much he upset me, refusing all solace, rejecting all advances. Such days reverberated into the night, when I'd wake up sweating with fear, pursued by a monstrous figure in nappies intent on murdering me. Then I'd creep, still damp from the nightmare, into his room to kneel by his small curled body and touch my fingers to his warm cheek. 'Poor baby,' I whispered sorrowfully. 'Poor melancholy baby, stuck with a mother like me.'

*

He was christened Michael at Our Lady of Hungary Church, a return engagement at the same venue with the same audience, and this time he and I were together in not understanding a single word. Nevertheless the infant star of the show played his part in the ceremony with a better grace than I did. Having given up on God myself I was incensed at having to watch my offspring being press-ganged into the Christian Army, Catholic Division, against my will and stood at the font huffing as loudly as I dared in protest.

'We should leave it to him,' I protested to István beforehand. 'Let him decide what he wants when he's older. Why should he be Catholic just because you are? None of you lot are real Catholics anyway.'

Like many people with an English Protestant background, real Catholics meant the Irish to me and I was indignant as only an unbeliever can be to discover that what I'd supposed to be iron-clad rules were openly flouted by István and his friends. Only a fortnight before one of the Dolly Countesses, normally an unruffled sort, had grown uncharacteristically hot and bothered describing a visit by the local French-Canadian priest.

'Can you imagine,' she said to István, tossing her head, 'he asked me how many children I have and when I said one, he gave me a lecture. I was so mad I told him to go and please not to come back.'

Her listeners bridled in sympathy at this example of priestly intrusion and the Prince growled, 'What can you expect? The Fathers here, they deal only with peasants and, *natürlich*, they are peasants themselves.'

'Oh, I see,' I said to István, eating up the potato crisps when they'd gone, 'one rule for peasants, another for aristos. Catholics aren't allowed to do things to prevent having children but you do and she does, probably you all do. Your precious Pope wouldn't half tick you off if he knew.'

'Ach, the Pope.' István, rinsing glasses, waved a soapy hand quite as dismissively as the Cleft ever had.

'And you never go to church,' I primly continued, 'or take Communion or confess your sins, same as if you were C. of E. How can you call yourself a Catholic? And why should Michael be one when you aren't?'

István chucked the dishcloth into the sink with a splash. 'Please. You must understand this is not your business. I am a Catholic as I am a Count, as I am Hungarian. All my family from my ancestor King Arpad of Hungary are Catholics and so shall my son be. The Pope is a peasant himself, he has nothing to say in it.'

Secretly, I rather approved of this bit of Pope-bashing but there were dodgy implications. Why should István, just because he was a Count, get away with breaking the rules and yet impose them on me and the baby? It was unjust. The Irish, whom I supposed he'd call peasants along with the Pope, weren't allowed such leeway, nor the French-Canadians. I said as much, edgily. István wasn't looking co-operative and he had a tray of our best glasses in his hands.

But he only sighed impatiently, said he refused to talk about it any more and added, 'Also, I do not want the baby's name to be Michael.'

At this, I rebelled. My favourite doll had been called Michael and I'd loved the name ever since. 'You can't have everything your own way,' I said hotly. 'All right, force him to be Catholic if you must. He can always give it up later. But then he has to be Michael for me. Otherwise . . .'

I'm not sure what otherwise I had in mind. At all events, István calmed down, put down the tray and came over to me. He cupped his hands round my scrunched-up face. 'Michael,' he said, 'was my brother's name, the one killed by the Russians.'

'All the better.'

'No. Not better. Michael is an unlucky name in my family. Bad things have happened to all the Michaels in the past. Believe me, it is so.'

For a moment I wavered. James? Adam? Luke? But no, I couldn't forever be giving way because István's family had done this and that since God was young. 'Honestly,' I said, sweeping the memory of the Star Lady aside, 'that's just superstition. There's no such thing as an unlucky name. I want Michael. I *do*.'

Four months after the christening a bad thing happened to our Michael when he was all alone in his crib at night. István went into his room in the early morning before dressing himself and came out with the terrible smile on his face, the one I feared so, and said, 'Mikey is dead.'

I remember things here and there. The doctor holding a big black bag with my baby inside, he said *Bonjour* as he left. The little furrow in the crib where Mikey had lain. Three bright red flecks on the sheet. His duck, knocked from the table, quacking across the floor. The bib crusted with the Apple 'n' Pear of his last meal. The Diaper Service delivering clean nappies – the man said, 'Gee, that's terrible. I know how you feel. My dog got run over this week.' The white glare of the lavatory bowl into which I retched and retched.

I remember the sickening scent of lilies. The man in the funeral parlour rubbing his hands, saying, 'We ave made *le petit* look so nice again, *voulez-vous voir*?' The tiny white coffin shining in the sun. Oh my melancholy baby. Everyone said I was brave because I didn't cry. They didn't mean it, I could tell by their eyes. They wanted me to cry to prove to them that I hadn't killed the baby but since I had, the healing tears of the innocent wouldn't come.

What was it? they asked each other whenever they thought I was out of earshot. What did the doctor say? An overwhelming infection, I heard. An infection? Overwhelming a big healthy boy? A cot death it's called, apparently. What does that mean? Nothing. A death in a cot. And if one of us died in the night, would they call it a bed death? Strange. Very strange.

Mother came to the funeral. She brought a letter from the Cleft. It said, 'Remember, everything passes, good and bad.' It also said, 'Poor child, what can you do but go on.' They were the kindest words he had ever addressed to me. Otherwise, Mother's visit is a blank: how she looked, what she said, what she did. One thing, though, stands out unfaded. Without a word to me she went to see the doctor. The significance of that escaped István, who mentioned it only in passing after she'd departed.

'What did she go for?' I asked him but I knew what for.

'To satisfy herself, I think she said.'

To satisfy herself. A black pit yawned inside me. To satisfy herself – and the Cleft, of course – that their wicked daughter hadn't picked up a pillow and suffocated their grandson. Hadn't left him alone to die of neglect. Fed him arsenic. Not fed him at all.

I went to the bathroom and was sick again. Then I hauled myself up from my knees. My face in the mirror was old and ugly, the face of the witch who killed children and ate them. 'I loved him, Mummy,' I whispered, but she didn't believe me. She knew I was no good. Both of them had always known.

Later I wept: in the apartment, in the dark at the movies, walking in a wood, sitting in a rowboat in the middle of a lake, in the car. Only István saw, his arms around me. Later still I was stricken by how invisible István had become to me. What had he done through it all? Was it he who had organized everything? How had he managed it? What had he felt? He must have cried too: where was I? Why couldn't I remember one thing about this man who had seen in that crib what he would not let me see, his child also, dead. Blind and deaf to him, I had taken the comfort he offered and given back none that I could recall. No good at all. Neither flesh, fish nor good red herring nor decent wife nor mother now. Kaput.

The Cleft was right, though; what could I do but go on? István and I trod with careful attention through the minefield that lay between us – I never mentioned the man who had blessed my child to death and István never mentioned the name that had, as predicted, destroyed his son. We both heard Mikey crying in the night, a forlorn heart-stopping sound. Perhaps we both thought of him in the cold earth, but that was the most unmentionable of all.

We moved from the apartment on Côte des Neiges to another where no dead baby cried and I started once more at the ever-accommodating CFCF. Life went back to normal, which is to say that the tangled undergrowth, full of foetid flora and fauna, had fresh topsoil dumped upon it until it vanished from sight. Our marriage should have been buried with it – what further torments we would both have been spared – but grief kept us together just long enough for me to become pregnant again, so the marriage went on.

I made friends of my own, of my age, and grew more and more reluctant to inhabit István's shadowy refugee world with its old hatreds, its impenetrable talk, its pride and suffering. I met Tony, an Englishman with a pink open face and the kind of wit that sent me into agonies of giggles. Tony and two other friends were with me one evening when István came home from work. He entered upon a chaotic scene, the children – two children now – crawling about, the floor covered with toys and orange peel and us convulsed by one of Tony's gags, moaning and clutching at ourselves, sobbing with laughter. The laughter did not long survive István's brooding presence and, as so often before, they soon made their excuses and left.

'I would like to make you laugh like that,' he said as the door closed behind them.

'Oh well.' I shrugged, wiped my streaming eyes and began clearing up the day's debris. 'That's Tony. He makes everyone laugh.'

'What jokes was he telling? Tell one to me. I would like to laugh too.'

'Nothing. I can't remember.'

István followed me into the kitchen. 'You like him very much?'

'Yes,' I said, quickly adding the obligatory, 'but not like that.'

'Uh-huh.' István sat heavily down on a chair and watched me as I started to prepare dinner. I could feel his eyes drilling into my back. After a while he went out and came back with a bottle of Scotch, which he poured out and downed. He said, 'I know the type of that Tony. Very much fun in every day but he would not have managed in prison camp.'

I turned to glance at him. His back was straight, his shoulders set. Sometimes the thought of István's wartime ordeals weighed on me dreadfully, exposing me and my friends as a silly, frivolous lot, children in his man's world, playing tiddly-winks while unimaginable horrors were happening to him. More often I just wanted out from under, like now. 'Oh, don't start on that again,' I groaned.

He took no notice. 'You should understand these things.' He poured himself another Scotch. 'There are men good in daily life but in bad situations they go . . . like this,' and he tore a page out of the newspaper on the table, crumpled it and threw it on the floor.

Already jumpy, but vexed by the aspersions being cast on my countryman, I said, 'Look, Tony happens to be a funny man. Does that stop him being brave?'

'Funny. Why is funny so fine to all you English? There are more important things for a man to be. I only say I can tell who would survive and who would not and your Tony would not. This I have learned.'

I put the frying pan down rather hard on the hob. 'Well, who cares. He's a hoot and I don't give a fig how he'd be in some boring prison camp. Can you get the children?'

As I spoke, István got up, not to get the children but to grab and half-Nelson me. Then he picked up the iron frying pan and hurled it at the ceiling. It hit and crashed back, smashing a fruit bowl on the table. Chunks of hamburger and tomato sauce rained down, apples rolled everywhere. Maddened by the uproar and the crashing in my chest I set up a howl. 'Bully! Hooligan! Beast! Let me go, let *go*!'

He gave a sharp extra twist to my arm, which effectively sliced through my vocal chords. In the humming silence the children began to wail. I joined in and he let me go. For the next two days I thumped about the house pumped up with righteous anger, blistering his eyes when I caught them on me with my own two flame-throwers. On the third day forgetfulness set in, except that I could not forget those eyes. I tried but I did not succeed, then, later, or ever, in blotting the look in them out of my mind: fierce, unflinching and utterly lost. Why was that look so familiar?

There were no excuses, it had been clear from the beginning. My husband was a violent man and becoming more so as the years passed. Nevertheless, I was not a battered wife. Once in a while, in a long while, he hit out, the sort of glancing blow that gives you time to duck and lands just off target, or gripped me so hard it left bruises, but broken ribs, split lips and ruptured spleens were not my lot. The terror of him lay not in what he did but in what he might do. Rage barely contained, held a breath away from mayhem by a single thread, is hard to contend with, for it gives you a choice. Shall I fight on and risk the thread snapping, or shall I wave the white flag before it's too late? I wasn't good at defeat but what fuelled my refusal to yield was rage too, twinned with fear. How dare he scare me half to death? How bloody *dare* he?

And so it went, skirmishes, rows and full-blown typhoons, often coming at me out of the blue as it seemed, so that before I could take defensive action, close the shutters, batten down the hatches, trees were being uprooted all around and the very house was slipping its moorings, off to Oz like Dorothy's. Two things could be guaranteed to blow up a storm: jealousy and what might loosely be called politics. The jealousy was initially confined to the men he suspected I fancied or who fancied me. Then it spread to include people of either sex whom I liked or who liked me. As time went on, he extended his range to cover anyone or anything remotely interesting to me. Thus he came to regard as rivals persons and things as diverse as Hemingway, Gregory Peck, Marcus Aurelius, Senator Kennedy, Chubby Checker, the Twist, Jack Kerouac, Proust, our Labrador dog, my hairdresser, *I love Lucy*, the Bee Gees, ice hockey, London. He would start by pointing out quite calmly, with a smile, their various flaws, and end up ten minutes later throwing my Chubby Checker records across the room, tearing my drawing of London in half, cracking the spine of poor Jack Kerouac and threatening to shoot Kennedy. Once, when I was fondling the dog, he picked her up by the scruff of the neck and hurled her, yipping frantically, down the stairs. Yet he did all this calmly, while smiling. I can see that smile now.

But Russia was the reddest of all the red rags. Whenever that subject came up, which it did with merciless frequency, I felt as trapped and fidgety as if he were a Jehovah's Witness on the doorstep. Unlike them, though, his foot was permanently in the door and nothing would make him budge or move on down the road to other sinners more open to being saved. He had been given a mission by God and it was to grind me, his wife, into a whimpering admission that Communism was, indeed, Satan manifest in political form. Driven by the old hatred of lectures, a gnawing boredom and a nagging sense of fair play, I obstinately resisted.

'You're only saying that because they put you in prison but that was the war. Communism isn't bad. How can it be? Communists think everyone should be equal, women too. No poor and rich, no workers and their bosses living off them, no Popes or God either, or Kings and Queens. Communists don't believe in an aristocracy, that's why you're against them.'

Already he was smiling far too widely. 'That is all propaganda. It is not true, I tell you. Communists believe in equality? Ha. They are dictators. They force people to confess, they will not let you believe what you want . . .'

'Like the Catholics, you mean?'

His shoulders hunched over and he lowered his head like a bull in a ring.

'Listen. *Listen* to me. Russia is full of rich Communists who have all what they want and do no work, while the masses are poor and sweep the streets . . .'

I heard the bomb ticking but I said it. 'Like your family and the peasants in Hungary?' That time, while I screamed abuse and wept, he meticulously broke every plate we possessed.

In view of István's twin triggers it was fortunate for me that politics and jealousy in the parochial world I inhabited hardly ever coincided. Politics was an old man's game and no one that I ever came across outside the *émigré* community had the faintest interest in it, partly because we made no connection between politics and a general feeling that justice and freedom were good things. We cheered the leaders of the Black civil rights campaign in America and Castro and Che Guevara in Cuba for the same reasons as we cheered Gary Cooper, my Coop, taking on the villains in *High Noon*. It was a simple case of goodies v. baddies, and if anyone had mentioned left- or right-wing we'd have thought they were talking ice hockey. Thus heros and politics remained poles apart and only twice in those years did I encounter the sort of sexy political men that were to pop up all over in the sixties along with the Kennedys. The first was John Turner, a thrusting young Canadian lawyer and rising politician with knitting-pattern good looks whom I met through Aunt Jen and briefly fell for – the same John Turner who, in 1984, ran for Prime Minister. The second was appealingly shambolic Gerry, a student at the University of Montreal. We'd met when we were both nineteen and at CFCF, and we'd kept in touch after he married and I was a full-time mother, seeing each other now and again for a coffee or a snack when he would talk about politics in a way that made the subject sound as intriguing as, well, sex. I didn't advertise this friendship to István but after one such meeting I relayed some of Gerry's political views with incautious warmth and István went on red alert. Politics and jealousy fused and the resulting explosion was not long delayed.

A week later, while István was away in Toronto, I left the children with a baby-sitter and set off to spend the evening with Gerry and his wife Liz, who lived an hour's drive out of town. At midnight, István rang to announce his return.

'Who are you with?' he asked. 'You left only this number and address.'

'Gerry,' I said, 'and now that you're home, I think I'll stay overnight.'

His voice sharpened. 'Why?'

'Because I'm enjoying myself,' I unwisely said, 'and it's late. I'll be back first thing.' I added rather tartly, 'Don't worry, I've got Gerry's wife as chaperone.'

'You have been drinking, I can hear. Come back now.'

'I haven't. Why should I?'

'Because I wish it. I want you at home.'

Immediately my heart started bumping up and down. Humiliated by this Pavlovian reaction I felt honour bound to ignore it. 'See you tomorrow,' I said and put the receiver down.

Some time later, when the house was quiet and I had fallen asleep on the sofa, the front door was assaulted. I woke to hear shouts in the hall and then, like a gangster complete with gun, István charged in. Before I had time to say a word he had whipped off my covering sheet and was shovelling me up from where I lay, naked as the day I was born. Shouldering bug-eyed Liz and Gerry aside he carted me, too stunned and stitch-less to struggle, out through the sagging front door and down the mercifully empty street to dump me in the car a block away, throw his gun on the back seat and drive off. The row that episode engendered took a week to cool off, after which, when István was safely absent, I rang Gerry.

'Sorry about the other evening,' I said weakly, too hot under the collar at the knowledge of what he'd seen to go into more detail. 'Any damage, send the bill and István will pay.'

"Fuhchrissake," said Gerry, instantly igniting, 'no bloody wonder they call him the Mad Magyar.' After asking if I was OK and drawing a few choice parallels between me and workers who had nothing to lose but their chains, plus a précis of the dynamics of the feudal system as applied to my marriage, he launched into a diatribe containing rather more down-to-earth analyses like the guy's a son of a bitch and he wants a good kick up the ass, the bastard.

I would like to have used Gerry's outrage to fan my own, but as so often before an inner voice undermined this intent. 'Gerry's pride is hurt,' it whispered, 'that's why he's angry, it's a cover up, what he really minds is not standing up to István. He was scared. István wasn't. István doesn't give a damn, that's why he wins.' A tangled knot of conflicting emotions lodged in my throat and like a cat with a hairball I tried but couldn't hawk it out.

Another kind of knot, dark and jumbled, blocked what should have been the clear passage of motherhood. The children were now two and three, well past the first hazardous months that had seen my Mikey Mouse off, but it was rarely that I could feel unalloyed pleasure in them. A miasma of anxieties clung about them, which I tried to dissipate with an unnatural adherence to order. On the days they slept well, ate satisfactorily, played peacefully and did not cry, I could begin to relax, join in with their games and sometimes, in a too-abrupt swing of the pendulum, catch them up in my arms and smother them with kisses, declaiming as they laughed themselves pop-eyed with terror, 'Mummy loves you so much she could eat you up.' But on fractious days when noses ran, cheeks paled, food was rejected and mysterious grief abounded I was catapulted back into panic and no amount of bolstering from István, friends or doctors could ease the inner quiverings that too often translated into distraught upbraidings and tears all round.

'All very well,' I'd rail at my would-be comforters, 'for you to say don't worry. They said don't worry about Mikey, tough as old boots they said he was but he wasn't, he wasn't!' On those days I yearned to put words into action and, indeed, eat the children – unhinging my jaw like a snake wider and wider to swallow them whole so they would be safe and I free of worry forever.

Fourteen

I was now nearly twenty-four and gravely aware of ageing. Was I doomed to spend the rest of my life in a Montreal kitchen, aching with loneliness, cut off half the year from the world outside by snow and minus zero temperatures? Were there no adventures in store for me beyond quarrels with István and motherhood? As for the Star Lady's predictions – if I didn't get a move on soon there wouldn't be enough years left to pack in the two more husbands she'd promised. For the first time during one of our rows I found myself shouting at István that I meant to leave him. He was shocked, I was too.

'Never never never do that,' he whispered in bed that night. 'I will not let you, it would end my life,' and, 'No,' I said, still reeling at the enormity of what I'd let slip, 'no, I won't.'

But wild words blurted out in the heat of the moment have a way of cooling into hard little bricks for future structures. I said them again and yet again until the idea of leaving began to seem real. Now István countered by telling me over and over that I'd never find any other man, did I hear him, any other in the whole world who would love me as he did, never, never. This I found depressing and quite likely true – after all, there was no logical reason why István should love me as he did except for him being a Mad Magyar, which meant the future offered either the sane but tepid affection of the Anglo-Saxon or, if I roamed further abroad, insanity again. While I was dejectedly considering this prospect, István switched tactics, giving up on the sweet words in favour of militant action. During one six-week period of continuous upheaval he almost daily put a gun to my head, grabbing one or other of the ten in his study and pressing the cold muzzle against my temple. Then came the dry click of the trigger while I shook in silent terror and fury and he smiled his anguished smile. At the end of the month he went away on a hunting trip and I committed adultery.

Looking back, I can only think that this was attempted suicide at one remove. Montreal wasn't a big place then and István had his *émigré* spies everywhere. He found out – besides I confessed at about the same time, half in the mad hope of bringing things to a head, half to relieve myself of the intolerable burden of lying. Astonishingly, almost as if he himself was relieved that the worst had happened and was over with, István stormed not that much more than usual while extracting from me under minimal duress the man's name. Evidently the fear of God was then visited upon the poor devil, for before I could turn round he had left town, as Hoagy had seven years before, and was never to my knowledge heard of again.

There came a lull. I remember thinking it was like that Christmas Day in the First World War, when the Germans and the English sang carols together. István bought me a beautiful amethyst ring, a beaver coat and a second-hand Mini. He made tea in the mornings and brought it to me in bed. He hired an au pair, saying he wanted a wife, not a housekeeper. My heart grew heavier at every effort he made, knowing as I looked at his pleading face and thanked him, kissed him, thanked him, that I was no nearer to loving him and that dragons lay ahead. Few things are so corroding to the soul as the rising certainty that some time soon you are going to have to drag on a pair of steel-capped boots and kick the love proffered by another human being back down his throat. But the knowledge was there and could no longer be dislodged. Under all his trappings of familiarity and, yes, the bulwark he still represented against the chaotic unknown, István was already half-way to being the stranger I knew he would one day become. Sometimes, watching him as he slept or sat reading or turned from the stove to offer me a taste of the goulash he'd made, I heard my heart crack as sharply as the first ice on the St Lawrence cracked before it broke apart in spring, for I could see the Damocletian sword hanging over us and he could or would not.

'I'm no good for you,' I said often at that time. 'You'd be much better off without me. Happier with another kind of woman altogether. A nicer, kinder woman . . .' cautiously adding, '. . . who would love you more.'

But he only laughed, put his hands round my waist and bounced me in the air, said there was no other woman in the world for him, said his love was enough for two, didn't I know that by now, silly girl, silly English girl? Anyway, who else would put up with me?

What man, echoed the Cleft from across the sea, would put up with you?

As I had known it must, the truce ended and the carol-singers hunkered back into their trenches. Though I tried hard not to admit it to myself, the woeful fact was that I found István's violence far easier to bear than his love, which drained the very atmosphere around me of oxygen and substituted instead such a choking smog of pity, self-hatred and grey dejection that there seemed no other possible reaction than to fight my way out to the nearest exit for life-giving gulps of fresh air. In dreams my husband bent over me, smiling his smile, then lowered his face to one side of my neck and gently milked the blood from my jugular vein. I lay quite still, letting him, because I knew he had to have such regular transfusions to keep up appearances. This was the secret between us that no one else shared: in spite of his best and bravest efforts, in spite of his most tenacious illusions, my sad lost soul of a husband had not survived that Siberian prison camp after all; they had merely forgotten to bury him.

This was the knowledge that encumbered me as he watched and watched me, his finger pressed to my pulse, monitoring my every mood, siphoning my laughter, my joys, the ruthless vigour of selfish youth into his empty veins. Only when we fought could I work up the necessary anger to slough him off and, naturally enough, he fought like the devil to remain close to the source of his nourishment. Or so I saw it anyway, and thus, clamped together, we struggled on.

Then, at last, István was given Canadian citizenship and a brand-new Canadian passport to replace his brittle bundle of stateless papers, whereupon he was seized by the conviction that if we returned to Europe a permanent cease-fire would result. He announced that he intended to take three weeks' leave, go to London, look for a job and send for me and the children when he'd succeeded: would I like that? Would that please me?

In a surge of hope, half-believing with him that such a radical uprooting might work miracles — London! London! — I acquiesced, stiffening myself against the foreboding of being even more lonely without him. Off he went. Immediately, and cruelly, the weight of him lifted from me. Immediately the friends who had kept their distance for fear of István flocked in. 'Confucius say, when cat away, mice play,' said Tony, popping up with two six-packs and three blondes. 'Sure he's not gonna burst out of that cupboard waving a bazooka?' said Gerry, sidling in with his arms up, grinning. Liz said, 'A few slugs of this and we'll all be in the buff,' and plonked down a bottle of caribou juice. Silly frivolous lot. Unfit to survive in prison camp. Oh, how glad I was to see them.

A gregarious young woman on her own in a place of her own is unlikely to lack company. As the word spread that István had gone, the flat became an unofficial H.Q. for a bevy of friends and friends of friends. Soon the territory was more theirs than mine, half club, half flophouse. Almost always, when I got up in the mornings to dress the children, there'd be a body sleeping-bagged in the bath, another body sprawled on a sofa and two of the Un-dead stumbling about the kitchen searching blearily for hangover cures, while every flat surface everywhere presented mute evidence of the night before: take-away cartons, empty beer cans and bottles, half-empty glasses, full ashtrays. As the day went on, a floating population ebbed and waned, eddied and whirled without much if any direction from me. Men only slightly more known to me than Adam stood at my elbow as I fed the children, arguing the case for *Québec Libre* or the merits of the Pontiac versus the Chevy; girls whose names I never caught confided over my ironing board tragic histories of male duplicity while in the sitting room, where music blared day and night, love affairs born on a Monday were worse on Friday, died on Saturday, were buried on Sunday like Solomon Grundy and started all over again the following week. And in the hall stood a man with a beard, permanently attached via Bell Telephone to an unseen sweetheart in Baton Rouge.

The children, whose feet hardly ever touched ground and were never left for a moment unentertained by some passing clown, thought they had entered the pearly gates and so did I.

The three weeks came and went. Next thing two months had slipped by. István wrote that he hadn't yet found a suitable job, though quite why it was taking so long wasn't clear. Perhaps – and my heart leapt up at the thought – perhaps he'd fallen for a proper woman, cool, sophisticated but adoring, who sang to him in a husky voice, preferably 'O solo mio' or something heart-breaking in Hungarian, with violins pulsing in the background. But while I was hoping for this to happen I fell in love myself.

He appeared one evening out of nowhere, a bear of a man with long hair the colour of marigolds, wearing a black velvet suit, carrying a guitar and many cans of Heineken. Ten minutes after he arrived it was as if he'd been there for ever. He swung my son on to his back, settled my daughter on one beefy thigh, laid the guitar across the other, lifted a hand the size of a baseball mitt and hit the strings.

> O-ho let the midnight spe-cial
> Shine its light on me
> Oh let that midnight spe-cial
> Shine its ever-lovin' light on me.

His voice boomed out, extinguishing the babble around, and in no time everyone was stomping and swaying and singing along. After the last Midnight chorus, he slowed down and sank to a mournful baritone:

> There is a house in Noo-oo Orleans
> They call the Rising Sun
> It's been the death of many a poor girl
> And me, oh Lo-ord, am one.

'Who is he?' I asked Tony, beery tears springing to my eyes. So many poor girls and me too, oh Lord.

'Some actor, isn't he? Dutch, I think. Didn't he come with that guy over there? "*Oh* the Rock Island Line is a mighty fine line, oh the Rock Island Line is . . ."' and Tony was off at the top of his lungs, though still more or less swamped by the Dutchman's roar and the bizz-bazz-buzz of the guitar.

He was there when the kids and I came down next morning, flat out across the bottom of the stairs with one hand still laced into the guitar strings as if gunned down in mid-song. As we edged round him, he opened one blue eye. 'Hi,' he said hoarsely. 'Oh man, do I need a bullshot.'

'What's that?'

'Wassat?' echoed my daughter, gazing at him with worshipful eyes.

'Come here and I'll show you.'

With a giggling child under each brawny arm he lumbered into the kitchen. 'Consommé?' he said.

'I haven't any.'

'Sure you have. Put it in the freezer myself last night.' He reached in and took out two cans, slopped the contents into a bowl and, taking a hip flask from his pocket, dispensed a liberal dose from it. Then he ladled the mixture into a tumbler and, after yawning hugely, poured it down. 'Wuff!' He shook himself like a wet dog. 'That's the stuff. You want some?'

I had some. The day picked itself up and roses began to bloom on its cheeks. Dutch fed the children, whistling each spoonful down from his great height to their wide-open mouths. 'No breakfast for us,' I said, 'unless you fancy Coco Twists. I'm out of everything.'

'No problem.' That funny muzzy Dutch accent of his made nothing seem much of a problem.

He sluiced his face in the sink, mopped it dry on a handy child's bib and raked back his glowing hair. Then he stomped out the front door and came back shortly with two cartons of food, most of which he stashed away, moving from cupboard to cupboard as confidently as if the kitchen were his. When only a few things were left on the table he said, 'Hey kids, you want a real Amsterdam breakfast? Looky here.' He buttered two bread slices, smeared them over thickly from a jar of chocolate spread, cut the corner off a small packet and sprinkled over the chocolate a rainbow of hundreds-and-thousands. The children, enchanted, clutched at his knees with their mouths open like starved chicks as he swooped over them and stuffed the goodies in. Then he sliced a black sausage, cut up two apples and fried them together for him and me. '*Donder en bliksem*,' he said as he shovelled the black-and-white rubble on to my plate. 'Thunder and lightning – that's what we call it in Holland.'

'Makes a change from goulash,' I said and set to.

Dutch was there the next morning for breakfast and all the mornings that followed, for the unvarnished truth is that he walked in that night and never left, moving into István's place so naturally and in such a comradely manner that his bulk on István's side of the bed seemed instantly normal, harming no one, nothing to do with adultery, just a brother and sister, twins perhaps, lost in the forest at night, comforting themselves with a bit of incest until the sun rose and the path ahead became clear. My grip on reality loosened further as I saw the children take him to their hearts as easily as their quisling mother, jumping up and down on his barrel chest wherever he sprawled, hung about him like monkeys whenever he moved. Dutch and I asked no questions of each other, past, present or future, we made no plans, no tender emotions were touched on, no jealousies emerged, we came and went without comment or inquiry like a married couple long accustomed to each other's ways, but I came and went on air. No one else asked questions either, the usual crowd turned up as usual, but since the Dolly world was no part of mine now there were no spies to worry about. István's image grew dim in my mind and oddly benign, a man I once knew who had had many troubles but who now, praise be, had found the happiness he so richly deserved with a good woman far away.

Quite how I managed this nifty reversal of our two situations I cannot now comprehend, but manage it I did and accordingly felt innocent, clean of wrong-doing, indeed often positively uplifted, as if I were fornicating for István's sake, in his best interests, with a saintly disregard for mine.

Until, one morning, my feet hit earth with a jolt that had my heart in my throat. A letter from that stranger, my husband, informing me that he had found work and a flat near Peter Jones and would I join him as soon as I had sold the house, which he was arranging for me to do by giving me something called Power of Attorney; my treasure, my darling, I long to hold you in my arms again.

'Don't be like that, honey,' mumbled the eternal man with the beard into the telephone beside me in the hall. 'You know I love you, only you.'

I set up a wail of shock and dismay that was certainly heard in Baton Rouge. Then I went into the kitchen, sat down and wrote back saying I didn't want to come to England after all; what I wanted was a divorce.

Things become jumbled after that. Telephone calls, telegrams, more letters marked Express, Urgent. Tears, hysterics, long-distance storms. Dutch was there to pick up the pieces, incurious but ever present, a sturdy blue-eyed listening post, though I did perceive now and again that the blue eyes had a faint cracked glaze on them, like the finest old Delft china. 'What shall I do?' I sobbed, often, and, 'Whatever you want,' Dutch invariably replied.

Eventually, a compromise was reached. István put it to me that the least I could do was to come to him with the children, where we could do what he called 'talk about things'.

'I cannot come back now and I cannot live so far from my children. Please, you owe this to me.'

By this time delayed guilt, like jet-lag, was catching up. My daydreams of István's new love were just that, idle, selfish dreams. Here was a man I was dreadfully hurting and it was my duty, it seemed, to hurt him face to face. That's what he wanted, therefore it must be done. Somehow, amid the herds that continued to stampede in and out, bearing ever more booze, I contrived over the following month to sell the house and contents, all but our most personal possessions, crying as the old French-Canadian pine corner cupboard was carried out, distraught to see my precious oak dressing table, rumoured to have been saved from the Titanic, sink into the arms of auctioneers – and all my fault, of course, all on my head.

The day of departure eventually came, after a night of carousing farewells. I stood limp as a rag in the echoing house waiting for the cab to take us to the airport, a child at each hand, Dutch looming over us, a doleful shade. The cab arrived.

'Goodbye,' I said, burrowing into Dutch's leather jerkin. 'It was lovely, every minute.'

He swung the children into the air, hugging them. 'See you soon,' he said.

'Don't say that. They'll miss you as it is.'

'But I will see them soon. In London. OK?'

'You'll come?' I was incredulous. No hint had been vouchsafed so far, nor had I asked for any.

'Sure thing.'

I left him then, waving on the steps of the door, full to the roots of his marigold hair with his everyday breakfast of bullshots. Full of bullshit too, probably. There was no way of telling. Nevertheless, the spark of hope that had always been there ignited and flickered for a moment or two, clearing the mist in my eyes.

István met us at Heathrow. He was easy to pick out, a

Eating Children

lighthouse in the midst of a choppy sea, but I was startled
anew by the erect formality of his appearance, light years away
from the bronchitic slouch and cowboy hobble favoured by
the young men of my recent acquaintance. He looked as if he
ought to be meeting some visiting Head of State, I thought, not
two sticky kids and a frazzled harpy with a large Ribena stain
on her T-shirt. The journey from Canada took close on sixteen
hours then, just before the advent of jets, and seemed longer
than the *Mayflower*'s voyage to me, buffeted and battered all
the way by fretful kids jumping on my lap. István, I noted as
he came towards us, looked drawn and older than he had when
he left, but since I was feeling at least eighty-five my stock of
empathy was in shorter supply than it might otherwise have
been.

We were both formal in our greetings to each other, however,
only brushing cheeks and exchanging diplomatic courtesies. I
had had some anxieties about what indiscretions the children
might let slip of our recent house-guest but I needn't have
worried; they were shy with their father and too owl-eyed at
the newness of everything to bother with prattle, while István
and I were too constrained. What talk there was during the
drive in to London was confined to inquiries from István
concerning the financial details of the sale of the house.

'You have the cheque with you?'

'Yes,' I said, proud of having negotiated this mighty transaction all by myself. 'It's in my handbag. The whole $80,000.' I
still hadn't got over the sight of so much money written out,
with my name inscribed above it.

London town at last, and a foggy day. On stalls by the
roadside piles of oranges gave out a dim amber glow like
Hallowe'en pumpkins. Stalls. Of course! I'd forgotten. And
butcher shops with sides of pork and unplucked birds hanging
and fishmongers with whole fish on the slabs! Food in Canada

came only from supermarkets, conveyer-belt produce wrapped in plastic and clearly labelled 'Stewing beef', 'Chicken Boilers', or 'Casserole Tuna', so you understood what everything was and what to do with it. How was I going to shop here, where you had to know the parts of real animals and confront their bloody carcasses? The people looked pretty unpackaged too – what a variety of noses they had, what chins! How did they cram so many bumps and crevasses into one face? Canadians, compared to this bran-tub of features, were stamped out by a cookie-cutter: every face to similar scale, blunt and even, hair clipped neatly, not a bit like the unpruned bushes here. And look at all the black people, where had they come from?

Apart from two fleeting visits I'd been away from England since the gloom of post-war shortages. Now so much had changed and I was back in a London on the brink of Swinging, though even I was aware that the Bay of Pigs meant we might all be nuked before I had a chance to experience the rumoured wonders of a Liverpool group called the Beatles.

The flat was tucked away in a mews behind Sloane Square, not rented, István told me, but lent by a friend. I had never seen a place so titchy yet so grand, all gold, red velvet and crystal drops, like a Versailles ballroom badly shrunk in the wash. Was the friend who lent it extremely rich and this just a bolt-hole or extremely poor with some chattels rescued from his ancestral château?

'Her,' István said, 'it belongs to an Italian girl I know. She is not in town at the moment.' Did he look a little shifty as he said that? Had I been right and here, as ordered, was the woman who sang 'O solo mio' and was set to take my place? Things were looking up. Then István said he had something for me and took a bottle of Moët et Chandon from the toy fridge. I was at once touched and harrowed by his efforts at gaiety as he poured the foam into my glass.

'To us,' he said, his eyes fixed on me. 'To us,' I echoed feebly. Things were not looking all that up, after all.

The expected storm broke not long after in our borrowed teacup, a travelling storm that rolled back and forth, now distant, now directly overhead, its thunderbolts increasingly laying waste to the possessions of the absent Signorina. It began with faint rumblings; István flatly rejecting the idea of a divorce and suggesting, with an attempt at briskness sadly belied by his white face and shaking hands, that we should now put our past conflicts aside and begin afresh in a new country.

'No,' I said, a nasty tremor affecting my own hands, 'I can't. It won't work, honestly. You must see that. We can't go on forever making each other so utterly miserable.'

To which István replied, kneeling before me, 'I would rather be utterly miserable with you than happy with anyone else.'

Unexpectedly, this statement caused a small volcano to erupt inside me, spewing out a river of lava that instantaneously combusted every one of my carefully prepared arguments. I felt I'd been thrown alive into some anonymous mass grave and must claw my way out, a shameful, instinctive scramble for life from the piteous cadavers around me.

'Don't *say* that.' I clapped my hands to my ears as if against a blasphemy. 'It's horrible. Dreadful even to think. You could be happy, I know you could, but if you won't, I will. I *will*.'

'Who with?'

The lava turned in one heartbeat to a glacier of ice.

'Who will you choose to be happy with? Tom? Julian? Eddie? The football player? The Dutchman? Tell me, my unfaithful wife, which one?'

He knew. These affairs I had concealed almost from myself, he knew of them all. The week in New York seeing Tom. The nights with Julian on a London visit, Eddie at CFCF, lunchtimes in his flat, Charlie the footballer, a one-night stand not long before Dutch appeared on the scene. Excitement, vanity, grief, lust. Irresistible men who said I was too, who chased me with such winning energy and in whose arms I could briefly imagine I was carefree and unfettered, just myself again. This was the gold I'd found at the end of some rainbows after too much rain, but once exposed to István's gaze, what did it amount to? A load of shit.

Silence. What was there to say? István said, 'Whore. You whore.'

Whore. It was a word I had not heard aloud since Miss Needham had said it at school, and it had a prophetic ring, like a curse. I pressed my fingers to the hinges of my jaw, a trick I'd learned to stop tears coming, and got up wondering if my legs would hold me.

'Where are you going?'

'Nowhere. To wash up.'

He let me go that time but not the next. I wouldn't sleep with him, I couldn't. That was injurious; a whore refusing her services made it the more humiliating – and her more covetable. Corruption bloomed in that dinky flat outfitted like a high-class brothel. Forays, rebuffs, coercion, cries, a noisesome quiet. Love spat out full of hatred, hate crooned like love. The reek in the place of desire gone putrid, and dark blue flowers on my skin. I fled one day to my parents, whom I had talked to on the telephone but not yet seen. István had been in touch with them, though, that was soon clear. The Cleft, iron-grey now, was iron all through. 'Well, gurl, what's all this I hear?' he said, lips curling back from the teeth as of old, as they had in the days when I was innocent on all charges. Mother looked worn but well-armoured, managing to greet me without contacting more than a kiss-shaped inch of my infected body.

'Can we come and stay?' I forced myself to ask. 'There's

nowhere else, you see. Just till I get myself sorted out? For the children's sake really. The flat's so small and . . .' and, I wanted to cry out, the walls make moan as they used to all the time in this house when I was a child, but refrained.

'Out of the question,' the Cleft said. 'You're not dumping the mess you've made on us.'

'The thing is,' my mother said, 'we've just had every room redecorated as you can see and, well, though we're both longing to see the children of course, it's . . .'

'It's a sorry business, that's what it is,' said the Cleft, 'but not unexpected, not at all. Put your house in order is my advice to you, though you will not listen, I've no doubt of that,' and he stalked from the room.

'How can Daddy *be* like that?' I demanded idiotically of Mother when he'd gone – when hadn't Daddy been like that? 'He's against me from the start and he hasn't even asked me one question.'

Mother went over and bent to poke the fire, keeping her face away from me. 'You know what István called you to your father. A dreadful word to hear about a daughter.'

'Whore, you mean. And you believed him, of course.' My mouth tasted bitter.

'How many men have you lived with?'

I looked up and caught her glancing over her shoulder at me. There was an odd gleam in her eyes, hungry, almost avid. Such despair seized me that I laughed out loud. 'Lived with? None. If you mean slept with, six. Isn't anyone ever going to ask me why?'

Mother dropped her eyes, staring at the flames. 'I have no wish to know. Oh, how could you, how *could* you?'

'The question is,' I whispered, 'how couldn't *you*?'

'What do you mean?'

'Mother, you know. You've told me often enough.'

'How dare you,' she hissed, her face distorted. 'I am a Christian, I kept my marriage vows. No other man but my husband, that was the promise I made to God, as you did – as you did.'

'I take this man in sickness and in sickness, till death does us both a favour. Mother, I will not take sickness. I want to be happy, can't you understand that? Oh, please try.'

She went on staring into the fire. The clock ticked. Ages went by. Finally, 'Those poor children,' she said. 'That poor unhappy man.'

In the end I left the flat in the middle of the night, ran down the steps into the darkness with nothing but a vanity case containing a nightdress and a sponge bag. All that evening the battle had raged; laments, curses, knives thrown with a hunter's skill to quiver in the jamb of doors, objects hurled to be fielded or ducked, the thin steel of a curtain rod whipping round in the tiny room as I skipped and dodged: a nightmare circus with a crazed ringmaster, a performing seal and two frightened children for audience. That was the worst of it. That could not be borne.

'Stop it. Stop it,' I sobbed at István, carting a pyjama'd little girl back to bed. 'Look, she's crying, you see? Please, you must leave. This is killing us all. Go to a hotel, go to a friend, just get out of here.'

'I will not go anywhere.' He sat with his head in his hands, the corpse of a chair beside him, kicked to death. 'You go, whore.'

'But the children, they need me.' My eyes were so swollen I could hardly see. 'And where can I go? There's no one to go to. Where, *where*?'

Nevertheless, twice, as the evening dragged on into night and the bellowing reached a crescendo, I made a dash for the front door. Twice István got there before me and stood with his arms out barring my way, the crucifier crucified. But he slept suddenly in the end, sodden with Scotch, his mouth open in a frozen howl. I fumbled in the unlit bedroom for my case, then tiptoed to the children's room where they lay breathing peacefully at last. Better an absent mother, it crossed my addled mind, than a murdered one and Daddy the murderer. Then I crept away.

A taxi took me to Fulham, to the only London contact I had, a friend of a Canadian friend. Dorothy, fortyish and single, was understandably less than enchanted to find at three a.m. on her polished doorstep a piece of flotsam washed up by some tedious domestic hurricane, but she let me in. I slept in her spare bedroom until the next afternoon and then got up, bathed my eyes and descended. The house was empty, no sign of my reluctant hostess except for a note on the kitchen table saying, 'Please double-lock and post key through letter-box when you go.' Vamoose a.s.a.p., in other words. I collected my case and vamoosed.

Though my flesh crept at the thought of going back to the little velvet hellhole there was nothing else to be done. Anyway, this must surely be the head to which things had been coming and something could be settled now. Jogging along on the top of the bus, peering down at the teeming pavements, a faint flush of optimism returned. Probably half the people bustling about below had gone through much the same as me, fighting like cats and dogs with their spouses and then getting divorces and starting anew. Probably they hardly remembered how awful it had been. They might even be quite friendly with the partner they'd once wanted to hang, draw and quarter. I slipped into a half-dream in which I, the children and a man who closely resembled Dutch came tumbling out of a rose-covered cottage to greet with great warmth a transformed István, animated and cheery, with his arm round, yes, the Italian flat-owner, tastefully swathed in red velvet with crystal drops in her ears. 'O solo mio', she sang merrily and István, joy of joys, serenaded her back with 'I only have eyes for you'.

The real István looked a little better too when he opened the door and the children, rushing to be kissed, appeared to have emerged relatively unscathed from the night's traumas. Never again, I vowed to myself, cuddling them to me, never again, no matter what.

István said, 'I drank too much last night.'

'Oh well,' I said, brushing cornflakes out of the carpet.

'Where did you go?'

'A friend's.'

'Girl or boy?'

My heart gave a thump and I looked up but, miraculously, he seemed to be teasing. 'She wasn't a bit pleased to see me,' I said. 'I can't go there again.'

'Look.' He patted the chair beside him and I sat down. 'I have made some arrangements this morning. I will stay here for one week more, to be with the children, and then I will leave.'

'But how can you . . .?'

'I have taken the time off.' István's new job was selling Daimlers in Berkeley Square. 'They do not mind. It is my commission I lose. After that . . .' He looked down, twisting the gold signet ring on his finger, then cleared his throat. 'So. You must find a place to stay for that time.'

Relief bubbled through me like champagne and I looked down too, to hide it. 'Thank you,' I said, 'and, honestly, you can see the children any time you want, be with them here or take them out or whatever you . . .'

'Yes.' He got up, cutting me off. 'Now, the finances. We must be practical. Where is that cheque?'

I delved in my handbag and held it up.

'I have a bank account here, you not yet. I will put the

cheque in my account for safety and then we can go together
to a lawyer and make proper arrangements. Sign the cheque,
look, on the back . . .' he bent over, pointing, and took out a
pen.

'But what will I do for money till then?' A hot embarrassment
enveloped me. Awful to have to ask this man I'd wronged.

'I have money for you. Here.' He pulled notes from his
pocket and smoothed them out so that they almost covered the
teetery side table between us. 'Fifty pounds. That is enough,
no?'

'Yes of course. Thank you.'

'Now sign, please.'

Just for a moment I hesitated, glancing up at him with a
wonky grin. 'You will give . . .?' I flushed a darker red and
covered my mouth. 'You won't take . . .?' Oh, this was daft.
'It'll be fair shares, won't it?' I finally got out.

István put his hands on my arms and drew me up until I was
facing him. He shook his head and gave me a rueful smile.
Then quietly, solemnly, he said, 'We have had many fights
about too many things in our marriage, I know, but not ever
one time about money. Is that not true?'

It was true. He had always been generous. I nodded, not
quite able to meet his eyes and quite unable to douse my
unbidden grin.

'Then let us not spoil that one thing now, uh?' He tipped my
chin up. 'Huh?'

I signed.

Well, somewhere I must have known what I was up to. Pay
him off, pay my dues, clear my conscience, something like
that. No idea of it then, of course, or at any rate not up there
on the dashboard where the warning lights flash, indicating
the need to get more petrol, recharge the battery, replace the
brake pads before disaster strikes. No, not up there. But

somewhere at the back of the neck, ah, a different matter. That's where the real stuff is, coiled in the ancient hindbrain where reptiles nest. That old hindbrain lies low with a lizard's patience, monitoring every vibration from the brash young forebrain above that thinks so much of itself, always monkeying about, showing off, putting on its sparky pyrotechnic displays. Look at me! Look at me! I'm the King of the Castle!

But the hindbrain wasn't born yesterday. It plays a waiting game and comes into its own whenever calamity looms and the green forebrain panics. A swift lunge then and its claws are on the strings, yanking things its way, forcing the human puppet to jig to its primeval tune, painting upon the puppet's face its own reptilian grin.

So, grinning, I signed the cheque and thought only, thank heaven the worst is over, things are going to work out, it'll be all right in the end and we'll all be the happier for it.

That evening I put the children to bed, packed a few more clothes, exchanged some civil words with István and rented myself a nearby room. The next four days I spent looking for a suitable flat for me and the children and maybe Dutch, if he ever came. I missed Dutch's staunch detachment, the way his glazed china eyes never seemed quite to focus on me, the way he never said 'I love you'. So comforting, all that, after István. Sexy too. How odd life was, how unfathomable, how profoundly unjust.

London had a reasonable supply of flats to rent then, if you were quick on the draw, and I found something adequate in World's End, 1 recep. 2 bed., brambly garden, abysmal furniture. 'I'll have it,' I said to the agent who had accompanied me and took out the required down-payment.

'Ah,' he said, palms up against my notes, 'but first we need the signature of a male guarantor.'

'A what?'

'A gentleman to sign the lease with you. Since you, er-hum, are a lady alone. A professional gent, British citizen. To guarantee payment of the rent, should anything go wrong. A mere formality.'

István was no good, then, not being British. No one else to ask but the Cleft, however much I shrank from the thought. Still, needs must. I rang home and got Mother. I told her, trying hard to cushion the blow with apologies and euphemisms, that István and I were separating and that I needed Dad's help to get a flat. She said not a word.

'Mother?'

'Mmm.'

'I'm sorry, really, but there it is. I know you don't approve but there are reasons . . .' I could go no further. If I was to be a leper, I would not ring my bell for alms.

'Speak to your father,' she said and went.

The Cleft's voice, when it came, slammed at my ears. 'Don't bother to ask. The answer is no.'

Sweat glands in every part of my body squirted out droplets like a showerhead. Hardly able to control the quaking, I said, 'But Daddy . . .'

'No buts. I will not be involved in this mess you've created. Anyway, I wouldn't trust you as far as I could throw you to come up with that rent and I certainly have no intention of doing so. Go back where you belong, my lady, if he'll have you, that is.'

A feeling far worse than fury, the kind you get when something truly hideous is about to bob to the surface, something you pray you'll never see – the bloated body of a drowned man, maybe – dried my throat so that I could only gibber: 'Why, why? How can you say . . .? What have I . . . you can't . . . oh *why* . . .?'

But he cut me off then with a sharp little click and just as

well, for I was about to ask the most useless of all the questions
there are, the one István asked continually of me: why don't
you love me, why can't you love me? *Why?*

I dropped the dead receiver and bayed like a hound. Then I
stumbled upstairs to my rented room, slapped water on my
salt-encrusted face and peered into the sliver of mirror above
the basin. If only I could pack up the kids and go back to
Montreal, a thousand miles from the Cleft and Mother, back to
Dutch and my friends. But that wouldn't be fair on the children
or István, they needed each other. There was no way out of
that. Never mind. Something will turn up, it has to. Meanwhile
I would move into the mews when István left and hope for the
best.

I abandoned flat-hunting and went to the mews each morning
for the remaining days of István's occupancy, staying there
until I'd put the children to bed. Mostly, István was out and
thank God he was, for one afternoon Dutch phoned.

'Hell's bells,' I shrieked, euphoric at the sound of his deep
bumble, 'what are you doing, phoning here?'

'Where then? This is the number you gave me.'

'I know, I know, but I shouldn't have. Don't phone again for
another week,' and I explained what was about to happen.

'Great,' he said. 'So I'll see you soon.'

'Why? How d'you mean?'

'I'll be over.'

'When?'

'Dunno exactly. But I'll be there.'

I put down the telephone, aglow.

The following morning I stopped on my way to the flat, did
a bit of food shopping, milk, butter, bread, and bought two
wind-up clowns for the children. No one answered when I
knocked at the door. I stepped back on the cobbles and hul-
looed at the windows. No response; they must be out for a

walk. Then I spied a piece of paper protruding from under the door and pulled it out. My name in István's writing: 'Ring at No. 15 next door.'

I rang at No. 15 and waited, admiring the lobelia that dripped from the window boxes. An aproned woman opened the door, affording me a glimpse of swirly lino and ducks on the wall. Nice to see that not everyone in the mews favoured velvet and chandeliers.

'Oh yes, dear, your hubby, he was round last night. Left these for you.' She retreated behind the door for a moment and produced two suitcases, mine. 'And a letter. Here. All right then? Must dash. Got me mother-in-law in the back. Don't want her poking her nose in my cupboards while I'm not there, do I? Cheers then, dear,' and off she went, banging the door behind her.

I stood outside with my suitcases and tore open the letter. It said he had taken the children and left the country – 'Do not try and look for us because you'll never find us.' It said the children were his and he wouldn't have them living with other men – 'You are the one who chose to break up our marriage and you must pay for that. You were the love of my life. Goodbye,' it said.

I walked back with the two suitcases to the rented room and had a go at killing myself but I botched that too, the meter ran out as I crouched on all fours with my head in the oven. The smell of gas faded before I had taken more than three decent gulps and for the death of me I couldn't find a sixpence to set the meter off again. After that I lay down on the bed and stayed there through the day until the daylight went and the night began and went on and on until the light came again and there was another day.

When he heard the news, the Cleft precisely summed up my future for me: *You made your bed, my lady, now lie on it*. This I did and in some part still do.

But life went on as it tends to do unless militant action is taken to truncate it. I discovered early on that the will to die requires quite as much energy for its transaction as the will to live, in the short term probably more, and for some time the energy reserves available to me for any project at all, even feeding myself, remained severely depleted. This inertia, however, had the effect of keeping me ticking over until energy returned wearing its other hat, hope. This was in large part due to Dutch who, two months after the children had gone, arrived at Heathrow and, like so many after him in the sixties, was promptly ejected for having long hair and a guitar. He retreated to Amsterdam where I later joined him. Much later, true to the Star Lady's prediction, I completed my complement of three husbands and the children, after years of legal battles, at last returned. But all that is another and scarcely more edifying story.

What is not another story, merely a continuation of same, is that though I hardly saw Mother or the Cleft for years afterwards either, indeed not until they had grown too old for grudges to be harboured with any enthusiasm, both continued to pluck away at my strings, fervently abetted by me. My old knee-jerk resolve to be their polar opposite signally failed to grow dog-eared with time, in spite of having proved itself again and again to be toxic to me and all about me.

Hardly surprising, then, with hindsight, that when finally they died, the Cleft forging ahead, Mother close on his heels, their fifty-year-old daughter found herself adrift upon a starless sea and there, bereft of rowlocks against which to pull, she set up a shocking racket and shortly after went down.

In the year that followed this unmourned demise, I managed to wrest from the wreckage another self. Once the pasting and patching was done I suppose I looked much the same to the outward eye. Nevertheless, the interior landscape had radically changed. No thought, idea, opinion, belief, no single memory remained undisturbed of that whole collection that had provided me with ground cover for so long. Each bare rootstock was subjected to meticulous inspection for signs of rot before the decision was taken as to whether it should be dug in again or discarded for good. Which among them, I continually asked myself, was truly an indigenous plant, suited to my particular soil and prevailing climatic conditions, therefore likely to thrive and propagate well if replanted, and which had been mindlessly scavenged in childhood, mainly from the Cleft's rejects?

Many turned out to be just that, scions severed from the parent plants and badly grafted, cuttings that had never properly taken, layerings with shallow roots, all of them apparently healthy but in fact requiring a whole kit of artificial props and fertilizers to provide staying power. This time round I meant to ensure that though what went in might look rudimentary and often unaesthetic — lumpy tubers, rhizomes with barely visible shoots, a few dry twigs here and there, some minuscule seedlings — they were at least my choice and would flourish without leeching unduly from the soil around. For far too long, busily resisting my father, rejecting my mother, I had raised and nourished a hybrid persona which had produced the odd fruit but at far too high a price. Now, with any luck, the real thing had been dug in and the roots would hold.

Frightening People

If you have to do some suffering in life, try and get it over while you're young. For one thing you can cry a great deal without looking like a three-day corpse fished from the sea, and then, crying itself is good for you, as a release and because each teardrop contains minute particles of toxic matter that, unshed, could do you bodily harm. Besides, there's a built-in bounce to youth that's given extra impetus by the touching belief that once you've hit bottom there's nowhere to go but up. This, of course, is an illusion: life can always, if the fancy takes it, flip open a trapdoor in one of its cellars to reveal darker chambers beneath, or whip out a spanking new anguish just when you thought you'd weathered the worst, like a conjuror producing yet another rabbit from a demonstrably empty hat. But when you're young you don't know this, and therefore the illusion cheers.

In the hey-nonny pretty springtime of 1961, with John Fitzgerald Kennedy newly enthroned in America, the Russians in space, London about to start swinging and the Beatles about to become more famous than Jesus, I was twenty-five and curled in a foetal position at the rock bottom of my life. Only three months before I'd had a husband and children, a four-bedroom, centrally heated home with a breakfast bar, a carport, a rumpus room, a fully automatic washing-machine, a tumble-drier, a fridge, a chest freezer and a dishwasher. Then came the decision to move back to London, where the marriage, always unstable, had finally exploded, embedding wicked shards in us all. István, my Hungarian husband, had walked out of our rented flat one morning and vanished into the blue, taking with him our two-year-old son, our three-year-old daughter and every penny in the bank. I knew not a soul in the city I'd left seven years ago, I was in debt to the landlord of my bedsit – a failure even at suicide (the meter had run out when I tried to gas myself) and my parents had washed their hands of me, as I'd done my best to wash mine of them at approximately the same time.

All in all, clouds had nothing on me when it came to loneliness and there were no daffodils dancing that year on the Old Brompton Road.

In addition to this plight, I was fast discovering that I had no more idea of how the world worked than a chimpanzee. Nothing in the way I'd been brought up and educated connected with what I dimly apprehended as reality; the one seemed entirely sealed off from the other. It was as if I'd learned the *lingua franca* of a particular country but, unfortunately, it was not the one I was currently inhabiting. I was haunted by disturbing intimations of another language entirely, other rules, other modes of behaviour which, if I could only grasp them, would rip the veil from my eyes and allow me to see clearly at last. My skull rattled with bits of a jigsaw, but where each piece fitted in with the next I couldn't fathom. Vaguely I felt there must somewhere be a key which, matched with the right door, would let me into that real world outside my head. So far I hadn't found it, nor had I the remotest idea where to look.

I was also oppressed by a growing suspicion that whatever was wrong might not be without but within. Possibly I congenitally lacked some small but vital cog or spring – for want of a nail the battle was lost, that sort of thing. It is hard to envisage the anatomy of one's own brain, let alone spot an abnormality and put it right. Nevertheless, there were times when I felt a chilling conviction that it wasn't running as it should. Some fragile inner circuit, meant to connect to other circuits, had failed to link up, one synapse dangling loose, another fused, leaving me badly wired in certain areas, a fool in parts. The sensation this produced was of treading on terra that appeared to be firma but could at any moment – and frequently did – collapse under my feet like one of those big-game jungle traps and pitch me down. Mere IQ offered no protection, the fault was elsewhere. I had the five functioning senses all right, traces here and there of a sixth even, but the rungs of the ladder that led up to these were untrustworthy, sometimes wobbly in the extreme, occasionally non-existent. If I put two and two together I often came up with quite interesting sums, but hardly ever four.

The symptom that troubled me most, however, was a crippling inability to distinguish what was normal from what was not. Other people seemed to emerge from the womb equipped with a handy yardstick for measuring the boundaries of things, the limits of deeds, the perimeters of behaviour, what was acceptable, what not. You could tell because they said things like *that's the last straw*, or, *this time he's gone too far*, or, *I wouldn't put up with that if you paid me*, or, *don't you worry, I showed them what's what*. That last phrase, above all, set me floundering. I longed to ask what exactly *was* what but knew eyebrows would only shoot up in a depressing manner. My father's eyebrows shot up like that at the zoo once when, having seen the camels, the giraffes and the monkeys with rainbows on their bums, I asked where the unicorns were. 'Ye Gods,' said Father to Mother, 'will that child never learn what's what?'

Still, one thing stood out clearly enough in this muddle. I had to find a job, and quickly, for my own survival and in order to hire a lawyer to get my children back. Briefly I considered the two jobs I'd had in Canada before motherhood intervened and dismissed them both as useless here. Dreaming up shopping-centre promotions? There were no shopping-centres in England. Chatty weather forecasting at Radio CFCF Montreal? What would the BBC make of my Canadian qualification for that task: a twig of seaweed whose moistenings and dryings I passed on to listeners as proof of the day's humidity levels? Anyway, the English didn't have local radio, all jazz and jingles. They took their broadcasting seriously, not to mention their weather, and the very thought of entering the awesome portals of the British Broadcasting Corporation shrivelled me. Why, I hadn't one suitable outfit and moreover I knew that, confronted with a plummy BBC gent, the words would dry in my throat. Worse, how could I guarantee that tears, those saboteurs that had dogged my every hour recently, wouldn't of a sudden pour out from their ambush and strike me shamefully down?

Brooding on all this, I sat late one afternoon on a slope by the Serpentine. Misery leant heavily on me like a faithful but smelly old dog. Children played, where were mine playing? Children laughed, were mine laughing? The dreams that nightly bedevilled me, of chasing after an endless trail of little bloody footprints, of struggling up the steps of a tower to reach my babies before they fell, spread a livid bruise across the otherwise cheerful scene.

'Hi.'

I glanced up. A man with dark, slicked-back hair, dark glasses and a white mac stood nearby. He appeared to be addressing the ducks.

'You know who I am?' he continued when I didn't reply.

Dumbly, I shook my head.

'Derek Niven van den Bogaerde,' he said. 'My father was Dutch.'

Dutch. That's what everyone called him, the man I'd left behind in Canada, the last of the men who'd heralded my downfall, but, all the same, far the nicest. How I wished he was here.

'I have a Dutch friend in Canada,' I offered.

Understandably he ignored this, merely repeating his name. 'Derek van Bogaerde. Ring a bell? Well, what about my stage name? Dirk Bogarde.'

The collar of his mac was up, concealing half his face. I squinted sideways at the top half. Was it? Who cared.

Tucking in the rubbery flange of his mac, he hunkered down a little way from me. 'You look like you got problems.' There was a transatlantic twang to his voice which made me feel at home. But surely Dirk Bogarde wasn't American?

'One or two,' I said.

'Like?'

I brought forth the least personal. 'I need a job.'

'Uh-huh.' He was still staring hard at the ducks. 'Which of my films did you like the most?'

My mind went blank. I tried to look as if I were making a difficult choice.

'How about *The Blue Lamp*?' he suggested.

'Yes,' I limply agreed.

He nodded, apparently with approval, and, edging himself a little closer, went on to draw my attention to the lesser known Bogarde oeuvres: *Hunted*, *The Spanish Gardener*, *Quartet*. *Doctor in the House* he dismissed with a shrug: 'Well, you gotta make a living.' I listened meekly, glad of any distraction. He wasn't Dirk Bogarde, I'd seen that by now, though he bore a fair resemblance. It didn't matter. As far as I was concerned, he could be the Queen of Tonga if he wanted. Nobody had talked to me for ages. Now that someone was, I had no wish to argue nomenclature.

After some minutes of wide-ranging monologue concerning Bogarde's lynchpin role in shaping the post-war film industry, my companion asked if I'd have dinner with him at the end of the week, somewhere quiet he knew where they didn't pester him for autographs. At the mention of dinner my stomach leapt up and what scruples I had were instantly crushed. We arranged time and place, then he shook my hand and got up.

'Oh yeah,' he said as he turned to go. 'You wanted a job. There's a notice in the window of a shop in Beauchamp Place, saw it this morning. For an assistant. You could do worse. *Ciao*.' And with a surreptitious glance over his lapels, presumably to check for pursuing fans, off he strolled.

Mr Shamir, the owner of the shop in Beauchamp Place, turned out to be a Polish Jew, very short and old, his English so bad and his accent so thick that when he said I wasn't right for the job I thought he said I was and turned up on his doorstep at 8.30 the next morning.

'Ach,' he said, wheezing as he unlocked the door. 'You again. Vat you vant?'

Anxiously I prodded his poor decayed brain cells. 'It's me. You hired me yesterday. Don't you remember?'

He stared. He hunched his shoulders. After a pause, he splayed his hands, rolled his eyes to the ceiling and let out a curious Mickey Mouse squawk. Then, with a jerk of his head, he indicated that I should enter.

The cabinets inside were still shrouded, as they had been the evening before. Together we folded the coverings away and there before my ravished eyes sprang out a whole midget company of manikins and thimbelinas, dancing, bowing, curtseying, strumming, flirting, all dressed to the nines in crinolines and breeches and lace mantillas, or costumed in masks and diamond-patched tights, clowning, leaping, pirouetting. There were monkeys too, dressed up like the Lilliputians, orchestras of them fiddling, fluting, drumming. The hushed room whistled with their clamour, the thin scrape of their violins, the high pipe of their laughter.

'Lovely,' I breathed. 'Dresden, aren't they? Oh, I'll *love* selling these.'

'Na,' sneered Mr Shamir, 'Nat Dresden. Meissen. An' I sell only. You vash. Every day, vash. Come, I show.'

I followed him to the back of the shop, where he bent and pulled at a ring in the floor. A trapdoor creaked open. We clambered down the ladder into profoundest gloom. Mr Shamir switched on a light, which merely turned the gloom a murky yellow. We were in a cellar, crumbling brick walls, earth floor, no chink or channel to the outside world. On one lightly iced wall was a stained butler's sink. Mr Shamir pointed to it. 'Dere you vash,' he said.

'Vash vat?' I pulled myself together. 'I mean, what am I to wash?'

'De Meissen, Miss. It get alla time dirty, you must vash, vash, vash.'

'Can I wear my fur gloves?' I inquired, trying to boost my spirits above freezing point.

'Gloves? You mekka joke?' He waddled over and positioned himself so close to me I could feel his breath gusting round my midriff. I looked down, he scowled up. 'No jokes, Miss. How much you tink my Meissen cost? Mebbe each one tousand pound.' He stuck a pudgy finger under my nose to illustrate this astronomical sum. 'So ven you break, den you muss pay me back one tousand pound. OK fine?'

Was he serious? I didn't know and couldn't afford to find out. 'OK fine,' I said.

For the rest of the week I washed away in the sulphurous dark, peering into the crannies of tiny china limbs, pompadours and lace, dabbing at the dust with a pastry brush. I wore my Canadian beaver coat against the cold, hoping that beavers, being aquatic, could cope with a daily soaking. My back hurt, my eyes ached almost as much as my feet, my nose sprouted stalactites and my hands became two wrinkled flippers. Every now and then Mr Shamir's face appeared at the trapdoor to grumble down at me: 'Too much water you take, I can hear. Dis not Buckanam Palace. I give you electric bill when it come. You pay.'

'Sure, why not,' I yodelled back, misery having escalated to surreal dimensions. One thing about working in a dungeon, come six o'clock and there really was nowhere to go but up.

On Friday evening, bloater-eyed and famished, I met Dirk Bogarde, still in Bogarde costume, at the appointed bistro. While he enlarged on the travails of fame, I wolfed down the food he was paying for, grateful for that and for company, however noncomformist. Happily, Dirk shared my minimal needs, requiring no more of me than my ears and a sympathetic expression, after which he escorted me out of the restaurant and paid a taxi to take me back to my room. These nourishing assignations continued twice weekly for the next six weeks while, back at the shop, Mr Shamir, perhaps because I didn't yet owe him a penny for breakages, relented enough to shout through the trapdoor whenever he had a well-known client coming in. On such occasions he permitted me to leave my sink, scuttle up the ladder and stick my nose over the rim of the trapdoor for a peek. Most of those I glimpsed were a sad disappointment – the years in Canada had left me unprimed as to British VIPs. Once only was my goggling rewarded, for there, prowling among the Lilliputians, was the squat, froggy figure of Edward G. Robinson, a 100 per cent paid-up member of any Hall of Fame.

That evening I informed Dirk of my sighting. 'Guess who: Edward G. Robinson,' I said proudly. 'He looked just like he does in the movies.'

This news appeared to shake my companion to the core. 'You think he's a better actor than me?' he barked, letting his fork and knife fall from his hands with a clatter.

'No,' I hastily reassured him. 'You're quite different.'

'How d'you mean, different?' His eyes were hooded, but small muscles began sliding about in his jaw.

'Edward G.'s ugly. Edward G.'s old.' I racked my brains for further comparisons in Dirk's favour, unsettled by the whitening knuckles of the fists on the table opposite me. 'He plays villains, you don't. Well, mostly you don't.'

Dirk was not consoled. His demeanour changed dramatically. 'Fucking Hollywood,' he growled. 'They got the money, they can make any fat fucking bastard a star. They wanted me out there, you know, but I wouldn't go. I'm no Hollywood sell-out. Fuck them.'

I had never until then heard that word said aloud, and the impact of it three times in one sentence took me severely aback. Glancing round at the other diners, I implored him to shush.

To my relief he complied, but his cheeks had gone grey while mine burned, and the way he was chewing at his lower lip didn't bode well. 'Let's go,' he muttered finally. 'I need a drink.'

Obediently I followed his stalking figure into Trafalgar Square and up St Martin's Lane. Halfway along he suddenly dodged sideways into a narrow alley. For the space of two heart-beats I hung back. It was dark and deserted. What might he . . . ? Quickly I suppressed the ugly thought. He'd been kind, he'd found me a job, he'd fed me. So what if he had a kink or two. Resolutely I turned in after him and there, at the end of the tunnel, a pub sign glowed. Relief laced with remorse made me take his arm and we entered together.

At the bar Dirk greeted the barman, who nodded briefly

back. I lingered over a tomato cocktail, Dirk threw down several scotches. Then, excusing himself, he headed not altogether steadily for the men's room. The barman, polishing glasses, watched him go. As the door swung shut behind him, he leant over to me, funnelling his lips conspiratorially.

'If you don't mind my asking, how long have you known that gentleman?' he said, and immediately ducked his head down, polishing furiously.

'Six weeks. Well, actually, a bit less really. Why?'

'Hey, Joe.' A large man elbowed in beside me with a clutch of empties. 'Fill 'er up, eh?'

The barman complied, after which he turned back to me.

'Look,' he said under his breath, 'if you was my daughter, I'd have you out of here now. That one's a . . .' He shook his head, apparently fresh out of words to describe what my absent companion was. Instead, in a sudden frenzy, he batted his dishcloth at me as if I were a large bluebottle. 'Go on,' he hissed, 'take it from me. Scarper while you've got the chance. Get out, go on.'

Overwhelmed by such urgency, I grabbed my handbag and scarpered.

I never saw Dirk again, though I made several attempts to retrace the evening's route, agog to learn the nature of the perils I'd fled. Mysteriously barman, pub and all had melted into the London fog like *Brigadoon*, leaving me to puzzle endlessly over the familiar *what's what* conundrum. Had the barman marked Dirk down as mad merely because he claimed he was what he wasn't? It seemed to me you could barely turn round for men claiming they were what they weren't – clever, sexy, important and right. Take the pope, for instance, the one I'd met in Rome with my husband, the one who'd blessed my not-yet-born baby who would be found dead in his cot a year later. He believed he was God's Rep on earth, and infallible, which would have been more impressive if it weren't for the fact that my father, along with hundreds of other men past and present, from kings and dictators down to any old husband on the street, believed much the same of themselves with as little proof. Dirk's claim, compared to some of theirs, looked positively humble.

On the other hand the barman might have been about to divulge that Dirk was something worse than not-Dirk – a rapist, say. Even so, in six whole weeks he'd shown no sign whatever of such criminal intent, whereas men no one dreamt of warning you against – Lords, colonels, solicitors, friends of your father – showed no qualms at all about trying if they got half a chance, and they didn't buy you twelve whole meals beforehand, either. It was all very confusing, and the only definite *what's what* that I managed to retrieve from the debris was how sorely I would miss the free dinners.

The need to pay my landlord the month's back rent, plus the ongoing rent and my daily bus-fares, took most of the weekly tenner I earned, leaving hardly anything over for frivolities like food. For that reason alone, Dirk had been a lifeline. Now my stomach bit painfully at me, making me fear that, like some trapped hyena, it was already chewing up my innards and would soon set about demolishing my bones, causing me to plop to the ground of a sudden, like a decanted jelly. Yet despite the constant inner gnawing I couldn't convince myself that I was actually starving. The idea was too preposterous. People starved in places like Calcutta and Cairo, not London. In London, people went to Government offices and were given food stamps or soup or something, or they borrowed money from friends; they didn't just keel over on the pavement. The trouble was, I had a job, which meant I wouldn't qualify for Government money, and I had no friends to borrow from.

Then the worry and the pains disappeared and a dream-like apathy overtook me. Day by day I drifted ever deeper into a strange seascape, unable to resist its hypnotic allure, the brilliance of its fauna, the seductive undulations of its flora. My ears rang with eerie buzzings and hummings, my vision doubled, my head untethered itself from my neck to bob about like a stray balloon. At night I lay sleepless, kept alert by the firework display in my head and I moved through the days like a sleepwalker. Indeed, if my landlord hadn't owned a stout, greedy spaniel, there is no knowing how I would have ended up.

'Vat dis?' Mr Shamir demanded one midday, descending to my underground grotto with yet another box of grimy china. 'Vat you eat?' He peered over my hunched shoulders, making disdainful Middle European noises.

Clumsily, I tried to shovel my lunch back in its bag. 'Nothing. Nothing.'

'Nutting? Vat is dis nutting? You eat stones from ze road?'

My landlord kept a sack of doggie snacks in the hall cupboard. I'd seen him doling out the stuff in handfuls to his beloved pet a few evenings ago. Here was a source of salvation that required no awkward explanations, no humiliating pleas. Every morning since, I'd siphoned off a day's ration, not enough to be noticed, just enough to stave off the dizzy turns.

'They're called Spiller's Biscuits,' I blustered, counting on Mr Shamir's ignorance of British dogdom. 'Very good for you. Full of vitamins and things.'

Mr Shamir picked up one of the biscuits and sniffed it. '*Gott in Himmel*,' he said. Then, with a sly sideways glance at me, 'English food, *ech*. Vat rubbish. Come, Miss. You try Polish food. Come, come.'

We left the shop in silence, he forging ahead through the bustling streets, me trailing behind him, perfectly indifferent as to my fate. Eventually we arrived at a large house where everyone spoke Polish and scents of a near forgotten kind wafted around a dining room. Inhaling, my stomach stirred like a shark from its slumbers and began to nose upwards. We sat at a table and mirages appeared before me – beetroot soup, stuffed cabbage, potato salad, a rum-soaked cake – and magically evaporated. Meanwhile Mr Shamir leaned back in his chair, exchanged Polish gossip with other old men and kept the dishes coming. At the end of the meal I excused myself, reeled off to the Ladies, reached its refuge just in time and upchucked the lot.

Afterwards, still weak, but less so, I expressed fervent gratitude to my boss before plunging back into the cellar for the afternoon's washing.

'Never mind mit de tank yous,' he called as I went. 'I keep de bill, don't worry. Next week you pay me back. OK fine?'

Thus Mr Shamir stepped into Dirk Bogarde's vacated shoes and stayed there, feeding me three times a week until my hollows had begun to reinflate, my debt was paid, the spaniel was again in sole possession of its bikkies and my benefactor was accusing me anew of causing the Fall of the House of Shamir by my reckless use of hot water, soap, electricity, dishmops, dishcloths.

'Next thing you'll be saying I'm wearing out the sink,' I countered once, enspirited by nourishment.

'Is true,' Mr Shamir agreed. 'I vant you buy me a new sink ven you go.'

Early one morning I woke to hear the pay telephone on the landing outside my room shrilling away. This time, for the first time, it was for me.

'*Dutch!*' I squawked. 'Where are you?'

'Heathrow. They won't let me in. You got any money?'

'No. Well, twenty quid.'

'That's all?' He gave a sad croak. 'No good. They're going to deport me to Amsterdam.'

'Oh, Dutch, no,' I moaned. So near, so far.

'Listen. Will you come?'

'To the airport?'

'To Amsterdam, dummy. To live with me.'

Pips began to bleat, there were muffled oaths, then a terminal click. I put the phone down and felt the vice that had gripped my heart ever since the children had gone loosen just a little.

Full of apologies and lies designed to spare my boss's feelings – an aunt fallen ill, no one in the world to look after her but me – I gave Mr Shamir a fortnight's notice that day.

As he had on the morning I'd arrived, he shrugged, cast his eyes skyward and embarked on his repertoire of guttural squeaks. Finally, 'OK, go,' he said. 'I never vanted you here anyvay. I tell you so ven you come first for ze job but did you listen? No.'

When I took leave of him, bending down on an impulse to drop a kiss on his scrunched forehead, he beat me off, growling, 'Ach, you. Go away, Miss, please.' But a few yards down the street I heard his raised voice and turned. There he stood outside the shop waving a bunch of papers at me. 'Miss. Miss. Look at all vat you owe me. Ven you come back, you pay.'

Faintly alarmed – had he meant it all the time? – I took two steps towards him, whereupon he threw his stubby arms in the air and the papers fluttered down all around him like snow in a Christmas paperweight.

'OK fine?' he shouted.

'OK, fine,' I shouted back. 'Goodbye and thank you, dear Mr Shamir.'

*

Shamir was gone but not quite forgotten: the first hot words Dutch and I ever exchanged concerned him. In the short time we had been together in Montreal, Dutch moving into my absent husband's place as if it had always been meant for him, there had been no arguments at all. We had settled immediately into harmonious adultery, asking no questions, asserting no claims, making no promises and above all steering clear of any word of love. This restraint appeared to come naturally to Dutch, I had to work at it but did so with a will, determined this time to fox the Furies that had until then set themselves to wreck my relationships with men the moment simple attraction showed signs of escalating. All through our turbulent marriage they had pursued István and me, and I had no doubt they were still quartering the sky overhead, waiting to swoop at the first intimation of two hearts beating harder than was biologically necessary. Better lie low for a while and hope they would soon take off in search of meatier targets. Love and all the turmoil it had so far caused me I could presently and happily do without.

And now here the two of us were at Schiphol Airport, about to take up where we had left off. After the first hectic embraces – Dutch's arms closing around me to swing me off my feet, his whole big warm body engulfing me – I heard myself laughing for the first time in months, a series of rusty creaks rather than a pretty tintinnabulation but still, I congratulated myself, better than tears. Men hated tears.

My resolve didn't last. Standing by, watching Dutch stow my two suitcases into the car, something about the familiar bulk of him, the reassurance of it, the refuge, unexpectedly popped the cork on my bottled-up woe and let loose the deluge. All the way into Amsterdam I sobbed and shook and ranted, hiccuping out from layers of Kleenex a disjointed account of the shocks that had assailed me since last we'd been together in

Canada. Out it all came, the sorry story, the pleadings and fury of István at my wanting to leave him, the velvet hell of the flat in Cadogan Mews where, caged together with the children, we had fought like wild beasts, me to free myself from him, he to hold on. How, worn but calm at last, he had agreed to parting and I, seeking to show good faith, had handed over to him the cheque I'd brought from Canada, proceeds of the sale of our house and possessions, all the money I had in the world. He would share it with me, he promised, he promised. And thence to the morning I'd gone out shopping and returned to find the flat empty, my chicks gone, both my pretty chickens at one fell swoop. Nothing left but my clothes and a note: *I have taken the children, do not try to find us, this is your punishment, you brought it on yourself.* No help from my father – *Your mess, my lady, clean it up yourself.* No comfort from Mother – *Marriage is forever, you should have stuck it, I did.* But, Mother, I don't love him, I never could, I told him so from the start but he wouldn't listen, he scared me into marrying him, he scared everyone. Mother, I want to be happy. *Happy?* she said in a voice from the tomb. Oh my babies, my babies.

Throughout this flash-flood Dutch remained impassive, he who had known me only in the good times, when István had left me in Montreal to find a job in London and all the friends who had hitherto shunned my husband's brooding presence had flocked back to party. The big hands webbed with golden hairs stayed steady on the steering wheel, the blue eyes never left the road as he raced for the city. Only when, nearing the end of the dismal saga, I gasped out a sentence or two concerning the job I'd just left and how Mr Shamir had saved me with transfusions of stuffed cabbage did Dutch suddenly react.

'Sonofabitch,' he grunted.

'Who?'

'That Shamir. What a bastard.'

'What d'you mean?' I was bewildered.

Dutch slapped the wheel. 'If he'd paid you a living wage you could have bought your own food. My God, you were starving right under his nose. As for that hell-hole he made you work in. Jesus. I wouldn't keep a rat in those conditions.' He punched the wheel again, his jaw tight and red. 'Talk about exploitation. Man, that takes some beating.'

'No, you don't understand.' A sort of desperation seized me. 'It wasn't his fault, I had debts to pay back. He fed me. He liked me. He was kind.'

'Liked you? Kind? You gotta be kidding. He just didn't want to have you die on him is all. Afraid he'd have to shell out for a coffin. Kind, my ass.'

At that point I set up such a piercing wail that Dutch was forced to swerve across two lanes and judder to a halt on the hard shoulder. He switched off the ignition and turned to hold me, but I fought him off. All my fears of inner malfunction, always nagging at the back of my mind, exploded into panic, more suffocating, more frightening than ever before, a jumbled mass swelling inside my head, pressing hard against my temples. If Dutch was right about Mr Shamir, if Dutch could spot instantly what was what, then something was truly askew in me. My hands clamped over my face, I saw in darkness the knobbly features of the old Pole, watched them shift ever so slightly, and lo, where before I'd discerned a gruff affection, there was now only cunning and contempt. Mr Shamir, laughing up his sleeve, sneering at my gormlessness, gloating in it, his chance to squeeze a few more pennies his way. Not kind but cruel. Not generous but grasping. A joker, oh yes, but the joke on me. Again I'd failed to recognize boundaries, blundered past limits, accepted the unacceptable. Again I hadn't grasped the obvious except, now, with awful clarity, that I was a fool, a sucker, a pitiful booby and the world was a bitter cold place.

'Leave me alone,' I sobbed. 'I'm no use to anyone, I wish I was dead. All I do is cry and cry. Oh God, my life is such a mess.'

'No it isn't,' said Dutch calmly. 'I'm here.' Whereupon, after patting my shoulder a couple of times, he revved up and looped back into the traffic while I tried not to think what he'd have said if I'd told him about Dirk Bogarde.

All this, the psychic re-run of my physical eruption in the Polish Club, left me feeling as empty as my stomach had then, but by the time we reached the outskirts of Amsterdam a fresh emotion had moved in to fill the vacuum and while Dutch, nudging into the old city, diligently named the sights therein – Rembrandt's house, the Dam Palace, Prinsengracht, the Rijksmuseum – I was crouched over a mirror busily repairing the recent flood-damage. *Down and down I go*, I hummed under my breath, coating my lips with Pink Pearl, starching my lashes with mascara, *in a spin, loving the spin I'm in*. The church called that old black magic a sin, one of the seven deadly, but to me it seemed pure as a mountain stream compared to the grey-green Limpopo of love. Already I felt braced by its effervescence, as if I'd downed a foaming Alka-Seltzer to cure a bad hangover. No matter how hopeless I might be at sorting out the rest of life's realities, I had no trouble recognizing this delicious sensation when it hit me. Cupid's dart was lust, not love, as they pretended. The Greeks knew what was what.

Just then, Dutch swung off a cobbled lane, manoeuvred the car into a courtyard and cut the engine. In the loud silence that followed, our eyes locked. One second to take in the rapid dimming of his blue gaze, one more to register the slumberous weight of my own eyelids, the sudden clotting of the blood in my veins, and then we were out and heading up the stairs of the building ahead, up and up to the topmost floor and through a door and so to bed, plunging like two famished falcons upon each other.

Oh, glorious! Tan-tan-tara! There the ancient battlefield, lit by fires and flashing stars in a purple sky, and lo the gallant body rising in splendour to flush from ambush each fear and horrid recollection of the craven mind. Chasing, weaving, clashing, fleeing, the mind at last is cornered, surrenders and is purged by joy. Then the body, merciful in victory, enfolds its erstwhile quarry in gentle embrace and both drift together into sweet sleep.

Or as Dutch put it before he drifted, 'Oh man, that was one great fuck.'

Late in the night, uneasily stirring from a blissful coma, I took two half-waking breaths and was roused to full alert. The darkness was thick, but made thicker by a rich, unnatural reek. Beside me Dutch lay undisturbed, flung out like Icarus on the rocks. I shook him.

'Waa?'

'There's a funny smell. What can it be?'

Still with his eyes shut he inhaled. Then, coughing, he staggered up and stumbled across the room into a far corner. Mechanical sounds emanated. He groped his way back, fell on the bed and reached for me.

I prodded at his encroaching chest. 'Well? What was it?'

'Gas.'

'*Gas?*'

'New canister,' he mumbled. 'Changed it this morning. Must've . . . I dunno. Come here, woman.'

I sat bolt upright, pushing him off. 'My God. If I hadn't woken, we'd have both been dead by tomorrow. We *would*. What was wrong? Did you forget to . . . ?'

'Uhuhuhuh . . .' Hand over my mouth, Dutch cut me off. 'It's OK. Don't worry. I'd have woken too, sooner or later. Come on, come here.'

An unwanted edge sharpened my voice. 'Later? *Too* late.'

His arms cradled me. 'You're safe with me, sweetheart. Forget it.'

Sweetheart. He'd never called me that before. I forgot it.

Leaving London, I'd had every intention of returning in two weeks, maybe three. All I desired was a brief respite from my troubles, a little rest and relaxation in a lover's arms so that I could work out in peace what I should do next and boost my spirits for the battle ahead. The hatred I felt for my husband, hating him for what he had done, hating him for making me hate him, great waves of hatred that welled up and burned like acid, was pitting my insides with holes and I had to dilute it with some tenderness or end up a human colander, dribbling away every drop of vital energy. One day I'd take up Dutch's invitation and live with him in Amsterdam but not now, not possible, not until my children were with me again.

Yet, once with Dutch, I kept postponing my departure. Tuesday, Thursday, Sunday, well, next Tuesday then. Each morning as I swam up from sleep my first thoughts were of my babies: where they were, how they were, how I could find them and bring them back. The thoughts attacked like a flock of crows, dozens of beaks pecking away, the pain forcing tears to stream silently out of my eyes as the early sun streamed in through the windows. By the time Dutch woke, luxuriously stretching and yawning with the gusto he greeted each new day, a drowned rat lay on the pillow beside him, watery eyes, snotty nose, soaked cheeks in a sodden frame of hair. I'd turn my back to shield him from misery's infection, half-fearing, half-hoping that today would be the day he'd decide he'd had enough and I'd have no further excuse to linger. After all, how long could any man endure this Chinese water torture – drip drip drip until madness struck?

In the event, Dutch turned out to be impressively waterproof, though whether the proofing was synthetic or natural I could never make out. At any rate, he appeared impervious to the Niagara Falls at his side. Looping his sheet into a toga, raking his fingers through the nimbus of his marigold hair, he'd beam down at me like the sun on a puddle, full in my wreck of a face, kiss the tip of my reddened nose and head for the kitchenette, raising his voice to holler as he went.

'We all live in a yellow submarine, a yellow submarine, a yellow subma . . . Coffee? You want a hot croissant? Croissants and honey, how about that? Hey, it's gonna be a great day, look at the sun, man. Wahoo!'

And so grateful was I for his tolerance of me that when he returned, plates piled high, crumbs and honey trailing in his wake, I was able to produce a wobbly smile, already drying out in the warmth of him.

Then we made love, then the morning began and the next and the next, leaving me ever more loath to tackle the thundery future. Better live for the day, as Dutch did so well. Best not to think for a while.

Soon after my arrival Dutch landed a production job with a television company and a freelance commission to act as a live interlude between programmes, accompanying himself on the guitar, one cowboy boot up on the rungs of a stool, singing the songs he had learned in Canada, songs of the West and the dispossessed. For this he was paid just enough to allow us to scratch along. But thanks to Mrs Reemrev, our landlady, we were able to eat well above our income.

'She's Indonesian,' Dutch told me before I met her, 'from Java. The Indonesians didn't go in for surnames until we came along and colonized them. Then some of them took the names of their bosses and turned them round. Reemrev, you see,' he ended with a flourish, 'is Vermeer spelt backwards!'

'Gosh,' I said, 'was he out there?'

'Who?'

'Vermeer.' Then, since Dutch looked blank, I said, 'The painter. You know.'

'Not *him*. Vermeer's quite a common name in Holland.' Suddenly, he hooted. 'You thought Vermeer, the painter, was in Java? For God's sake, woman, that Vermeer lived in the sixteen hundreds.'

Swiftly I distracted him – 'Good thing Rembrandt wasn't out there either or Mrs Reemrev'd be Mrs Td-narb-mer' – and the humiliating moment passed but, oh dear, how familiar such moments were. Why did I know so little? Why did men know so much? Ever since I could remember, my father had presented himself as the ultimate authority on everything, dismissing all other opinions with a contemptuous wave of the hand. Later, boyfriends took over, expounding with shattering confidence on any subject that came up, from the state of the nation to the quickest way to get to Norwich while avoiding Stratford East. Then, when I married, István began his own series of lectures on world affairs, instructing me on topics as diverse as the iniquities of Communism, the virtues of feudalism, what Italian women thought about sex, why Rudyard Kipling was England's greatest poet, how to track, shoot and dismantle a moose, how to cook paprika chicken and why America was right, meanwhile correcting my mistaken views on banning the bomb, not hunting moose and America being on the whole wrong. But at least István was ten years older than me, had fought in the war, been a prisoner in Siberia, spoke a daunting five languages and was some sort of cousin to most of the grandees of Europe. Dutch was my age, hadn't done much of anything and wasn't related to anyone special, yet still he knew more than I did. What was it about being male?

Mrs Reemrev, source of my latest *faux pas*, turned out to be a cheerful little butterball, miraculously ageless, with wrinkle-free skin and high taut cheekbones. Her extended family of equally little sons, daughters and grandchildren took up all the storeys below our bed-sit, yet in spite of this amplitude of offspring, Mrs Reemrev's abundant maternal instincts easily enveloped the two giants who stomped about on her top floor. Whenever she detected our steps on the stairs of an evening – and we soon learned to make them very detectable – there she was, leaning over the banisters, tiny hand fluttering to catch our attention.

'You like a nice Indonesian food? I cook *rijsttafel* now. You come down, eat with us seven clock. Yes?'

Soon we were descending nightly to take our places at her kitchen table, Brobdingnagians among the Reemrevs and with appetites to match. The *rijsttafel*, dish after spicy dish of it, was delicious and on occasion so hot my nose would start to run like a tap. The first time Mrs Reemrev noticed my embarrassed sniffs she clapped like a child given a treat.

'I see you,' she crowed. 'Your noses, it run, ah-ha.'

Blushing, I owned up to nasal incontinence.

'No, no. It is good. It say I fine *rijsttafel* cook. Come, I show you how we do.' And gesturing to a nearby son, she shooed us out of the door to watch the son pinch his nose and snuff its contents down the stairwell to peals of merry laughter. I never managed to shed my inhibitions to this extent but always, afterwards, I armed myself with tissues and snorted noisily into them as a compliment to mine hostess.

Climbing back to our room at the end of one evening, pot-bellied with rice, I said to Dutch, 'I was right, you know. It *could* have been Vermeer.'

'What could?'

'Holland occupied Indonesia at the beginning of the seventeenth century. Mrs Reemrev told me. So you see, Vermeer might have been there.'

'I didn't say he couldn't,' Dutch said.

'You did.'

'No, I didn't.' Patiently, he added, 'All I said was, he wasn't. I know about Vermeer. He was never in Indonesia, take it from me.'

'That's not the point.'

'So what is?'

I gave up then as I usually did on such occasions, feeling my brain dissolve into a porridge and not wanting to argue anyway. However, a vague resentment lingered, as was usual too. It struck me that men might not, after all, know so very much more. Perhaps they only talked and acted as if they did, and were smarter at covering up if they didn't. Those pauses to let their words sink in, the way they closed their eyes if you interrupted, the way their voices sharpened ever so slightly to warn you off. But, apart from all this, how odd that they should think they had to have an answer to everything. No wonder it was hard to have a proper conversation with them. You'd start out all right, chatting away, and then, abracadabra, you were back at school, he the teacher, you the pupil. Even Dutch, who was good about not holding forth, never admitted straight out that he didn't know something or dreamt of asking a question himself. If he got lost in the Sahara, I brooded, without me with him to inquire where the nearest oasis was, he'd die of thirst rather than ask himself. Questions, it seemed, were women's work. 'Eve,' said Adam, 'ask the snake over there to pass us an apple.' She did, and got blamed ever after.

During the day, while Dutch was working, I embarked on my love affair with his city. Amsterdam had all the attractions any Michelin-toting tourist could wish: four-star buildings, palaces, cathedrals and churches, world-class paintings and sculptures, bustling street markets and shops, the added glamour of water everywhere and a red-light district well worth the detour. But it had something extra no other city could claim: Amsterdamers. They were the icing on the cake, the big, fair, friendly men and women who thronged the narrow pavements, bicycled along the cobbled streets, strap-swung on the jouncing trams, gossiped around the herring stalls, greeted each other under the awnings of the street cafés and played dominoes all day in the corner taverns. As a lone foreign female in any other city I'd have felt at best an outsider, at worst continuously harried, dogged by bum-pinchers and kerb-crawlers as in Rome or Madrid, or scared to wander on my own, as in New York.

But in Amsterdam I felt entirely at ease, so much so that one afternoon, footsore and thirsty, I did what I had never done anywhere before: I went into a tavern on my own. A big step then for a woman, if a small one for womankind. And no one stared or leered or sneered, nor was I ignored. Instead room was made for me at the bar and, when I had my drink and was looking around, still nervously, for somewhere to sit, several people at a nearby table beckoned me to a chair quite as if I were an old friend and, as I said 'thank you' and sat down, continued with their noisy discussion – Amsterdamers never talk if they can shout – but in English now, for my sake. Just my luck, I thought with a kind of guilty relish, to land in this particular city. The prospect of leaving Dutch was bad enough but had his home town been anywhere else I'd have found the willpower to tear myself away ages ago.

Or so I weakly told myself as one month became two and three and still I remained, hanging on like some junkie endlessly promising and failing to kick a habit. My addiction was to Dutch for his lightness of heart and good humour, such a contrast to the grim passion of my war-wounded husband, and also to Amsterdam for its treasure chests of beauty. I had lately become quite ravenous for the stuff, seizing on beauty's every manifestation for use as a poultice, a balm for disquiet, a healing antidote for hate. Greedily I stared at the sly squinting faces of Flemish madonnas on canvases and carvings, hungrily I feasted on enamelled Vermeers, the flow of Rembrandts, Van Dyck's sumptuously lace-trimmed burghers, Van Gogh's flaming landscapes and the legion of Low Country Masters with their wide skies, rumbunctious drunkards, discreet glimpses of domesticity and cornucopias of the countryside, pheasants, partridges, blood-gouting rabbits, fruit, grapes and wine in bacchanalian abundance and cascades of peonies, tulips, roses, camellias, studded here and there with one exotic butterfly, a humble spider, a glossy house-fly.

Beauty was also rampant in the streets. High wimpled houses, row upon row, leaning every which way like tipsy nuns; the organ-grinders pumping at their gaudy machines; the plump matrons up from the country, clogs peeping from under starched petticoats, in flyaway caps with coral at their necks; the neon-pink prostitutes posing in tiger-striped undies and, lacing everything together, reflecting every beauty back, Amsterdam's broad, stately canals. On a sunny day, walking their banks hand in hand with Dutch, wind dimpling the water, boats scudding by, the air ringing with the cries of gulls and the jingle of hurdy-gurdies, every nightmare that plagued me ceased, for that blessed while, to exist.

By the time I'd been in Holland for four months, however, even Vermeer's *View of Delft*, the most wonderful painting in the world, had begun to lose its hypnotic translucence, dimmed by churning anxieties that could no longer be allayed. The dragon barring the path ahead grew larger and more menacing every day and it would have to be confronted, however inadequate I felt for the task and however much I dreaded defeat. It was, in large measure, that dread that had rendered me thus far paralysed. While battle was not yet enjoined I could at least hope, but how would I survive the death of hope if the outcome, the return of my children, went against me? The mere thought, whenever it slunk into my mind, caused such an eruption of raw red grief that it blew the rest of the day apart and half the night too.

My return was finally triggered by two ads in a copy of the *Sunday Times* that Dutch brought home from work. Both required someone called a Home Editor, one for the newspaper itself, one for a woman's magazine. The salaries on offer were so far above Mr Shamir's tenner a week that I fell back, dazzled.

'Look,' I cried, tearing out the ads and waving them under Dutch's nose. 'Home Editor, see? That's one thing I know about, homes.'

'Journalistic experience necessary,' Dutch read out.

'I wrote the whole of that supermarket promotion thing in Montreal and all my own links at the radio station.'

'Ability to produce imaginative room sets,' Dutch went on.

'Room sets?'

'That'd be the same as film sets,' he said confidently, 'only smaller. You put furniture and stuff together in a studio and they photograph it.'

'I could do that.'

'And it says you have to have established contacts in the design field.'

After a longish pause I said, 'Well, they can't have everything. I'll apply anyway.'

The letters took Dutch and me two evenings to compose and were small gems of dissimulation, relying heavily on the prospective employers' ignorance of all things Canadian and accounting for my Amsterdam address by explaining that I was currently doing a stint as film-set adviser for Holland's Vara TV Station – Dutch's employer.

He read the final versions aloud. 'Sounds great, huh?'

'Yes,' I said and went to peel some potatoes. From the kitchen I called, 'It's all lies, though. Is that awful?'

'Don't send them, then. Don't go,' Dutch called back.

Fiercely I gouged at the eyes of the potatoes.

In a little while, Dutch said quietly, 'Not *all* lies.'

Ten days later answers came, both offering interviews. Dutch hugged me, I hugged him, we capered about the room. Then, 'Oh Dutch,' I panted, stopping suddenly with his arms about me, 'now I really have to go.' Dismal reality was setting in. If I got either job I'd have money to start a custody case. Inevitably, then, the lid of Pandora's box, which I'd managed to keep firmly closed in Amsterdam, would be pried open to spill out its horrid contents and I'd be all on my own to face it, no Dutch to mop me up of a morning and cheer me on. How would I bear it?

'Don't worry.' Dutch beamed upon me. 'I'll be close behind you.' Twisting his lips into a gangster sneer, aiming two fingers at the wall, he said, 'Rat-tat-tat. Next visit to l'l ol' Heathrow, baby, I'm gonna *shoot* mah way in.'

I stood rigid in the only half-decent outfit I possessed, a moulting mohair sweater in funereal purple and a black lint-flecked skirt. The room was dauntingly bright, high up and built almost entirely of glass. On the carpet at my feet lay sprawled an elegant stick-insect of a man in a lettuce-green suit.

'Mark Boxer,' he drawled, extending a hand.

I bent stiffly to take it. Silence fell as he surveyed me. I hoped I looked better upside down.

'Why,' he said finally, 'd'you want to work for the *Sunday Times*?'

First question and I was stymied. For the money, of course, I wanted to scream, for the money, money, *money*. I knew nothing of British newspapers except that they evidently paid their staff fortunes. My father had taken the *Daily Telegraph* and *The Times*. Were they the best? He'd always claimed so but, then, he would.

'Because it's the best newspaper?' I replied. Oh God, that question mark had tilted my voice, making me sound like a half-wit child.

'Ah ha,' said Mr Boxer, absently reaching up to pluck a fleck off the hem of my skirt. 'Why, in your opinion, is that?'

In between arriving and finding a room, I'd only had time to buy and read one issue of The Best Newspaper. Hands twisting damply, I began reciting in a Dalek monotone: 'Because it's serious. But it has humour. It's knowledgeable. But not pompous. It's . . .' At this point, my eyes rolled backwards like a horse baulking at a fence. Hastily, Mr Boxer changed tack.

'OK. Now tell me, who do you know?' he said, linking his arms behind his head and scrutinizing the ceiling.

If the first two questions were bad, this was worse. Tacky to drop the names of the gaggle of princes, counts and barons, my husband's relatives and friends, and pointless besides. Knowing foreigners, however impressive, wouldn't help me here in London and in London the bleak fact was that I knew no one at all.

'How about Sir Paul Reilly?' nudged Mr Boxer. 'Head of the Design Centre?'

Glumly, I shook my head.

'Tony Snowdon, perhaps?'

'Tony . . .?'

'Princess Margaret's husband.' By now he was enunciating slowly and clearly, as to the deaf. 'The. Earl. Of. Snowdon.'

'Oh yes, of course.'

'Yes? You know him?'

'Oh no. I mean, I know *of* him.'

Mr Boxer's eyebrows rose. Below them, his eyes were now showing as much white as mine. He cited the names of six more people, each of whose acquaintance I was forced to deny.

'You see, I've been in Canada for seven years,' I added in feeble extenuation.

'Uh-huh,' he said, clearly suspecting that I'd spent those years in a Canadian jail. In which supposition, I mournfully thought, he wasn't far wrong.

Out of courtesy, he extended the interview a little longer but then men in shirt sleeves began poking their heads round the door and glamorous girls in mini-skirts dashed in and out. Mr Boxer sprang to his feet, invigorated, and I backed into a corner, awed by the brief exchanges that occurred, so witty, so matey, so full of mysterious jargon. Everyone exuded such confidence, such cheer, as if they'd never known a care in the world. Half of them were apparently on the verge of flying off to exotic locations and an air of sophisticated bustle suffused the room. I felt dowdy, defeated and a hundred years old and when I edged up to Mr Boxer as he chatted away and mumbled about another appointment, he ushered me to the door with such warm expressions of goodwill that I knew I'd convinced him I was unemployable. Just then, I heard one of the glamorous girls asking did anyone know how to get hold of Princess Ira Furstenberg?

'I do,' I whispered as I sidled out.

The door slammed behind me.

Back in my rented bed-sit I slumped down in front of the cracked mirror on the dressing table and watched myself cry – a drearily familiar sight. Lord, what was happening to me? Why should a room full of perfectly amiable people start up that sickening pulse in my stomach, making it nearly impossible to form a coherent thought for the wicked thump-thump, like a boiler-room engine throbbing deep in my guts? Even to produce a decent smile had been foiled by the tremor on my lips. I'd never felt like this before. Before, I'd been blithely confident and the jobs I'd applied for were easily got, though I possessed even fewer qualifications than I had now. Before, I'd taken for granted that each worldly oyster on offer would instantly and gladly yield me its pearl. But before *what* exactly? Was my unhappy marriage to blame for this shrinking violet I'd turned into or was it the shock of the children vanishing? I closed my eyes, trying to pinpoint the source and saw, painted on darkness, the baby features of Michael, my first-born, my little Mickey Mouse. One morning there he'd been in his crib as usual, cooing, gurgling, kicking his legs and the next, he lay silent, rosy face white as snow, chubby limbs still. Five months old, healthy and dead. A cot death, they'd called it. Words. Four years had passed since then and the volcano of anguish had subsided but the questions remained. How could it happen? What did it mean?

It meant there was no safety anywhere. Under the cheery surface of life, a sliver below the hubbub, the laughter, the fun and games, was a secret place where horrors not only could happen but did, to anyone, to babies, without reason, at random, sweeping in like the sea. It meant that beneath all the meanings lay meaninglessness and beneath all the somethings, nothing. Understanding this, I saw for the first time that I was altered forever. Adrift without the usual moorings. Aware that all was not for the best in the best of all possible worlds and cut off by this knowledge from others of my age, marked by it like a plague victim whose sores, however carefully concealed, seeped through the bandages to repel the passerby. Shame made me awkward, tongue-tied in company, the spy, the spectre at the feast, carrier of a foul virus that threatened every innocent around. The Furies, as if they still doubted their new convert, had gone on to take my two surviving children. Ah ha, they shrieked triumphantly as they flew off, you thought because we'd struck once we wouldn't strike again. Know better now?

I knew better now but the comfortless knowledge, which might conceivably have come in handy had I planned to be a nun in a flagellant order, was a crippling disadvantage in everyday life and especially, it seemed, in the newspaper world, where natty clothes, an easy bonhomie and a huge appetite for the gloss of things were paramount. A rotten outlook, given that a job was now vital rather than the pastime it had hitherto been. I peered at the lopsided face before me. Somehow I was going to have to learn to pretend: first, that I didn't know what I knew and, second, that I knew a great deal about what I didn't.

Egged on by visions of ending up back in the Black Hole of Shamir, I must have lied with some skill at the second interview, for I got the job, floating back to my room in a rosy haze to try out in front of the mirror suitable home editorish expressions – happy-housewife smirk, mumsy twinkle, snooty executive stare – before succumbing to fright once more. I'd be a disaster, unable to cope. My lies would be exposed and I'd be sacked in disgrace. In a dream that night, the sacking took on a ceremonial aspect: an arch formed by cackling women under which I was forced to scuttle while being belaboured with various Hoover accessories. Conducting events in the cunning disguise of the magazine's editor was a certain Miss Needham from schooldays who had once predicted I would end up on the streets.

In fact the job turned out to be almost embarrassingly easy and I quickly learned the obligatory house behaviour – mad squeals of joy on discovering, say, a new gadget for unblocking drains ('Isn't it fab? My God, isn't it simply divine? How did we ever exist without it?'), interspersed with loud yelps of panic ('Oh no. Oh. My God. Can you believe it, they've sent the wrong mop. Pardon me while I slit my throat'). The whole staff contributed selflessly to the general frenzy, which rose from andante at the start of each month to a screaming climax on the thirtieth day whereupon, as from the hell of childbed, out popped a new-born issue. Occasionally I paused to wonder how journalists on daily newspapers coped. Hit high C on day one, I supposed, and screeched non-stop from then on, like so many boiling kettles.

The thing that did rattle me, though, was the unforeseen social whirl. The job itself provided luxuries beyond expectation, an office to myself, a padded chair, half a secretary, my own rubber plant, but then the invitations began pouring in: callers, mainly female, who announced themselves as public-relations officers for every sort of household appurtenance from sink tidies to three-piece suites and implored me to let them divulge the wonders of their products over long lunches, money no object. From being a non-person I was suddenly an object of compelling desire and my bed-sit diet of baked beans forked from the tin transformed itself overnight into four-course meals at smart Soho trattorias.

I knew perfectly well, of course I did, that all this wining and dining was a matter of business, yet some swaddled part of my mind kept itself tight clenched against the knowledge. This had the unsettling effect of leaving me as touched and grateful for hospitality received as if my various hosts had shelled out from their own pockets for no other reason than sheer goodness of heart. A number of them added to my confusion by shelling out true confessions at the same time. Over shrimp cocktails they mourned being too fat or too flat, over steak Diane they wailed of lost loves and by the time the Beaujolais had run out they were sobbing into the Black Forest gâteau of untimely pregnancies and shock-horror backstreet abortions.

Consequently it seemed tactless, even brutal, to recall that we'd been drawn together not by soul calling unto soul but the merits of Johnson's Wax. I did my best to hold to the magazine's interests and not indiscriminately to promise plugs simply to staunch my companions' tears, but the temptation pressed and the human debt I often felt weighed heavily. Power, I was discovering, didn't suit me at all. Even the minuscule amount in my gift – a two-line mention of a new wallpaper, a glimpse of fabric in a photograph – carried with it all sorts of sinking anxieties concerned with upsetting or letting down others.

For me the working world was another country, that was the rub. They did things differently there. Different language, different customs and habits, a different religion, other gods, and I'd stumbled across its border without a notion of how to adapt, without even being aware of the need to do so. My father, and all the men in my childhood and adolescence, daily travelled in and out but appeared to be bound by some Mafia oath never to talk of what happened there to wives, daughters or anyone else of the female sex. The Office, the Ministry, the City, these were the Stonehenges of no woman's land, mysterious constructions of obscure provenance and purpose. How had they come about? What were they for? What esoteric rites were enacted within them? No answers were vouchsafed but, then, there were no questions. My mother, her friends, my aunts, my friends' mothers, none asked questions that I heard, not even about the financial rewards these strange places offered. Indeed, for ages I suspected that my father, at least, went there solely to rid himself of me and Mother. The only women I ever encountered who worked themselves were teachers, but what use were teachers as guides to anything that lay beyond school walls?

Later, it became permissible for daughters to contemplate

taking what were called 'little jobs', in legal or financial firms safely inside City walls, EC1, EC2, or, at a pinch, arranging flowers at Constance Spry, W1. The aim, however, was to fill the interval before marriage and not in any way to foster that aberrant thing, a career. Little Jobs were strictly temporary, for supplementing a dress allowance, for meeting nice girls and, above all, nice men.

Like pretty well everything else about the way I was brought up, I regarded this attitude as antediluvian, ridiculous and deeply unfair. Having a brother had long since convinced me that anything the male sex had or did was by definition the best on offer, and men didn't go in for Little Jobs, to be picked up and dropped as the fancy took them. Men had careers, therefore careers were *ipso facto* desirable and my right too. Yet that penetrating insight was about as far as my rebellion went: all form, no content. Thus far I'd been happy enough to pick up and drop Little Jobs, as pastimes, for fun, for pocket money, exactly as convention decreed.

Circumstances had changed now. For the first time I had no parents or husband as bulwark and, besides, it had recently been forced to my attention that husbands as a species could vanish overnight. Little Jobs were clearly no longer adequate for the purposes of long-term survival and therefore I regarded this job as the Big One, my embarkation upon a career. Yet I set out as ill-equipped for the journey as my mother would have been, knowing no other way of treating the workplace than as a home from home and no other ethic or etiquette than was practised at home. Oblivious to everything but the day, without a conception of the path ahead, blind to any stepping stones or ladders to be climbed, ignorant of structures and hierarchies, illiterate in politics, office or otherwise, trailing clouds of wholly unsuitable emotions, I remained, as ever, unable to discern the divisions between public and private, contacts and friends, kindness and more venal favours, the business world and the personal; it was all one to me.

The chimpanzee was at its old tricks again, reacting on a chimp level. Body language, instinct, reflex, sight, smell, the belches that erupt from the unpatrolled unconscious, inchoate feeling and not much more: a primate's range. Complexity, ambivalence, the veiled motive, the necessary skills of dissimulation passed me by. Half-baked, my father had often called me, to no avail. Those raw, unrisen patches, the soggy bits round the edges, were to encumber the whole of my working life. I never much improved.

For the time being, however, being half-baked had its childish consolations. The impressively deckle-edged invitations that were always arriving for launches of new products, with drinks, with eats, at hotels, clubs and conference halls, made me feel warm and wanted. The parcels that came, full of fascinating samples of everything from cosmetics to pots and pans, never failed to produce a thrill of birthday excitement as I tore them open and my office soon looked as if Santa Claus dropped in every day.

The office next door, though, put mine in the shade. It belonged to the gardening editor, one of the few men on the staff, a middle-aged gent with a big, wine-dark conk. His room was so stuffed with boxes, sacks and implements that frequently only the conk was visible, poking like a gremlin's over the humps. One day, however, passing by while he was on the telephone, I discovered that his goodies were obtained by rather more creative means than mine.

'Take a pew,' he said, waving me in. I perched myself gingerly on a pile of some horticultural substance while he continued his conversation. 'Listen, old man, what I'm saying is, I've got a double-page full-colour spread in the mag next month. You know, April? Time to get out there, spring-clean the garden, all that sort of rot. But the mower you've sent me won't do, d'you get me?'

The receiver squawked.

'Yes, old man, I know it's a bloody wonder. Yes, just the job for our readers. The thing is, I'm in Bucks. Got an acre of rough grass to keep down, not some pocket-hanky Purley lawn. Ah, now you're talking. Yes, that's the one. The roto-thing. Perfect. So let's put it this way, between us and the bedpost . . .' – and here he gave me an avuncular wink – '. . . you get your pet wonder in headlines, page front, visible to a blind man at forty paces, and I get your roto-whatsit for the old homestead. Is it a deal? Good. Cheers then, old man.'

He hung up and gave me a beam. 'Old mate of mine,' he confided. 'Like to do him a favour now and then. A thousand quid's worth of free advertising I'm handing him, on a platter. Quite some favour, eh? Still, what are friends for, I always say.'

I gave him a weak grin back. Funny, I'd understood the conversation to mean it was him getting the favour. Oh dear. Wrong end of the stick again. Would I ever learn?

As the weeks went on, though, I learned. At every press launch of consequence, i.e., of merchandise that cost real money, I couldn't help remarking the presence of a certain rather grand older woman, columnist on a rival magazine. Her entrance invariably caused a stir, our hosts either flocking to her or veering off sharply in the opposite direction. Then I witnessed the lady in action. At the end of a demonstration of a new central-heating boiler she rose from her chair and sniffed the air for a moment like a retriever. The manager of the company, who was talking to me, saw her too, gave a sudden quiver, mumbled an excuse and dodged behind a nearby pot plant. Too late. She beat her way to him and pounced.

'Most impressive, that gadget of yours,' she hooted. 'Dare

say it'd go down a treat with my 400,000 readers. If it lives up to your handouts, that is . . .' and in a trice she'd wrenched out of the cowed MD a promise to install the boiler along with accompanying radiators 'for testing' at her country house.

As she sailed off, a nearby PR shook his head in awe. 'That house of hers must be a palace by now,' he remarked. 'Furnished from top to bottom, curtains, carpets wall to wall, fitted kitchen, all appliances plus a swimming pool. And everything, to my certain knowledge, for nowt. Or should I say, for "testing".' He peered at me then with narrow eyes, as if he suspected I'd just picked his pockets. 'You journalists, you're all the same,' he said, tut-tutting with awful archness. I blushed, he frowned, checked that his wallet was still there and departed.

Another eye-opener was to come. The rumour crackled through the building one morning. 'She's killed herself. Threw herself out of a window ten storeys up.'

Bewildered, I asked, 'Who? Where? Why?'

'Miss Pettigrew, you know. She was the first editor here, the mag's her baby. Then she went to the *Mirror*. Came back from holiday last week and found someone else sitting at her desk.'

'You mean . . .?'

'Yes. No warning. They'd fired her. So out she dived, head first. Isn't it awful?'

Miss Pettigrew. Awful. I listened, arms splayed out across my own desk as if to fend off invisible interlopers, thinking of her coming in one morning and seeing some anonymous Other in her place. I imagined a figure sleek as a seal looking up at her, eyebrows politely raised. Your office? So sorry. I'm afraid you're mistaken. Miss Pettigrew stuttering: N-no, that's m-m-my rubber plant. That's my c-coffee mug. The seal stares, expressionless. Sor-ry. And then the rush across the room, the hurtling down.

'It's happened before. They often do it that way.'

'Often?' I said, appalled by visions of bodies raining down all over Fleet Street.

'Not tell you you're fired. They wait till you're away for some reason and move the new person in.'

'That's right,' another girl chimed in, 'it happened to Helen, remember? And Mrs Whatsit in the Art Department. She was ill for a fortnight and she came back and . . .'

And on they went while I sat gazing at the rows of glossy magazine covers pinned on the wall: sweetly smiling housewives in frilly pinnies, cheery hubbies in hand-knit cardies, laughing kiddies hugging doggies and moggies. Girlies in the kitchen helping Mummy cook, Sonny in the garden helping Daddy dig. Christmas trees, Easter eggs, summer hols beside the sea, bonfire nights, toboggans, happy happy families. Not my experience, no. Not my mother's, either. Nor our current editor's, I knew. She had no family at all, just a cat in a bungalow in Esher. And what of Miss Pettigrew? Was she the Heart of a Happy Home like the women in her mag or did she dream it all up? Woollies-and-jellies was what we called that dream in the office and that's how she'd ended up, poor thing. A jelly on the pavement in a woolly.

Goose pimples ran right up my arms at the untoward image. Evidently this new career wasn't all thrills. There were spills, too, for some, maybe for me. Already I'd noted a few slippery patches. Little Jobs had no such peaks and troughs, what you saw was what you got. You did what you were told to do, had as good a time doing it as possible and at five on the dot you forgot all about it. Little Jobs didn't raise ripples in the mind, didn't disturb the surface at all. A career, on the other hand, seeped into evenings and weekends, popped up even in dreams, in fact took up so much of life that to all intents and purposes it *was* life, which might explain why it kept coming up with the same kind of questions: what am I here for, where am I going, is what I'm doing right or wrong? And, like life, the answers were never straightforward, often depressing. Very often there were none at all.

What of the gardening gremlin, for instance, with his matey telephone deal? Was that wrong? I'd thought so but obviously he didn't, indeed, he seemed sure he'd done right, and he was nearly twice my age, with years of experience in what was what. The grand woman at the press party had shown no qualms either. She hadn't tried to keep her voice down when she made her demands and the man who'd commented to me about her hadn't been shocked but admiring. And what had he added, admiringly? You journalists are all the same.

Well, if he was right – and why shouldn't he be, knowing so many more journalists than me? – then I was the one out of step, unadmirably dragging behind me an outworn and foolish schoolgirl code adults had long since discarded. Stupid to use priggish words like dishonest, immoral, wrong, instead of amused, uncensorious ones like crafty, bold, he's a rogue, she's a real character, what gall, some nerve. Those were the sort of things mothers said about a pet child, pretending to be cross but actually proud that their boy (somehow, it was always a boy) showed spirit, wouldn't buckle down, had the gumption to break their rules. That was how I longed to feel, but a tight little part of me wouldn't budge, just kept tutting away in the background like a maiden aunt. But a maiden aunt had her virtue. I hadn't. I was an adulteress, somebody's mistress, a failure as a daughter, wife and mother. I lived in a glass house and still I went on throwing stones.

This heart-searching process eventually brought me to the core question: was this precious career of mine the right one or not? Did its end product, the mag, help the readers or at any rate provide a bit of harmless fun? At times I had the uneasy suspicion that there might be something sneaky, deceitful, almost immoral – oh, not that word again! – lurking within its glossy pages. Certainly they reflected nothing I recognized as true but, then, who'd pay for a dose of my woeful views? Even so, the gulf between me and the magazine's credo appeared to be deeper than for most of my colleagues. They joked about it but that was a bluff, I could tell, meant to show they weren't serious when they actually were. The editor didn't bother with jokes. She was too devout, believed too passionately in the fantasy families beaming out from her pages, though their fantasy lives were as foreign to her as they were to me. Her inspired cover ideas – December (Christmas tree), April (showers), June (bride) and so forth – had her marvelling each month at her own genius, and ours if we conformed.

At her urging – September (Queen's birthday) – I'd written about Her Maj, what a wonderful mother she was, how despite all her duties her children came first, how loving she was, yet strict, yet fair, Heart of the Happiest Family of all. I'd had fun writing it, hunting through clippings for apt quotes, making a nice rounded shape of it with a cockle-warming ending. Everyone said they loved the piece, the editor adored it, sniffing with emotion as she read it, and, judging by the letters, the readers adored it as well. I alone, though pleased as Punch with the praise, remained unstirred by the subject. Experience of my husband's circle, a mixed bag of aristos that included two ex-crowned heads, had stripped me of any illusions concerning the nobility of the nobility. Nevertheless, here I was, painting the most saccharine of royal pictures and enjoying it, too. What did that make me?

And what about the monthly menu of perfect people in perfect homes doing all the right things? Fed this superhuman diet, were the readers uplifted or merely stunned, rabbits too dazzled by headlights to flee? Did so much perfection cheer them or infest them with guilt, sending them rushing for the Valium? And if it had no effect on them, what about me? While I dreamed up room after room to ornament my pages, each tidier, brighter, more spotless and polished than the one before, my own room sank to new depths of squalor, a residential version of *The Picture of Dorian Gray*. So was that what my precious career came down to, composing fairy stories for grown-up females? Not the Brothers Grimm sort either – they had their hardcore truths – but the goody-goody kind, full of elves in noddy hats and woodland creatures being sickeningly nice to each other.

The longer I mulled over these affairs, though, the plainer one thing became. No matter what moral conclusion I might finally come to, at the moment I couldn't afford it, for one aspect of the job overrode all the rest: money. In four months I'd saved enough to start the legal ball rolling that would bring my children back. So, shelving for the moment all whys and wherefores, I set off with high hopes one winter morning for Lincoln's Inn Fields, in pursuit of the Holy Grail of Justice.

'Did your um husband practise any er sexual perversions?'

We were huddled together knee to knee in an icy cubbyhole off the main office, me and the solicitor's clerk, a gangling lad of about my own age, mid-twenties. He had a Vesuvius of a cold, his nose all sore and bubbling with it, and his long face, wonky as a melting candle, was volcanic with spots that flared up like tiny indoor fireworks at each new burst of speech.

'Perversions?' I was taken aback. 'You mean, dressing up in women's clothes or something?'

The clerk nodded wordlessly and buried himself in the folds of a gargantuan hanky. I assured the nape of his neck that my husband's wardrobe had remained throughout our marriage strictly masculine.

'What about um enelinercourse?' my interrogator mumbled.
'What?'

A seizure gripped him. He struggled with it, angling his neck away from me, his Adam's apple yo-yoing madly. The sneeze, when it came, compressed him like a concertina. Afterwards, unfolding, he cleared his throat. 'Anal intercourse?' he inquired, overloudly.

'No,' I said. 'No.'

We stared at each other for a moment with a wild surmise, like two people trapped together in a sinking canoe. Then his eyes dropped to his notepad again. 'Er, cunnilingus? Um, fellatio?'

I heard my mother saying what's that when it's at home. Probably something disgusting Italians did. My husband thought everything Italian was marvellous, so maybe he had done whatever it was and I hadn't noticed. Well, I didn't intend to reveal my ignorance to this mere boy. 'No,' I said.

Another pause. I studied my frozen feet. He studied his. Then, 'Any sadism at all?'

Sadism. That at least I understood. 'Funny,' I said, determined to make clear my grip on the subject, 'de Sade was a Count, you know, like my husband. D'you suppose . . .?'

It was no good. The clerk's spots were on the verge of combustion. Hastily I affirmed that, Count or not, he wasn't sadistic. 'He scared me sometimes,' I went on, recalling the cold muzzle of his gun hard on my forehead, and the hard, lost look in his eyes. 'But he didn't enjoy it.'

The clerk scribbled on his pad. 'Excuse me,' I said after a pause, 'but what's all this for?'

He glanced up, looking stricken. 'Have to establish grounds for divorce. Unpleasant. Sorry.'

'Actually,' I said, 'I'm not interested in a divorce. I just want my children back.'

'Oh, yes. Oh, quite. But, see, divorce comes first, then custody. Have to follow procedure. Sorry.'

We followed procedure. We followed and followed and followed it. Soon I was on more intimate terms with the clerk's spots than if they'd been my own, watching them swell, erupt, die away and swell anew while their owner filled three more notebooks with details of my tattered marriage: sex, adultery, cruelties physical and mental, sex again. Conflicting emotions made me frequently stutter to a stubborn halt in mid-answer. The portrait of my husband being ground out of me was becoming increasingly distorted, unfair. Yes, he'd often terrified me but, no, he wasn't Jack the Ripper. Yes, he'd made me wretched. No, not because he didn't love me, because he loved me too much and I couldn't love him. Yes, he was jealous beyond all reason and yet there were reasons, he'd lost everything in the war, so understandably he feared losing me. Yes, he'd sometimes hit out in a frenzy, but being a prisoner in Siberia wasn't calculated to calm the nerves. Yes, no, but, so. Stop, go. That was the worst of it, the stop-go, more crippling than the shame, the embarrassment, the sweet-and-sour memories dug up and pinned out like a frog on a slab for the law's vivisection. Stop whenever a monster with slavering jaws usurped my tragic husband, but go the moment the pendulum looked like swinging too far his way, for if it did I might never see my children. At times I felt as torn as if a lynch mob had hold of me.

After five more interrogations over two more months, some with the solicitor himself, an elderly pot-bellied gent who called me his dear Countess but seemed a good deal less *au fait* with the other details of the case, I was informed that, most regrettably, divorce proceedings could not, at this time, be initiated.

'But why not?' I quavered, too stunned for anger, whereupon I was further informed that in order to start divorce proceedings a wife was required to establish her place of residence and since a wife had no legally recognized place of residence other than that of her husband, and since I was unable to furnish the court with my husband's place of residence, then, unfortunately . . .

'But that's the whole trouble,' I wailed. 'I don't know where he is. That's why I'm here. Oh, I can't believe it. Surely the law can do something. Oh please, please.'

As it turned out, the law could do nothing except, with exemplary speed, dispatch me the bill, which unfortunately wiped out my savings and plunged me in debt. Most regrettable, my dear Countess.

'Now don't cry any more, you hear,' Dutch said. 'I'm gonna give in my notice Friday. Four weeks, then I'll be over, OK? Hey, come on, speak to me.'

I had to take several deep breaths before a weedy voice emerged.

'They won't let you in.'

'Sure they will. This time, I got money. You got money, everyone lets you in. Four weeks from now, you take a look at the sky. Is it a bird? Is it a plane? No, it's your own personalized Suuuuperman.'

I put the phone down with a gulp that was almost laughter. Afterwards I cried some more but the tears flowed more easily now, the knot in my chest had loosened. Superman or not, Dutch wouldn't be able to change things, I knew that, but at least he'd bring comfort. Towards evening, the last tears were scalded off my cheeks by a sudden tornado of fury. Caught up, I spun about the room like a top, picking up and flinging anything to hand, saucepans, pillows, clothes, tins, shaking and yelling.

'Bloody law. Call that justice? Take all my money, then tell me to forget it, you don't exist. How dare they, how bloody dare they! What am I, a dog? Somebody's dog that can't even call its kennel its own without its master's say-so? I've *got* a residence! Right here! Paid for by me and nobody else! But oh no, that won't wash, not in bloody law it won't. To them I'm a hole in the air without a man, a bloody husband. Well, I'm not and I won't and I'll darn tootin' show 'em . . .'

And so I raged on into the night. In the morning when I awoke my room – everything all over the place – looked much the same as usual.

I said nothing at work, I had never said anything to anyone there about my circumstances. That was how I put it to myself, carefully, distantly. My circumstances. As far as the girls in the office knew, I'd spent time in Canada, which was why I used words like drugstore and sidewalk, but otherwise I was much like them: single, with a boyfriend, mine temporarily working abroad. No husband, no rings, no children, no hint of tasteless melodrama. Once or twice, when one of the girls, mopping her eyes, complained of quarrels with parents or a fickle love, I'd been tempted to pour it all out, but shame withered the words before they took shape, the shame of a leper confessing disease while the listener's eyes widen with shock, a shrinking pity, then an odious interest. I wanted no one to look at me like that, withdrawing even as they offered sympathy and afterwards running to spread the news – oyez, oyez, guess what, a leper is come among us. That was the comfort of Dutch, he'd never shrunk away, never tiptoed around me or tried to be tactful, didn't seem all that interested really, only cursing my husband now and again for making me wretched but actually, I suspected, for threatening to spoil his, Dutch's, day. I liked that in him particularly. It made me feel normal.

So I continued to say nothing, working as usual the rest of

the week, tapping out tips for readers on how to keep their houses clean, their kiddies happy, their marriages fresh, their armpits dry, their lips moist or the other way round, perhaps, since concentration was lacking. Then Friday lunch time, armed with my salary in its brown paper packet, I went to the bank, deposited it and requested an overdraft.

The teller grunted and lurched back as if I'd stuck a gun in his stomach. Recovering, he instructed me to put my request in writing to the bank manager, who might then consider granting me an audience.

'Now,' I said. 'I must see him now, it's very important.' Certainly I said it loudly, perhaps with a desperado's edge. I may even have tapped the counter a couple of times. At any rate, flashing the whites of his eyes, the teller scooted off. On his return, he flipped up a gate, beckoned me through and into the manager's office.

A small man with bushy eyebrows and a peppery moustache was seated sideways behind a large desk. 'What's all this?' he growled as I entered, swivelling round on his chair, eyebrows so close they looked like one long caterpillar in transit across his forehead. Then he saw me. 'Ah. Well, well. Come in, my dear. Sit down, sit down.'

I sat. He regarded me. The caterpillar split in half, revealing two eyes that were twinkling. 'An overdraft, eh? Very important, eh? Oh, you young ladies. What is it then? Want another pretty hat, do you? Haven't got a thing to wear for the next party, is that it? What's a poor man to do with you? Oh dear oh dear.'

Taking my cue, I began to wriggle my shoulders, bat my lashes, nip my underlip with pearly teeth.

The manager leaned forward and winked.

I simpered back. 'Just a teeny overdraft, oh please,' I almost lisped.

One pale finger rose and wagged itself at me. 'You're a naughty girl, I can see that. And you want me to be a naughty boy.' He chortled. I giggled. The finger dropped to some paper on the desk and ran down its columns. The caterpillar appeared on his forehead again.

'I'll pay it back as soon as I can,' I squeezed out in a little high voice. 'I'll be ever so careful. Promise.' And I bent my head meekly for fear he'd detect my wrathful heart and refuse me.

Through a thicket of cautions and admonishing clucks, I eventually extracted my overdraft and was sent on my way, only just avoiding a pat on my bum by a nimble two-step as I exited. An hour later the overdraft was spent, signed over in a grubby office behind a door that said PRIVATE INVESTIG ONS UNDERTAKEN. DISCRETION ASS RED.

All the following week I worried that Len, the man I'd hired, was too tall. He'd listened to my story so attentively and taken such copious notes that I didn't have the heart in the end to say, Look, Len, how private can your investigations be when you stick out so? I imagined him lurking behind a tree, his head nesting on the topmost branches like a giant bird's egg. No crowd could conceal him. He could not skulk. Disguise would be impossible: he was, without doubt, the most detectable detective. But he had sad pouches under his eyes, pulpy as if they were full of leaked tears. I felt sorry for him, all lonely up there, and could only hope for the best.

The hopes crumbled soon enough. Len on the telephone sounded strangely tinny, as if he was speaking from inside a bucket. 'He punched me,' he explained, 'on the nose. Near broke it. Your husband. When I found him.'

Found him! Oh Lordie. Oh heavens alive. Grabbing my bag, I raced over. Strips of plaster held Len's nose on to the rest of his face, which was streaked like a newly sprung rainbow. I expressed an ardent sympathy before starting to gabble: 'But you found him, you found him, did you see them, the children, how were they, what . . .'

Far above me, he raised weary hands. 'No,' he said, 'no children. I was shown off the premises PDQ, though I will say . . .' and here a mild pride suffused his Technicolor features, '. . . it took five of them butler fellows to one of me. After that, I hung around for a couple of days outside, keeping check, cars coming and going, then I slipped some deutschmarks to the chap on the gate. Told me he'd left with the kids in the night, destination unknown. See, I couldn't keep a round-the-clock watch, could I? Sorry about that.'

I'd guessed right then. István had fled to the castle in Germany where the two of us had stayed on our honeymoon, taken refuge with his relations there, the prince and princess who had so many servants he wouldn't have to look after the children at all, just park them and go hunting in the Schwartzwald as he had when we were there. Len, it turned out, had bearded him on the steps as he set out – 'There was a party of them,' he told me. 'Dogs, guns, those funny hats, all the gear' – and that was where István had punched him, standing two steps above, aiming down. Now he was gone and my money with him.

'You want me to sniff him out again? Don't take no notice of this.' Len gestured at his swaddled nose. 'That's par for the course. I don't mind. You give me a clue where he might of gone and I'll go after him. It'll cost, though, I have to say. Up to you.'

I thought of the children, scooped from their beds in the middle of the night, sleepy, bewildered, crying for a favourite toy left behind. It had happened in London, now this was twice and I thought of it happening again and again, because of me. Was that what I wanted, even supposing I could find the funds? Where would he go next? Venice? Rome? Madrid? István's rich relations were everywhere. Maybe, if I persisted, he'd dive behind the Iron Curtain, back to Hungary, taking the children into that bleak and dangerous barbed-wire world. No decent food, no vitamins, no fluoride toothpaste, no warm clothes, no free speech. Their dear little teeth would rot, their bones would grow weak, they'd be cold and afraid and . . .

'No,' I said to the Great Detective. 'Thanks all the same, but no thanks.'

Hope drained away, I trudged emptily back to the office and Happy Familyland.

Dutch came. I was in bed with my head under the blankets when I heard him come. The whole road heard him. It sounded like a small war had broken out, grenades exploding, gunshots, commanding shouts. Craning from the window I could see smoke at the end of the road, black whorls of it smudging the morning air. Then from the fumes lurched what looked like the husk of some fallen meteorite with a tail of youths pushing and shoving. The procession approached in fits and starts until, with a fusillade of backfire, the car jerked to a halt on the kerb below and out Dutch leapt like the sun bursting through clouds, gold hair flying, thumbs held high in triumphant salute to the bodies slumped gasping around him. The car gasped too and slumped but, unlike the bodies, it did not stir again. A fortnight later, despite Dutch's clandestine tinkerings – he had to work at night or be nicked in possession of a vehicle of no known provenance, half-buried in tickets – the police finally dragged it away, never to be seen again.

That morning, though, I skittered down the stairs as if my ship had come in.

'You should've let me know when you were coming,' I said later. 'It was just luck I was home with a cold. What if I'd been at work?'

'Well, you weren't.'

'But you didn't know that. You'd have had to wait hours and hours outside.'

'I'd wait years and years for you,' he said, the darling.

When the first ticket appeared on the car's windscreen, I worried about having to pay it. As they proliferated, so did my worries, leaping like a forest fire from imminent arrest to jail to lifelong ruin and a pauper's grave.

'Don't worry,' Dutch said. 'That car's on nobody's books, so it isn't there. So the tickets aren't there. So what's to worry about?' And he beamed like a conjuror.

When they took the car I said, wringing my hands, that I couldn't understand in any way whatsoever why he'd spent good money on such a useless lump of metal.

'It got me here to you, didn't it? What else matters? Don't worry.'

But I did. I worried all the time, something I'd never done before. That was the other change in me. Unspecified disasters of all sorts now hovered just above my head, sharpening their claws for the kill. I dreaded waking to the ominous rattle of their bony wings. I dreaded falling asleep in case they swooped in the night. The numbers on buses added up to bad luck, the sight of one magpie shadowed the day, and when it struck me that my room, wider at one end than the other, was the shape of a coffin, I dreamed of being buried alive. Though Dutch's buoyant presence held me up for a while, the black pit was waiting there, biding its time. Some months after his arrival, I fell into it.

'My dear,' said the editor, stopping me in the corridor one afternoon. 'Can you spare a moment for a little chat?'

In her office, full of flowers, greetings cards (from grateful readers?) and framed photos of herself and dog, she put her elbows on her desk and her chin on clasped hands. I didn't like the way she was looking at me: head tilted, the kindest of smiles.

'My dear, just between us, is anything the matter?'

Alarmed, I shook my head.

'Nothing worrying you here? About the job, I mean?'

'No. No. Not at all. Why? Have I done something wrong?'

'We're all very pleased with you,' she said in the hushed tones nurses reserve for the dying.

In the drowned pause that followed, all my unpaid bills swam before my eyes. How would I pay them if I were sacked? How would we live, Dutch and me, him with no work permit and no money left?

'Any troubles at home?' the editor asked, swaying cosily towards me. 'I want my girls to feel they can tell me anything. It'll go no further. Guide's honour.'

I assumed an air of near-swooning surprise. 'Troubles at home? Goodness no. Everything's fine, thank you. Just fine.'

The telephone rang. While the editor talked, my thoughts raced about in a panic. Had she planned this as a cunning diversion? Was someone else, at this very moment, moving her things into my office, crating my books and unpacking hers, elbowing my rubber plant aside for her African violets? Would I return to discover my chattels in boxes outside and everyone waiting expectantly for me to follow Miss Pettigrew through the nearest window?

As the telephone call ended I said, 'Why?' rather loudly.

'Why?' The editor put up a restraining hand while she scribbled. Then she looked up. 'Why what, dear?'

'Why did you think I had troubles?'

'Ah.' She focused again. 'Because, my dear child, you've worn the identical sweater, the same skirt and the same shoes for the last two months. That's eight weeks. That's forty working days. I'm no clothes-horse myself, far from it. Few but good is my motto. Nevertheless, one outfit for such a length of time does raise questions. People notice. People talk.'

A blast of heat hit me, making a bonfire of my cheeks. 'I wash them,' I blurted, 'all the time. This sweater's drip dry and the skirt too, nearly, and . . .'

'Now, now. Calm down, child. Nobody's accusing you of BO. No complaints there.' She gave a powdery chuckle. 'But I do feel we pay you well enough for the occasional change of attire. Isn't that so?'

'Oh yes,' I fervently agreed.

'You see, when you girls go out and about on business, you represent the magazine. You are It in the Flesh, so to speak. If you never change, never wear anything new, then people could get the idea that the magazine you work for never changes either, never comes up with anything new. D'you get my point?'

It occurred to me briefly that I was, so to speak, more It in the Flesh than she had any idea of, but the thought left me unamused. I stammered out contrition and promises of a new leaf and departed with my guts in a horrid stew.

That evening, rushing home, I wailed to Dutch, stretched full length across bags of laundry watching the telly he'd recently rented, 'What on earth shall I do? I've got to have some new clothes.'

'Sure. Why not?' he said. 'Look at that goalie, will you, he hasn't moved for the last three tries. You ask me, he's dead.'

'Why *not*? Because we haven't a bean, *that's* why not, so I'm going to lose my job and we'll be out on the streets and I'll never get the children back, never, never . . .' And I gave a great sob of despair at fate and the shrill fishwife it was making out of me.

'Hey hey hey,' Dutch soothed. 'Wait till you see what I've cooked for you. Veal escalopes in a white wine sauce. How about that?'

'We can't afford veal,' I cried. 'We can't afford wine. We can't afford any damn thing.'

Thus the pit opened beneath my feet, tumbling me into solitary confinement, and, since there was no ray of light down there, I went on wearing that sweater, skirt and shoes pretty well daily for the next two years, until, one day, on a work outing to Paris, Mel Calman said, 'I can't stand it any more. I'm going to buy you a new pair of shoes,' and did, and made me put them on. Then he said that in his opinion I was clinically depressed. 'I've been there. I know a clinical depression when I see one and, madam, you are in it.'

'Mel says I'm in a clinical depression,' I told Dutch when I got back.

'What's that?'

'Dunno.'

Looking back, I see that Mel was probably right. Either that or I'd gone a bit clinically mad. I had no idea what depression could mean, not many people did then. Depressed was what you said you were when it rained or someone didn't telephone or you got a spot before a party. *Honestly, I'm so depressed,* you moaned, and your friend moaned back, *Oh, I know, so am I.* At the other extreme, if someone took to their bed and wouldn't get up, then that might be acknowledged as depression too but if you kept moving, if you walked and talked and smiled politely and only collapsed in private, then unless they'd known you before, people simply put you down as the quiet type and never noticed that your hands grew damp and your throat went dry when you met them because you felt dull, said all the wrong things and looked terrible. And nobody in London had known me before except Dutch. He was my sunshine, my only sunshine, because he alone remembered the way I'd once been.

That chat was the trip-wire that did for me. Afterwards, I

saw very clearly how unfit I was for the outside world, too deformed by My Circumstances to cope or, more likely, a born failure. I'd been puffed up with empty pride for a while, thinking I was as good as the next, thinking I could have a proper career, but reality had exposed my pretensions. While I carped and picked holes and took up moral postures, others got on with the job, managing their lives with skill and style and neatly side-stepping the fixes and plights that had dogged me for so long. Nor was luck involved – lack of luck, until now, had been my craven excuse. They simply knew better, *were* better. Therefore the only option left was to give up and accept my inferior destiny with as much grace as I could muster.

This I did, though I held out for a further fortnight, trying to keep my promise of sartorial change by digging out the last shabby bits of my wardrobe and doing what I could to brighten them up with big hoop earrings, a bit of lace, a scarf tied *so*, like it said in *Vogue*. But such tricks were no substitute for new clothes, and since my overdraft had long ago hit the ceiling, the old uniform soon surfaced again. At that point I wrote to the editor that I'd had a life-and-death summons back to Canada and never went near the place again. It was, I suppose, an indication of my incoherent state that dumping the only source of income to hand because I was sunk under ever-inflating debt seemed the only possible course.

Thus I set myself adrift alongside Dutch on the tides of the city and as we floated out, *sans* provisions, *sans* rudder, *sans* everything, I saw to my astonishment that all around were other drifters bobbing about, young like us. Suddenly London was awash with a whole generation. There they were, fleets of them on the move, as though they'd been summoned together from all over the globe for some grand if mysterious enterprise. There was even a word for us: drop-outs. It was eerie. I began to wonder if I'd really ditched my job for the reasons I thought or had I simply heard the Pied Piper and obeyed, like the rest. Certainly my distress at being unable to stay the pace of a job wasn't shared, that I soon learned. In pubs, in parks, in bed-sits, on the streets, everyone seemed quite at ease with their unemployed state, proud of it, even smug. To them the working world was a rat-race, and they looked down upon, with pity shading into contempt, its denizens, the squares, the abject nine-to-fivers. Some had cut loose on principle, rejecting the very possessions, the money, the clothes, whose yawning absence in my life had driven me to join them. And some, I discovered, were actually working but pretended they weren't, mortified at having what I was mortified at losing. No wonder they called it the alternative society. Everything was upside down. I couldn't believe it.

Dutch could though. Oh yes. He took to it like a duck to water, sailing about as if he'd always been there. Because of him, large and loud and ebullient, covered in no time with right-on jumble, beaded leather bracelets, necklaces of bells, scrappy velvet waistcoats, a kerchief binding his golden hair, we, him and me – his chick, as I found myself labelled – were immediately part of the flock. Everywhere we went, Portobello, the King's Road, the Fulham Road, Carnaby Street, we were in a crowd and somebody was always playing guitar, usually Dutch. Half of me went along with it all in a stunned sort of way, my boring old outfit concealed beneath a Tibetan blanket from Oxfam, but the other half remained unabsorbed, subdued but ill-at-ease, hide it though I most earnestly tried.

And, of course, we were more broke than ever. Bread, as I'd learned to call it, might be despised in our new circles but it remained the only currency unenlightened landlords and shopkeepers would accept, and here Dutch and I had a problem not shared by our companions. Neither of us, unlike them, qualified for the safety-net of the dole, he not being British, me having been abroad for too long. When this was revealed to me by a monosyllabic official at a grille at the end of a shuffling queue, I iced up with fright. Dutch didn't care. He wonderfully, boldly, defiantly, didn't give a toss, and immediately became a most talented scrounger, setting off like a hunter into the jungle when we hit rock bottom (which was every third day), and returning with a huge grin to fan out pound notes in front of me. To begin with the sight of such dubious loot brought me out in a sweat and I peppered him with questions I didn't want to ask: where, how, who, when, oh how could you, the shame, the shame! Then I stopped and bought takeaway pizzas instead. Dutch came up with a plan for a commune, arguing that we could live cheaper that way, so we did a split from our coffin of a room, leaving a mountain of unpaid rent behind, and with contributions from Jean-Claude, Esther, Josie, Karen and Nancy, rented a much bigger place a stone's throw from the Queen's Elm, Dutch's most favoured hunting ground.

Gunter Hall Studios, where my old self finally gave up the ghost and another self began, was at the poor-white-trash end of Chelsea, a yellow-brick conglomerate purpose-built for artists in the 1920s that now belonged to Renato Cimatti, the dapper Italian owner of a chain of fish restaurants with names like the Contented Sole, the Happy Trout, the Orgasmic Cod and so on. Our unit constituted one gigantic hangar with steel rafters and great glass slabs for a ceiling, a gallery jutting over and a warren of amateurishly partitioned rooms, all papered like the sky at night, inky, with rashes of stars. To furnish this mausoleum we brought with us a one-bar electric fire, three bean-bags, one sagging sofa, a furry rug that looked like a dead Yeti, some charred pans and yards of foam rubber for beds. Renato, his plastered hair gleaming and a crisp ascot tucked into a spotless white shirt, hopped nervously from one natty pump to the other as he watched this assortment arrive, making little Italian sounds of grief. Already we were more than he'd bargained for, while we mutually agreed there was a lot less to him than met the eye.

We settled in, if settle is the word for adapting to living in a vast refrigerator. Jean-Claude, a spry young Frenchman who described himself as *un alpeniste*, was the best equipped to cope. He immediately donned his climbing gear and spent his time whizzing up the walls and threading himself nimbly through the steel beams that crisscrossed the ceiling, watched with adoration by small, cherubic Esther from Algiers. In their room we could hear them every evening, twittering at each other. It was like keeping canaries. Now and again, though, mournful silences fell, marking the end of another of Jean-Claude's patient explanations as to why, although he loved her most sincerely, he could never marry Esther, due to her being *une pauvre petite Arabe* and him being *d'une très bonne famille*. Everyone took turns pointing out to him, on behalf of tear-stained Esther, the appalling nature of his views – '*Tu es fasciste*, Jay-Cee, you know that? *Un* bloody Nazi' – but he was not to be moved and after a bit one got dizzy, arguing upwards at someone hanging upside down from a rafter. Anyway, by evening they were twittering again.

Josie moved in with nothing but a suitcase and a paper bag full of chicken bones. Back in Jamaica, she explained, they threw them to tell the future and she frequently scattered them about to tell ours, not that anyone believed her predictions of the wildest good fortune for each of us, including becoming Hollywood stars and also winning the football pools. Josie was far too kind to trust with anything as threatening as the future. She was my best friend of them all. I loved her rubbery, smiling face, and the comic grace of her grasshopper body, all joints and high angles. Best of all I loved her laugh, so rich and gurgling and full of glee it would have made a bloodhound snicker. I only saw her downcast once, at a party.

'Come with me, go on,' she pleaded, coming into my bedroom and leaning her weight against me, as if I were a wall.

'No way,' I said, 'I hate parties, specially ones I'm not invited to.'

'I'm inviting you. Oh go on, pur-leeze.'

'No,' I said firmly. 'Pur-leeze push off.'

Naturally I didn't know anyone there but, one good thing, there was lots of food. I remember stuffing myself while some loon smelling powerfully of joss asked me what sign I was.

'Capricorn,' I said through pastry crumbs.

'Oh yeah, man, I knew it. I'm really into astrology. Capricorn, huh? Hey, that's groovy. Me, I'm Libra, man. We're, like, twin signs, you know? You wanna split? I gotta pad round the corner.'

I wanted to be nice to him but I couldn't, due to the way he clicked his skinny fingers. 'Hey, too bad, man. I'm already twinned with Frankfurt,' I said and edged off in search of Josie. After a bit I glimpsed her with a group of black men in robes. Her head hung down like a tulip someone had forgotten to water while the men talked at her urgently, wagging their fingers. As I came up she turned, and her great dark eyes were full of woe.

In the hall, grabbing our coats, I said, 'What was all that about?' but she only hunched her shoulders and shook her head. When we got home I had to sit on her and pull her hair hard before I got it out of her.

'They said I shouldn't be with you. You shouldn't be my friend.'

'What?' I was outraged. 'Why on earth . . .'

'Because you're white,' she wailed, the tears welling up. 'They said Jamaicans had no pride, not like Africans. We have to learn, they said, that black is beautiful and whites are the enemy and stuff like that. They made me feel so bad, like a tart, you know?'

I rocked her in my arms crooning comforting things. Black is beautiful. I'd never heard that phrase before. It sounded OK. Josie was black and beautiful. So why did my stomach feel as if I'd swallowed ice?

Karen and Nancy were both Americans, but that was all they had in common, Karen being small, clever and poor, while Nancy was large, dumb and rich – her daddy owned most of Hawaii. It was Karen who passed on this nugget, rolling her eyes to show how unimpressed she was, but she was unable quite to stifle the reverence in her voice. We felt pretty reverent also. Money in the abstract was easy to despise, but Nancy's sort, solid, Hawaii-sized and in our flat, had us whispering as if we were in church. It was visible, too. All her possessions down to T-shirts and jeans had a sheen and substance to them that made our collective belongings look sad ghosts of hers. Nevertheless, after the first flurry no one referred to the subject again or thought to inquire of the heiress why exactly she'd chosen to slum it with us. But then we were habitually an incurious lot, not given to questioning each other about anything further back than the day we'd met. Everyone else we knew was the same. We existed solely in the present, a characteristic apparently programmed into all who were young at the time, as if the strains of the Pied Piper, gathering us together, had simultaneously erased our memory banks. The tacit understanding was that each of us in that floating world had emerged from some uncongenial past, a home, parents, a way of life that did not in any detail suit and which was as well forgotten.

Nothing particularly unusual about that, it pertains to some in every generation. Our distinction was in our numbers. So many of us in the same boat and no wonder, really. Something in the century's works had long ago jammed up, failed to move on. We grew up breathing air that was musty and stale, hamstrung by rusty rules and empty beliefs, surrounded by adults who trotted out the sort of opinions that, despite the odd refurbishment, the occasional lick of fresh paint, would have seemed familiar to their parents before them and their grandparents too. It was as if a set of ideas, the traditions and habits of an entire society, had been plucked in their prime by some Victorian Mrs Beeton, who pickled them in aspic and put them up on a shelf, where they sat gathering dust, mould and mouse droppings, quietly festering inside, until suddenly the lids began to bulge and shift and loosen and then – whoosh – the whole lot blew. Some such eruption may occur in any age to individuals. This one, like the Blitz in the war, had happened to us all and in doing so demolished a vast acreage of ancient constructions. They could blame us if they wished, they could call it what they liked – a rebellion, a Youth Revolution, the world turned upside down – but to us, surveying the wreckage, there seemed nothing for it but to get out from under and start rebuilding from scratch. You were where you were and you did what you did because you had to. Therefore, no questions.

Renato, our landlord, at forty-something was one of many still appalled by the upheaval. Already thrown off balance by the sight of our ramshackle possessions, he evidently found us so gruesome in person that despite his best intentions he couldn't keep away. He was like someone in the Reptile House at a zoo, repelled by the snakes and lizards but unable to resist staring and poking. During our first month in residence he kept knocking at the door with various landlordish excuses, but you could see from his shifty glances around that his hope was to catch us in some outrageous act involving either sex or vandalism. Josie claimed that his real thrill would be to come upon all of us fucking while simultaneously demolishing the walls. Soon he dropped any pretence at an excuse, simply knocking, coming in and hanging around, always bringing with him a newspaper so that he could sit on it and protect his immaculate trews. Later, he moved into messianic mode, picking on me as a soul that might still be saved and insisting that I taste his wines or inspect a new acquisition in his studio, which was as luxurious as ours wasn't, jungle-hot and full of bits of wild beasts – tiger rugs, zebra sofas, a whole menagerie of horn and tusk chairs. He watched me minutely during these excursions, longing, I could tell, for me to crumple at the sight of such marvels, fall at his tasselled feet and beg him to let me move in with him. Not because he fancied me in my tattered Oxfam blanket, far from it, but in the interests of some personal vindication.

As usual, Corinne was drunk, but this time she was also blocking the stairs with a knife in her hand. I could hear the two children above, mine and hers, waking from their afternoon naps and beginning to call. Again I tried to push past her, and again she lunged at me. The knife, a blunt instrument pitted with rust, which I used to open the cats' tins, looked unappetizing. If she stabs me with it, I thought, I'll die of lockjaw complicated by Whiskas.

'OK, OK,' I said, retreating. I'd already said all the rest: come on, Corrie, calm down, for heaven's sake, it's only me, don't be like this, you'll be sorry later, and once, because six months of Corrie was five months too long, if you don't stop waving that bloody knife I'll bloody kill you but nothing had worked and now my heart was bumping nastily, thinking of stranded Luke and Mark. When chaos threatened them, it was time to turn copper's nark. Back in the kitchen I pounced on the telephone.

'Police?' I said, low for fear she'd hear and come lurching down. 'Listen, I need help. This woman who lives here, she's got a knife, she won't let me get to the children upstairs . . .'

'Pardon?' said a male voice. 'Who is this? Speak up.'

I spoke up, giving my name and address. Then I went on. Eventually the voice said, 'Let's get this straight. This friend of yours, she's assaulted you, has she? Caused you bodily harm?'

'Yes. No.'

'Which is it, then?'

'If you mean has she stuck the knife in me yet, no, she hasn't.'

'Domestic,' muttered the voice to someone at his end. To me he said, 'Look, love, the way things are, we can't do nothing

379

for you. Why don't you call back when you've got something definite to report, all right?'

'Like I'm bloody dead, or what?' I hissed and banged down the receiver. Typical. Bloody typical.

Corinne had been at school with me in Switzerland. A quiet plump girl, appealing in a Victorian Christmas card way, I hadn't seen much of her there, we weren't close. Ten years after we'd both left school and two years after my children had been taken, she appeared at the door of the Chelsea flat Dutch and I shared, holding her little boy Mark by the hand. Woe poured out over coffee. An unhappy marriage that had led to her drinking too much. Divorce proceedings started by her husband, falsely accusing her of being an alcoholic, unfit to have custody of their son. She'd thought of me instantly. Heard that my husband had run off with my children, knew I'd understand her plight. Men, wicked men.

Wicked men. Oh dear. Have a biscuit.

She unfolded her strategy. A social worker had been deputed by the court to report on her maternal fitness for a period before the divorce hearings. If she and little Mark could only stay for that short time with me, Dutch and our baby, *en famille*, the social worker would be impressed, would report favourably back to the court and Corinne would confound her malevolent spouse by getting custody of little Mark, please say yes, please or I'll kill myself.

They moved in. Mark was enrolled at the local primary school and the social worker made her first appointment. I knew nothing of social workers except that they were a branch of Them, the Grown-ups, and must therefore be highly qualified professionals with hawk eyes trained to penetrate all camouflage, drill straight through to the soul within and deliver impartial righteous judgement. Awed by this vision and determined to pass muster for Corinne's sake I put on my only frock, tidied the flat, hollered upstairs to Corrie, sent Dutch out to the pub – he could not be made to look respectable at any price – and sat down beside Luke in his playpen to await the visitation.

Miss Battersby turned out to be middle-aged, her hawk eyes behind pebble glasses. The authoritative calm I had been expecting was not in evidence. Indeed, she seemed as jittery as me. I plied her with tea and cupcakes while her eyes darted here and there and I explained that the walls were black because the people before us were photographers and we hadn't managed to repaint them yet. After far too long, Corinne appeared, descending the stairs to the sitting room like Aida in the Funeral March.

'Ah, Mrs Drummond,' Miss Battersby said, hand outstretched. Corinne, giving a Queen Mother smile, allowed her hand to be taken and pumped. Thereafter, having settled herself on the only piece of furniture with all four legs, she said a great deal in oddly monotonous but beautifully modulated tones, mostly concerning the doings and opinions of her father and mother: he ex-Governor of an Indian province and she connected to a ducal dynasty. She also touched upon her own Presentation at Court, adding that that sort of thing, didn't Miss Battersby agree, was really too silly in these days when we were all equal and class no longer mattered one bit.

'Oh, ra-ther,' breathed Miss Battersby, transfixed, and when eventually Corinne, with a gracious little nod, begged us to excuse her since she had to dress for dinner with boring old Lord X, Miss Battersby stood up and almost curtsied as she watched Corrie very slowly mount the stairs. Afterwards she remarked in a hushed voice what a very nice person Mrs Drummond seemed, a real lady, and how good it was to see that she'd overcome her little . . . er . . . problem. Oh ra-ther, I said, whereupon the good woman took her leave and I followed

Corinne up to her room, where she lay upon her bed as regally as ever, surrounded by empty whisky bottles, one hundred per cent blotto with drink, out for the count.

There were other episodes. Corrie, young, pretty and for short stretches plausible, was forever being adopted as a cause by those far better equipped than I to cope with her binges and alleviate her addiction. Churchmen of all denominations couldn't wait to tuck her under their wings, a variety of doctors and psychiatrists involved themselves with her and various prestigious institutions took her in at one time or another, vowing that their particular regime would have her steady on her feet in a jiffy. Each of these well-wishers, as they whisked her off, gave me to understand that though they were sure I had done my best with little Corrie I was not, after all, qualified as they were. And each of them, after at most a fortnight, would inevitably eject her and send her back to me, outrage in their voices on the telephone as they listed her misdeeds and their own profound disillusionment. I came to regard them one and all as I did my son's baby-sitters, temporary stop-gaps who allowed me to draw breath between the apparently lifelong task of Coping with Corrie. I noted what they said, registered what they did and drew my own conclusions from the contradictions.

Eventually – with Miss B.'s enthusiastic support – Corinne was awarded custody of Mark. At that point I embarked on a three-month nervous breakdown which took the form of a violent jaw-ache, as if some iron vice had clamped shut, trapping my face. Three dentists could find nothing wrong.

Dutch diagnosed the cause. 'It's her,' he said, indicating with rolling eyes the upper regions of the flat where bottles clinked interminably. 'You are not the type who can cope with her. I am.'

'But you wouldn't have taken her in in the first place, you said so,' I argued.

'Exactly,' he replied.

It took us three months to persuade Corinne to leave. Several times Dutch physically ejected her, scooping her drink-sodden body up in his arms, dumping her outside on the steps, chucking her suitcases after her and locking the door while I sobbed within. She was always there in the mornings, sitting on the steps or curled up in the telephone box opposite, with a bottle of course, and looking more grubbily pitiful than ever.

But at long last she was persuaded and moved into a flat nearby, where she spent most of the rest of Mark's childhood lying in bed in a stupor. I was reinforced in what I had already guessed: 90 per cent of the Great and the Good could not tell their arses from Charlie Chaplin but no good came of saying so, for the shit on the fan would rebound on you. Once, in despair for Mark's welfare, I tried to explain to another of the Great and Good, his headmistress, the un-merry-go-round of his home life. 'Mrs Drummond? Oh now, I find that hard to believe,' she drawled and ice filled the room as she raised incredulous eyebrows. 'Mrs Drummond always speaks so highly of you,' was her parting shot as I slunk hot and sweating from the room, dismissed as the most debased of God's creatures, the female Iago, the two-faced friend, the school sneak.

The day before, Scotland Yard had held a press conference. I'd come home loaded with bumf concerning the ardent desire of the Boys in Blue to strengthen their bonds within local communities, share ordinary people's concerns and troubles, be close at hand to help them. The day before that I'd talked to the press officer of a famous drying-out centre for alcoholics. The PR's voice had been low and caring, he'd discoursed at length on the Centre's philosophy, how they never gave up on anyone, how they strove to see through the drink-sodden wretch to the eternal soul within. That was the day they turfed my knife-wielding friend out in spite of me pleading on the telephone, in my capacity as an ordinary person, not a journalist on an important newspaper, for them to keep her in, I can't cope any more, I've got our two children, give me a break, just a few more days . . .

I read the newspapers afterwards. Nice articles on the police, nice on the drying-out centre. Full marks, well done, bouquets all round. Everything in the garden rosy for retired colonels in Tunbridge Wells, but for many others, no.

Afterword
by Alan Brien

The manuscript of Jill's second volume of memoirs, *Frightening People*, breaks off here, part-way into an episode of London life in the sixties. She had embarked on this second instalment of her autobiography with a rare (for her) confidence in her own ability, even before the first had been delivered to the printer. She went so far as to make a casual comparison to George Sand, who frequently penned 'The End' on one page, and then went on to write 'page one' at the top of the next, in the middle of the night.

What then stopped Jill one day, 20,000 words into *Frightening People*, at the door of her office in our hidden-away Holloway mews house, as if she had seen a ghost sitting in her chair? Why did she whisper the words that haunt me still? 'An ice cube has formed around me, cutting me off from the world outside.'

Ironically, the mortuary chill that was to rob my wife of the urge to continue began to creep through her on what she was looking forward to as a wonderful night – the Viking book-party for *Eating Children* at the Café Rouge in Kensington. Though many of the guests were the usual professionals, critics, literary editors, gossip columnists and so on, most of these were also friends, and there was a bubbling core of long-term intimates, and family members from both sides. As we got out of the taxi, I was able to tell myself that the aura of gauntness around the fringes of her precisely chiselled face was nothing more than tiredness. After all, I thought, creating a masterpiece is hard work.

As we climbed the stairs to the party room on the first floor I saw from behind that she was suppressing a limp in her right leg, and I smoothed it out, hoisting her onto each step, my large hands around her still-girlish waist, as if giving a lift to a ballerina on stage. This too I dismissed, as a hangover from a not entirely successful hip operation of the previous year. Did she not arrive at the top expanding like a star, absorbing the star's intake of hugs and kisses, praise and admiration?

Of all the embraces, the wrap-around bear-grip of TV Channel 4's Jon Snow was the one few women forgot, especially big girls like Jill, who appreciate being shrunk to petite, fragile Meissen figurines. He told her she looked terrible. And she must have medical advice immediately. Soon every one of us at the party saw what he had seen but had persuaded ourselves was an illusion. 'A case of the Empress's old clothes,' Jill observed later.

Within twenty-four hours, thanks to that marvellous network Jon can switch on to aid his lucky friends, Jill had been examined at home by a top consultant for nervous diseases, who just happened to live round the corner from us. All we learned from that first informal examination was our specialist's assurance that Jill's original, secret fear would almost certainly turn out to be groundless. This was that she might have inherited from her father the dreadful motor neurone disease which his doctors diagnosed only on his deathbed, a wasting ailment that saps the connections between the muscles and for which there is no treatment and no cure.

For the rest of the week the pair of us trailed round from clinic to clinic, lab to lab, like twin sacrificial sheep waiting to be given the place and time of our slaughter, though I was always conscious that I was the one to be divinely reprieved. Somehow all power to make decisions, utter protests, even ask or answer the simplest questions, was fading from us. As we huddled together in the corridors, hand in hand, staring ahead, outside door after door, I saw us twain as the couple in Ford Madox Brown's *The Last of England*, paying pole-axed farewell to our homeland before sailing steerage to a strange New World.

I had just settled on this image for my Afterword when Jill's Amstrad disgorged the following paragraphs she had written for the *Guardian* after she had learned she was ill. I thought she had destroyed them, taking them with her when she died.

I'll pass on a curious observation I've made about doctors in the last fortnight. When they're about to tell you whatever it is they think you've got, and they gaze blankly at you as you enter the room, get your name wrong, look mildly bored or rather tetchy, thank your stars, for the chances are there's nothing much amiss. But the day they bounce up from behind their desks rubbing their hands, full of chat and banter and Santa Claus ho-ho-hos – man, you're dead.

Come to think of it, this is not very curious at all. Ever since the Greeks shot the messenger, nobody likes to be the bearer of bad news, least of all doctors. Their job, after all, is to know about illness and how to cure it, so it discommodes them extremely to have to say to the patient, as a doctor had recently to say to me, look, you've got this disease we know hardly anything about and there's no cure or treatment or drugs and you're going to die of it, rotten luck and all that, did you hear the one about the Scotsman, the Irishman and the . . .

'How long have I got, Doctor?' I asked, cliché from a thousand B-movies.

'There's no way of knowing.'

'Weeks? Years?'

'There's no way of knowing.'

Out in the corridor again, I sat down. Next thing, someone was kneeling beside me, a young woman in white who seemed to have sprung from the skirting board. Absently, I swatted her away.

'I'm Cindy,' she said brightly. 'Just thought I'd measure you up while you're here.'

Dumbly, I stared at her smiling face.

'For a wheelchair?' she explained, enunciating clearly while nodding a lot, the way Americans do. 'They take two months to order, see. Best to get in quickly.' She whipped out a tape and measured me from ankles to knees and knees to bum. 'Tall, aren't you?' she said.

'Not,' I answered, 'in a wheelchair.'

After this rite of passage, they guided me, still stiff and unresponsive as a Dalek, along a maze of corridors into a kind of mock house of bedrooms, bathrooms and kitchens, whose Ideal-Home-Show veneer had cracked to reveal the ugly workings beneath: dangling ropes, steel bars and poles, lumpy black boxes concealing batteries, plastic in unaesthetic mode. This is the Pit and the Pendulum Room, I thought, donated by the Friends of Edgar Allan Poe, and galvanized by terror and water on the eyes, I rose, made some excuse to the nice smiling girls and stumbled out of there like a half-blind bat out of hell.

I have always been healthy, taken health for granted, filled in all those forms over the years that ask 'Any serious illnesses?' with a firm and virtuous 'No'. My diet is balanced and nicely varied, supplemented now and then with vitamins, and I am long-accustomed to possessing a physique more flexible, able and fitter than most. Until quite recently I could still divert the easily amused by doing the splits, a cartwheel or two, a backward flip, leftover skills from youthful ballet classes.

Afterword

Having come to terms with the fact of ageing, I confidently expected to live into my eighties as my long-lived family had always done, dispensing gems of accumulated wisdom to anyone I could buttonhole.

Now I think of Michelangelo's fresco, the one that precedes *The South Bank Show*, the hand of God reaching out to touch the hand of Man and the electric bolt between them, the same that struck life into Dr Frankenstein's monster. But God's life-giving bolt has in my case gone into reverse. I have blown my fuses for good and all, blown them every one. I remain as healthy as ever, but the web of nerves and muscles within which I exist is unravelling fast, and there is nothing anyone in the world can do about it. The name given to this oddly biblical phenomenon is motor neurone disease.

There were few signs of the looming disintegration. An occasional unsteadiness, as if I'd had a bit too much to drink, not to be taken too seriously by one who has sometimes had a bit too much to drink. One hand began to show an irritating weakness. I had to use both to squeeze toothpaste. The price of laziness, I thought, must take more exercise. Aerobics, swimming, come the autumn I'll join some classes, promise.

One April morning my breathing altered. Not for the worse, exactly, more as if something had shifted at the pit of my lungs. Must give up smoking I said to myself for the umpteenth time. Then I fell over. One knee gave as I went up a step and I keeled forward into a doorjamb, blacking an eye. Plenty of scope there for comedy of the unalternative walked-into-a-door variety. Forget it.

Nevertheless I eventually went to the doctor, a new GP who knew me not at all. 'My breathing,' I said. 'It's changed.'

The stethoscope came out, she listened front and back. 'Clear,' she said, 'quite clear.'

'And I feel . . . well . . . rather weak,' I added.

She instructed me to walk on my toes and on my heels. 'You're all right,' she said.

I sat rather glumly looking at her until she got up, like a society hostess with a dilatory guest. My allotted time was over.

The next thing I knew was Jon Snow, and then the hospital, and then the tests and the diagnosis, and I hear myself saying, 'Doctor, how long have I got?'

The room we sat in was small and stuffy. My husband stood up and put his hands on my shoulders. The doctor looked out the window. I felt like a Tragedy Queen in the wrong opera. Perhaps I ought to rise, clutch my bosom and belt out some heart-breaking aria. On the other hand I felt like a schoolgirl. Better behave in front of the teacher.

Jill's obedience to the school rules did not last long. They were talking about her life, her future, her death. She had told them everything they wanted to know. She wanted the same courtesy in return. Typically, Jill could not bear evasiveness, any insultingly obvious softening of a blow. She instructed me to find out what was really involved.

I simply could not accept such a huge gap in the prognosis. There had to be statistics, actuarial figures – after all, we were talking about medical *science*. My informant, a kind, honourable man, told me that, if I really wanted to know all that he knew, I should accept that the majority of sufferers from motor neurone disease were dead within two years of being diagnosed, though a minority lingered for a few years longer.

As an optimist, against any odds in any circumstances, I perked up. So the chances were *more* than two years, I stressed. I looked at Jill's face. Not a pessimist, but always a realist, I saw, as though it had been typed up on her forehead, she was convinced she would soon be dead, at the best not survive beyond Christmas 1993. She died on 12 November.

But, back in June, I moved into overdrive, encouraging her to leave behind *two* wonderful books. She had always wanted a bestseller, even a mini one. The first bore every sign of being well on its way. The second had an even more impressive pedigree. I was right. As I type this – how she laughed at my inability to manage any kind of computer, relying instead on a sit-up-and-beg, heavy metal Imperial, built pre-war, and solid as a desk-sized field gun – I see Jill's *Eating Children* is climbing the *Evening Standard* list. Why could she face one part of her past and not another?

She sat me down like a child that has to be told the news of some terrible accident.

'You see, that was the sad half of my life. The cot death of Michael. The growing estrangement from István, who was like a zombie. His theft of my boy and girl and all my money. The growing fears that I was doomed to repeat patterns I had rejected. István was just Daddy all over again, and I was the Little Daughter still hoping for presents and praise. With Dutch I had the Big Boy and I was his Little Mother. Neither understood what I wanted, what I was, that I was a woman first; that I wanted to be loved by men for what I loved in myself.

'But I could still tell this painful story because I knew it had a happy ending. I *would* start to write. I *would* become well known. I'd meet you, my darling. I was travelling out of bad times into good times, fast. Now I was in the cheerful half. My two lost babies coming back as teenagers. My new family love my old family. My daughter going to university in London. You know it all, you are it all. Six months ago I wrote about myself with pleasure, with joy, as I'd never done before. But now, now it is all going to have an unhappy ending. There are grandchildren I'll never see, books I'll never write, houses we'll never live in, an old age we'll never share.

'When I sit down at the word processor, I have to throw my mind wide open to remember everything, to re-live everything, and then the weasels and stoats come pouring in, devouring and miring everything. The ice cube that was melting is now freezing again into permafrost.'

Secretly, after her death, I hoped to discover the manuscript of the second half or two-thirds of *Frightening People*, hidden in plain sight among so many near replicas. For the only time in our relationship, I wished Jill had been an academic who kept drafts and copies, outlines and skeletons, of what she was writing. Instead here is a typical sample of the potted notes she made to pin down her memories.

> Still don't feel part of the sixties, bird, chick etc. Weighed down. Get pregnant. Benn parties, gets Dutch work permit. Leave work for freelance. No success. Bailiffs in and out. Dutch gets appendicitis, scene. Job at IBM.

Her pursuit of her two missing children, Adam and Ilona, had piled defeat on defeat, driving home the message that in this world to be victim is to invite all the more injustice and, outside of Westerns, the good 'uns are not a good bet to win. She had just survived a life-threatening ectopic pregnancy, with pains that were like torture, and now she was being given a second, possibly last, chance to be a mother of a child that would not be snatched by death or demon husband.

And what was Dutch doing? Dutch had lifted her from a depression fuelled by irrational guilt and shame at being a failed mother unable to protect her children from an obsessive husband who really wanted her not them, but if not her, then them. Dutch had done this largely by ignoring all her symptoms, physical and psychic, agonies of the teeth and the uterus, the heart and the head, but in the short term it worked. Dutch lived for the moment. It was a seductive illusion for those able to delude themselves day by day. But Jill could not survive for long in a land of make-believe. She did not fit the role of anybody's 'old lady'.

With her career, after *My Home*, stuck in the mud, it was obviously Dutch's turn. Tony Benn's parties were where everybody who was going to be anybody crowded in and even such things as Dutch's work permit could be negotiated. Despite being legal, he still refused to attempt any job that would allow her to count on a regular income for what was now to become a family.

Dutch did not mind bailiffs. You could always store the furniture in the next flat, leaving only a bed, a typewriter and a beautiful pregnant lady by an empty crib. He earned enough from their stall on Portobello, with nights strumming the guitar at the Russian café Luba's, for his needs. If that got dull, he could always revert to multi-lingual courier and guide for a travel agency in Italy, Greece or Yugoslavia. He was vague about income and expenditure, but she couldn't help noticing that he seemed to be earning enough for lovely silk suits, expensive writing paper with his name at the top proclaiming his doctorate in nuclear physics from a university in Canada, usually a couple of cars (one of them a Porsche), a bank account and one of those new-fangled credit cards in his name only. And what was he doing for her, and their future child? Lounging around in hospital having appendicitis!

She stormed the hospital, thumped his pillow, rattled his drip, tugged his hair and threatened that he would never see either her or his child for the rest of his life unless he got off his bum and acted like a proper husband and father. It must have been quite a performance, for he discharged himself that night and by the weekend had a job in the film-making department of IBM. Dutch and Jill and baby Luke moved from the Chelsea flat to the Georgian house in a ruined square off the Old Kent Road which she wrote about in the fragment of *Frightening People* that survives.

It was 1970 and Jill was thirty-four when I saw her across a crowded room at a Posy Simmonds' party. She was wearing her hair in a particularly unflattering way, wound round and piled into a top-knot at the back of her Modigliani head. The style — if such a word can be used to dignify the way she happened to tug the comb that morning — drew attention to her Alice in Wonderland neck and emphasized what I was to learn she thought of as her 'heron nose'. Her clothes, too, were hardly calculated to more than hint at the subtle grace of the body beneath. Though, of course, nothing could obscure the cunningly chiselled, impossibly extended legs that might have been models for that famous Polly Peck poster of the period which, blazoned on gable ends and railway bridges, had dazzled more than a few male drivers into half-demolishing walls and railings.

Despite the scruffy sweater that seemed to have been knitted from dog's hair, the baggy skirt creased at as many angles as John Birt's Armani suit, plus a defiant last-minute waistcoat of gold lace scaled with tiny mirrors, it seemed to me I could see, through this somewhat neurotic disguise, not the grown woman, but the teenager and schoolgirl hiding within. Though I had no other picture to go by, except the illustration at the top of Jill's page which (typically for the *Guardian* of those days) represented a dull worthy creature with a naive stare and shy smile, I held my vision of a fiery, wiry beanpole in a gym slip, eyes like pitch balls, hair like a golliwog, drumming her heels on the carpet in fits of fury at parental promises unkept, wailing for full and honest answers to her questions about God and sex and capitalism and death and war and truth and beauty — answers that decent parents would never ponder even behind locked doors. Desdemona to her Othello, I loved her for the dangers she had passed and she loved me that I did pity them.

As a guide to her feelings for me, I offer her portrait of me written later:

He has none of the attributes of the mythic lover. He is not chivalrous, he is not even very polite. He cannot dance, he is tone-deaf and colour blind, he has no moods, he does not day-dream, he does not dream at all. He brings home no flowers, he remembers no birthdays, he does not try a little tenderness. He has no god, he worships no one, loyalty is not a word he recognizes. He does not know the meaning of the word romance, or care to know. He never says don't worry your pretty head about it. He loves me for what is lovable in me and distances himself from what is not. He looks at me carefully with the world's eyes as well as the eyes of love, I know him to be accurate in his assessments and so I know where I am. If I ask him a question he will answer it as truthfully as he can and if the truth hurts, he will comfort me, for a while.

Our wedding three years later was a quiet, sober formality in a north London registry office, attended only by the children and Sally Vincent as my witness, Mel Calman as hers. Just one thing bothered her: I had registered her as 'spinster of the parish'. 'Why not "mutton dressed as lamb"?' she whispered. I explained that I had inserted this deliberate inaccuracy so that the whole charade would be invalid and she could walk free as soon as she wanted. She purred with pleasure.

I never met anybody who laughed at themselves the way Jill did. Nearly all her stories were about failures, mistakes and setbacks. Once, when we had been living together for a couple of years, we took Luke, her son by Dutch, to see a psychiatrist. It was something many middle-class parents did from time to time in the seventies. Jill explained that the eight-year-old never seemed to be sure where he was or what time it was. 'Um,' said the shrink leaving a long, long pause. 'You do know, Jill, that your appointment with me was for yesterday?'

*

Afterword

Ever since *Eating Children* was published, I do not think I have met anyone who knows I was married to its author who does not say 'I must find out what happened to the children.'

Before I met Jill she had suffered for nearly ten years the dreadful ache of Adam and Ilona's disapperance. It was as if they had dropped into a chasm. 'If my husband had stolen a necklace of mine,' she wrote much later, 'I would probably have had it back within weeks. But he had not stolen my necklace and I had no redress.' It was, she told me, 'almost literally like having a limb wrenched off. You can't see it. You don't know where it is. But still you feel the pain where it used to be . . .'

She had for a long time no address at all for them. Then somehow she found out where they were being kept. She wrote to them, at first regular monthly messages, presents at Christmas and birthdays. But the strain of shooting arrows into the dark, and not a single one returned, made the pain too great.

As it turned out, István was intercepting and destroying them all. There was to be no mother, not even only a photograph and a scrawl, for them. They felt they had been deserted, rejected, scorned – the way children tend to do even in amicable separations.

Then, just after Jill and I started living together, we began to renew the contact. István had married the boss's daughter, an executive of the firm for which he was a salesman. She had become a Countess, but he was hardly living like a Count. He did not seem to be having such a great time of it, I was happy to think. My fantasies, very real and bloody, of creeping up on István and killing him began to ebb. There were possibilities of a visit from the pair to us in London. Then in 1972 Jill and I went to Russia for a year. We travelled about 25,000 miles. I wrote a weekly diary for the back page of the *Sunday Times* and researched my novel on Lenin. Jill, for once, did nothing but try to find something for us to eat and sightsee — the longest holiday from writing she ever had.

Jill's Luke and my children Adam and Jane were booked to fly to Moscow and spend the summer vacation with us. What about Ilona and the other Adam joining the party? István was against the idea. He had formed the view that Jill and I were internationally notorious Reds — some knowledgeable customer in Baden-Baden had vouched for this as a well-known fact. Perhaps we would defect to the Soviet Union and rob him of his two little aristos.

Another year slipped by, but at least we were getting the occasional card, even the odd phone call. Then in 1974 suddenly the barriers all fell down. We were waiting at the airport for Adam and Ilona. I watched the emotions, every one there was it seemed, surging through Jill. She was hot, cold, blue, pink, shaking, fainting and deliriously happy.

Then, there they were, a boy of fifteen, a girl of sixteen. He was tall, nearly as tall as me, with raven hair and eyes, a noble Wellingtonian conk. She had ugly spectacles, but a wonderful rounded figure, and spoke excellent English. We took to each other instantly.

Their grandparents, Jill's father and mother, insisted the visitors must stay with them for beginners, but they soon changed their minds. Meal times, with the emphasis on *times*, were sacred to them. But Adam and Ilona rarely showed for the gong, slept till noon, had no table manners, stuffed themselves and then went off together. This was the way they lived on holiday at home, Ilona told us, like hermits, or lovers, feeding and keeping to themselves in their own separate flat. The new Countess did not allow the Count tobacco on the premises, and so he spent his time alone in his study, drinking, smoking and reading Westerns.

Afterword

He is dead now, unforgiven and unspoken to by Jill. The children with their spouses visit us here at least once a year. They were part of a family party of twenty-two last Christmas. I cooked and then we all played charades and drank like mad. I could feel Jill's spirit in the air. Adam and Ilona are a wonderfully handsome pair and I regard them as mine.

Jill's life illustrates her insistent desire to show her readers how it looked on the other side of any situation. She knew what it was like because she had been there herself. So had many of her *Guardian* following. They recognized themselves. But even those who had not shared experiences realized that she was a trusty foreign correspondent reporting back from the badlands and killing grounds they had not seen even at a distance.

After her first feature was accepted by Katharine Whitehorn on the *Observer*, Jill got a job on the *Sunday Telegraph*. She remembered those days with happiness: 'There was a wonderful woman called Winefride Jackson who was just like a mummy to us ... One day, however, "Mummy" did something that changed my life. I remember her sweeping through the office crying, "Girls! Yoko Ono says women are the niggers of the world. Does anyone know what that means?" I thought to myself, I do; and it means I have to move on.'

One crippling problem was her inability to know except in the broadest outline what she was going to set down on paper until after she had done so. The first editor to trust that she could deliver what she promised without being able to explain what that was had got himself the best woman journalist of our era. His name was Alastair Heatherington, and he edited the *Guardian*. In 1969 he gave her a whole page a week she entitled 'Off-cuts', to accommodate the overflow of her commentary on our times.

Incidentally, Heatherington asked her at the end of her

interview – out of mild curiosity, he explained – why she had not replied to his invitation to join the *Guardian* the year before. She said that she had often wondered why he had not replied to her offer to join the *Guardian*, also the year before. 'Cor!' I remarked when she told me. 'It's like *Romeo and Juliet*.' 'Yes, it is,' she said, 'but then, I never thought *R and J* was about star-crossed lovers. I always thought it was an indictment of the disgraceful inefficiency of the Verona Post Office, didn't you?'

On the *Guardian* as in life, Jill was a doughty opponent, tackling current problems and also problems that at the time no one even thought *were* problems. Consider her campaign over a decade ago urging that rape in marriage should be made a crime in law. How they all laughed and jeered, the right-wing, realistic men of the world, particularly the satirists on Richard Ingrams' *Private Eye*. Such a thing, they crowed holding their sides, was a contradiction in terms. What would these jack-booted feminists dream up next?

I have a letter I found in the back of a drawer, written by Jill to Dutch in December 1961. He is in Amsterdam, she is in London with the children, and the Count is momentarily out. She writes:

My husband, after a flying start of extreme generosity (when I last wrote to you) has now crumbled completely and is being as mean and miserable as can be ... No lawyer would give me much encouragement, since my husband wants me back, says he will never marry again and that 'There's a candle in the window' when I wish to take advantage of it.

He knows about you from the children, bless 'em, which I think was one of the reasons he suddenly changed his tune. He thinks me immoral, irresponsible and a slut, although he does his best to sleep with me. Wotthehell.

I have felt rather ill ever since I've been back, it's a ghastly experience living with a man so closely, who actually makes your skin crawl, as he does now for me. I can't even sleep at night for fear my virtue will be taken, as indeed once it was and believe me, I was quite physically sick . . .

Well, now marital rape is an offence on the statute books.

Another column inspired Erin Pizzey to set up the first refuge for battered women. Today they are to be found across the country. And those are only two instances from hundreds of columns that influenced and shaped people's lives. In 1994, Jill was posthumously honoured for her lifetime achievements in newspapers. She already had an award from 'What the Papers Say' on Granada TV soon after she joined the *Guardian*, and another the following year from IPC – Woman Journalist of the Year. After her death Jill was awarded the Gerald Barry Award for lifetime achievement in journalism. This was the first time it had been awarded posthumously.

Jill's constituency, her heartland, her power base, her oxygen supply, her praetorian guard, her extended family, her reservoir of new friends and old pen pals, lay in the *Guardian* readers. They supported and cheered her in long, funny, clever letters, when her colleagues and the paper's executives went through troughs of no-enthusiasm for her latest campaign expressed in outspoken language that caused the delicate stomachs of male essayists to heave. She sometimes worried that the 'Open Space' letters column on the Woman's Page was slanted to be more anti than pro her. This was due, however, to the facts of newspaper life. Those against you write direct to the office and their comments are shown to the editor. Those in favour write to you by name and their envelopes are then forwarded, unopened, to you at home.

Of course it was up to Jill to make a selection of the most

favourable and enthusiastic from her large post-bag, many of them from famous and bankable names, and circulate them among influential executives. But this was too near office politics for her: 'I'm strictly an amateur paranoiac.' The way she saw it, it was *their* job to know who sold papers and who did not. The result was she was rarely given the satisfaction of being told by those supposedly on her side how important she was – the archetypal wild woman, man-eater and bimbo-trasher – admired, feared, hated but talked-about, known far beyond the pages of her paper. If they felt, in the *Guardian* seats of power, that just her name was of value to the paper's commercial image, they seemed determined she would be the last to know. Until the nineties, she lagged below the pay level commanded by several male writers. Yet, as foreign correspondent Suzanne Lowry (once Woman's Editor of the *Guardian*) said: 'She understood what the women she wrote for were feeling, she had experienced so much pain herself and she was able to expose the feelings women hadn't realized were there. Her writing was about the world she inhabited.' Polly Toynbee, now the BBC's social affairs editor, said: 'She influenced so many women writers and touched so many women's lives.' And Sally Belfrage said, 'She saved my life once a week.'

In 1988 Jill left the *Guardian*. She had already published a collection of essays, *It's Only Me*; a study of sexual desire, *In the Name of Love* (1979); *Letters from a Faint-hearted Feminist* (1982) and *More From Martha*, a comic correspondence that was later turned into a TV series. Two novels, *Bliss* (1984) and *Internal Affairs* (1986), followed. To her surprise she found that she could positively enjoy producing books, especially fiction. Free from the restrictions of libel laws, the Damoclean knife-edge of the deadline, the discipline of routine checking through the cuttings or on the telephone, the necessity of timeliness and topicality, the short sprint across the half page, she was able to give her imagination and her intuition the chance to explore wider horizons, to see further and think deeper, as if floating at will in the gondola of a hot-air balloon, over an uncharted landscape.

In her own life story, *Eating Children*, she found the perfect theme and style for her continually flowering talents. It was undoubtedly the finest thing she had ever written. The next volume, *Frightening People*, gave every sign of equalling, or possibly excelling, it. For once she was eager to get to her desk each morning, showing every sign of actual physical delight in play of fingers on keys, while the soft shuffle of the Amstrad rarely fell silent. Normally Jill distrusted any mechanical device powered by electricity, gas, petrol or paraffin. She asked only one question — 'Will it explode?' But she adored her word processor, coaxing, wheedling, flattering it, as if she were playing with some kind of robot pet.

Jill almost never consulted me when producing journalism, apart from the occasional Trivial Pursuit question that saved her the bother of opening a reference work. She herself would put every piece out of her mind once it had been collected by motorcycle courier, or, in later times, fed into the fax, and never ever read what she had written in the next day's paper. After a while we settled into an agreement that I was allowed, without comment or argument, to correct errors of fact about life in the big, boring male cosmos, thus avoiding the possibility of some oddity such as 'when Einstein split the atom', but I kept my fingers off her thoughts, theories, confessions and boasts about what was going on exploring the fascinating, molecular, inner space of women.

But with *Eating Children*, and the overlap into *Frightening People*, I was authorized each night, around six, to take up a comfortable stretch on my sofa, pour myself a scotch, and listen to her read aloud the five, six hundred words she had put together that day. These were the happiest minutes of my life. In bouts of depression I sometimes think the last ones.

Between the revelation of death sentence by MND in June 1993, and Jill's death in November, my life had narrowed to two activities. One was looking after my wife, something one out of every couple may need, and want to do, as she regressed from reliance on my arm to a stick, to crutches, to zimmer, to wheelchair. I was the only one authorized to bathe and dress her, though I sometimes made a mess of the job in a way that provoked her to invoke Laurel and Hardy. Then there was the twice-daily torrent of mail. I read all the letters and acknowledged around a thousand of them. I was taken aback to discover that at least a third of them were from men, and they too contained the same phrases. Over and over, her readers wrote: 'Dear Jill, How could you have anticipated what I was thinking, feeling, suffering, dreading? It is as if you are inside me, walking about in my mind . . . You are the mother, sister, wife, lover, daughter I never had because I never believed you could really exist . . . We talk about you in our family as if you live next door . . .'

She always loved me telling her stories of what we were going to do . . . in the next house, on the next holiday, on the next shopping expedition, at the next party. Now we did much the same but in the past, living among what used to be, arguing over what we really meant when we said or did that, imagining alternative existences. No death can take that away.

She would listen wide-eyed as if it were a fairy tale about some other woman when I explained how I had sworn an almighty oath that she would be mine forever after I saw her at Posy's party. How she had chucked lunch with me at an hour's notice, pleading as she often did that she was catching a plane. How, discovering she was on a freebie to the new Hilton in

Kenya, I bullied the PR-man into bumping the editor of the *Bolton Evening News* on the promise of a whole column in the *Sunday Times* and how she turned deep pink when she found I was in the next seat on the plane. It was my birthday, March 12th, so I never forgot our first real encounter. On her birthday, May 22nd, I got myself on a trip to the Lebanon even though the excuse was a fashion show. Instead we bunked off in a taxi to the southern front, where the Israelis were invading, a joint scoop. We got into the habit of going on assignments together, each covering our notebooks from the other's prying eye, peering round to see what could be important enough to record, competing for the most picturesque metaphor, the most clinching quote.

For nearly a quarter of a century, we worked within feet of each other round the clock. If one woke in the early hours, the other was already listening. She would expound to me her vanities, her terrors, her snobberies, her dreams. 'I know how ghastly they are,' she would remind me every now and again. 'I just like to hear how they sound. Remember, you heard it here first.'